A Concise History of Bolivia, Second Edition

Bolivia is an unusual high-altitude country created by imperial conquests and native adaptations, and it remains today
the most Indian of th   rtic-
ipates in the world e   )cial
and economic mobil      s in
Latin America. Thes   this
historical survey. In i   in's
A Concise History of   :hin
Bolivia as the new sta........ ....y .. .... important nation.
Surveying Bolivia's economic, social, cultural, and political
evolution from the arrival of early man in the Andes to the
present, this current version brings the history of this society
up to the present day, covering the fundamental changes that
have occurred since the National Revolution of 1952 and the
return of democracy in 1982. These changes have included the
introduction of universal education and the rise of the mestizos
and Indian populations to political power for the first time in
national history. Containing an updated bibliography, A Concise History of Bolivia remains an essential text for courses
in Latin American history and politics. This second edition
brings this story through the first administration of the first
self-proclaimed Indian president in national history and the
major changes that the government of Evo Morales has introduced in Bolivia's society, politics, and economy.

Herbert S. Klein is the author of 22 books and 163 articles in
several languages on Latin America and comparative themes
in social and economic history. Among these books are *The
Atlantic Slave Trade*, Second Edition (2010) and four studies of
slavery, the most recent of which are *Slavery and the Economy
of São Paulo, 1750–1850* (co-author, 2003); *African Slavery
in Latin America and the Caribbean* (co-author, 2008), and
Slavery in Brazil (co-author, 2009), as well as four books on
Bolivian history. He has also published books on such diverse
themes as *The American Finances of the Spanish Empire,
1680–1809* (1998), *A Population History of the United States*
(2004), and *Hispanics in the United States Since 1980* (co-
author, 2010).

CAMBRIDGE CONCISE HISTORIES

This is a new series of illustrated "concise histories" of selected individual countries, intended both as university and college textbooks and as general historical introductions for general readers, travelers, and members of the business community.

Other titles in the series:

A Concise History of Australia, 3rd Edition
STUART MACINTYRE

A Concise History of Austria
STEVEN BELLER

A Concise History of Brazil
BORIS FAUSTO, TRANSLATED BY ARTHUR BRAKEL

A Concise History of Britain, 1707–1975
W. A. SPECK

A Concise History of Bulgaria, 2nd Edition
R. J. CRAMPTON

A Concise History of the Caribbean
B. W. HIGMAN

A Concise History of Finland
DAVID KIRBY

A Concise History of France, 2nd Edition
ROGER PRICE

A Concise History of Germany, 2nd Edition
MARY FULBROOK

A Concise History of Greece, 2nd Edition
RICHARD CLOGG

Series list continues following the Index.

A Concise History
of Bolivia
Second Edition

HERBERT S. KLEIN

Stanford University

CAMBRIDGE

CAMBRIDGE UNIVERSITY PRESS
Cambridge, New York, Melbourne, Madrid, Cape Town, Singapore,
São Paulo, Delhi, Dubai, Tokyo, Mexico City

Cambridge University Press
32 Avenue of the Americas, New York, NY 10013-2473, USA

www.cambridge.org
Information on this title: www.cambridge.org/9780521183727

First published 2003
Second edition published 2011

Printed in the United States of America

A catalog record for this publication is available from the British Library.

Library of Congress Cataloging in Publication data

Klein, Herbert S., 1936–
A concise history of Bolivia / Herbert S. Klein. – 2nd edition.
   p.   cm. – (Cambridge concise histories)
Includes bibliographical references and index.
ISBN 978-1-107-00568-6 (hardback) – ISBN 978-0-521-18372-7 (paperback)
   1. Bolivia – History. I. Title. II. Series.
F3321.K54 2011
984–dc22   2010049861

ISBN 978-1-107-00568-6 Hardback
ISBN 978-0-521-18372-7 Paperback

CONTENTS

PREFACE TO THE SECOND EDITION

In this fourth version of my history of Bolivia (two editions with Oxford University Press and two with Cambridge University Press) I have been faced with the usual problems of defining periods in contemporary history. As readers of the earlier editions will note, I have been constantly changing the post-1952 periodization. What constitutes key turning points is a continually changing perception among Bolivian historians and social scientists. Thus I have used the election of 2002 as the break between the last two chapters since national commentators have stressed its political significance in presaging the emergence of a new political system. It should be recognized that this periodization does not work for the social and economic trends that clearly straddle this divide, and that this breakdown will most likely be redefined in the future. I also recognize that I am making judgments about contemporary trends in the midst of some very profound changes that are occurring in Bolivian society and polity, and that future historians will see these changes from different perspectives. It is clear that some of these contemporary political, economic, and social changes will lead to unanticipated developments. Although some readers may feel that it is too early to evaluate what has been occurring in the last eight years, I would simply note that I have reached an age when I will not be around to see how this all turns out. But my fascination with Bolivia compelled me to undertake this latest version since I felt that I could offer some insights, even at this early stage in the process of change, based on my reading of the past and my long experience with this country that has fascinated me for most of my academic career.

In the eight years since the last edition, a whole new generation of social scientists and research centers have emerged and have produced an important literature analyzing contemporary change. There has also been a subtle change in social definitions within Bolivian society in recent years, with a slow abandonment of the word "cholo," which is now considered pejorative, to the more generic term of mestizo. I would stress that the Bolivian definition of mestizo differs considerably from the more general meaning of this term for most Latin Americans. In Bolivia the mestizo more closely identifies with his or her indigenous past than with the Western part of their culture and tends to maintain clothing and other symbols of identity even when adopting Spanish as their primary language. Equally the term "indígena" has become the standard to define all those who identify themselves as pertaining to an Amerindian group, even if they are mestizos. Although I have adopted this new terminology in the later chapters of this book, I have left the older terminology intact in the pre-1980 chapters since their contemporary meanings were then not current.

Unless otherwise indicated, all the current statistical information that I cite comes from Bolivian government sources, above all the National Census Bureau (INE); the Presidential Planning Commission (UDAPE); the Central Bank of Bolivia (BCB); and the relevant government ministries. For comparative Latin American statistical data I have relied on data provided by the UN and its Latin American research groups CEPAL and CELADE. In undertaking this new edition I have been greatly aided by the research assistance of José Alejandro Peres Cajias. As usual, my friends, colleagues, and former students listed in the earlier edition have continued to provide me with support and advice.

Menlo Park, California
June 2010

PREFACE TO THE FIRST EDITION

The evolution of the peoples of Bolivia is one of the more complex and fascinating of human histories. It is the most Indian of the American republics whose monolingual speakers of Spanish remain a minority to the present day. The Amerindian languages of Quechua and Aymara still predominate, and even such pre-Incan languages as Uru are spoken. Thus, Bolivia is not simply a colonial replica of its last conqueror, but a complex amalgam of cultures and ethnicities that go back centuries. A society that has successfully adapted to one of the highest altitudes of human settlement on earth, the Bolivians have created a constantly changing and vital multiethnic society.

For the mass of Bolivians, their culture is a blending of pre-Columbian and post-Conquest norms and institutions. Spanish systems of government were grafted onto pre-Spanish kinship organizations, ecologically disperse settlements were converted into nucleated villages, and local and state religions were syncretized into a new folk Catholicism highly mixed with the symbols and myths of Mediterranean popular religion. Traditional exchange systems coexist with a highly developed market, and wheat is grown along with pre-Columbian staples such as quinua and coca. In the Quechuan and Aymaran languages, Spanish loan words form an important part of the vocabulary, while among the popular urban classes, pre-Columbian belief systems can be found mixed with modern Western norms.

But this description of Bolivia as a dual society does not mean to imply that Bolivia is simply a laboratory of peasants developing a new cultural idiom in a difficult environment. For Bolivia is, and has been since the sixteenth-century Spanish conquest, a capitalist Western class-organized society in which the Indians were for many centuries an exploited class of workers. The government, which extracted the surplus from the peasants and workers, was traditionally run for and by the "white" Spanish-speaking and Western-oriented elite. While, phenotypically, the Bolivian "whites" look much like their Indian ancestors, their economic, social, and cultural position has placed them squarely in the classic mold of a Western European society. Educated by Europeans to European norms, and even practicing a religion distinct from the folk Catholicism of the peasants, the "whites" ruled over and exploited the peasantry.

But the elite itself has slowly miscegenated, as in all such multiracial societies, and over the centuries there has emerged a new biological grouping of mixed background. Thus, Bolivia, like most multiethnic societies in the Americas, has come to define race as a social rather than a genetic or even phenotypic term. The upper classes, speaking Spanish, wearing Western dress, and consuming nonindigenous foods, were the "whites," or, as the peasants called them, the "*gente decente*." The urban lower and middle classes, and the rural freehold farmers who wore European dress and spoke Spanish and one of the Amerindian languages, were the *mestizos* or, as they are called in Bolivia, *cholos*. The monolingual peasants speaking Indian languages and consuming traditional Andean foods were the "Indians." Indians were denied access to power except as they abandoned their traditional norms and languages and integrated into the national society as cholos or whites. Thus, the more marginal, ambitious, or able of these peasants have constantly fed the white and cholo classes. Even among the traditional monolingual peasantry, there were internal divisions between rich and poor, hereditary high-status individuals and commoners, original members of the communities and later migrants. Although these dichotomies changed over time, and especially since the introduction of mass education and effective political democracy, Bolivia still contains many of the elements of a racist society, although with a far more powerful and aggressive cholo class than is found elsewhere in Amerindian America.

In its political evolution, Bolivia has been typical of such multiethnic societies in the long domination of one ethnic group and its fight to maintain its monopoly on power. In fact, there is considerable debate as to whether the Indian masses did better under the Crown than under the Republic. Much of local politics of the nineteenth and twentieth centuries involved the white elite's attempts to organize themselves into a cohesive group capable of denying power to the cholos and Indians. The limited parliamentary republican regimes that they created were the exclusive preserve of the small elite of Spanish speakers. But, like most such systems in the Americas, the impact of modern economic change in the second half of the nineteenth century forced the disintegration of these closed political worlds, and the elite were forced to expand the political system to include the middle class and urban workers. But this process of partial inclusion and increasing democratization eventually broke down. At this point in its political evolution, Bolivia sharply diverged from the common Latin American pattern when a massive popular worker and middle-class revolutionary movement swept aside the entire preexistent political system in the National Revolution of 1952. The resulting social, economic, and political reforms, while they did not destroy the dual society, radically reduced the level of exploitation and even opened the door to an alternative means of acculturation to modern society without abandoning Amerindian culture and languages. Indians were finally given political power, along with their lands, and the basic export sector was nationalized. With its polity, economy, and society so drastically altered, Bolivia's evolution in the last several decades, while sharing the Latin American horrors of military rule, has nevertheless continued to evolve in a manner distinct from the rest of the hemisphere.

In its economic development, Bolivia also has shown itself to be a relatively unusual nation. In a spectrum of economies in the world, Bolivia stands somewhere at the extreme as an almost classic case of an open economy. Concentrating on mineral and primary exports from the sixteenth century until today, the Bolivian economy follows world market conditions to an unusual degree. International changes in supply and demand are immediately felt in a national economy totally dependent on primary exports. Given the small size and extremely low density of the national population (the lowest in Latin America), a national industrial structure is virtually precluded from developing except under the most extreme conditions of world crisis or international integration. Bolivia thus differs from most of the developing world in its loyalty to the system of comparative advantage.

Despite this external dependency, Bolivia also has had an unusual degree of national control over its own resources, especially in the national period. Bolivian entrepreneurs made up of whites and cholos dominated the mining industry and succeeded in passing their control to the nation without the massive intervention of foreign entrepreneurs until the last few decades. Bolivia has obviously not been immune to the machinations of its neighbors or of more distant world powers. Yet, the creative spirit of its peoples has enabled it to survive and to condition these external interventions in the context of its own needs and concerns.

For all its fascinating historical evolution and the rapid changes that have occurred in the contemporary period, Bolivia still remains a poor and relatively backward society and, in terms of human survival, one of the harshest regions in the Americas. Even today, its eight million nationals, despite significant improvements, still have among the highest death rates, lowest life expectancies, and lowest per capita wealth in the Western hemisphere. Yet, even here there have been profound transformations in the past couple of decades, which have finally brought public education to the entire population and reduced illiteracy to a low level even by Latin American standards.

Unique as it is in so many ways, Bolivia forms an intimate part of the common history of mankind, from its development as a multiethnic conquest society to its contemporary emergence as a nation that has undergone profound social and political change. It is this fascinating interaction of Western patterns and pre-Columbian traditions, of class organization and dual social systems, of poverty and exploitation and vigorous independence and social creativity, that I will attempt to explore in the pages that follow.

In undertaking this survey of Bolivian history, I have tried to distill some forty years of reading, research, and participant observation on this subject. Although one not born into a culture will miss many of its nuances, I hope that my distance from the subject will compensate for potential distortions. Equally, as a member of an advanced industrial society, I have tried to remain as objective as possible without suspending my own moral or intellectual judgments or going to the extreme of being patronizing.

In my long education as a "Bolivianist," which began in the late 1950s, I have had the advice, instruction, and constant support of a large number of scholars and friends. Bernardo Blanco-Gonzalez and Teresa Gisbert introduced me to the subject in formal courses, and Gunnar Mendoza and Alberto Crespo guided me in my researches when I arrived in Bolivia in 1959. Antonio Mitre, a long-term friend and former student, has constantly challenged my assumptions, and I am also indebted for guidance, criticism, and support to Silvia Rivera, Xavier Albó, Josep Barnadas, Philip Blair, Thérèse Bouysse-Cassagne, Tristan Platt, Terry Saignes, Karen Spalding, Enrique Tandeter, and Nathan Wachtel. As intellectual mentors and close friends, Marcello Carmagnani and Nicholás Sánchez-Albornoz have been of inestimable value to me on this project. At various times this manuscript has been critically read by Stanley Engerman, Harriet Manelis Klein, Richard Wortman, and Maria Ligia Coelho Prado.

In undertaking the revisions from earlier versions of this work,[1] I have continued to receive the support and criticism of friends and scholars including Ricardo Godoy, Erwin Greishaber, and Eric Langer. I also would like to thank my former students Brooke Larson, Clara López Beltrán, Manual Contreras, Mary Money, and Ann Zulawski for sharing their ideas and research with me. Manuel Contreras has been especially helpful to me in getting access to the latest social and economic data on Bolivia and critically examining my interpretations of this material. In turn, Clara López Beltrán has been my constant source of current information on the latest in historical studies. Finally, Judith Schiffner made this whole process of writing a wonderful experience.

---

[1] This work was initially published as *Bolivia: The Evolution of a Multi-Ethnic Society* by Oxford University Press, in 1982, and revised in 1992.

In this new age of electronic access to materials, Bolivian government agencies have been extraordinarily generous in providing vital data on their society and polity: this has included the Banco Central de Bolivia, the Instituto Nacional de Estadistica, UDAPE, and the Bolivian National Congress as well as the United Nations and the World Bank, to which I am deeply grateful. I would like to thank as well the journal *Annales* for permission to reprint the map "Les señoríos aymaras" in T. Bouysee-Cassagne, "L'organisation de l'espace aymara: urco et uma," *Annales, E.S.C.*, 33 (1978) 1059. Map 1-2 is adopted from E. Boyd Wennegren and Morris D. Whitaker, *The Status of Bolivian Agriculture* (New York: Praeger Publishers, 1975), p. 20 and reproduced with permission of Greenwood Publishing Group; and map. 1-3 is adopted from Rex A. Hudson and Dennis M. Hanratty, eds., *Bolivia: A Country Study* (Washington: Library of Congress, Federal Research Division, 1989), figure 3. Finally, I would note that I have adopted the most common current spellings of Aymara and Quechuan Indian terms used in the national literature, though recognizing that these are constantly changing, and I use the Spanish term *cacique* for Indian noble, which is the norm in the Bolivian literature, rather than *kuraka*, which is the quechuan term used in Peruvian studies.

Menlo Park, California
August 2001

Chapter 1

Geography and Pre-Columbian Civilization

Bolivian society evolved in a highly complex and unusual environment. Although situated in tropical latitudes, it was in fact an unusual high altitude society only comparable to those few similar societies found in the Himalayas. From the earliest human settlement to the present day, a good part of its people have lived at altitudes over five thousand feet above sea level, with the majority of the population and its most advanced cultures being found at twelve thousand feet or above. While not a totally prohibitive environment, the highlands have poorer soils and much colder and drier climates, and face constraints that do not hinder the lowlands. This ecology required the domestication of plants and animals unique to the highlands and even had a dramatic impact on human physiology, as highland populations were forced to adapt to the limited supply of oxygen and quite different degrees of air pressure.

Although some two-thirds of Bolivia's territory consists of tropical and semitropical lowlands, from the Pacific coast deserts of the Atacama region (until this past century) in the west, to the vast stretches of eastern lowlands and flood plains forming parts of the Amazonian and Pilcomayo river basins in the east, humanity has been concentrated in the highlands from remotest times until today. But the highlands and their associated intramountain valleys (see Map 1-1) formed but a small part of the total Bolivian landscape.

While the lowlands may have offered better soils and the potential for a richer life, their inaccessibility until modern times rendered them useless to all but a small number of seminomadic hunters and

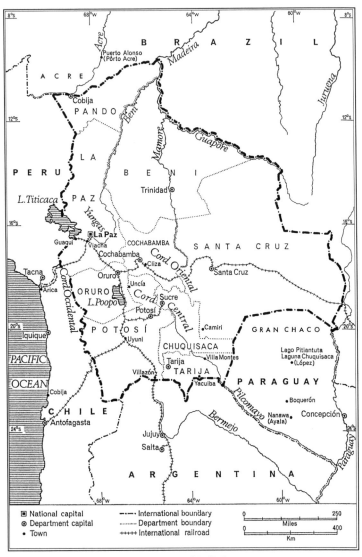

1-1 Map of Bolivia

gatherers isolated from significant contact with the major centers of advanced civilization. By contrast, the high plateau was well articulated with the dense populations and advanced culture areas of coastal and central Peru. Thus, despite its limitations in terms

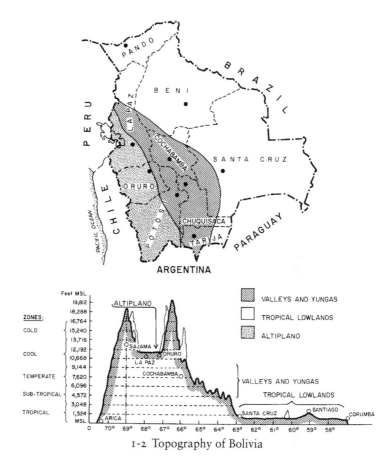

1-2 Topography of Bolivia

of crops and life in general, the broad expanse of its arable lands, its potential as a major grazing zone, and its deposits of accessible minerals made the Bolivian highlands the logical center for human settlement.

The Bolivian highlands, known to the Spaniards as the *altiplano* (or high plateau), consisted of an enormous level tableland at an extremely high altitude (see Map 1-2). Beginning just north of Lake Titicaca, these highlands extend some five hundred miles to the south at an average altitude of some thirteen thousand feet. Created by an opening of the Southern Andes into two distinct mountain ranges at around nine degrees south of the Equator, the altiplano grows from a width of a few miles at its beginning to approximately one hundred miles across in the central areas. A great elliptical sphere with the enormous lake at its top, the altiplano is the largest and most level plateau in the Andes, which in its turn is the most extensive mountain range in the world. Two-thirds of the approximately fifty thousand or so square miles that constitute the altiplano falls within the current borders of Bolivia.

The mountain ranges that define the altiplano contain quite different features. The western branch is known as the *Cordillera Occidental*, and is an extremely narrow and well-defined range averaging some 16,500 feet, rising at its highest point to over 21,000 feet. It contains few river valleys or habitable plateaus and forms a steep barrier blocking the high plateau from easy access to the sea and the desert of the Atacama coast. Although formed from volcanic activity and highly subject to erosion, it contains relatively few minerals worth exploiting. On its eastern slope touching on the altiplano, it has very arid soils and some enormous salt flats, those at Uyuni being greater in size than Lake Titicaca itself. Thus, the western Cordillera stands as a harsh barrier preventing easy access to the coast. At its northern and southern edges, however, the Cordillera breaks up into more accessible routes to the sea, encouraging Bolivia's integration with the coast in a more northern or southwestern direction. This western mountain range offers few attractions for human populations either within or near its borders and so defines the western half of the altiplano as the most sparsely settled area of the region.

Quite different is the eastern range of mountains known variously as the *Cordillera Real, Central,* or *Oriental.* Far broader and much more broken than the western Cordillera, the Royal Cordillera contains numerous fertile plains and river valleys at altitudes from fourteen thousand feet down to a few hundred feet above sea level. Because of its numerous valleys, it also provides easier access to the eastern foothills (known as the *montaña* region) and the lowland plains to the east.

The valleys and plains of the Cordillera Real are quite complex but can be roughly defined by altitude and extension. The higher altitude plains, defined as subpuna valleys, for the most part have a temperate environment and good ground water, although relatively dry climate, and average about eighty-two hundred feet above sea level. They are usually long open plains with relatively easy accessibility from the higher altiplano; the most densely inhabited are the valleys of Cochabamba and Chuquisaca, the western part of Potosi, and the region of Tarija. These broad middle altitude valleys were major zones of pre- and post-Conquest production and settlement. Best exemplified by the Cochabamba Valley system, these valleys were the primary producers of maize in the pre-Columbian period and of wheat after the Spanish Conquest. They also were the major manufacturers of *chica*, the alcoholic beverage made from maize. Given the importance of all these crops, these subpuna valleys were in constant contact with the core highland populations. Here, too, would develop cattle production after the conquest, while the altiplano became the center of Spanish-introduced sheep.

Below the subpuna valleys or just off the altiplano itself were the steep river valleys in the central part of the Cordillera known generally as the *Yungas*. At anywhere from thirty-two hundred to eighty-two hundred feet in altitude, these valleys are characterized by high humidity because of the Amazonian winds and thus have intensive cultivation of tropical and semitropical crops. The most important of these Yungas are those located close to the altiplano city of La Paz and called the *Nor* and *Sud* (or North and South) Yungas, the regions of Larecaja, Muñecas, and Inquisivi. Historically, these valleys were the center of maize and coca production, two fundamental products in high demand on the altiplano and incapable of being cultivated there. They also were the zone of intensive citrus, fruit, and coffee production in the post-Conquest period, and thus were complementary to the highland centers. Another series of semitropical valleys were the more isolated ones to be found in the provinces of Cochabamba and Santa Cruz. Capable of producing the same crops as the Yungas valleys, they remained largely unsettled and inaccessible until the twentieth century.

Before reaching the flat plains of the Amazonian and Chaco lowlands, the eastern Cordillera turns into a series of small hills and mountains called the montaña area. Passing these one enters the open sea level plains. These are divided into two quite distinct zones. In the north are the *Llanos de* (or plains of) *Mojos*, sometimes called the Northern Humid *llanos* or those of the Beni. These tropical savannas are usually heavily flooded in the December–April summer rainy season. In their center is the Rio Mamore, which forms part of the Amazonian basin system. To the south of the Mojos plains are the highlands of the *Macizo Chuquitano*, named after the old province of Chuquitos. At slightly higher elevation, this area shares much of the Mojos environment but is also a center of important hydrocarbon deposits. Then to the south are the dry plains or *llanos del Chaco*. Stretching from Santa Cruz south to the Brazilian, Argentine, and Paraguayan borders and beyond, these sandy dry *chaco* plains, which form the Pilcomayo river basin, are covered with scattered scrub forest and form a large part of the territory of the nation, yet contain only one-fifth of its population.

Because of inaccessibility and harsh seasonal variations, these lowlands were unexplored and unexploited until recent times. While some coca production and cattle-raising were developed in the colonial period along the eastern montana edge of the lowlands in those areas close to the cities of Santa Cruz and La Paz, it was only with the development of commercial production of wild rubber in the late nineteenth century that systematic exploitation began. Only the opening of rail and road transport in the twentieth century finally permitted the development of commercial agricultural production in sugar, cotton, soybeans, and coca and the exploitation of the region's oil and natural gas deposits. In turn, cattle-raising become centered on the northeastern plains regions of Mojos and Beni. Even with all these recent developments, these lowland regions still only contain a third of the national population.

Throughout the history of human settlement in Bolivia, the altiplano and its associated eastern valleys remained the primary zone of human activity, with the altiplano the core of the system. But, despite its centrality and the density of its population, the altiplano was not uniformly hospitable for human settlement over its entire area. The western half of the altiplano contained few minerals, largely infertile soils, and extraordinarily dry climate; the eastern half, however, had reasonably fertile soils, enormous mineral deposits, and a relatively more humid and warm climate resulting from the presence of Lake Titicaca. With its thirty-five hundred square miles, Lake Titicaca exerts an enormous influence over the local climate and provides humidity and relative warmth unavailable on the rest of the altiplano. As a result, intensive agriculture and herding became essential occupations of the peoples surrounding the lake and provided the ecological support for the creation of an important food surplus. This in turn provided the incentive for the creation of more complex cultural systems. The settlement around the lake took place in a series of open plains defined by foothills, known as *cuencas*, which stretch south to the great river valley that would become the city of La Paz, some fifty-six miles south of the lake. The cuenca on the shores of the lake and the one of Jesus de Machaca are the most valuable in terms of soils and humidity and are linked by the Desaguadero River. This in turn binds together the two lakes, Titicaca to the north and Poopó to the south, and also passes through the two southern cuencas of Oruro and Uyuni. The Oruro cuenca is moderately populated, while Uyuni – the driest zone in all Bolivia – is the center of salt flats and largely uninhabited.

It was on the altiplano that the domestication of the staple products of Andean civilization took place. In the Lake Titicaca region the potato was domesticated – a development that was to have a profound impact on the populations of Europe – as well as quinoa and a host of nutritional root crops. Frozen and dehydrated, these numerous roots have been fundamental staples in the Bolivian diet.

The altiplano also was the scene of the domestication of the American cameloids: the llama, alpaca, and vicuña. Beasts of burden, producers of wool, and sources of meat, fertilizer, and heat, these cameloids were to play a fundamental role in the Andean ecology and economy. From the remotest times, these animals were found in close contact with human populations on the altiplano, although it was during the epoch of the historic Aymara kingdoms that the domestication and use of these animals reached its fullest development. So important were their herds that in all their fortified settlements the pre-Incan Aymaras provided space for their animals as well as their people.

An excellent grazing zone of natural and artificial pastures, the altiplano also became the home of the European domesticated sheep after the Spanish Conquest. While usually incompatible with other grazing stock, sheep successfully integrated with the American cameloids, and the two today remain integral parts of the Amerindian herding economy. Thus, between the great herds and the intensive root crop agriculture, the altiplano Indian populations were able to produce both sufficient foodstuffs and woolens for their own survival and replacement, as well as surpluses to exchange for fish, fruits, condiments, maize, and coca, which could not be produced in the highlands.

The altiplano also contains a wealth of mineral deposits that have been exploited from pre-Columbian times to the present and that mark this region as one of the great mineral zones of the world. The distribution of these minerals closely parallels the primary agricultural areas of the altiplano. Just as the best soils were in the eastern side of the altiplano, some 80 percent of Bolivia's vast mineral deposits are to be found in the same area. Concentrated in a zone that has been given the general name of the *faja estanifera* (or tin belt), most of Bolivia's minerals are found in the Cordillera Real and its associated plains and upper valleys, running from just northeast of Lake Titicaca, through the eastern Cordillera range, to the Argentine frontier in southern Bolivia. Going from north to south, the minerals belt is divided into several roughly defined areas. From southern Peru to about the level of Mururata is the oldest geological section, which contains all the gold deposits, taken mostly through placer mining since pre-Columbian times, as well as wolfram and other metals. From Mururata south to Oruro are more deposits of wolfram and the first important deposits of tin. But the major tin districts appear in the third zone heading south, in the region from Oruro through Potosí to the southern frontier. Known as the "poli-metal province" because of its unique association of tin with silver, this region is the heartland of Bolivia's mineral deposits and contains not only tin and silver in extraordinary abundance but also a host of rare metals, many of them unique to Bolivia, and minerals such as lead, bismuth, zinc, and antimony. The only major metal deposits located outside this zone are copper in the eastern altiplano, and the large nitrate and copper concentrations on the other side of the western Cordillera in the Atacama desert. The Cochabamba Valley contained a host of nonferrous metals. In the eastern foothills are large deposits of natural gas and petroleum and the only iron ore in the whole region. Thus, the only minerals or hydrocarbons Bolivia lacks are coal, bauxite, chrome, platinum, and precious stones. This extraordinary mineral heritage, while only modestly exploited in pre-Columbian times, would become the basis for Bolivia's importance in the world economy once the region was discovered by Europe. Moreover, even during its more modest pre-sixteenth-century beginnings, the metallurgy of the highland populations was an important trade item between themselves and the high civilizations of the Peruvian coast, and it was in metallurgy and in their creation of a unique highland ecology adaptive to man's needs that the early Bolivian populations showed their greatest originality.

Given the extraordinary importance of minerals, root crops, and cameloid products in the Andean economy, the highlands remained the primary zone of exploitation for the peoples of pre-Conquest Bolivia, and thus set the pattern that would predominate down to the present day. But the utility of the altiplano environment, for all the creativity of its human populations, was limited. For this reason, the highland populations have constantly interacted with the valley and lowlands peoples to obtain basic complementary food products that they could not produce. This so-called vertical ecological integration, involving exchanges of products from sharply different ecological zones, has been a common feature of human life in this region from the beginning. From earliest known times, colonists from the altiplano were to be found in all the valleys to the east and also as far away as the Pacific coast on the west. Intense interregional trade became the hallmark for all the advanced cultures on the altiplano. Trading root crops, meat, and wools from their vast cameloid herds of llama, alpaca, and vicuña, the highland peoples obtained coca, maize, fish, fruits, and beans from the lowland areas and maintained a varied subsistence base. Through centuries of expansion, change, and finally European conquest, the highland peoples kept this vertical ecological integration intact, and fought all attempts to isolate the altiplano from its regional sources of trade. To this very day, in fact, vertical ecological integration is a dominant theme of social and economic organization in rural Bolivia.

In this, as in so much else, the area that would eventually make up the Bolivian nation shared much in common with the entire Andean region, of which it formed only the southern sector. In the central and southern highlands of what is today Peru, similar geographic settings created similar patterns of integration, especially in the region immediately north of Lake Titicaca. Moreover, the entire Andean area would share a common cultural history.

The arrival of early man in the Andean area dates back at least twelve thousand years, although the remnants of their presence in the highlands have been less well preserved than along the Andean Pacific coastline. But both highland and coastal cultural areas in the period prior to 2500 B.C. shared a largely hunting and gathering subsistence with seminomadic settlements. Whereas in the coastal zone, human population concentrated on the resources of the sea, the highland peoples engaged in wild-animal hunting for subsistence. From the end of the last glacial period (c. 8000 B.C.), there began the slow development of domestication of plants and animals. Agriculture and herding finally became the predominant forms of subsistence only after some six thousand years of experimentation. By 4000 B.C., herding of Andean cameloids became a major highland activity; by 3200 B.C., pottery could be found in the region, and spun cotton cloth has been recovered from coastal burials dating from 2500 B.C.

By this latter date, the highlands of Peru were the scene of a major transformation to settled village agriculture. Permanent settlement, increased population density, and more complex social organization in terms of multicommunity governments became the norm. For the next thousand years, both the coast and highlands experienced this increasing tempo of settled agricultural life. More truly urban centers were formed, and the establishment of religious ceremonial centers marked the beginnings of non-food-producing specialists who provided services to the full-time agriculturists.

Although the process that moved village horticulturists to sacrifice some of their surplus to non-food-producing groups is not fully understood, the record from the Andes suggests that it was primarily technical and/or religious motivations that led to the formation of complex intercommunity governments. The existence of unfortified ceremonial centers isolated from agricultural settlements and the creation of complex irrigation systems across several valleys and around the major lakes seem to reenforce this interpretation.

The next major phase of Andean development involved the widespread use of metals, the development of metal technology being an important indication of the creation of increasingly larger states and more dense populations. Copper dates at least from 2000 B.C. and in the highlands, copper pieces of the Wankarani culture from the region near Oruro date from 1200 to 1000 B.C.

Around 800 B.C., the development of the "Chavín" civilization, the best studied of the earliest advanced cultures in the area, brought changes throughout the Andean area. This culture, the core of which was in the central highlands and associated coastal valleys, saw the first massive spread of influence of one major culture over a very large area. It was a period marked by extensive use of textiles and gold, as well as the development of advanced pottery techniques and urbanization. Major ceremonial centers were built along the coast and highlands, and almost all of the valleys and plateaus were now fully and permanently settled. In all of these developments, the southern highlands of Bolivia, although sharing many of the traits found elsewhere, seemed to concentrate on metallurgy, of pure metals such as gold and silver, but refined alloys as well. Although Chavín culture did not reach as far south as Lake Titicaca, a coterminous and later culture known as Paracas did influence the southern coastal and highland areas, but the extent is still not fully known.

At about 100 B.C., the Chavín style disappeared from the Andean area and was replaced by vigorous local styles confined to a given valley or drainage area. On the coast appeared the Moche and Nazca cultures. In the highlands, Waru culture developed near Cuzco, and a major center appeared at the small town of Tiahuanaco just south of Lake Titicaca. These cultures saw the final introduction and domestication of all the known plants and animals and the full development of Peruvian technology. In the Bolivian highlands, the copper and tin alloy, bronze, was discovered. Although fully developed in the southern highlands, bronze was not universally adopted in the Andean area for use in war or agriculture and, unlike Eurasia, had little technological impact.

The growth of a viable and important center of culture at Tiahuanaco represented a major development in Bolivian history. Situated some thirty miles south of Lake Titicaca on the altiplano at an elevation of 13,120 feet, Tiahuanaco was an advanced religious settlement with pottery and metal objects from approximately A.D. 100 onward. It was only after A.D. 600, however, that its influence began to spread beyond its local site. Its importance in Andean history was due to both its unusual location and its dominance within the entire southern Peruvian highland region from approximately the seventh century until the thirteenth century A.D. Because its distinctive art styles and designs influenced pottery throughout the highlands and most of the coastal areas, it initially was thought that the Tiahuanaco empire was established through conquest. But all the major Tiahuanaco cities so far discovered have been unfortified settlements with a religious style of architecture. Some scholars have assumed that Tiahuanaco influence was purely religious, and that such secular kingdoms as that of the Waru (A.D. 700–1100) in the region of Ayacucho were more important in spreading its influence. The continued discovery of new Tiahuanaco "religious" centers with their characteristic square, or rectangular platform surrounded by sandstone and basalt blocks (called a *Kalasasayas*), has suggested a possible third interpretation: that of Tiahuanaco religions and/or commercial colonies distributed among the highlands, valley, and coastal regions that spread the influence of Tiahuanaco culture through direct contact.

In the highlands, this period is associated with an intensification of agriculture and a major expansion of mountain terracing, floating gardens in Lake Titicaca, raised fields in highland flooded valleys, and complex irrigation works. It appears that Tiahuanaco civilization was associated with a major increase in the tempo of highland economic and social change. It has been suggested that the hydrologic engineering of the Tiahuanaco civilization was quite advanced even for the Andes, which may explain its rapid expansion after A.D. 1000, and the progressive drying of the climate after A.D. 1200 had a profound impact on its agricultural base and thus explains its rapid decline.

With the collapse of Tiahuanaco and the parallel breakdown of the Waru empire, there emerged in the Andean area over the next three centuries a number of regional states and empires. Among the most distinctive of these were the Chimu on the northern Peruvian coast, with their large urban center at Chan-Chan. In the highlands around Lake Titicaca, the most important groups were the Chanka federation just north of Cuzco, and the kingdoms of the Aymara speakers on the shores of Lake Titicaca and in the southern altiplano.

T. BOUYSSE-CASSAGNE   L'ESPACE AYMARA

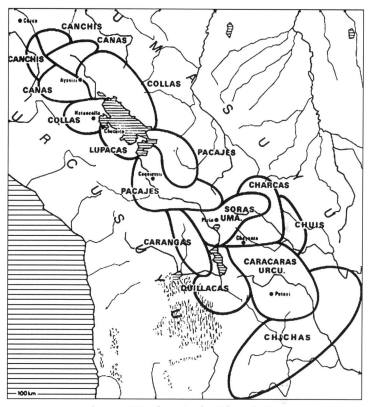

1-3 Aymara Kingdoms in the Fifteenth Century

The development of the Aymara kingdoms marks the beginning of the historic period of Bolivian history, that is, the period for which written records exist (see Map 1-3). It is the Aymara who dominated the central highlands of Bolivia from the end of the twelfth century until the arrival of the Spaniards in the sixteenth century. From the oral traditions recorded in the Spanish and mestizo chronicles and from the archaeological record, it is clear that the Aymara kingdoms represent an important departure from the previous Tiahuanaco period. The concentration of towns along the lakeshore in open communities, the commonality of pottery styles and decoration, and the importance of terraced agriculture were now replaced by fortified towns (or *pucara*) on hilltops well back from the lake, a much more intensive development of a cameloid herding culture, and a more localized religion as represented by the *chulpas*, or local burial and ceremonial houses, in all the communities.

The rather warlike and aggressive Aymara-speaking peoples seem to have carried the Peruvian penchant for moiety organization to an extreme. While it is currently assumed that there were at least seven major "nations" of Aymara speakers, it appears as if each nation was divided into two separate kingdoms. Thus, the Lupaca and the Colla, to mention just the largest of these nations, both had an *Urcusuyu* and *Umasuyu* government, each with its own separate "king" and each controlling different territories. Linguistic and geographic evidence suggests that the Urcusuyu division of any nation was primarily concentrated in the mountaintop fortified centers to the west and southwest of Lake Titicaca, with their colonies grouped along the Pacific coast, while the Umasuyu of any nation were in the eastern highlands and had most of their colonies in the eastern associated valleys and montaña region.

The Aymara "kingdoms" extended from just south of Cuzco into the northern highlands of present-day Bolivia. The core of the region was the highland settlements of the altiplano, and the moiety division of the "nations" ran more or less uniformly along a northwestern-southeastern axis intersecting Lake Titicaca. The most powerful states were those centered on the lake, and this can be considered the heartland of the Aymara peoples. Between them the Collas and the Lupaca controlled most of the Titicaca shore, and, with the Canas to the north, were considered the most important of the Aymara kingdoms.

Just as with the better-known Incan society, the pre-Hispanic Aymara kingdoms also were organized in a complex amalgam of corporate and class structures. There existed the *ayllus*, or kin groupings, with each ayllu divided into an upper (*hanansaya*) half and a lower *(urinsaya)* half, to which everyone belonged. But the nobility in any particular kingdom were associated with the *hanansaya ayllus*, and the commoners with the *urinsaya* part. Although ayllu membership was vital to all Indians, and its common rights to land suggest a communal corporate style structure, the Aymara also had regional chiefs, or *caciques*, who held land independently of the ayllus and extracted free labor from the ayllu members they governed. In turn these caciques were served by assistants at the local ayllu level who were known as *jilakatas*, who seem to have been the moiety leaders.

Thus, among the "kings," the regional nobles, and the local elders there existed a group of individuals with access to private property and with inheritable rights to land and labor independent of the basic ayllu structure. It is not known if these rights were ultimately dependent on royal favor or were truly personal, thus suggesting an incipient class structure. Also, there existed some groups of artisans and special workers who may not have pertained to any ayllu but depended directly on the nobility. In Incan times, these were called the *yanaconas*, and they appear to be either serfs or slaves.

Besides the complex sociopolitical and economic structures that existed in the core highland regions, both caciques and ayllus also had colonists working for them in different ecological zones. Called *mitimaq*, these highland colonists were the vital link binding the interregional and multiecological economy that was so crucial in maintaining the core highland populations. Each ayllu and each nation and its nobility had colonists farming the temperate and semitropical valleys. In exchange for highland meats, potatoes, quinoa, and woolen products, these colonists paid with everything from fish and salt from the Pacific coast villages to corn, coca, and fruits from the Yungas and subpuna valleys. In these distant regions, many colonists coexisted with the local non-Aymara populations. Thus, many of the eastern escarpment valleys held a complex of institutions, communities, and properties, ranging from private estates of caciques and colony communities of altiplano ayllus to native ayllus of local groups. Thus, slave and free labor, dependent villages, and even independent nations coexisted in these valleys and lowlands.

This whole system of vertical integration of microecological systems (which has been likened to an archipelago), based on the production of different crops and bound into a nonmarket economy through elaborate systems of kinship, exchange, and labor obligations, was fundamental in maintaining a powerful and economically vital society on the altiplano. So extensive were these colony-core arrangements that even full-fledged gold and silver mining colonies were maintained by highland peoples in Carabaya and other eastern valleys, making the Aymara the premier gold producers of the Andes as well as the leading herdsmen. Such was the wealth of these kingdoms that, despite Inca and Spanish conquests, they were still considered to be unusually wealthy provinces in the sixteenth and seventeenth centuries.

But the Aymara were not alone on the altiplano. Along with these peoples there coexisted a large number of Uru and Puquina-speaking peoples known generically as Uru. Grouped like the Aymara into dual ayllus, the Uru were nevertheless denied access to lands and herds, although they lived among the Aymara. They had no broad-based political organizations and worked primarily as fishermen or as laborers for the Aymara. Whether they were a subjected and conquered peoples held in control by the Aymara is difficult to judge. The Puquina speech of the Uru represented one of the three major altiplano languages in pre-Conquest Peru, along with Quechua and Aymara. By the time of the Spanish Conquest, the Uru were a poor people living in small groupings among all the highland kingdoms, although they still retained scattered colonies along the Pacific coast and in the eastern valleys. Moreover, the cultural – if not political and economic – deference paid by the Aymara to the Urus seems to imply that the Uru may have preceded the Aymara and may have been remnants of an earlier and more advanced civilization. Some have even argued that they were the people of Tiahuanaco. Whatever the situation may have been, by the time of the Spaniards, the Uru, although still quite numerous, were all so poor that most of them escaped Spanish taxation.

Warlike, economically potent, and covering most of the altiplano and the regions to the east and west of it, the Aymara by the late fourteenth century were the dominant peoples within Bolivia and in an important section of southern Peru. But, given the growth of population and wealth throughout the Andes by this time, it was inevitable that a new imperial organization would again be attempted for the region. While many powerful states flourished on the Peruvian coast, the highland cultures had become the vital centers of expansionist states following the epoch of Tiahuanaco. By the late fifteenth century, the numerous Aymara kingdoms found themselves in direct competition with the emerging imperial state of a Quechua-speaking nation in the region of Cuzco north of the lake.

By the early decades of the fifteenth century, the various competing states in the central highlands had sorted themselves out into major groupings, and the Cuzco-Quechua speakers emerged as the most powerful of the new nations. By the middle decades of the century, the expansionist Quechuans, who came to be known as Incas from the name of their rulers, had spread into the northern highlands and were slowly penetrating south toward the Lake Titicaca district. In the 1460s, they were able to extend their influence over the Aymara kingdoms, which were incapable of uniting against the Inca threat because of traditional animosities among themselves. That weakness, despite the relative military power of the Aymara – who undoubtedly were the strongest possible contenders to Inca hegemony in the entire highland region – led to the gradual loss of independence for the Aymara kingdoms by the end of that decade.

The arrival of the Incas in the second half of the fifteenth century, surprisingly, changed little of the social, economic, and political organization of the Aymara kingdoms. Retaining the traditional rulers and contenting themselves with extracting surpluses through tribute payments, the Incas did little to disturb the fabric of Aymara life. This wealthy region was organized into its own province known as *Kollasuyo* (one of the four of the empire). Nevertheless, integration was not peaceful, and in 1470 there was a major revolt against the Incas in the lake kingdoms area. The result was that the remaining independent kingdoms were conquered and Quechua-speaking mitimaqs established in colonies in all of their areas, especially so in the valley of Cochabamba. In fact, this revolt and associated wars would determine the linguistic composition of Bolivia from the fifteenth century until today.

Among the Aymara, the Lupaqa and Collas retained the most autonomy; but even they were now integrated ever more tightly into the Inca empire, as roads, warehouses, fortresses, new urban centers, and military colonists spread throughout the Bolivian highlands and valleys. Like the three other sectors of the Inca empire, Kollasuyo was required to pay tribute, to send its sacred objects to Cuzco, and to allow its youthful nobles to be educated by the rulers of that city. That the Aymara of Kollasuyo retained their languages and autonomous social, economic, and even political structures to such an extent is a tribute to their wealth and power in the pre-Incaic times as well as their sense of powerful ethnic identity. Even the Spanish Conquest, with its deliberate support for increased "Quechuanization," could not wipe out the Aymara culture.

By the time that the Incas had completely dominated the Aymara kingdoms, their allies, and the smaller subpuna valley and Yungas groups within the highland cultural zone, they had already fully elaborated the basic outlines of their imperial organization. Yet, the principles of a coherent economic, social, and political system were still only being slowly implanted when – some eighty years later – the Spaniards ended the experiment in Inca organization. The early demise of the Inca state just as it was beginning to mature has made it extremely difficult to analyze the exact nature of Inca society in the late fifteenth and early sixteenth centuries.

As officially recounted to the Spaniards, the Inca state was an authoritarian and benevolent organization based on rational principles of equality and justice. Prohibiting private property, the state distributed goods and services by taxing up to two-thirds of the produce of the Andean peasantry. The peasants in turn were organized hierarchically into decennial groups of tens, hundreds, and so on, and finally the empire itself was administered in four basically homogeneous regions by a state bureaucracy dependent totally on the Inca and associated by clan groupings with the rulers of the state. A state religion that stressed the civic virtues and was totally syncretic to all previous religions was the instrument that guaranteed the consensus of the popular masses.

Although the rulers of the empire may have perceived their society in quite coherent and rational terms, in fact the rapid and recent conquest of all types of peoples made for a relatively heterogeneous society. True, the road network was fully constructed and the incredibly large warehouse system was in place so that in fact the Incas could store surplus from any area for use throughout the empire during times of emergency as well as maintaining nonagricultural artisans and a professional army. But there did exist important elements of private property within this broader nonmarket system. Thus, nobles who had surrendered peacefully to the Incas retained their lands and their workers, just as distinguished Inca nobles were able to obtain private lands and the use of *yanaconas*, or landless servants of the state. Equally, the preexistent states retained many pre-Inca forms of government, despite their incorporation into broader provinces in the Inca empire. The removal of religious objects to Cuzco and the forceful Quechuanization of the local elites did not change the dedication of the peasant masses to local religions or lead them to abandon their local languages. Moreover, as in the case of the Aymara, pre-Conquest arrangements of highland colonists and dependent peoples were left largely intact by the Incas, who did not seriously challenge the viability of the old social and political structures so long as they were not a threat to their own control.

Thus, the Inca empire retained a mosaic of political structures, religions, and languages and even had an important element of private property within its borders. Although not completely congruent with its perception of itself, the Inca empire was nevertheless a powerful and cohesive force and probably the most sophisticated state and economic structure elaborated by the peoples of pre-sixteenth-century America. It also performed some of the most amazing engineering and agricultural projects in America. From Ecuador to the southern Bolivian borders, a maze of roads was built that facilitated the easy access for man and animals from all parts of the empire to Cuzco. Thousands of acres of new agricultural lands were created through complex terracing of the steep Andean mountainsides, and vast compounds of warehouses were built to store enormous quantities of cloths and nonperishable foodstuffs for the entire population. The empire, thus, functioned as a major distributor of goods and services in a nonmarket manner and probably created a well-being and wealth among all the population unmatched from those times to the present. Finally, its extremely coherent economic and social organization provided an unusual measure of social and economic justice, as even the Spaniards recognized, for the Incas went to great lengths to alleviate onerous working conditions through carefully selected labor drafts, which were of a short term and fully insured by the state in terms of providing maintenance and compensation for the workers' families. Thus, the peasantry were called on for *mitas*, or forced draft labor in the mines, on engineering projects, in the armies, or on personal service for quite limited periods and were fully and effectively compensated for this work.

So efficient was this Inca organization that it proved to be a military power that none could oppose. It could mobilize large numbers of troops, feed and supply them over long periods of time, and thus remained impervious to agricultural cycles. The Incas were able to wear out their opponents by their numbers, equipment, and persistence. In the period of less than a hundred years that the empire existed, it swept all before it, easily taking both coastal and highland societies – in fact, any state where a settled peasantry was the primary base. By the end, few states could resist the *Pax Incaica*, and many societies voluntarily joined the powerful new empire. It was, by the time the Spaniards arrived, one of the greatest experiments in human organization that the world had seen.

But there were limits to the Inca expansion, and these were defined more by social and economic organization than by military activity. Despite all their use of colonists and armies, the Incas proved incapable of subduing cultures that were not primarily based on peasant agriculture. This was especially evident in the region of Kollasuyo, the zone encompassing Bolivia. Here the Incas had been successful in the conquest of the Aymaras, their Uru dependents, and the smaller populations living in association with the highlanders – that is, the cultures of the subpuna valleys and the Yungas. Although evidently speaking languages distinct from Puquina, Aymara, and Quechua, these valley peoples were easily subsumed in the Inca state, and both during Inca times and in the post-Conquest Quechuanization programs, their languages were lost and replaced by Quechua. Clearly, the dominance of Quechua over Aymara as the major language in the entire Bolivian region has as much to do with the conversion of these local language groups to Quechua as with the placement of Quechua colonists in these formerly Aymara-dominated territories.

Outside this highland system stood an important human frontier in the montaña region and the lowland plains. Here a complex combination of hunters and gatherers, village agriculturalists, and even multivillage states existed, which prevented the highland peoples from expanding eastward. Although the Incas attempted the conquest of this region, they were unsuccessful, and the peoples of these areas blocked highland cultural penetration and domination. Generically called the Chiriguanos by the Spaniards in the post-Conquest era, the lowlands peoples consisted of a large number of different groups that ranged from the Siriono-type hunters and gatherers at a primary level of development to the sophisticated dwellers of the Mojos floodlands. The latter, probably the most advanced group in the region, would disappear by the time of the Spanish Conquest. Nevertheless, it was evident from their remains that they were major causeway builders who maintained a year-round settled agriculture in the lowland floodplains of northeastern Bolivia. Constructing wide causeways, which stretched for hundreds of miles in some cases, the Indians living in the Mojos region successfully resolved the crisis of annual flooding and maintained fairly dense populations and complex governmental structures on this artificially constructed high ground.

So powerful was this frontier that blocked access to both the Amazonian and Pilcomayo river basins to the northeast and southwest that even the Spaniards were unable definitively to conquer and settle this region. In fact, some of the lowland tribes remained isolated until the twentieth century, and overall, until recently, the lowland tribes have preserved a surprisingly large part of their languages and cultures.

To the southwest, another frontier of resistant Indians successfully opposed Inca access to the Chilean coastal plains. These so-called Araucanians (or Maupuches), although fairly advanced materially, were governed by loose intercommunity confederations. Nevertheless, they proved to be an extremely effective military group. Despite repeated attempts by the Incas, they successfully prevented highland penetration to the southwestern coasts. In this case, however, the frontier seems to have been slightly more porous than the eastern lowlands, for trade and contact were fairly frequent between the two regions.

Only to the direct south, in the Andean foothills where the two Cordilleras again merged, in what today is northwestern Argentina, was there strong highland conquest and penetration. Quechua military colonists successfully entered this territory and clearly would have fully settled the northern Argentine plains region, had it not been for the early destruction of the Inca state by the Spanish Conquest.

While the potential for expansion was not totally blocked, the Inca empire had found its natural limits by the time of the Spanish Conquest, and these limits, interestingly enough, were to prove to be the limits of Spanish expansion for most of the colonial period; for advanced and complex state organizations in the Andean area ultimately depended on the existence of a stable and taxable peasantry. Where that peasantry existed and survived, the Incas and their successors could construct powerful state organizations based on the surplus of the peasant class. With land resources abundant, it was the labor input that was always the expensive element in American society, and the stability and productivity of that factor was essential for the existence of non-food-producing classes.

Thus, at the base of the Andean culture stood the peasants organized into tightly knit fictive kin organizations known generically by the term "ayllu," which organized work and distributed land among its members. While some classes existed outside the ayllu structure, the overwhelming majority of all commoners, nobles, and rulers were members of an ayllu. Unlike the contemporary Indian peasant *comunidades*, or the free communities organized by the Spaniards and called ayllus after the Conquest, the pre-Columbian ayllu was essentially a kin group that was not defined by a single residential community. Ayllus had members in all the various ecological zones and, while retaining a central residential area, were not confined to one space. Although land rights ultimately resided in the ayllu, to be granted to its members on an individual basis, members could hold land in a widely spaced and dispersed regional setting, from the coast to the highlands and the eastern valleys. This relatively unstructured geographical setting was an inevitable response to the harshly different ecological zones inhabited by the Andean peoples. It was in sharp contrast to the clustered village pattern of the Mediterranean peasants, which was the distinguishing feature of Spanish culture. It also was quite different from the closed corporate-style community described by anthropologists that would emerge as the dominant form of peasant organization in the post-Conquest period.

By the first decades of the sixteenth century there had emerged within the southern Andean highlands a highly developed society and state organization firmly anchored in a dense and complex village agricultural system. Something like three million Indians were to be found under Inca control (compared with some seven million Spaniards in Spain at the time), with close to a third of them within the southern province of Kollasuyo. Here, a multiplicity of societies speaking numerous languages were grouped together into a vast nonmarket exchange system that involved a continuous transfer of products among starkly different ecological systems. It also was one of the world's richest mineral zones and one of the more densely populated peasant societies at this time. Given this potential, it was inevitable that the southern Andean region would become one of the most important centers of Spanish colonization in the Americas. In turn, the Bolivian highlands, once integrated into Western Europe's expanding overseas empire, would become a source of new foodstuffs and minerals that would have a profound impact on the entire world economy.

Chapter 2

The Creation of a Colonial Society

The Iberian Peninsula in the fifteenth and sixteenth centuries was the leader of European expansion on a global scale. The Portuguese initiated European world domination through the conquest of the oceanic trade routes of Africa and Asia. And Spain – and more specifically the Castillian kingdom within the Spanish state – undertook the conquest and settlement of vast territories of the Western hemisphere. America, unlike Africa and Asia, was unknown and unintegrated into the Eurasian world prior to the fifteenth century. By its American conquest, Spain provided a whole new arena for exclusive European settlement and development that in turn gave Europe a decided advantage in its race for world influence. Thus, the Castillian conquest of the lands of America, along with the Portuguese conquest of the international sea lanes, finally tipped the balance of world economic power to Europe and helped prepare the way for its ultimate industrial domination as well. The conquest of America in the late fifteenth and early sixteenth century was thus crucial in changing the relative importance of Europe in the world, and in defining a new world historical era.

Whereas the Europeans may have initially viewed America as an empty land filled with simple peoples to be exploited for European benefit, in fact America also would change what contemporary social scientists call the "cognitive map" of the Europeans themselves. America did not fit the worldview of early modern Christian Europe, since it was totally outside the Mediterranean cultural tradition and its Christian subcultural perceptions. The Bible did not mention

America, and its Indians had never heard of either Christ or the older religions of the Eurasian land mass. At first, the Europeans ignored these worlds in their conceptions of historical reality, but in the following three centuries the existence of America would begin to help erode some of the traditional beliefs and verities of European cultural norms. Moreover, the new American plants and animals that slowly expanded into the older world regions would profoundly affect the societies and economies of Europe, Africa, and Asia.

The possession of American empires defined the relative power within Europe itself of the various contending nation states. New World territories provided a European state with an important new market and required a powerful navy to make itself felt in the intra-European struggles. That Castile first entered the race for an American empire and possessed most of its lands, resources, and peoples gave the new Spanish state a power over its European contenders that remained unbroken until well into the seventeenth century. For close to a century and a half, Spain was the dominant power in Europe, just when Europe itself was establishing its economic hegemony over the rest of the world, and it was America that made this difference.

The Spanish state, which unleashed the resources of Europe on America, was then the most modern and one of the most recently formed within the European continent. As a result, it was able to combine a broad range of private initiative in the conquest and settlement of America with a very rapid integration of these newly won territories into a centrally controlled and coherent empire run from Europe. Just as their Inca predecessors were known for their administrative and organizational ability, so the genius of the Spaniards would ultimately reside in their ability to integrate the powerful European drive of private enterprise into the context of formal government structures. They were also the first people in world history to create and maintain an intercontinental empire for four centuries.

Thus, the conquest of America meant both its integration into the world market and its organization within the world's largest imperial structure. Until the eighteenth century, no European power could rival the Spanish empire. And this empire stretched from Tierra del Fuego to the Puget Sound and from Sicily in the east to the Philippines in the west. But despite the vital importance of the American colonial empire to Spain in providing the resources to dominate European politics, it was not the only resource of the Spanish state. Even without America, Spain entered the sixteenth century as one of the wealthiest nations in Europe with a thriving international trade in wool and a complex set of exports of the classic Mediterranean crops. It also had an important mining sector and a very dense and commercially active population. Thus, it was able to mobilize enormous internal resources that, with those coming from America, were used to create Europe's most powerful army and navy. With this invincible force, Spain not only fought the Turkish power to a standstill in the eastern Mediterranean but also conquered large parts of southern Italy and Sicily and maintained an important colonial area in the Low Countries. It actively intervened in the politics of the German states and in the French regions, and even was involved in the dynastic struggles of England.

Thus, both within Spain and within the rest of Europe, there were numerous areas for personal opportunity for the upwardly mobile members of Spanish society. Spain itself expanded tremendously: its bureaucracy was growing into the largest in Europe, and its army and its commercial sectors were developing apace. The distant and relatively dangerous Americas therefore attracted only the most daring and the most marginal of the nonpeasant groups within Spain. It was the poor journeymen and not the master craftsmen who went to America, the bastard sons of poor gentry and not the eldest or even second sons of the very well-to-do large landowners. The junior nephews of the leading merchant families in Seville left for America, as did the poorest of lawyers and notaries who had not the funds to purchase a position after obtaining their degrees. It was, in short, the lowest groups within the potentially upwardly mobile classes who left for America. The upper and middle nobility, however, were all doing well enough on the Continent and in Spain not to need to risk the long Atlantic crossing, whereas the vast peasantry were too poor to undertake the voyage.

This background helps explain the surprising nature of the social structure that would be created by the Spaniards in their American empire. To begin with, there was the total absence of the Spanish peasant class, which was replaced in the New World by the American Indian peasants. Moreover, with no preexistent institutions or classes to compete with, and with human resources scarce, all those going to America experienced an extremely rapid elevation of status in relation to their former positions within Spanish society. For many of these individuals, their success in America would in fact make it impossible for them to return to Spain. Although it became the classic myth both in Spain and the rest of Europe that one could go to make one's fortune in America and return, in fact successful Americans could find no place in the more rigid Spanish society. Thus, while the rare conquistadores like Pizarro and Cortés would obtain wealth equal to the greatest of Spanish grandees, they found that the Spanish nobility refused to incorporate them within their ranks, and their wealth could not buy them a place in Spain equivalent to their status in America. Many of these famous conquistadores, after a brief visit to Europe, returned to America. The same occurred at all ranks of society, with the journeyman who never finished his apprenticeship in Europe quickly becoming a powerful and wealthy artisan in America and being unable to transfer his new status back to Europe. Only those who had gained their titles or had their connections established prior to migration could use the wealth they obtained in the New World to achieve position in Spain. The previously poor lawyer or notary could now buy a wealthy practice in Spain, and quickly did so. Moreover, the poor nephew quickly became the rich American merchant and in turn left his poor relatives behind when he returned to Europe. But these were the few exceptions to the general rule that it was difficult to go home again for those who migrated to America.

These factors made for an establishment of a permanent Spanish or Creole society in America virtually from the first days. It was also a society that in many ways proved to be far more mobile than the home society. While the first generation of conquistadores would maintain their station, even when their wealth and status changed, their children knew no such restraints. By the second generation, the honorific titles of Don and Doña were no longer carefully restricted to the elite but were becoming general to all Spaniards, whether born in Spain or America. The rigid guild structure of Spain could not be established in America, where the skilled trades became relatively open to all persons who wished to participate in them.

This open quality does not mean that Creole Spanish America became a classless society. In fact, the Creoles worked very rapidly to establish class lines and quickly absorbed the best resources in an unequal distribution. Thus, a class structure quickly took form and even existed at the very moment of conquest, the spoils of the wars being strictly divided according to the initial economic investment of the soldiers in the conquest expedition and their relative rank within the conquering army. The new elite also used such extra-market mechanisms as free land grants and kinship and marriage alliances to cement land, resource, and capital acquisitions, to close entrance into their ranks as much as possible. But the jealous Spanish Crown never permitted them to create as rigid a class structure as existed in Spain. Entail and primogeniture were rarely used in America until the very end of the colonial period, so the upper class had to maintain itself in the context of a wide-open system of partible inheritance in which all children of both sexes participated equally. That they succeeded in maintaining class lines is obvious when one examines the class structure anywhere in America. Nevertheless, these societies had far more mobility built into them than was apparent in metropolitan Spanish society.

Just as the Spanish-American elite was more mobile than its metropolitan counterpart, it also was less politically powerful. It was denied control over the local government and had to share its power with a royal bureaucracy alien to local influences to an extent unknown in Europe. That the elite influenced that bureaucracy was obvious, but even with all their wealth they could not control or dominate the government as was the case in Europe. In one area, however, they exceeded their counterparts in Europe. In relation to the Indians, all Spaniards exercised more power and control than the equivalent groups did in relationship to the peasants of Spain. The excuse of conquest and cultural-racial differences gave the arriving Spaniards, of whatever class and background, a dominant position unknown in Europe.

The establishment of American society was as much influenced by the nature of the conquest process itself as by the social background and political structure of the metropolitan society. For the Spanish-American empire, especially as it was established in the Andean world, was fundamentally and primarily a Conquest creation.

A minority made up of whites and their black slaves would dominate an initially separate and wholly distinct mass of American Indians. However differentiated internally, the Indians were still considered as an isolated and repressed mass, lower in status than even the poorest and most illiterate conquistador.

At first, the Spaniards appeared to the Andean populations merely as a more powerful foreign conquering group that did not differ significantly from the Inca conquering host. For this reason, and because of the relatively recent Inca subjugation and the existence of antagonistic non-Quechua groups still not fully assimilated within its borders, the Spaniards initially had an easy time overthrowing the Inca empire. As the Spaniards seemed to promise a continuation of internal class structures, recognition of traditional Indian nobilities, and all other types of special privilege accorded to a supportive group in the midst of a war of conquest, many Indians joined the Spaniards as allies. The future pattern of racial discrimination and class oppression was not apparent in the first phase of the Spanish Conquest in the 1530s.

Thus, the Spanish Conquest of Peru, as the area that is now divided into Bolivia and Peru was called, proceeded much as had the conquest of Mexico. Metal weapons, gunpowder, and horses permitted several hundred Spaniards to overcome Indian armies of thousands. At the same time, the Spaniards effectively used the restive non-Quechuan Indians, and the results of the internal civil war between the Inca brothers Huascar and Atahualpa to further their own ends. Initially, they convinced the Inca leadership that they were a simple mercenary force that would leave once their appetites for gold and silver were satiated. To the former independent states and tribes conquered by the Incas they proclaimed themselves liberators, while to the losing Huascar side of the famous Inca civil war they claimed to bring justice and recompense for all their losses.

Astutely using all of these appeals, the Spaniards effectively isolated the recently victorious Atahualpa and his professional Quito armies from the rest of the population south of Ecuador and obtained much needed intelligence, supplies, and auxiliary Indian military allies. Once the Quito troops were dispersed and Atahualpa was killed, they created their own puppet Incas from the previously defeated Huascar faction. When these leaders in turn rebelled, they got the support of their own Indian yanacona servants and anti-Inca forces, which helped them overcome the great last Inca rebellions. Such Indian assistance, combined with their unqualified military superiority, meant that only in rare and special instances were many Spaniards killed in all the fierce and bloody fighting. Spaniards suffered more deaths from battles among themselves than they suffered from the Indians. Finally, whatever hope local Indian victories may have engendered, the onslaught of new Spanish troops and immigrants arriving daily clearly meant that the loss of a few hundred soldiers in no way crippled the Spanish ability to mount a century-long war of conquest and colonization.

It was only the progressive hardening of Spanish rule, with its increasingly odious extraction of surplus resources from the Indian elite and peasantry, that finally drove the various Indian forces into even a moderately unified antiwhite front. This alienation was inevitable, given the constant flood of hungry colonists intent on extracting whatever they could from a population that had already been totally despoiled. But by then the Spaniards were too powerful and the Indian rebels too weak to throw the conquerors back into the sea. The Inca-led rebellions from the late 1530s onward were thus doomed to total defeat.

It was in the context of this intricate web of alliances and rebellions that altiplano groups south of Lake Titicaca finally entered into the history of the Spanish Conquest of Peru. The great rebellion of the supposedly puppet Manco Inca in April 1537 brought about the need for the various Aymara groups finally to choose sides. Whereas they had initially supported the Spaniards because of their own earlier alliance with the losing Huascar faction in the pre-Conquest civil war, the desertion of the leader of that faction from the Spanish cause forced them to rethink their loyalties. In the siege of Cuzco by the rebel Incas, levies of militia were sent from many of the highland areas, with the Lupaqa being particularly strong supporters of the rebellion. The Colla, however, remained stubbornly pro-Spanish, a fact that finally led to a combined Inca-Lupaqa attack on the Colla.

In coming to the defense of the embattled Colla in 1538, Francisco Pizarro led a major expeditionary force to Chuquito and the Rio Desaguardero to destroy the Inca rebel armies and those of the Lupaqa. The end result was the usual one of total victory for the

Spaniards. Caught in the open plains, the rebels were no match for massed cavalry charges and were destroyed. At this juncture, Pizarro decided to leave his brothers in the area to undertake the full-scale colonization of the Bolivian highlands and valleys while he returned to Cuzco. It was thus some six years after the beginning of the Conquest that the Andean region from Lake Titicaca to the south was finally pacified by the Spaniards.

The arrival of the Spaniards in 1532 for their definitive conquest of Peru initially had not been felt in the altiplano and valleys south of Lake Titicaca. A region rich in peasants, herds, wools, and traditional Indian food crops, it initially contained neither the armies nor the readly available gold and silver so sought after by the Spaniards. The urban centers of the Aymara kingdoms and Quechua colonies were small and relatively less developed by the standards of Cuzco. Also, the region had been intensely loyal to the Huascar faction in the Inca civil war and as a result initially welcomed the Spanish intervention as a victory over their enemies. Because of this loyalty, none of the Quito armies that so concerned the Spaniards in the early years remained in the area, and thus they did not attract Spanish military concern.

Several expeditions, of course, had passed through the region prior to 1538. The first of these was led by Diego de Almargo, the contender against Pizarro for title to the southern territories, who first passed through the region in 1535 with a large contingent of loyal Huascar-related Inca troops under the command of Manco Inca's brother, Pullapa Inca, who had close ties to the Aymara kingdoms. The expedition quickly and peacefully passed through the western edge of the altiplano along the Desaguadero River and then south to Lake Poopo, across the Andes, and down into Chile. But Almargo and his followers concentrated their attention first on Chile and then on a long and bitter civil war with the Pizarro family for control of Cuzco. It was thus left to Francisco Pizarro, who beheaded Almargo in early 1538, to undertake the definitive settlement of the region south of Lake Titicaca that the Spaniards would call by the name of Charcas or Upper Peru.

In late 1538, Pizarro's two brothers, Hernando and Gonzalo, entered the southern altiplano and established several important centers. The first and most crucial was the town of Chuquisaca (today

Sucre) in a densely settled subpuna valley at the southern edge of the altiplano, and the second was a small mining camp at Porco to the east of the city on the highlands. With the establishment of these two Spanish communities, the settlement of the Charcas region finally began, some five years after the capture of the Inca at Cajamarca. With the Spaniards busy establishing effective control over Lower Peru and fighting among themselves to pay much attention to the southern region, the region remained relatively neglected until 1545. In that year, the Porco miners discovered the continent's richest veins of silver in the nearby zone, which would become known as Potosí. Thus at the height of the last major Peruvian Spanish civil war, in which Gonzalo Pizarro was attempting to defy the royally appointed viceroy, the *Cerro Rico* (or rich mountain) was first discovered at Potosí, and the mining rush was on. As soon as Gonzalo Pizarro was defeated in Lower Peru, the Lima authorities sent a new expedition into the Charcas region, and this expedition in 1548 secured the Chuquisaca-Potosí-Cuzco road with the creation of the crucial city of La Paz in the heart of the Aymara region. La Paz quickly became both an important commercial and trans-shipment center and a major agricultural market town.

But it was Chuquisaca that was to prove the dynamic frontier town of the new Charcas region. Whereas both Potosí and La Paz turned inward to develop their local regions, Chuquisaca became the staging area for a series of major expeditions into the northeastern Argentine regions around Tucuman. In fact, during the next few decades, Chuquisaca attempted to make Tucuman and the northern Argentine towns into a satellite region. While eventually losing administrative control to Santiago de Chile, Upper Peru nevertheless made the northern Argentine region an economic dependency through the latter's close involvement in the highland mining economy.

Meanwhile, the Pizarro-sponsored thrust from north to south had been met by a counterthrust of another Spanish group coming from the distant eastern regions of the Rio de la Plata area. In the mid-1530s, the Spaniards finally settled the riverine port of Asunción on the Paraguay River, and the local entrepreneurs, deciding that their future wealth could be obtained in the western interior heartlands, proceeded to explore the entire Chaco region. In 1537, a Paraguayan group had successfully crossed the Chaco. By the early 1540s, they were establishing permanent outposts in the Chuquitos and Mojos region at the foothills of the Andes. Quickly running into opposition from the Lima and Cuzco entrepreneurs, the Paraguayan conquistadores were finally forced to accept the lowlands as their frontier and after several expeditions settled the region of Santa Cruz in the late 1550s, finally establishing the settlement of Santa Cruz de la Sierra in 1561 with Paraguayan troops.

By the 1560s, the outer limits of the frontier of Charcas were thus fully established. The Paraguayans had opened up a route to the lowlands and secured a few strategic towns guarding a thin communications link to the east. But this frontier region, filled with hostile and seminomadic Indians, with no metals and few settled peasant agriculturalists, proved uninviting to Spanish settlement. The Chiriguano, Toba, and other Chaco and lowland Indian groups quickly adapted their warfare to that of the Spaniards, many becoming horse nomads, and succeeded in killing many Spanish troops. This same hostile eastern and southeastern Indian frontier sometimes extended westward, where seminomadic Indians often disrupted the vital southern communications links to the Tucuman region and thence on to the Atlantic ports of the Rio de la Plata. The *Gran Chaco* lowland plains region was such a violent frontier that it would take missionaries and permanent fortifications to hold it against the local tribes, and even by the end of the colonial period it still remained fully independent of direct Spanish control.

Within the settled Charcas territory the primary orientation was thus north and south. With the mining center at Potosí becoming one of the primary reasons for the Spanish presence in the Charcas region, the supplying of those mines with animals and equipment became the reason for existence of the northeastern Argentine towns. At the same time, Chuquisaca became Potosí's administrative headquarters and its nearest agricultural supply center. La Paz both served Potosí as its major linkup city on the road to Arequipa, Cuzco, and Lima – and thence by sea to Spain – and itself became a major provisioning center of laborers and goods for the mines.

The Charcas region also was rich in that other extraordinary resource that was so limited in America: Indian labor. The Cuzco and the La Paz regions were the most densely settled Indian peasant areas in Peru, and the Spaniards were aware of the wealth potential of this scarce resource. Leaving the lands in the hands of the Indian peasants, they attempted to continue the Inca patterns of domination through indirect rule. Thus, the ayllus were maintained, and the local nobility – the caciques (or kurakas in Quechua) – were confirmed in their rights. In return, the goods and services that formerly went to the Inca government and the state religion now went to the Spaniards alone. The Indian peasant communities were divided up into districts and these in turn into *encomiendas*, or grants. A grantee of these labor taxes, the so-called *encomendero*, was a Spaniard who was required to pay for religious instruction and otherwise acculturate the Indians into Spanish norms, in return for which he was granted the rights to the labor and the locally produced goods of these Indians. Such grants, which were the single largest source of wealth to be had in sixteenth-century Peru, were given to a very small percentage of the Spanish conquistadores. The granting of encomiendas thus created a local Spanish nobility in everything but name. The encomenderos in fact became the governing authority in their regions and had at their disposal vast labor power. Although a highly exploitative system, the encomienda was fundamentally postulated on the idea of the preservation of the preexistent Indian society and government.

By the 1650s, Charcas had some eighty-two such encomiendas, twenty-one of which contained over one thousand Indians each. While the total of Upper Peruvian encomenderos was small compared with the 292 encomenderos found in the Arequipa-Cuzco region alone in the same period, the latter region had only fourteen encomiendas that held over one thousand Indians. Thus, the Charcas encomenderos, although far fewer in number, tended to be wealthier and more powerful on average than their southern Peruvian compatriots. The average Cuzco-Arequipa encomienda contained something like four hundred Indians, whereas the average Upper Peruvian encomienda encompassed double that number, or over eight hundred Indians. Also, this group of elite Upper Peruvian encomenderos was relatively new, or at least had sided with the anti-Pizarro factions in the various civil wars, for, by the 1560s, the overwhelming majority of them had received their grants from the Lima viceroys. But this was probably the high point of the encomenderos; already by this date, over half of the encomenderos were second-generation grantees, and the Crown had succeeded in taking over some twenty encomiendas in its own name.

Although the reorganization of Charcas rural life had followed fairly well-established Spanish principles that went back to Cortés and the conquest of Mexico, the creation of an effective mine labor force was something new, and in Peru a whole new set of institutions was developed to extract Indian labor for the mines. Here the Spaniards tried everything from slavery to wage labor and finally settled on a system of corvee labor that was rotated among a large number of Indian towns. But to standardize this system and solve the problems of governance in the rural area, it was necessary to reorganize totally local law and custom. And this, in effect, was the task laid out for the famous Peruvian Viceroy Francisco Toledo, who visited Upper Peru in the period 1572–6, in the midst of his viceregal reign.

The Toledo reforms marked a major turning point in the social and economic organization of the Spanish empire in the region of Upper Peru, since Toledo had to resolve crucial problems in the area of rural social and economic organization. The Spaniards had attempted to preserve as much of the existing population and government as possible so as to obtain the greatest benefits at the cheapest costs. But the European diseases they brought with them decimated the lowlands Indians and severely affected the highland population as well. By the 1570s, it was clear that all regions of Peru had experienced severe population declines since the arrival of the Spaniards, and this decimation was continuing. Thus, the encomienda was no longer as financially remunerative an institution as it had been before.

Second, the Crown had informed Toledo of its hostility to the idea of creating a local colonial Spanish nobility based on encomiendas and sought to pressure the elite into giving up this institution altogether and allowing the Indian towns to revert to royal control as regular royally "owned" villages. But even here, Toledo faced the problem of maintaining the village populations in the face of their constant overexploitation and their demographic decline. For him, the only solution was a reorganization of the social and economic bases of Andean life. To this end, he decided to "reduce" the Indians into permanent fixed villages and attempted to convert the remaining ayllus into nucleated communities. The model he used was evidently the Mediterranean agricultural community, but in the highlands the communities were made up of many ayllus, all of which had colonists in various ecological regions. It was the aim of Toledo to force these highland ayllus to separate themselves from their colonies and also to regroup themselves into more permanent larger settlements with fixed and contiguous lands so as to be managed and taxed more easily. Thus, the model of the *comunidad indígena* (or rural Indian community) comes from the time of Toledo, and, despite his rapid creation of numerous *reducciónes,* or new towns, his reforms took at least a century or more to be consolidated. Just how massive an operation this reducciónes campaign was can be seen in the numbers involved. In some five sampled districts of the many that made up Upper Peru at this time, nine hundred communities involving over 129,000 Indians were reduced to just forty-four pueblos. Whereas prior to this "congregation" of the Indians their villages averaged 142 persons, the Toledo reduction policy created towns containing some twenty-nine hundred persons each. Large numbers of these "reduced" towns created by Toledo were abandoned, and many of the lowland and valley communities were never successfully separated from their highland core ayllus, as the Indians fought to preserve their ecologically diverse interregional system from destruction. But by and large the system he created eventually became dominant in the Andes.

In other areas, Toledo was more immediately successful. He broke the power of the encomenderos and limited most of the encomienda grants to three generations, thus recapturing direct control over the Indian populations for the Crown. Moreover, he systematized the tribute that the Indians would have to pay to either the Crown or the few remaining encomenderos. The landowning Indian communities were henceforth to pay the majority of their taxes in specie, rather than in goods. This action standardized the Indian tax structure by making the unit of taxation common to all, with variations then being based not on the changing market value of the goods taken by the tax collectors but on some agreed-on principle of the relative ability of the Indians to pay. The amount of tribute was made to correspond to the amount and quality of the land that the Indians possessed.

This apparent rationalization of the tax structure ultimately proved to be a major weapon forcing the Indians to integrate into the Spanish economy. Because currency could be obtained only by selling goods on the Spanish markets where money was exchanged for goods and services, Indians had to supply either goods demanded by the Spanish or their labor for wages on that market. In the end, they did both things. Wheat and specially produced cloth fit for the urban market were produced and/or traditional products were brought to the new Spanish urban centers for sale. Equally, the demands of the Spanish farmers, merchants, and artisans for harvest and seasonal labor were met by free community Indians who sold that labor on the Spanish markets for cash. Although traditional markets for the exchange of Indian goods continued to thrive in the Andes, especially as the ecological imperative for mixed cropping remained, a large part of the Indian peasant population was forced to enter the monetary market created by the Spaniards. Thus, the need for specie to pay royal taxes proved a major factor in integrating the dual markets developing in the Charcas region.

Just as Toledo was to reorganize the rural structure of Upper Peruvian society, he also was able to reorder dramatically its mining economy. From 1545 until the early 1560s, Potosí had produced an ever larger quantity of silver, quickly becoming the single richest source of this mineral in the world. But this growth was based on extraction of surface deposits that had extremely high ore contents and were easily refined through traditional pre-Columbian smelting processes. But as the surface deposits gave out and shaft mining developed, the purity of the ore declined, the costs of smelting rose, and productivity fell. Thus, when Toledo arrived on the altiplano in the 1570s, the industry was in full crisis, with production declining and the Crown desperately concerned to preserve this enormous resource.

Toledo attacked the Potosí problem on several fronts. First of all, in 1572, he introduced the amalgam process, whereby the silver ore was extracted from the other metals by amalgamation with mercury. This enabled the miners to extract silver from minerals with ever-lower content of silver ore. This change led to the Indian control over refining being broken, and the more than six thousand Indian open-hearth smelters were replaced by a few hundred large refining workshops controlled by Spaniards and driven by water power. To guarantee the mercury supply needed by the Potosí miners, Toledo also organized the royal mercury mine at Huancavelica in Lower Peru, which thenceforth became the exclusive supplier of mercury to the highland mines.

To deal with the problem of government control over the industry and the classic problem of smuggling and evasion, Toledo also created a royal mint at Potosí and demanded that all silver mined and refined in the city had to be turned into bars and bullion in the royal mint. It was at the mint that the Crown extracted its one-fifth royalty on production, as well as minting taxes. Moreover, now that mercury was a fundamental necessity in the extraction of silver, the Crown established a mercury monopoly. This monopoly not only gave it a profit on a basic necessity but, equally, allowed it to determine actual production and guarantee itself against tax evasion. With all mercury purchases registered by the Crown, the smelter owners, or so-called *azogueros,* had difficulty in shipping out unminted and untaxed silver, since the combination of mercury with ores was a fairly fixed ratio. Thus, the potential silver output of all the smelters was known.

Toledo also established the basic mining code. He reiterated standard royal claims to the ownership of all subsoil rights, requiring miners to pay one-fifth of their output for the use of the royal properties. Moreover, the registration of claims and the rights of use of shafts and other technical matters were all codified by Toledo. The establishment of legal rules was especially important in Potosí because of the extremely complex nature of mine ownership. Unlike other mining areas in the New World, the concentrated nature of the silver veins in one huge mountain of ore at Potosí resulted in a multitude of mines constructed virtually on top of each other. No one miner owned anything greater than a few mine heads leading into one of the countless veins of silver, with numerous owners using different shafts often working a common vein. By 1585, there were about 612 separately owned mines in the Cerro Rico mountain, each representing a different shaft. Elaborate rules of determining ownership of veins were essential to prevent constant armed conflict.

Finally, and most important of all, Toledo resolved the labor question for the miners. Shaft mining was an extremely expensive enterprise, with labor being the highest cost item in the entire process. To construct and maintain a proper shaft cost as much as it did to build a cathedral. Moreover, the enormous quantities of water needed to drive the grindstones in the smelting processes eventually required the construction of a complex series of dams and some twenty artificial lakes, the total cost of which was estimated at the extraordinary sum of over two million pesos. At the wages paid for free labor in the mines in the 1570s, it was evident that there was simply not enough capital available to continue the massive mining output that the Crown wished to maintain. Since he was already reorganizing the rural communities and standardizing their tax structure, Toledo went one step further and decided to use a pre-Columbian corvee labor system, the so-called *mita*, to extract forced labor for the mines at Potosí.

Some sixteen districts stretching from Potosí to Cuzco in the highland area were designated as mita supply areas. Here, one-seventh of the adult males were to be subjected to a year's service at the mines, serving no more than once in six years. This provided an annual labor force of some 13,500 men, which was in turn divided into three groups of over four thousand each. These latter groups worked on a rotating basis of three weeks on and three weeks off, thus maintaining a continuous labor supply and yet providing rest periods for the workers. While the miners were obliged to pay the *mitayos* (as they were called) a small wage, this was not even a subsistence amount. In fact, the mitayo communities were required to provide the food for their workers as well as maintain the families of their absent mitayos and to pay for their transportation to the mines. Most of the food and coca consumed at the mines were in turn paid for by the workers themselves. Thus, at one stroke, a good half to two-thirds of the mine labor force was now provided to the mine owners by the Crown at extremely low cost, which greatly stimulated production. Although the mita system was used to extract mercury at the Huancavelica mine, such a forced draft labor system was never applied elsewhere by the Corwn. The mines of Mexico were all worked with free wage labor, and even when the Oruro silver mines north of Potosí came on line a century later, miners were only allowed to use free wage labor. Even at Potosí a major part of the miners were free wage laborers. But there is little question that the mita and the mercury amalgamation process gave Potosí another century of profitable exploitation. With the Toledo reforms production once again soared by the late 1570s, and silver production now reached extraordinary levels between the 1570s and the 1650s.

Having resolved the issues of rural organization and mine industry reorganization, Toledo then turned toward problems of Spanish settlement in the region. While the frontiers of Upper Peru were now well defined, there were many interior regions that as yet had not been fully exploited by the Spaniards. Thus, Toledo sponsored a whole new wave of Spanish settlements. The single most important of these new towns promoted by Toledo was the city of Cochabamba, which was established in 1571. Situated in the heart of a broad series of subpuna valleys, Cochabamba also became the central city for controlling the valley Quechua Indians. It also quickly became Upper Peru's major wheat- and maize-producing region and would be intimately tied to the Potosí market in the next century of economic growth. Toledo also better integrated the southern Andean region with the establishment of the city of Tarija in 1574. Like Cochabamba, it was situated in broad subpuna valleys well populated with Indian peasants. Finally, to secure the eastern frontier against the Chiriguanos, Toledo encouraged the settlement of the town of Tomina in 1575.

With the final settlement of the frontiers and the interior towns, the growth of the silver mine industry, and the integration of the older Indian agricultural market with a new Spanish one, Upper Peru became one of the wealthiest centers of the new Spanish empire in America. Its dense populations of settled Indians provided a seemingly inexhaustible labor force, while its mines were quickly recognized as the principal source of silver in the Americas, if not in the entire world at this time. Thus, the Crown was forced to establish a viable and semi-autonomous government to control the destiny of this region and guarantee its adherence to the empire.

While Lima and Cuzco had always wanted to dominate the southern highlands, in fact, all the rebellions during the period of Spanish civil wars in Peru showed that Upper Peru could easily operate as an independent and quite dangerous element. Reluctantly, the Lima authorities therefore agreed that a separate and powerful government under ultimate viceregal authority would have to be established in the area south of Lake Titicaca. This decision led in 1558 to the creation of an independent *Audiencia*, or royal court, which was placed in the city of Chuquisaca. The Audiencia of Charcas would prove to be one of the few such audiencias constructed in the New World that had both judicial authority and executive power at the same time. The president of the Audiencia, himself a judge, thus became the chief administrative and executive officer in the region.

To control the largely urbanized and western minority of the population, the Audiencia constructed a system of government much like that which existed in Spain prior to the Conquest. Municipal governments were created based on the free suffrage of its citizens (or *vecinos*), and these governments had quite extensive power. With their borders spreading well into the rural hinterlands, they were the primary granters of land titles in the earlier days, controlled local markets, and provided for local justice and police powers. In every principal town, there also were royal officials, going from an executive officer known as a *corregidor* (there were some four Spanish *corregimientos* by the early seventeenth century) through a series of royal finance officials whose job it was to tax trade and production. By the standards of Spain at the time, these local governments were rather responsive and representative of the interests and needs of the local elite.

The rural areas contained over 90 percent of the population, all but 10 percent of whom were monolingual-speaking Indian peasants. For these, the Spaniards devised a complex system of indirect rule. Toledo in his reforms had guaranteed local autonomy to the new "congregated" or "reduced" towns, and a complex government of elders of the community began to develop on the local level. Formally elected by the *originarios*, or original members of the community, these local administrations consisted of representatives from all the local ayllus, which went to make up the community and had charge of local land divisions and distribution, local justice, and the collection of all taxes, often in association with local caciques or Indian nobles. This same government also maintained the local community church and sponsored local community patron saint festivals. The community governments, although supposedly elected in the Spanish style, most probably continued pre-Conquest practices by selecting the most experienced and the most successful older men to represent them. Such men tended to be extremely conservative, being the eldest and most responsible members of the community, and the royal officials made them responsible for everything from the maintenance of local peace to the vital role of providing taxes and mita labor. So long as the exactions on the community were considered reasonable by the members of the community, such a government of principal elders (or jilakata) proved to be a bulwark of conservative stability. But once such leaders were convinced that the exactions of their surplus were beyond acceptable limits, these same elders proved the most dangerous of enemies, since they were able to call out the entire community in their support. The innumerable Indian rebellions in the period after Toledo, which lasted well into the middle of the twentieth century, were never disorganized individual affairs but were always movements of united communities led by their principal elders. This explains the often strange phenomenon of rebellions confined to a few clearly defined local communities, without affecting their neighbors.

Moreover, these community governments over time began to serve not only as an institution of governance and leadership but also as a means of internal redistribution of resources within the community. Faced by a hostile and threatening environment, in terms of both ecology and economic exploitation, the communities could not afford serious internal differentiation among their original participant members. Therefore, an elaborate "ritual impoverization" system came into play in many of these communities whereby wealth distinctions were considerably reduced through the forceful dispersion of savings of its more successful or lucky members. Only successful farmers were selected for offices in the civil and religious hierarchy that made up the local community government, and they were required to spend considerable sums of money and a great deal of their time in their offices during the year. Especially in the religious part of their duties, the so-called *cargos* (or obligations), these community leaders required large expenditures of their personal savings to sponsor local religious festivals. In return for the expenditure of time, food, drink, and money, successful elders were rewarded with honor and local power. But such expenditures usually reduced their lifetime savings and thus tended, through the whole ritual process, to reduce their income to the general level of the community. The system guaranteed that no original member of the community with access to land would dominate the others and accumulate an advantage that might threaten the communal nature of property and the integrity of the community. Civil-religious office holding and "ritual impoverishment" were the idealized norm, but were not totally operative in all places and at all times. Nor did this system prevent, as we shall see, the emergence of groups of nonlandholding Indians living in the communities. But for the landholding members, when it functioned effectively, it helped prevent the operation of normal market mechanisms from destroying communal unity.

For most of the colonial period, there also existed in the rural area a group of local Indian nobility known as the caciques who played much the same role as they had under the Incas. These Indian nobles were usually in charge of several villages and had recourse to their own private estates within the various communities as well as the rights to community labor and a host of other local resources. In return, the caciques were to protect the local religion and customs of the community members, to represent them formally to the Spanish authorities, and to act as a buffer between the local peasant and their jilakatas and the Spanish authorities. Theirs was a brutally difficult position, because not only was the kuraka a landowner and labor exploiter but also he himself was required by the Spanish authorities to guarantee all the local taxes and mita obligations. He of course relied on the jilakatas to carry out these demands in the local communities, but he, his lands, and his goods were made ultimately liable for the noncollection of taxes or the nondelivery of labor. For this, the Spaniards recognized their lineages as noble and they were honored with the title of Don and Doña and given numerous other privileges that clearly distinguished them from the Indian peasants. But over the three centuries of Spanish colonial rule the local Indian nobles would slowly be ground down by Spanish exactions and many would be reduced to peasant status if they remained in the countryside, or absorbed into the middle or upper classes if they escaped into the cities. Although the Indian nobles survived far longer in the Andes than anywhere else in America, the institution finally would be wiped out as an autonomous and effective force in the great Indian rebellion of Tupac Amaru in 1780, in which the caciques played such a key role as both rebel and royalist leaders.

However indirect their principles of governance, the Spaniards did ultimately control the system. For this reason, they divided up all the rural zones, much like the urban areas, into rural corregimientos under the control of royal officials known as *corregidores de indios*. These underpaid officials were in charge of the extraction of taxes and labor at the district level, and to pay for their offices could force their Indian subjects to purchase goods that they imported into the rural areas. The forced sales of Spanish products to Indian communities proved an enormous source of wealth and corruption for these officials and made them an object of continual hatred by the local Indian populations.

Finally, to guarantee loyalty to the state both from Spaniards and the recently pagan Indians, the Crown forcefully sponsored the establishment of the Catholic religion in the region of Upper Peru. With the arrival of the first Spanish settlers in 1538 had come the secular clergy to minister to the needs of the conquerors and begin the conversion of the Indians. These seculars were quickly joined by the "regular" missionary clergy from all the major orders in America: the Dominicans, Franciscans, Augustinians, Mercedarians, and, after midcentury, by the Jesuits. The direction for all such activity came from Cuzco and ultimately from Lima. But this system changed in 1552 with the naming of the first bishopric in the region. Called the bishopric of La Plata, it was placed in the city of Chuquisaca, where a decade later the royal Audiencia also was situated. The establishment of a dominant ecclesiastical authority was crucial in the formation of an independent center for Upper Peru.

Meanwhile, the entire Peruvian Church was concerned with evangelization and in 1561 began a series of all-Peruvian Church Councils, the results of which were to provide direction for the regular and secular clergy in the evangelization process. The first council of 1561 ordered that the catechism texts be translated into Quechua, while the third Council in 1582–3 finally ordered a full set of materials in Aymara as well. The result of this was the publication of the first work in Aymara in Lima in 1584. By the first decades of the seventeenth century, the Jesuits Ludovico Bertonio and Diego de Torres Rubio published full-scale Aymara grammars and dictionaries. This was almost a generation behind the publication of Quechua catechisms, grammars, and dictionaries, also undertaken by the various missionary priests. Given the predominance of Quechua, even in Charcas, this late start for Aymara is understandable. But this meant that Quechua became far more of a lingua franca, pushed as it was by the missionaries, even in the traditional highland areas and surrounding valleys. This earlier concern of Lower Peru with Quechua evangelization helps explain the disappearance of all non-Aymara or non-Quechua languages in the subpuna valleys after the Conquest, to be replaced most often by the dominant Quechua brought by the missionaries.

In other aspects, the Church was not slow in striking out into the Aymara populations. Already, by 1582, the bishop of La Plata had granted the caciques of Copacabana the right to establish a brotherhood in honor of the Virgin in this traditional pre-Conquest Lake Titicaca Aymara religious center. The sanctuary built here to the Virgin of Copacabana, along with the sanctuary to the Cross built around the same time at Carabuco, became vital syncretic symbols of the evangelization process. The Virgin at Copacabana became the region's unquestioned central religious symbol. This creation of the outward forms of Christianity does not mean that precontact religion disappeared, or that the clergy had universal success in its evangelization among the Indians. The existence of private encomiendas in most areas until late in the sixteenth century prevented direct clerical access to Indians, and even with the division of Charcas into effective provinces of the missionary orders there were far fewer clergy than were needed. Every reduced town and older settlement now had a church, but most Indians saw a priest only rarely. Thus, traditional beliefs, especially as related to family and work, were preserved to a large extent, and also systematically protected by the local jilakatas and caciques. It was at the higher spheres of state religion and the broader cosmological order that Christianity made itself most effectively felt. The best evidence for this change is to be found in the progressive decline of anti-Christian revolts throughout the century, and their replacement by the end of the sixteenth century with revolts, steeped in messianic Christian symbolism, that at the same time were both heavily Catholic and totally anti-Spanish. No longer were the local *huacas*, or community religious objects (usually stones), called on for support in battle against the hated Spaniards, but now the dark Copacabana Virgin was called on to lead the Aymara and Quechua against the white oppressors.

That local belief changed little is also evident in the late sixteenth- and early seventeenth-century bishopric pastoral *visitas* (or visits) and inquisitorial investigations, which show that in curing, in activities associated with planting and harvesting, and with all those events associated with reenforcing family, kin, and local ayllu ties, precontact religious belief and practice predominated, often practiced by the sacristans of the local Catholic Church. While the more zealous and consistent high church clergy attempted to destroy these beliefs, the weakness of their numbers and the concerns with the preservation of indirect rule essentially guaranteed the continuance of local belief so long as it did not challenge the statewide and societal legitimacy of Christianity.

The formal church, like the royal government, responded to changes in the regional economy and society by organizing new bishoprics and parishes. In recognition of the growth of the La Paz district as the center of Aymara highland civilization, the Crown and Papacy created a new bishopric in La Paz in 1605, while the entire frontier area of the lowlands was recognized as a separate zone with the establishment of a bishopric in Santa Cruz in the same year. For the missionaries, work with the Aymara and Quechua peasants quickly lost some of its romantic appeal, and so the various missions in the eastern lowland Mojos zone, near Santa Cruz and southward into the Gran Chaco, all attracted vigorous missionary activity, especially in the seventeenth century. The elevation of Santa Cruz to a bishopric gave impetus to this work. To complete the colonial organization, the Chuquisaca bishopric was raised to an archbishopric four years later and the archbishop of Chuquisaca was made the primate of the Charcas Church. The preponderance of the Chuquisaca administrative and religious center was finally crowned with the establishment of a university in the city in 1624. Thus, Charcas now could graduate its own clergy in all the advanced degrees, and by 1681 this essentially theological center also was offering legal degrees as well, becoming the premier legal institution for the entire Rio de la Plata and southern cone area until the end of the colonial period.

Thus, with its state bureaucracies and state church, the Spaniards quickly consolidated effective rule in the settled peasant areas of Upper Peru. Some six major towns of Spaniards (La Paz, Chuquisaca, Potosí, Cochabamba, Santa Cruz, and Tarija) were strategically located to control vast hinterlands and different ecological and economic zones. Secure frontier towns were established, along with an effective mission frontier in the eastern lowlands to prevent the seminomadic Indians from entering into the settled areas, and finally a complex system of indirect rule was introduced to control the Indian peasant populations. But all of these plans conceived of Charcas, or Upper Peru, as essentially a dual social, economic, and political system. There was to be a Western-oriented Spanish-speaking white elite, more or less divided along peninsular class lines based on birth and money, and alongside them a vast self-governed but fully exploitable Indian peasant mass, also differentiated into a class of peasants and nobles but otherwise interacting little with their conqueror's world. In fact, the conquest process and the nature of the conquerors themselves would slowly erode this relatively simple model and create a complex amalgam of new classes, castes, and groups both within the rural Indian world and in the Spanish-dominated urban centers as well.

To begin with, the conquerors brought with them a new set of European diseases unknown to the highland Indians. A system of exploitation based on a population of something like one million peasants would soon find itself oppressing just half that number with the same taxes by the end of the century. Each generation of post-Conquest Indians suffered repeated epidemics of endemic European diseases in roughly twenty-year cycles, epidemics that did not end until well into the seventeenth century. Moreover, the ten thousand or so Spaniards who reached the Charcas region were predominantly male and thus uninhibited by the tight European family restrictions that they had left behind them in Spain. They also brought with them almost an equal number of black African slaves. The result was the creation of a whole new racial grouping of mulattos and mestizos (known as cholos in the Andes). Thus, the Indian population loss would be replaced somewhat by an intermediate racially amalgamated group mixing the parentage of Indians and whites, and, to a lesser extent, of Africans.

Nor was the rigid and unchanging social order projected by the Crown the one that was to be, in fact, created by the Conquest. Just as the racial composition of the population was slowly changing, so, too, was its social structure. The base of the entire economic and social order was the Indian male head of household aged eighteen to fifty who was an original member (or originario) of his ayllu with direct access to land rights. This originario Indian was the primary producer in the Charcas economy. He paid the basic tribute tax – which was the royal equivalent of the encomienda tribute obligation now directly collected by the Crown – and was the only one subject to the mita labor tax. Moreover, the originarios also were the primary producers for their own caciques, who continued to collect their own tribute obligations and for the local church taxes. Given the land base and the labor supply that the Spaniards initially inherited from the Incas, the levies on the originarios were not excessive and could easily be borne by the large numbers of such originarios initially available in each community.

But the demographic collapse of the Indian population caused a shrinking of the originario class without any consequent relief from the extractions of their surplus product. The pressures on the originario continued to mount throughout the two centuries of demographic decline. The result of this was both the wholesale abandoning of communities and the massive withdrawal of Indians from the originario status. Given the amount of community abandonment and the policy of new community foundations under Toledo and his successors, there quickly developed a floating Indian peasant population. Arriving as migrants to the old communities or latecomers to the new ones, these *forasteros* (foreigners) – sometimes also called *agregados* – were given lesser land rights or no land at all, and simply took up residence as landless laborers on the plots of the *originarios*. In changing status, they may have lost their lands, but they removed themselves from all their tax and mita obligations as well. Until the early eighteenth century, forasteros did not have to pay the tribute tax.

The same demographic and economic pressures that created the forasteros also created an entirely new group of Indians who pertained to no free communities but were living on the estates of the Spaniards. As the value of the encomiendas declined and the Crown forced their revocation, wealthy Spaniards found alternative sources of income in direct agricultural production. With the decline of

Indian populations and the constant reorganization of communities, much land in traditional areas became available for private exploitation. These lands were quickly absorbed by the wealthier Spaniards and a new class, the *hacendados* (or large landowners), was created. Initially obtaining their labor from the floating population of Indian servants known as yanaconas, the Spaniards soon found that ex-originarios were more than willing to work the Spanish estates in exchange for usufruct land use. Moreover, the Spaniards made no attempt to destroy the ayllu structure, which functioned in the communities and on the haciendas as well. Although the term "yanaconas" came from the Inca period and initially meant those workers without ayllu connections or land who were assigned to leading nobles and other officials by the Inca as their servants or almost slaves, by the end of the sixteenth century the term came to mean simply landless worker. The early conquistadores may have used some pre-Incan yanaconas, but this new yanacona class came primarily from the labor force released by the breakdown of the more traditional communities.

Although the haciendas quickly developed from the second half of the sixteenth century, they soon reached a limit in growth once the free communities stabilized themselves in the second half of the seventeenth century. This resulted in an end to the first epoch of hacienda expansion. By that time, the haciendas were to be found throughout the highlands and major subpuna valleys, but they absorbed only about a third of the Indian labor force in the entire region of Charcas. The free communities remained the dominant form of social organization and landownership in the rural areas, absorbing two-thirds of the Indian peasantry. But unlike the homogeneous ayllus of the pre-Conquest period, the seventeenth-century free Indian communities contained two distinct classes, the original landed members and their families and the later-arriving forasteros who had little if any land rights and were obligated to perform free labor service to the originarios in return for access to usufruct lands. While the communities were still corporate entities controlled by their members and in turn held ultimate land title for all, they now contained second-class citizens, who in fact made up a significant minority of most of the free communities. But these various categories were not fixed and immutable. Many originarios gave

up their rights in their lifetimes, and became either yanaconas
on the estates of the Spaniards or forasteros in other communities.
Equally, yanaconas moved relatively easily into forastero status.
Only entrance into the originario status proved to be difficult, and
marriage into that status seemed to be the sole possibility for those
not born to that right.

This change and movement within the rural areas was also accompanied by much interregional and rural-to-urban migration.
Indian originarios who did mita service in Potosí often found it
difficult or unattractive to return to their original communities, and
many became free wage laborers, or *minganos*, in the mine region.
Many originario Indians also decided to give up rural life altogether
and moved to the Spanish towns. These towns of several thousand
quickly began to fill up with Indians who took on all the urban laboring work tasks and became the dominant element among the urban
working class. Speaking both their native languages and Spanish,
these new urban Indians often gave up their traditional costumes
and began to dress in an adaptation of the Spanish manner and con-
sume Spanish-style foods, such as bread. They became urban cholos,
even though they were of a pure Indian stock. The designations of
Indian, cholo, and white thus quickly lost their biological significance and became cultural or "social caste" terms determined by
such externalities as speech, dress, and food consumption. Nor were
the miscegenational Spanish elite immune to these changes, as con-
cubinage and illegitimacy became the norm, and bastard offspring
of multiracial backgrounds were brought into the elite class itself,
along with the Hispanicized caciques, who became members of the
local landed classes.

The pace of social change in Bolivia was influenced by such negative factors as the demographic decline and the exploitation of the
mita. But the tremendous economic growth that affected the entire
region after the reforms of Toledo also was influential. The first
mining boom of the 1540s and 1550s had been spectacular, but it
was as nothing compared to the massive growth of silver exports in
the great boom of the 1570–1650 period. During this period, Potosí
alone produced over half of the silver of the New World. The impact
of Potosí on Europe and on its trade with Asia was staggering. For
Europe, Potosí silver was influential in causing the long-term trend

toward rising prices. Equally in its trade with Asia, Europe was finally able greatly to increase its importations of Asian goods, because of its ability to make up for the ongoing negative trade balance with the payment of Potosí silver.

For Charcas, the growth of Potosí in the late sixteenth century was even more traumatic than it was for Europe. The location of Potosí in the center of the Upper Peruvian region in an arid and poor agricultural and grazing zone meant that everything used in mining, from the food and tools to the animals and labor, had to be imported. With its mines so far from the sea, it was also necessary to develop a complex communication system to supply both the European imports and export the finished silver. Thus, the backward linkages between this export sector and the local regional and international markets were extensive. The growth of the town of Potosí and its silver industry was to be felt from northern Argentina to southern Peru, as one vast economic supply area was integrated into the Potosí market. Equally, the merchants, traders, and shippers from Lima, Arequipa, Cuzco, and La Paz came to play a vital role in linking the mines of Potosí and its satellite elite of Chuquisaca to the outside world.

Potosí's growth from a settlement of a few hundred Spaniards and their Indian laborers to a population estimated at between 100,000 and 150,000 by the early seventeenth century had a profound impact on the growth and settlement of other highland regions. Cochabamba and its associated valleys became major producers of maize and wheat for the Potosí markets, and the growth of the haciendas in the areas was so rapid and powerful that the free communities were pushed early into a minority position within the region. In addition, the demands for labor and the very early breakdown of the ayllus and communities meant that the Cochabamba Valley would become the most "choloized" and bilingual Indian zone in all of Upper Peru. While Quechua remained the predominant language of the valley, Spanish language and culture spread quickly. Many of the agricultural peasants became bilingual and gave up most of their traditional Indian culture to adopt a new mestizo cultural norm that emerged between the two old groups of conquerors and conquered.

At the other extreme, the growth of mining at Potosí led to the expansion of Aymara culture in the eastern valleys known as the

Yungas through the development of the new areas of coca production. Whereas coca leaf mastication had been an important source of stimulants in the diet of the pre-Conquest Indian nobility, and thus a native domesticated plant from well before the arrival of the Spaniards, its use would now undergo a major transformation. With the state apparatus of the Incas destroyed, coca chewing after the Conquest spread to all classes, and the Spaniards quickly found that its consumption was an absolute necessity for the miners working the high-altitude silver mines. Thus, the demand for and production of coca increased enormously after the Conquest, and the traditional centers around Cuzco were no longer sufficient to meet demand, especially in Upper Peru. While coca had been grown in the Yungas near La Paz and even in the Chapare region near Cochabamba from pre-Conquest times, its production was quite limited compared to Cuzco. Now, however, demand outpaced supply, and the Yungas, above all, became the prime center for the growth of Upper Peruvian coca that soon displaced the Cuzco variety from the mine center markets. The increase in Yungas production, which would grow steadily throughout the colonial period, meant that the nomadic Indians of these valleys would be replaced by Aymara peasant settlers from the highlands; and this process of settlement, once begun in the sixteenth century, continued uninterrupted into the nineteenth century. The Yungas colonization even involved some African slaves, who quickly adapted to the dominant culture and became monolingual speakers of Aymara by the end of the period. Thus, from zones with only a sprinkling of Aymara colonists, the Yungas became a totally Aymara culture stronghold, even to the extent of having a black Aymara subculture.

Potosí also was vital for the development of the Tucumán region, with the ranches and farms of the northeast of Argentina becoming the vital suppliers of mules, wine, and sugar to the Potosí market. In between Tucumán and Potosí, the region of Tarija became a major grain supply area, while the subregion of the Cinti Valley saw the development of irrigation agriculture, largely owned by Potosí miners, which became the source of local wines. To the north of Potosí the altiplano became the prime supplier of labor, traditional foodstuffs for miner consumption, and the vast llama herds needed for shipping out the silver to the coast. Beyond Lake Titicaca, the mines of

Huancavelica became the exclusive providers of the vital mercury for Potosí; mita labor demands also were to be met from this region as well. Moreover, tropical fruits, wines, and other food consumption items came to Potosí from both the highland valleys and the coastal plains. This enormous trade and movement of goods and services was financed by both the Potosí and Lima merchant classes. The latter, in fact, appear to have been the primary source of capital, financing the movement of most goods from the north to Potosí and exclusively controlling all of Potosí's international trade until well into the eighteenth century.

The late sixteenth-century boom and expansion of Potosí also had an impact on further settlement and development of the interior spaces of Charcas. At the end of the century, the search for mineral deposits was intense, and even the poorest altiplano communities had some mining activity. Gold was being panned in the Sorata region in the northeastern Cordillera valleys, and such communities as Berenguela just south of Lake Titicaca continued to develop as a small but important mine center. It was from among these highland small-time miners that the initiative came to settle the Uru Indian region just north of Lake Poopo. The whole region of the corregimiento of Paria, as it was then called, was filled with small mines, but in 1695 the very biggest mine of the area was discovered near the site of what would become the city of Oruro. The mine took the name of San Miguel and was soon producing important quantities of fine silver ore.

The result of this discovery was to create a new silver rush among the highland miners from all the nearby small mine centers. It was the Pacajes region miners who supplied the capital and expertise to get these new mines in operation, and by the first decade of the new century the mining camp counted some three thousand Indian workers and four hundred resident Spaniards.

Without royal provisions for mita labor, the Oruro miners, like those elsewhere in these northern regions, had to rely on free wage labor. They began by offering wages of five *reales* per working period (*jornal*) for basic miners, and much higher wages of over one peso per day for skilled workers. Such wages were effective in quickly drawing a large free Indian labor force to the mines, but at the same time kept Oruro mine costs high so that production developed only slowly. In 1605, the local miners felt that the settlement had become important enough to obtain official status, and after much negotiation the town of Oruro was formally established in late 1606. From then until the 1680s, the town grew at a rapid pace. By 1607 there were thirty thousand inhabitants, of which six thousand were Indian miners, and by the 1670s the town reached its maximum size of some eighty thousand persons.

Despite this rapid growth, however, Oruro never rivaled the power of Potosí, as its production at best was no more than a fourth of the latter's output. Nevertheless, the town and its mines quickly took on great significance. It became a crucial transit stop on the Lima-Arequipa-La Paz-Potosí route, on the one hand, and the chief highland port of entry for the vital mercury shipments, on the other. Since the cheapest route for the Huancavelica-produced mercury to Potosí was that by sea from Lima to the Pacific coast port of Arica and then by mule to the highlands, Oruro turned out to be the closest highland city to the Arica port. Oruro was thus able to secure its mercury at more favorable terms than Potosí, and to obtain an important income from provisioning and financing the mercury shipments.

Just as important as its central location was Oruro's crucial development as the largest free mine labor center in all of Charcas. As long as its richest veins of minerals lasted, which was until late in the seventeenth century, the Oruro mines became a lodestone for free Indian laborers throughout the region and kept wages high elsewhere, to the bitter complaint of even the Potosí miners. Although the higher wages made shaft mining, when it came, an extremely expensive undertaking, it nevertheless provided the Indians with a welcome alternative to the harsher Potosí conditions. This combination of factors led to the establishment of a more permanent settlement, so the city quickly developed a lively and thriving cholo population. It also proved to be one of the more open and violent cities in the Charcas area, with mestizos reaching even the upper levels of power. Oruro became known as a relatively unruly place and one with a taste for political independence, which in the eighteenth century would lead to several important antiroyalist revolts.

In terms of its regional impact, Oruro tended to reenforce the market patterns developed by Potosí. It, too, was forced to rely on lower

Peruvian mercury production, and it generated the bulk of its labor force from among the Aymara highland Indians. Like Potosí, the majority of its foodstuffs came from eastern valley sources, although in this respect Oruro was even more heavily dependent on the nearby Cochabamba Valley system, which became the city's single most important producer of temperate and semitropical foodstuffs. Oruro replicated much of Potosí's market impact because it, too, was situated within an essentially poor and infertile agricultural zone, and thus forced to import virtually all of its basic necessities.

With the permanent establishment of Oruro, the basic period of Spanish settlement in the highlands and principal eastern valleys came to a close. Although the next century would see the growth and expansion of the eastern lowlands mission frontier, the core area of Charcas by the beginning of the seventeenth century was now fully defined. From then until the end of the seventeenth century there was a constant growth of the Spanish and cholo populations, accompanied by a slowing but still evident decline among the Indian populations.

This initial period of extraordinary urban expansion and unusual wealth, which lasted until the end of the seventeenth century, created with it a major cultural and artistic boom. For the riches pouring into such cities of the realm as Chuquisaca, Potosí, Oruro, and La Paz led to a massive construction of churches and cathedrals with the consequent growth of the plastic arts.

In the first century of the Conquest, the Spaniards brought their artists and artistic ideas with them. Spanish, Italian, and Flemish artisans, artists, and architects predominated in the sixteenth century, and many of them were priests. It was in the churches that the most advanced artistic ideas of colonial life were expressed, since the Europeans most conspicuously expended the great wealth they extracted from the mines and the Indians in the construction and adornment of their temples. An average-sized church took decades to construct and adorn and was often the most costly item of construction in the entire region. A large urban church or monastery could absorb hundreds of thousands of pesos and be equivalent to the total royal revenues of a given city.

Before 1600, major church construction and artistic activity were concentrated in the city of Chuquisaca, the administrative and religious capital of the region. In this first period, the predominant influences were European, as mature artists were brought in directly from Europe to undertake the construction, painting, and sculpture desired by the colonials. The clerics – migrating for the needs of their various orders – were the most accessible and inexpensive artists at hand, although by the end of the first century noncleric artisans began arriving in ever larger numbers. While Indians were taught the rudiments of all the plastic arts, since they formed the working class everywhere, it was the Europeans who provided all the initial models, ideas, and techniques. Given the fact that Spain itself was a major world artistic center for most of the sixteenth century, and a good part of the seventeenth as well, it was evident that the latest of European styles – filtered through Spanish concerns – would predominate in the colonies.

In the earlier part of the sixteenth century, the architectural norms were determined by traditional Renaissance themes and ideas, while in the last two decades of the century there was a rise of Iberian *Mudejar* influences. In the plastic arts, influences were more varied, with Italian and Flemish styles of the period having a profound impact on the migrating artists. Given the wealth of Upper Peru, the altiplano cities were able to draw on the most advanced artists coming to America, and soon the churches of Chuquisaca were being adorned by the same artists who were carrying out the artistic development of Lima and even of Sevilla. The most outstanding of these early artists working in Upper Peru was the Italian Jesuit Bernardo Bitti, one of the most original painters working in America in the sixteenth century. As was typical of such men, Bitti had developed his formative ideas in Europe, being much influenced by Michelangelo, and was to pass through all the major centers of population of both Perus from his arrival in the 1570s until his death in the first decade of the new century.

By the last two decades of the sixteenth century, the dominance of European and white artisans was being challenged by the appearance of the first Indian and cholo artisans. Sculpture was their first field of effort. As wood and stone craftsmen were prevalent among the Indians from the beginning, and it was Indian workers and artisans who did all the basic church constructions under European direction, it was natural that they made their first impact in sculpture. The most important of these early Indian artists was the sculptor Tito Yupanqui of Copacabana. Trained by Europeans in the cities of Upper Peru, Yupanqui was famous for his rather original style and for the important sculpture he did of a Virgin for his native city of Copacabana, which became a cult figure for the entire region. Beginning with European forms, Yupanqui quickly developed his own style and created several important and innovative pieces for local churches.

By the early seventeenth century, there was a subtle but important shift of influences and origins among the artists and artisans of the region. With the incredible amount of religious and civil construction that had taken place, there had developed important workshops of European masters and Indian assistants to help them in their work. Since the time needed for the full construction and adornment of a given church could take decades, either master artisans began projects and moved on to other churches or buildings, leaving their Indian assistants to complete their designs, or they died and could be replaced only by their Indian assistants. Thus, by the seventeenth century, a new *criollo* (or native American) style developed by Indian and cholo artists and artisans would begin to emerge in the region.

While architecture and the plastic arts were undergoing a vital growth in the sixteenth and the early seventeenth century, the first century of Spanish rule was not a particularly fertile period for nonartistic intellectual endeavors. Charcas was still in many respects a rough mining frontier dominated by a nouveau riche mentality. Thus, its expressions of an intellectual "high culture" were left to priests and government officials, who in turn were primarily concerned with conversion and governance of the Indian population. Given the limited intellectual marketplace, Upper Peru did not obtain a printing press until the end of the colonial period, and its few authors were forced to send their works to Lima or Europe to be published.

Aside from the grammars and dictionaries of the Aymara and Quechua languages, the most important single work produced by a Charcas writer in the sixteenth century was undoubtedly the treatise on "Government in Peru" written by the *oidor* (or royal judge) of the Audiencia of Charcas, Juan de Matienzo, in 1567. A profound analysis of local Indian conditions and patterns of government, the Matienzo work was of fundamental importance in determining the shape of the Toledo reforms. Aside from Matienzo, however, there were few if any Charcas writers to compare with the contemporaneous group of Cuzco and Lima ethnographers and chroniclers. Upper Peruvians produced few works of any significance on pre-Columbian developments, in contrast with the extraordinary productivity of the Lower Peruvian writers of both Spanish and Indian background.

Rather, the Spanish writers of Upper Peru concentrated in the late sixteenth and the early seventeenth century on the writing of their own post-Conquest history. Missionaries wrote the histories of their respective provinces, or the histories of local shrines, the several written about Copacabana being the most important. Finally, the first of a famous series of chronicles was begun about the history of Potosí, the most important of these early historians being Luis Capoche, who wrote in 1585.

It was this intense concern with the present and the future development of the region that most marked the writers of Upper Peru in the first century and a half of Spanish rule. This was also a period in which intensive colonization had occurred in response to the rising level of silver production. But the eventual crisis in silver production, which began to be felt in the middle decades of the seventeenth century, had an adverse effect on the economic, social, and political opportunities of the more recently arriving immigrants. This background of declining opportunities and increasing stratification helps explain the series of urban conflicts among the Spaniards, which came to be known as the "civil wars" of the seventeenth century.

The most important of the new urban conflicts occurred in the heart of the export sector itself, the city of Potosí. The early seventeenth century was to prove a period of particularly intense conflicts among Spanish miners and merchants over the control of the mining industry, disputes that finally led to open warfare among the various factions. The most notorious of these conflicts involved a long and protracted series of violent confrontations between the Basques and all other Spaniards – known generically as vicuñas because of the type of clothing they wore – over control of the urban government of Potosí. This so-called civil war between *vascongados* (or basques) and vicuñas occurred between 1622 and 1625 and essentially involved an attempt by the non-Basques to remove this entrenched group from their control over both the mines and the *cabildo*, or town government. Despite a fair amount of rioting, the total number of deaths was relatively small, and the end result was the retention of power by the traditional Basque miners.

But the increasing tension among the urban Spaniards, which involved similar power struggles in many of the other urban centers, was another indication of the seriousness of the long economic decline that was beginning to be felt by the middle decades of the century. Already the available resources were becoming exhausted, with the result that the stranglehold of key groups over those resources meant the elimination of opportunities for newly arriving but unconnected Europeans who wished to make their wealth. Having failed to dislodge the entrenched elites from their control over mines and Indians, newly arrived or poorer Spaniards would migrate from Upper Peru during the next century, and a long-term decline would begin in all the major urban centers. Thus, the end of the first century of economic expansion was to be followed by a century-long period of depression, which would have profound and long-term effects on both the urban and rural sectors of the Bolivian society and economy.

Chapter 3

Late Colonial Society: Crisis and Growth

With the peaking of silver production by the middle decades of the seventeenth century, both at Oruro and Potosí, and its subsequent secular decline, a fundamental shift in the economic space and social organization began to occur within Upper Peru, the American region most profoundly affected by the so-called seventeenth-century crisis. The most immediate impact of the precipitous decline in silver output over the next hundred years was a steady fall in the population of most of the region's urban centers. This in turn would lead to a major retrenchment in the regional economy and affect institutions such as the hacienda and the free community. In imperial terms, the importance of Upper Peru now began to fade. By the end of the century, Mexico surpassed total Andean mining production and became as well the major source of American tax income for Spain. By the last quarter of the seventeenth century, Peru and the Charcas region had ceased exporting surplus revenues to the metropolis and were no longer to be the center of Spain's New World empire.

The dramatic decline in the cities was the first response to the silver mining depression. Both the number of miners and the number of townsmen fell sharply in the century from 1650 to 1750. The annual number of mitayos going to the mines fell from 13,500 – in groups of 4,500 in three different periods – or so Indians that were serving each year in Potosí in the 1570s to some 2,000 Indians at any one time by the 1690s. The decrease in mitayos was both a consequence of the diminishing pool of originarios in the sixteen "obligated" provinces – either through death or escape into forastero or yanacona status – and a shrinking in demand at the mines. The reduction in the labor market also seriously affected free Indian miners, many of whom returned to the countryside. But it was among the whites that the depression in silver production had its greatest impact. At least one hundred thousand Spanish-speaking whites migrated out of the mine centers and away from the region seeking their fortune in more economically dynamic areas of the empire. In this century-long depression, both Oruro and Potosí lost over half of their respective populations, with Potosí falling to just thirty thousand persons and Oruro to some twenty thousand by the middle of the eighteenth century. In fact, every city either lost population or stagnated in the depression period.

The contraction of population and of silver production led to a constriction of the extensive hinterland markets serving the mining centers. This was well illustrated in the fate of the important food-supplying region of Cochabamba. With the grain demands from Potosí lessened, it was found that the region around Chuquisaca was productive enough to supply most mining needs, so the more costly Cochabamba products were less competitive. Cochabamba thus exported less from its valleys and turned more toward a subsistence economy, exporting its surplus wheat and maize to the highlands only when the latter suffered severe local harvest crises. In turn, the end of significant exports meant the decline in the power of the Cochabamba hacendado class and the conversion of their large estates into smaller rented parcels. Because most of the free communities of Indians already had been replaced by landless laborers on the estates of the Spaniards, these divisions of land led to the rise of a whole new group of cholo small farmers producing on rented properties. Cochabamba thus became the major center for small-scale, noncommunity, freehold-style farming and the most important region of *minifundia* agriculture in Upper Peru. Its local Spaniards and cholos also turned toward specialization in cloth production and the central valley became a significant producer of crude popular textiles (*tocuyo* cloth).

As production declined in response to declining urban and mining markets, the haciendas producing for these markets also suffered. The general depression in most regions led to a decline in hacienda creation and expansion by the end of the seventeenth century, in contrast to the feverish growth of such units in the first half of the century. Although the Crown had carried out major sales (*composición de tierra*) of "empty" lands (*tierras baldías*) on a periodic basis early in the seventeenth century, these sales became less frequent as the century wore one. By 1700, the frontier had stabilized between Indian ayllu lands and those of the Spanish haciendas, especially as the Indian population stabilized within their new post-Toledo *reducciones*.

This Indian community consolidation was reenforced by population expansion, since the period of the great colonial silver depression in Upper Peru corresponded to the period of renewed growth in the Indian population. It was only in the late seventeenth century and the beginning of the eighteenth century, a good half-century after such a change in Mesoamerica, that the native Indian populations of the region finally were capable of surviving endemic European diseases with a level of mortality little different from that of their European conquerors. This change did not occur until the last decades of the seventeenth century, but, once begun, there developed a long-term trend toward growth throughout the eighteenth and well into the nineteenth century, when epidemics would again become an important check on population expansion. But, by then, there were new diseases such as cholera, which affected all classes and ethnic groups. Until then, however, population growth in the rural areas was impressive, and this increase prompted a strengthening of the free community system.

Thus, a combination of declining pressure on their lands and increasing population created a major period of growth for the free communities at the time of the urban and mining decline. Mita labor obligations lessened as mining declined, and this obligation was now spread over more population. Tribute lists only slowly adjusted to the increasing number of Indians, which somewhat reduced the burden of this tax. There also was more labor in the countryside, and the communities began to pick up immigrant workers who received only minimal land rights in return for their labor for the original (originario) members of these communities. From the late seventeenth until well into the nineteenth century, the communities tended to grow through the expansion of this new immigrant forastero or agregado population. In a partial colonial census of 1646, such new migrants to the communities averaged about a quarter of the total ayllu population, and by the tribute census of 1786, they represented just over half of the total community population in the province of La Paz – which in turn housed half the region's Indian peasant population. This internal stratification within the Indian communities enabled them to accumulate surpluses and even promote church construction in their regions. In fact, the late seventeenth and early eighteenth century became a period of major artistic flourishing among Indian artisans who worked in the highland churches during this period. Both communities and caciques promoted these constructions and the latter patronized the cholo and Indian artisans who built and decorated these churches. Although the Crown controlled communal funds and often forced these communities to grant mortgages to the Spanish hacendados, with the slowing of hacienda expansion, the need for such funds declined, and the pressure on the *cajas de comunidad* (or treasuries) of the communities also declined, allowing them to retain more of their income.

The late seventeenth-century crisis in mining also led to a relative shift in the importance of given districts within Upper Peru. The city of La Paz, in contrast to Oruro, Potosí, and Chuquisaca, seemed to have only stagnated and then for only a short period in the late seventeenth century and then continued to grow, so that, by the middle of the eighteenth century, it emerged with its forty thousand inhabitants as the most populous city in the entire region. The growth of La Paz at the time of the relative decline elsewhere can largely be attributed to the growth of the local Indian markets and production. With its hinterland of some 150,000 to 200,000 Indian peasants, close to half of the region's total Indian population, La Paz thrived as a major administrative and market center both for the area's most densely populated highland zone as well as the thriving eastern Yungas valleys, which were now major coca producers. In these valleys were the richest Indian communities as well as newly arrived Spaniards who began to terrace previously empty lands and to plant coca bushes to produce the highly desired leaves.

The local Spanish elite of the province based its income on regional commerce and agricultural production. It had become a major landed elite after the land sales of the Crown in the region, most especially that of the 1640s, which saw a very large number of the Spanish-speaking merchants and well-to-do locals buying rural properties. By the last quarter of the seventeenth century, this elite was becoming primarily native born. By then half the wealthy members of the community were born in the city of La Paz and only 20 percent came from Spain, the rest coming from other American regions or other parts of Europe. As was to be expected, more women than men were native born, and there was by now a high mixture of mestizos in the elite population, given the lack of Spanish women through most of its history. Even more impressive of the more open nature of this elite, compared to metropolitan Spain and even other more advanced centers in America, was the extraordinarily high incidence of illegitimate births that elite women experienced. In the elite Spanish parish of San Agustín, over half the births to elite women were listed as illegitimate in the period 1661–80, an extraordinarily high rate even by elite standards in America.

With expanding local markets, increased Indian consumption and the largest rural population in the region, La Paz also became the center of an ever-expanding coca plantation production. A crop confined to the pre-Colombian elite, coca had become a basic consumption item of miners and all high-altitude workers. From earliest times it had been grown in the tropical Yungas Valleys just to the east of the city of La Paz. These step valleys had been terraced and worked by local Aymara speaking communities. They now became the object of exploitation by the local Spanish-speaking elite as well. Such an owner of *cocales* – lands dedicated to the production of coca – was Don Tadeo Diez de Medina, a native and resident (vecino) of La Paz who from the 1750s to the 1790s emerged as the leading hacendado in the Audiencia of Charcas. With his wealth based on merchant activity in the first half of the century, he only obtained rural properties with his first marriage in 1752. But through this marriage and continual purchases, he invested large amounts of his commercially generated capital in terracing and planting new coca fields. Like the Indian communities before him, he also purchased major estates on the altiplano and in other valley regions so that he created a multiecological farm system in which he often exchanged coca leaf from his Yungas estates for cheese, wool, meat, and other products from his highland ranches. Although a very wealthy merchant, he did not engage in mining – which was a highly specialized activity.

Probably the most extraordinary of the specialized miners/mineral merchants/smelters in this period was Antonio López de Quirogas who arrived from Galicia to Potosí in 1648 and died there in 1699. By the first decades of the 1600s, the Potosí mining industry was fully matured. There were in place some seventy-two water-driven refining mills plus some thirty dams and sophisticated canals bringing water to these ore crushing refineries. Despite the decline in the Indian population, there was always a ready supply of salaried miners (*mingas*), if not mitayos. The real problem was the progressively declining quality of ore. New explorations and numerous experiments were tried to reach the ever deeper veins, but almost all the old mines ran into problems of flooding and high costs of extraction. The smaller returns on capital invested in mining and smelting help to explain the already noted violent elite urban confrontations that occurred in the city of Potosí between the Basque and non-Basque merchants, smelters, and mine owners, which could only be resolved through the necessity of royal government intervention in 1625 in favor of the Basques. But the base cause of this conflict remained, which was the continued decline of mining profits. The originality of López de Quiroga in this new more difficult age was to come up with the idea of investing huge sums to revive mining by cutting shafts below major veins in the Cerro Rico, so as to drain the older mines and gain access to new silver lodes from below. López de Quiroga came from an upper level Spanish background and learned the mining profession by entering the market as a silver trader (*mercader de plata*). His extraordinary success in this endeavor not only made him very wealthy but also gave him an intimate knowledge of the industry. By the late 1670s, he was renting mines and was owner of two refining mills picked up through defaulted loans to the original owners. These investments were still relatively modest and his primary activity was in the purchase of unminted silver and loans to miners and smelters. By the late 1660s, he was working twelve mines, but began grouping them into larger units through constructing large galleries used to cut across several veins and smaller mines. The genius of López de Quiroga was to open up old and abandoned sources of ore. By the end of the decade he was the region's largest smelter and now had the funds to construct far more costly adits (or *socavónes*), which were large horizontal shafts built below the water table and passing under many old abandoned mines – these were then drained, which permitted them to be exploited. Each of the adits that he built at several mining centers were opened with blasting gunpowder, the first such use of this mining technique in America, took half a dozen years to build, and cost in excess of several hundred thousand pesos each. The five adits he built at Cerro Rico by 1689 were over a mile and a half in length. His efforts and those of other miners to revive old mines led to a temporary stabilization of production in the last quarter of the century from the 1660s to 1690, but soon even these efforts proved of little utility. Moreover, after his death, the mining industry became far more fragmented and no single miner would come to play such a dominant role in production until the nineteenth century.

López de Quiroga in 1689 sponsored his nephew in one of the last military expeditions to conquer the Upper Amazonian lowlands, in this case the northeastern region of Moxos. The result was total failure. But the seventeenth and early eighteenth century was no longer a time of civil frontier expansion. In fact, the arrival of the Jesuits, Franciscans, and other missionaries in the second half of the seventeenth century would finally lead to partial settlement of this frontier zone of "uncivilized" Indians via the famous mission frontier. In 1587, the Jesuits set up a residence in Santa Cruz and began to learn Guaraní, Chané, and other native languages of the region. By the 1590s, they were venturing further afield into the northern regions, but did not get permission to set up missions until the last quarter of the seventeenth century. Eventually establishing some twenty-five missions between 1682 and 1744, the Jesuits settled some thirty thousand Indians on the Upper Mamoré river and surrounding regions. In 1701, they published the first grammar of the Arawak language spoken in the region. European diseases, Indian unrest, and even revolt did not destroy the mission culture that even survived the expulsion of the Jesuits in 1767. The exploitation of chinchona bark for quinine and rubber trapping in the nineteenth century was the final event that would lay waste to these old mission towns. Another Jesuit style mission republic was established to the south of Moxos in the province of Chiquitos where some ten Indian missions were established between 1691 and 1760. These mission settlements with their farms and herds eventually housed some twenty thousand Indian neophytes. Here they built some magnificent mission compounds and churches that have survived to this day. Here as well as in Moxos the Jesuits had to fight off incursions by Portuguese troops seeking Indian slaves, and as in Paraguay had to arm and defend their towns. A third center of missionary activity developed out of the southern city of Tarija where the Jesuits sent expeditions to christianize the Chiriguanos, Tobas, Macobies, and other Indians of this Gran Chaco region. Although other missionary groups replaced the Jesuits after their expulsion from America by the Crown, the powerful mission frontier after the late 1760s went into decline.

Although the eastern lowland frontier had seen major activity in the late seventeenth and early eighteenth century, in the rest of the colony the long economic depression had brought about long-term structural changes that were not reversed until late in the nineteenth century. Although silver production and exports would begin a long-term rise in the 1750s, and a prosperous industry would develop, peak production during this period reached no higher than 50 percent of late-sixteenth-century output. For this reason, the late colonial silver boom was incapable of renovating the urban populations. The Upper Peruvian populations of Europeans and their supportive urban Indian and mestizo workforce never revived. Production increased, but it did so on the basis of relatively stagnant urban populations, at least in the major mine centers. This would mean that the development of the late-eighteenth-century mining industry, while important in reviving the regional economic ties of local producers, was unable to recapture fully the enormous pan-Andean market that had existed before the crisis. Thus, everywhere the linkages between local markets and the mining centers were now greatly reduced in importance or had disappeared altogether.

While the eighteenth century was to prove a relatively productive period for colonial Charcas, and one in which artistic and intellectual life was well developed, growth in the urban sectors and regional economies was very modest compared to the glories of the fifteenth and early sixteenth century. Moreover, in the total American production, Potosí was now a distinctly secondary source of silver output. Mexican continued expansion from the seventeenth century to the end of the colonial period guaranteed that Upper Peru remained a relatively minor producer even despite the late eighteenth-century revival. Although Potosí and Oruro, even in their reduced production, were still major sources of silver for the world market, they were no longer the dominant center even for the Andes as silver production also developed within the Peruvian viceroyalty. In contrast to the Mexican viceroyalty of New Spain, where the Crown was able to export large quantities of bullion to Spain every year, the Peruvian colonies generated enough taxes to pay only for the royal bureaucracy of the southern region of South America. The eighteenth-century boom for Upper Peru was thus a relatively fragile and limited affair that would not survive a series of structural, market, and political problems that arose early in the nineteenth century. Limited as it was, however, Upper Peruvian mining still represented the region's single most important industry. Thus, a major power struggle developed in the second half of the eighteenth century for control over the Audiencia of Charcas, which pitted the older merchant wealth of Lima and Cuzco against the rising power of the new merchant groups of Buenos Aires.

Beginning in the late sixteenth century, the final site of the port city of Buenos Aires had been settled, and a small but prosperous regional economy had begun to develop on the basis of local trade and a grazing industry. But this growth was quite limited, as Buenos Aires and its hinterland were unable to use its primary asset – its seaport and fast European connections – to promote its growth until the second half of the eighteenth century. While contraband certainly thrived in Buenos Aires, it was not until the Crown of Spain officially changed its policy toward open imperial trade that the real growth set in. Once trade was officially permitted between Buenos Aires and Europe on the one hand and Buenos Aires and the interior on the other, the growth of the region was phenomenal. Already by the end of the seventeenth century the Crown was showing interest in this growth potential by forcing Potosí to send an annual subsidy (*subsidio*) to Buenos Aires to help defray local administrative costs and to sustain its long-term conflicts against Portuguese incursions into the Rio de la Plata estuary from its Brazilian colony.

Then in 1776 the Crown decided the growing conflict between Buenos Aires and Lima for control over trade to Potosí in favor of the former. Upper Peru and the Audiencia government were placed under the direct control of Buenos Aires, which now became a new and independent viceroyalty. In 1778, this control was reenforced when most of the trade restrictions for the Buenos Aires viceroyalty were removed. These political decisions were crucial in shifting the preponderance of Potosí trade from the northerly direction toward a southerly one. Whereas previously the southern route had involved only imports, from the northern Argentine towns, of mules and foodstuffs, and from Paraguay of yerba mate, Potosí now slowly turned its whole export system southward and opened up a major new exporting route all the way through its traditional northern Argentine satellite towns in the Tucumán district toward the sea at Buenos Aires.

The reorganization of the economic space of Upper Peru and its connections to the outer world meant a consequent decline of Lima. No longer did Lima merchants hold a monopoly over Charcas's trade with Europe, nor was it any longer its single major source of capital. This decline in trade dominance to their mining hinterland brought in a long-term decay of Lima's economic power. This decay, in turn, allowed the growth of alternative regional centers of economic power. The most powerful of the new centers was, of course, Buenos Aires. But the relatively marginal captaincy of Chile would also find the potential for growth developing rapidly at the expense of the former Lima monopoly. Thus, the reorganization of Upper Peru's trade links to Europe would in fact both reflect long-term changes in the relative economic and political power of different South American regions and help foster these trends to such an extent that the power of Peru itself, and to a lesser extent, Upper Peru, would now be much reduced, to be replaced by new and now more dynamic areas such as Chile and, above all, the Rio de la Plata.

All of these trends would, of course, continue well beyond the eighteenth century and have important consequences for the relative position and power of the postcolonial regimes. But in the early decades of the eighteenth century such long-term changes were only beginning. Moreover, the Crown, in creating the new viceroyalty, hoped in fact to stimulate further the export economy of Upper Peru. Thus, the Audiencia of Charcas was soon staffed by a group of extremely able administrators with unusually broad backgrounds, whose efforts were primarily directed toward reviving the silver-mining industry of Oruro and Potosí by whatever means possible. As would be evident from later developments, it was quite clear that the silver veins were still plentiful in the Upper Peruvian minefields. But they were now to be found at much deeper levels, most often below the local water tables, and were more often found in mixtures with other metals and at lower quality per unit of crude ore than they had been in the early period. The collapse of silver production had more to do with the exhaustion of richer and more easily accessible surface and near-surface deposits than it did with the exhaustion of mineral deposits themselves.

To get at this next level of silver ore, large capital expenditures would have to be made, and the local mining industry of Upper Peru was incapable of generating that amount of capital. Therefore, it was essential that the Crown provide the financial support necessary to open up deeper shaft mining. The Crown finally recognized this need in the eighteenth century. In 1736, it agreed to lower its tax share from 20 percent to 10 percent of total output, a decision made much earlier in Mexico. Next, it assisted in the creation of a minerals purchasing bank in 1779, the Banco de San Carlos, which had been originally established as a credit institution by the smelters (azogueros) in the late 1740s and had become a semigovernment institution for minerals purchases as well by 1752. The bank's direct purchase of refined silver eliminated private silver merchants (rescatadores), thus guaranteeing high prices to smelters and miners and, even more important, providing credit for purchasing mine supplies. In short, it brought order into the chaos of the local capital market. When the bank went into a severe crisis in the 1770s, it had become such an important institution that the Crown was forced to take it over and directly support its functions. Finally, the Crown not only reorganized the mercury trade after the collapse of the Huancavelica production in the 1770s, and brought in major mercury shipments from Almaden in Spain via the port of Buenos Aires, but it subsidized the price as well. In 1784, the price of mercury to the local miners was reduced by almost a fifth.

While the population of Potosí continued its decline, going from an estimated seventy thousand persons in the 1750s to some thirty-five thousand in the 1780s, production slowly began to revive after 1730, especially after the systematic assistance granted by the Crown. After some debate, the mita, now much reduced to some twenty-five hundred mitayos per annum, was nevertheless maintained and strengthened, and still provided a crucial labor base for the miners. For, despite their severe decline in numbers, by the end of the eighteenth century the mitayos still represented close to one-half of the underground shaft miners and thus still made the crucial difference between profit and loss in the Potosí mines.

Supported by royal grants and the mita, the Upper Peruvian miners were able to foster steady growth in mine output in the late eighteenth century. This was matched by a growth in the agricultural sector of the economy and a general growth of the rural population. While this vibrant agricultural sector was limited to the regional and Andean markets, its activity was lively enough to provide the Crown with a growing income in the form of sales taxes and the Indian head tax. This tribute tax by the end of the eighteenth century had become the second leading source of royal income in the Audiencia of Charcas district.

The increased role of tribute income was due to essentially three separate phenomena that occurred in the eighteenth century. The first and obviously most important factor was the long-term positive growth trend in the rural population that began late in the seventeenth century. Second, the reduction of exploitation of the rural population as a result of the mining crisis had enabled the free communities to recoup their resources and to develop further their local production. Finally, the tribute tax was extended to all Indian males regardless of their land access status, and this in turn profoundly altered the burdens and the extension of the entire tribute taxation system.

Since much of the agricultural produce Indians traded among themselves or produced for local regional markets was exempted from taxation, the Crown was forced to rely on its tribute tax as the primary mechanism both to force the Indians into the Spanish markets and to provide the Crown with direct income. But given the tax laws, the Crown was exclusively taxing the originario members of the communities, and despite the general growth of Indian rural populations, the number of originarios either remained unchanged or declined. This failure of the originarios to grow along with all other Indian groups was obviously related to the fact that mita and tax obligations rendered the originario status less than profitable for all but the very few wealthiest peasants. Even the Crown recognized that it was destroying the legal class of originarios to its own detriment, and in 1734 finally accepted the advice of local royal officials and extended the head tax to include all Indians.

Maintaining its recognition of local distinctions, the Crown now provided a fixed tax of five pesos per annum for all forasteros living in the communities and yanaconas living on the estates of the Spaniards. While the former were required to pay their own tax, the latter had their tribute tax paid for them by the Spanish landowner, which was another inducement for encouraging rural labor to migrate to the haciendas. In both cases, however, the new extension of the tribute tax to all rural Indians increased royal tribute income by some one-half to two-thirds in the years that followed and also stabilized the originario class, as the advantages of changing status were no longer so great as they had been in the period prior to 1734.

With the tax burden more evenly spread and with taxes remaining relatively fixed, the increasing population in the rural area was better able to handle the state and private extraction of its surplus and to survive and prosper to some extent. Equally, while the Crown maintained the mita as an institution vital to the prosperity of the silver-mining region, it did not increase the number of mitayos by making the forasteros or yanaconas subject to this obligation; thus, the regional weight of mita obligation remained much reduced from its sixteenth and seventeenth century burden.

The community Indians also were less bothered by the haciendas. Although the mining revival had increased demand on the local urban markets, that demand was met by bringing in marginally productive haciendas or reviving production on the better estates. It brought little major expansion in the hacienda system, which appeared to remain relatively stable throughout the eighteenth century. Thus, the growing Indian population did not find themselves dealing with the problems of massive hacienda encroachment.

But despite the relative relaxation of exploitation of the expanding rural Indian peasant population, that population remained bitterly opposed to its overlords. The unending exactions of local corregidores and their forced sales of goods to the Indian populations (the so-called *repartimientos*) was particularly resented. Although the mules and other goods bought by the Indian population were useful to their work, they bitterly resented the forced nature of these sales and the brutal methods of collection. Moreover, whatever positive aspects of the system of providing credit to the poorest workers in the society, local corregidores, desperate for income, were known to abuse the system in every way possible. Indians also resented the demands of local corvee labor obligations which often went for private Spanish interests rather than state concerns. Moreover, the local caciques found themselves being constantly attacked in their own privileges and exploited by the Spaniards and were forced to the wall to defend their increasingly eroding leadership position. Finally, the more literate and cultured church of the eighteenth century was equally as opposed to non-Christian activity as the church ideologues of the previous centuries had been, and there was a never-ending attack on local religious belief systems that forced the Indians to defend themselves constantly.

It was this complex of factors that helps to explain the massive Indian rebellion that occurred in Upper Peru and the Cuzco area in 1780, at the height of the eighteenth-century expansion and economic and social revival. Such Indian uprisings in the rural area, or urban mestizo and criollo uprisings in the cities, as represented by the Great Rebellion of 1780–2, were not new to Upper Peru or to the Spanish empire. Local community or even provincial uprisings occurred periodically in Upper Peru throughout the colonial period. Usually responses to immediate local causes, these rebellions most often took place among the free communities because of the abusive taxing of a local corregidor who went beyond the usual norms of exploitation, because of conflicts over land with non-Indians, or, most important of all, because of local interference in the appointment of local caciques by the Spaniards. In the urban areas, such rebellions also were common, ranging from local subsistence riots in times of crisis and food hoardings, to protests against local taxes or royal officials. Such movements or conspiracies had occurred in Oruro and in Cochabamba in the 1730s.

But all of these endemic revolts were usually short-lived and quite local affairs that wanted nothing so much as temporary relief of taxes or elimination of corrupt officials. "Long Live the King and Death to Bad Governors" was the traditional appeal of these revolts. Such movements were an essential part of local government and were recognized by all as a more or less normal outlet for local protest. This did not mean that suppression could not be quite violent and lead to extensive killings. It was evident that, unlike comparable situations in Europe, such riots in the face of the general oppression of Indian masses provoked more violent responses from the authorities than might have otherwise been the case. But the pattern of such movements was well known, so the government never felt itself severely threatened in its ultimate power by such typical local protests.

In this respect, the great Túpac Amaru rebellion of 1780–2 was in fact a profound and fundamental departure from the norm. It was massive in its participation and its extension. Probably encompassing over one hundred thousand rebel troops in all its activities, the rebellion involved relatively well-coordinated activity from the highlands of southern Peru in the Cuzco area, through all of Upper Peru, into northern Argentina. It was a multiclass, multicaste, and extremely well-led revolt that ultimately had as its aim the establishment of an autonomous region under control of the local classes to the exclusion of all Spaniards. It was, in short, an independence movement. Although the leadership would come from a dissident element of the cacique class in the Cuzco region, there was a very important participation of Indian leaders from the Audiencia of Charcas and many of the crucial battles were fought in its territory. The two most important rebel leaders were the Aymaras Tomás Katari, the cacique of the pueblo of San Pedro de Macha in the province of Chayanta (Potosí), and the commoner Julián Apaza, who took the name of Túpac Katari when he emerged as the leading military leader of the rebellion in the La Paz region.

The case of Tomás Katari is truly an extraordinary history. Ousted from his traditional position of cacique by the local Spanish corregidor in 1777, Katari, who was neither literate nor bilingual, during the next four years used all the legal instruments available to him to retake his position. From formal petitions to the local royal court to a trip to Buenos Aires to speak with the Viceroy, Katari successfully fought his case at every level of government and usually won. But corrupt local officials kept rejecting formal decrees reappointing him to his position and not only jailed him several times, but fearful of his powerful local support, also killed his major ally Isidro Acho, another cacique, and then secretly ordered his assassination in the midst of the great rebellion in January 1781. It is evident that while pushing his legal case, Katari also was organizing powerful forces to oppose Spanish rule and began to have formal contact with the Túpac Amaru movement. On his death, his two brothers then led a massive Indian rebellion that laid siege to the city of La Plata.

More threatening to the Spaniards was the commoner Julian Apaza, or as he would call himself in honor of his two heroes, Túpac Katari. Without traditional claims to loyalty from his Indian followers, he yet emerged as one of the leading military leaders in the big rebellion itself, and through his personal abilities alone was able to organize and lead a powerful forty thousand-person Indian Army. An itinerant merchant in coca and cloth, he was only a forastero from the region of Sicasica and just thirty when he emerged in the midst of the rebellion in 1781. Little is known of his background, although he was married to Bartola Sisa who acted as one of his lieutenants in the war, and apparently spoke no Spanish nor was literate. But he proved to be an able military leader and generated intense loyalties from his followers.

The rebellion had its preparations well before November 1780, its official opening, in the contact that its able leader, José Gabriel Túpac Amaru, had with many leading caciques of Charcas and southern Peru, as well as with Julian Apasa and other potential rebel leaders. A direct descendant of the Incas and a leading cacique in the Bishopric of Cuzco, Túpac Amaru was a well-educated and literate member of the Indian noble class. Given the legitimacy of his background and his own undoubted intellect, he was able to convince an important minority of Quechua kurakas and a few Aymara nobles that Spanish rule had to be destroyed.

As the rebellion developed, there were essentially two major phases. The first was the actual rebellion led by Túpac Amaru himself, who seized most of the province of Cuzco and besieged its capital city from November 1780 to March 1781. Involving large numbers of troops on both sides, the siege of Cuzco was eventually broken by the local Spaniards, and Túpac Amaru and his immediate entourage were captured by the latter date.

But the execution of its leader did not stop the massive revolt from spreading, nor dissident local leaders from joining the rebellion. The second phase of the rebellion began just as the Cuzco activity was being crushed and took place largely in Upper Peru. First was the Chayanta rebellion which began in January 1781 with the assassination of Tomás Katari, led by the brothers of the dead cacique. Then in March the nephew of Túpac Amaru, Andres, conquered the entire province of Larecaja along the eastern shore of Lake Titicaca in the region of La Paz and after a three-month siege took the provincial capital of Sorata in August 1781, killing all the Spaniards. He then marched on the regional capital of La Paz and joined Túpac Katari in a formal siege of the city, which lasted in two phases for some six months from March until October of 1781. Although the city never fell, something like half the urban population lost their lives in the battles. Relief armies finally succeeded in breaking the siege and in capturing Túpac Katari in November.

In the meantime, in February 1781, a criollo urban revolt had begun in Oruro, led by Jacinto Rodríguez. The rebels, who were closely allied with Túpac Amaru, succeeded in seizing the city from the peninsular Spaniards. This was the most powerful mestizo and criollo support that the Indian caciques received, and Oruro was the largest Spanish city ever taken by the rebels. Although Rodriguez worked closely with the local caciques, the alliance between Indians, mestizos, and American-born whites or criollos was not an easy one as class differences quickly made themselves felt. Here, as elsewhere, the royal forces eventually seized the town, and the rebels were executed. The final group that joined the rebellion were mestizo artisans in the southern town of Tupiza who killed the local corregidor in March 1781. But this movement was quickly suppressed and had only a local impact.

But the defeat of the rebels was not exclusively a caste war. In fact, the majority of the Aymara caciques and a very important number of Quechuan nobles opposed the rebels and fought pitched battles with them, using their own Indian followers and allied Spanish troops. In fact, a large number of Indian noble houses were wiped out by the rebels in these intracaste battles. Most of the caciques among the Aymara along the southern shore of Lake Titicaca joined the royal cause and many died in opposing the armies of Túpac Amaru. Such was the case of the cacique Agustín Siñani of Sorata, who in the 1760s had paid for the extraordinary paintings of himself and his noble clan in the lakeside church of Carabuco, one of the classic works of the mestizo art style of the eighteenth century. He died defending Sorata against the troops of André Amaru. Another was Dionosio Mamani, the cacique of Chulumani in the coca-growing lower valleys of the Yungas. He organized his Indian vassals in armies to fight the rebels, fought several battles with them, was forced to flee to Cochabamba, and eventually died in his home community in a pitched battle with the rebels, who destroyed his homes and plantations. Another was Manuel Antonio Chuiquimia of the lake community of Copacabana, who like Mamani also joined the Spanish army of Sebastían de Segurola and was known as a particularly repressive leader in his official role of judge-pacifier (*juez pacificador*). Although some of the jilakatas and other principal men of their communities joined with the rebels, the aymara nobility as a class tended to remain loyal, especially as the maximum leader of the Aymara rebel troops was a commoner and not a member of their class.

By the end of 1781, the rebellion had been crushed in most rural areas, and all captured cities were again in the hands of the Spaniards. The rebel leaders were executed in the usual brutal manner, and there was a massive confiscation of property. All rebel caciques were removed from office, and a very large number of loyal caciques had died in the fighting. Whereas the crown recognized the titles of the loyalists who survived the rebellion, the destruction was so massive that thenceforth most of the free communities in the central zones of the rebellion were controlled by Spaniards, who now took the title of caciques. At the same time, the community elders, the jilakatas, henceforth took over some of the functions previously exercised by the old noble class. These events marked the effective extinction of the cacique class in Southern and Upper Peru, the last of the great Indian nobility that had survived the Spanish Conquest. Following the rebellion of 1780–2, the Indian noble class ceased to be a major factor in the social, economic, and political life of the region.

Despite its massive and far-reaching impact and its extraordinarily broad mobilization, the Túpac Amaru rebellion was soon a distant memory in the minds of the population of Upper Peru. It also was the last attempt to bring both social justice and independence to the region prior to the nineteenth century. Later rebellions and the ultimate winning of independence would finally come from the criollos and would be distinctly upper-class and largely non-Indian affairs. Thus, the Túpac Amaru rebellion, despite its actual and symbolic importance, had little lasting impact on Upper Peru.

The destruction of human life and property during the rebellion had been massive, especially around La Paz and the Lake Titicaca region. But general economic and demographic growth – quite pronounced in this decade – enabled most of the haciendas to be rebuilt by the end of the 1780s. Thus, in the immediate years after the revolt, local documents described the massive loss of farm implements, animals, and workers on abandoned haciendas, but by the end of the decade almost all of these haciendas were again operating at normal capacity and attained the same level of wealth that they had had prior to the revolt. The population losses also were soon made up, and by the 1790s most of the former rebel territory contained population densities equal to the pre-Rebellion period.

By the 1790s, the largest rural population – well over two hundred thousand person – and the biggest city of Upper Peru with over forty thousand residents – were to be found in the province of La Paz, which now accounted for half of the colony's total population. The rich highlands and valleys of this dominant province contained some eleven hundred haciendas worked by eighty-three thousand peons, or yanaconas, and were owned by 719 hacendados, most of whom were absentee landlords living in the provincial capital. Some 39 percent of the hacendados owned more than one estate and, like the merchant Don Tadeo Diez de Medina, spread their holdings over several ecological zones, thus complementing their production of agricultural products. Some two-thirds of these hacendados were men with the rest divided evenly between women and church institutions. In this respect, the Upper Peruvian Church, which had some forty monasteries and a total of twenty-four hundred clergy by the last quarter of the eighteenth century, was a wealthy institution but not a major landowner. It provided most of the mortgage monies (or *censos*) available for hacienda purchase and expansion. But unlike other colonial churches, it remained a relatively minor owner of rural properties. This relatively weak position of the church would prove extremely important in the nineteenth century, when Bolivia had little difficulty in controlling the church and its lands and incomes, in contrast to the bitter struggles that occurred in most other countries in Latin America.

Despite the late-eighteenth-century expansion of the hacienda in the department of La Paz, the dominant group in the rural area in terms of land ownership and population remained the Indian communities. There were some 491 such corporate landowning groups in La Paz with well over two hundred thousand Indians. Such communities even owned twenty-two haciendas with over eighteen hundred yanaconas. Of the Indians living in these communities, just over half were originarios and the rest were later immigrants with limited land rights, although the latter group would continue to grow faster than the originario class and would become the dominant group in the ayllus by the next century. Providing a major share of royal revenues through their tribute tax, these landed Indian peasants would become the single most important source of government revenues in the new republic, again on the basis of their tribute taxes.

The rapid recovery of Upper Peru from the effects of the Túpac Amaru rebellion had a great deal to do with the successful impact of the Bourbon reforms of the economy, which originated in Spain in the middle decades of the eighteenth century. The reforms of the mining economy soon brought a renewed prosperity to Oruro and Potosí production, and a general reform of the commercial structure led to a healthy rivalry between Lima and Buenos Aires for the trade of the Audiencia of Charcas. This in turn opened up a second set of economic networks and trading systems that increased the general tempo of commercial and market activity on the altiplano and the associated eastern valleys. Finally, to bring some order to its political structure, and thus to bring the administration in line with the more advanced policies of freer trade and open competition, the Crown carried out a major administrative reorganization.

The symbol of this new governmental structure was the creation of a new local administrator known as the intendant. Modeled on the institution that had such success in France, the colonial American intendants effectively superseded the old corregidores and created jurisdictions that now encompassed both Spanish and Indian territories under one regional administration. In 1784, four such intendancy districts were established in Upper Peru (or Charcas), covering the regions of La Paz, Cochabamba, Potosí, and Chuquisaca. These new officials were very highly paid and thus independent of the need to engage in local commerce as had the old corregidores in order to obtain funding. They also were carefully selected from among experienced administrators throughout the empire, and their primary function was seen as being promoters of regional economic and social growth.

This careful process of selection and the well-endowed salaries given to the new officials resulted in the creation of an extraordinary corps of literate and sophisticated administrators who governed Upper Peru in the last two decades of the eighteenth century. Figures such as Francisco Viedma in Cochabamba and Juan del Pino Manrique in Potosí were outstanding among these new officials. Concerned with reviving trade, experimenting with agriculture, promoting general well-being, and increasing royal revenues, these men left behind wonderfully detailed memorials on the life and times of the peoples whom they governed. They also appear to have examined all the major issues related to the problems of a social and economic nature in their areas and provided detailed debates on alternative strategies. To these intendants should be added the rather unusual roving *oidor extraordinario* of the Audiencia of Charcas, Pedro Cañete. Jurist, historian, and administrative investigator, Cañete examined and legislated on the mining industry, the government's tax structure, the issue of the mita, and even the relationship between the Crown and the church. Often he engaged in bitter disputes with the intendants, the results of which provided even more detailed memorials on the state of society. Viedma, Pino Manrique, Cañete, and the other intendants well represented eighteenth-century enlightenment thought and brought to Upper Peru both a new administrative structure and a new sense of leadership and development potential (see Map 3-1).

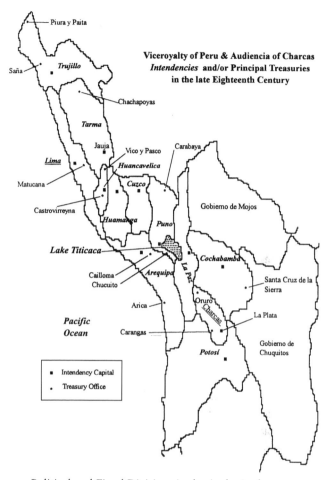

3-1 Political and Fiscal Divisions in the Andes in the
Eighteenth Century

There also had been a revival of higher education in the Audiencia
in the last quarter of the century. As a result of reforms of legal education in Spain in the 1760s and of the expulsion of the Jesuits and
the negative impact this had on the education system in the region,
the Audiencia obtained Crown approval in 1776 to set up a modern
legal center to train new lawyers in the capital city of Chuquisaca.
This was the first of such legal centers established throughout the

empire. The Academia Carolina eventually trained some 362 lawyers by 1808 in the most modern rigorous civil law legal training then available. Although the majority of its elite students came from the Audiencia, an important group also came from Peru, Chile, and the Rio de la Plata region. This elite quickly moved into the royal administration and provided a hard core of first-class and well-trained lawyers for royal service. Given the later history of the region, it is also no surprise that it supplied an important share of the republican revolutionary leadership in the early nineteenth century.

This new government concern with both the colonial administration and economy led to increased trade and commerce. Francisco Viedma of Cochabamba, for example, spent a great deal of energy promoting regional growth and seemed to have played an important role in breaking the pattern of stagnation that Cochabamba had suffered since the seventeenth-century crisis. By the end of the century, Cochabamba became a major Peruvian manufacturer of rough textiles (*tocuyo*) and was again being integrated into larger regional markets. As for the mining industry, the Crown's constant intervention in local affairs produced an ever-increasing subsidy of private miners with everything from guaranteed mercury supplies to support of the minerals' purchasing bank, which became a formal royal institution in the 1770s. All this activity, along with booming trade throughout the Spanish-American empire, produced a major growth in regional trade and population, if not a complete revival of the silver mining glory of the previous epoch.

Thus, the Túpac Amaru disaster was relatively easily absorbed by the Upper Peruvian economy, and within three or four years of the rebellion, treasury income was equal to pre-Conflict levels, and most of the rural hacienda system that had been destroyed was completely rebuilt. But whatever the long-term effects of governmental subsidization, freer trade, and general economic growth may have been, not all classes or groups benefitted equally. Thus, despite all reforms, and the change of their names, the Crown still retained the oppressive system of local corregidores de indios (now called subintendants) in the Indian areas, and these men still actively exploited their Indian subjects through the usual processes of forced sales, intervention in the election of officials and selection of caciques, and periodic shakedowns of community officials. Moreover, the increasing accuracy of the government census, established on a modern basis in 1786, meant an increasing impact of the more effectively collected tribute tax on all Indian male heads of household, and a more efficient registration of mita laborers. Although general growth softened somewhat the impact of the old tax structure, the more efficient government administration canceled out these gains by collecting the revenues more systematically, while at the same time leaving untouched the old exploitative mechanisms.

The patterns of decline and renewed growth, which were evident in seventeenth- and eighteenth-century Upper Peru, were to have their influence on the patterns of artistic activity as well. Whereas the first major urban construction and massive artistic adornment had occurred in the city of Chuquisaca from its foundation until about 1650, in the second half of the century, the city of La Paz and its hinterland became the new area of church construction, with Potosí following closely behind. The late start of this latter city was due to the initial commitment of the local elite to more prosaic construction in Potosí and to more refined architectural investments in the nearby city of Chuquisaca. By the second half of the century, however, just as its production was going into long-term decline, Potosí finally got around to developing an urban center of some distinction.

This new period of artistic expression not only occurred in a new geographic setting but also reflects certain fundamental changes in style and organization. Stylistically, the period from approximately 1650 to 1700 is dominated in Upper Peru by baroque themes, then much in vogue in Spain itself. But the artists who developed this style were more likely to have been born locally, even if they were white. The great age of the immigration of artists from European centers was drawing to a close, and there existed enough workshops and experts to supply local needs, with only the occasional European priest to give the latest news of styles and changes. Moreover, among the American-born artists, there appeared Indians and cholos even as painters, a field, like architectural design, that had been an exclusively European-controlled occupation until that time.

In the field of painting, there was so much intense activity in the seventeenth and eighteenth centuries that one can distinguish several different "schools" at work. There was first the abundant "popular" school of Indian and mestizo artists whose paintings were usually unsigned and lacked perspective. This anonymous group of popular artists were often sculptors and masons as well as part-time painters, and they left works everywhere in Upper Peru, even in the best cathedrals. By the eighteenth century, these popular painters were beginning to merge with one of the formal "schools" – that of the Colla – or artists of the La Paz and Lake Titicaca region. The other two formal schools, whose artists signed their works and used standard perspectives, were those of Chuquisaca – where mannerist styles coming from the works of Bitti were the norm – and Potosí, which tended to stress the current Spanish interests. While the fifty or so artists who signed their paintings seemed initially to be defined as a different class and group, the increasing sophistication of popular artists and the increasing influence of mestizo styles on the more professional elite led in the late eighteenth century to a virtual blending of popular, Colla, and the important Cuzco styles into a quite distinctive Upper Peruvian criollo or "mestizo style."

Whereas the Chuquisaca school had flourished in the first century of Spanish settlement, the Potosí and Colla schools were to predominate in the period from 1650 to the end of the colonial period. Of the two, it was the Potosí school that was most influential and powerful in the period from 1650 to 1750. Just as the economic crisis was at its worst in the city, Potosí began a massive construction of churches and public buildings and also supported the most prominent colonial school of painters. The most outstanding of these Potosí painters, and the greatest of the colonial period, was Melchor Pérez de Holguín, who was born in Cochabamba in the 1660s and arrived in Potosí to begin his career in the early 1690s. From the last decade of the century until well into the 1720s, Holguin was the dominant painter in Potosí, and spread his art through all the regular and secular churches, along with important private commissions for nonreligious persons. A classic baroque stylist of extraordinary ability, Holguin had an enormous output that was to be found in all the major churches of the city and whose style soon influenced many of the other leading painters.

As for the Colla school of painting, which also flourished after 1650, its primary center was not to be found in one of the provincial capitals, as with the schools of Chuquisaca and Potosí, but in a traditional peasant rural zone, most particularly the area around Lake Titicaca. This region was one of the primary centers of agricultural activity in Upper Peru and the heartland of Aymara settlement. The fact that churches of major artistic achievement were constructed in these small peasant villages, especially those that made up the provinces of Chucuito (temporarily a part of Upper Peru), Pacajes, and Omasuyos, would seem to imply the existence of unheard-of wealth for rural and primarily Indian Upper Peru in this time of generalized crisis in the mining export industry. The existence of this wealth suggests the relative decline in the level of exploitation of the traditional free communities of this zone; the Indians in this area were thus able to retain their savings, which in turn were now available for investments in a major program of construction and artistic activity – almost all of it related to church activity. That many of the artists in the Colla school were Indians and mestizos also implies an increasing specialization of labor in these areas, and this supports the idea of a relatively thriving rural economy that could permit such full-time artists to develop.

By the second half of the eighteenth century, the pattern of artistic and architectural activity again shifted somewhat, as a generalized mestizo art style came to dominate most of the painting of the region, with the Colla and popular schools essentially melding together and the other two schools reduced in importance. Furthermore, in architecture as well, the baroque style largely ended by midcentury, and was replaced, as in Spain, by a neoclassical movement. Construction of these new-style churches predominated in Cochabamba and in Chuquisaca, which again became major centers of activity in the last days of the Audiencia, while the cathedrals of La Paz and Potosí also were built in this style.

Although art and architecture were somewhat tamed by the neoclassical movement, apparently sculpture in wood and stone and worked silver retained the extraordinary vigor of the so-called mestizo-baroque style until the end of the colonial period, with the Indian and mestizo artisans becoming dominant in these skills by the eighteenth century. In this mestizo style, the themes of the baroque remained – mythic sirens, grotesque masks, and grotesques – along with pre-Renaissance Christian traditions. But now, typical American flora and fauna as well as pre-Columbian motifs and figures were added.

Whereas the arts flourished in Upper Peru from the beginning and achieved extraordinary quality in all areas, the field of letters was very underdeveloped even by Latin American standards. There was some minor church music, most of which has not survived. There was some theater, including a vigorous religious and historical theater written in Quechua and Aymara by Spanish clerics desiring to spread the faith among the Indians. But there was little serious poetry and no major theatrical work of distinction that has survived. Even in historical and philosophical works, Upper Peru was a relatively backward area even in relation to Cuzco, let alone to the rest of America, until well into the eighteenth century. And in science the only major work of distinction remains the isolated classic by the parish priest Alonso Barba, the "Art of Metals," written in 1640, the most important metallurgical study composed in America in the seventeenth century.

But this relative backwardness of letters changed somewhat in the eighteenth century as the region seemed to partake more of the mainstream of ideas and developments experienced in the rest of the American colonies of Spain. Several major historians now appear, the most prominent of them being Bartolomé Orsúa y Vela, whose history of Potosí in 1724 was a major study, and Pedro Cañete, whose work on Potosí in the second half of the century was extremely important. There also appeared a group of famous statesmen who provided significant studies of the functioning of colonial society, with Cañete being the most prominent, along with enlightenment writers such as the intendants Francisco Viedma and Juan del Pino Manrique and the protector of the Indians, Victorian de Villava. Finally, the German-born scientist Tadeo Haenke spent most of his adult life in the region, recording its flora and fauna late in the century.

The university life at Chuquisaca, especially after the foundation of the Academia Carolina also seems to have been quite vigorous by the eighteenth century. Early leaders, memorialists, and pamphleteers of the nineteenth-century independence movement included the extraordinary Bernardo Monteagudo, who participated in virtually every major republican event in the Wars of Independence in the region and was at various times a close adviser or lieutenant of Moreno, O'Higgins, San Martin, and Bolivar. One of the founding fathers of Argentina, Mariano Moreno, and Jaime Zudánez received their education there. But, on the whole, literary and political output in the late colonial period in Charcas was quite limited. Neither the academy nor private individuals appear to have created a significant body of literature in any of the humanistic or scientific disciplines. Given the relative wealth of Upper Peru and the long tradition and regional importance of its university center at Chuquisaca, this lack of a more substantial output is difficult to explain. Factors that clearly must have influenced this output were the very low rate of literacy, and the very limited number of Spanish speakers within the entire population, which in turn delayed the introduction of a printing press until late in the eighteenth century. Clearly, Spanish remained a distinctly minority language throughout the colonial period and well into the next two centuries. But in the only form in which language was unimportant, the arts, the Upper Peruvians flourished with an extraordinary creativity and output, marking the colonial period of Upper Peru as one of the great artistic eras in world history. The fact that this art was created by many Indians and mestizos along with Europeans also suggests that it was the only form of creative intellectual and cultural expression fully open to all persons within the colonial society, and therefore the form in which the greatest possible creativity was expressed without fear of racial oppression or class control.

Despite the important growth of the colonial economy in the period after 1750, which permitted a continuation of a very active period of new church and public construction throughout the highland cities, the Upper Peruvian economy was to show itself to be still very much affected by the long seventeenth-century crisis. It was to prove, in fact, extremely vulnerable to short-term changes in international market conditions, which in turn showed that the mining economy had relatively little reserve capacity to weather temporary trade crises or a weakening of governmental support.

This vulnerability became evident in the first decades of the new century. By the late 1790s, the mercury supplies for Potosí were no longer coming from the defunct Huancavelica mines but were being shipped directly from the royal Almaden mines in Spain.

The beginnings of the great international conflict known as the Napoleonic wars would soon lead to direct Spanish involvement, and a bitter dispute with England in 1796 led to open warfare between the two states and the effective disruption of Spain's sea routes to America. For Upper Peru, this meant the halt of mercury deliveries and thus an immediate drop in local smelting. More important, the sudden collapse of the international trade routes created a temporary but quite severe depression in commercial markets in general with a consequent credit squeeze in the colonies. This in turn suddenly left the miners with little capital to maintain their costly enterprises, and, as a result, a rapid decline in production set in.

By the first years of the new century, there was a general crisis in the mining sector, with production plummeting. Then, with its export sector severely reduced, Upper Peru was struck by a major series of harvest failures and epidemics between 1803 and 1805, which had a profound impact on both rural populations and regional markets. Thus, by the time of the French invasion of Spain in 1808, the Upper Peruvian economy was in a general state of depression, and the population was suffering from a temporary but severe loss of life. These conditions created an extremely tense atmosphere both in the rural areas and even more in the reduced urban centers. .

Chapter 4

Revolution and the Creation of a Nation-State, 1809–1841

The nineteenth century in Upper Peru began with a severe long-term depression that had a profound effect on its literate urban populations and its mining export economy. This decline and the serious agricultural crises that erupted in the countryside formed a crucial background to the region's response to the collapse of the imperial government in Madrid. In late 1806 and all of 1807, Napoleon's armies slowly invaded Spain and eventually forced the abdication of the Bourbon monarchy. In May 1808, the Madrid populace rose up in revolt against the new French-controlled Spanish government, and the rebels eventually established a formal resistance structure that proclaimed itself to be the legitimate government of the Bourbons. Known as the Junta Central, and controlling part of southern Spain, the rebel regime claimed legitimacy, despite the abdication of Ferdinand VII, and demanded loyalty from the colonial viceroyalties. Such a situation of divided government had occurred once before in imperial history at the very beginning of the eighteenth century, when the Bourbons and Hapsburgs had contended for control over Spain and fought a long and bitter conflict for the monarchy on Spanish soil. But at that time the colonies were passive and allowed all basic decisions about the fate of Spain and the empire to be made in Europe.

In 1808, however, the world was a different place. The two independence movements of former colonies, Haiti and the United States, had a profound impact on changing the dependent concepts of colonial American thinking. Moreover, the United States and England, both major powers, now provided financial support for potentially rebellious movements, as well as places of refuge. But, most important of all, Europe itself no longer possessed the same stable monarchic structure as had existed during the early eighteenth-century War of Spanish Succession. In 1789, the French Revolution had unleashed a new ideology and movement so unsettling that it affected every monarchy on the continent and suddenly made republican governments a viable alternative.

The American colonies of Spain were not unaware of all of these developments, as the many small plots and revolts throughout the hemisphere showed. The ideology of the so-called Atlantic Revolutions spread throughout the Americas in the 1790s and the first decade of the new century. But the stability of the Spanish-American empire was such that the royal bureaucracy had little difficulty in suppressing these movements. In this activity, the bureaucracy was supported by the white and mestizo classes because of their fears of potentially destructive social revolutions that might occur should the Indians be allowed entrance into the political debates of the whites. In this respect, the Haitian experience was a warning not only to the slave societies of America but equally to those who lived off the labor of an exploited Indian peasant mass.

But the sudden disruption of both the metropolitan government and the rise of conflicting central authorities created enormous problems for the local elites. Each local American colonial government had to make fundamental decisions as to who could best guarantee their own legitimacy and stability. There was the new monarchy of Joseph Napoleon in Madrid, the Spanish Junta government that ruled in the name of the abdicated Ferdinand VII; and Ferdinand's sister Carlota, who arrived in Brazil in 1808 as the wife of the Portuguese monarch and who attempted as well to claim the allegiance of the American empire. Finally, with Spain in disarray and under French control, and with its European allies quickly succumbing to the armies of Napoleon, the English turned their energies toward their traditional interest in imperial expansion beyond Europe. They began providing strong support for potential revolutionaries and even to make plans for the formal invasion of Spanish America.

The arrival of the disturbing news from Spain slowly spread an ambience of crisis and indecision throughout the Americas in the months of July, August, and September 1808. In each case local royal officials were forced to make a series of unpalatable decisions. They also had to decide who should take part in the decision-making process. In most cases audiencias, governors, or bishops made the decision for the status quo, which they defined as a wait-and-see attitude, with preference being given for the Junta government that was slowly retreating toward the peninsula of Cadiz. A few called open meetings of the citizenry (*cabildos abiertos*) to sound out local elite opinion as to which course of action should be taken. And a few decided to support actively either the French or Carlota's pretensions. But these temporizing measures pleased few and in no area were all the Creole and Spanish-born elites fully content with any particular solution. This climate was conducive to local power struggles, conflicts between individual governors and their audiencias or local bishops, and between these royal officials and the local municipal councils.

This background explains many of the events that took place in Upper Peru in 1808 and 1809. The region became the first area in Spanish America to be severely disturbed by all the conflicts developing in the imperial and international scene, and the first center of an independence movement. Partly because of its isolation from the sea, partly because it still formed an independent zone of economic power between two conflictive viceroyalties – those of Lima and Buenos Aires – and partly because of its traditional autonomy, the conflict between differing groups was allowed to develop for quite some time before being suppressed.

The first conflicts began with the arrival of the news of the Spanish crisis, which reached Upper Peru in September 1808. Immediately the archbishop and the president of the Audiencia demanded affiliation with the Junta Central, while the judges of the Audiencia refused to recognize the Junta's authority. Tensions grew quickly, and in late May the president of the Audiencia was seized by the independent judges, who feared their own imprisonment. Although the Potosí intendent Francisco Paula Sanz opposed the movement, he offered no immediate resistance, so the semirebel judges proceeded to send emissaries seeking the support of the other cities.

Despite the tensions and some limited mob action, the whole affair up to this time was confined to the bureaucracy and was almost exclusively a Spanish *peninsulares* affair. This was not the case with the popular revolt that now occurred in the city of La Paz. On the sixteenth of July, also in 1809, popular unrest among the city's vecinos, many of whom included convinced revolutionaries, led to demands that an open town meeting be called to make some basic decisions about which regime to support. The fact that the local elite was demanding the right to make its own decisions on these events independent of what the central Audiencia bureaucracy had decided in Chuquisaca well reflected the growing power of La Paz itself. Now the largest city in Upper Peru, it was beginning to feel resentment toward southern domination, and thus the conflicts in both Spain and Chuquisaca provided an excellent opportunity for the local elite to express its own version of independence.

Under the leadership of a vecino by the name of Pedro Domingo Murillo, the La Paz creole elite seized the local governor and the Bishop of La Paz and declared themselves a *Junta Tuitiva*. They immediately voiced their opposition to the Junta regime of Spain and proclaimed an independent American government in the name of Ferdinand VII – a classic ploy used by all the later rebellious leaders in America to legitimate their independence movements.

This was the first declaration of independence by an American colony of Spain. It was to initiate the long period of American Wars of Independence, which would last from 1809 to 1825. But it proved only a short-lived revolt. The "shout" (*grito*) of independence by the creole rebel leaders of La Paz found no immediate echo among the Indians, nor positive response from the other urban creole elites. On news of the revolt, the Viceroy of Lima ordered immediate reprisals and sent President Goyeneche of the Audiencia of Cuzco to La Paz with five thousand troops to put down the movement. Murillo and his supporters, for their part, were able to organize a local army of some one thousand poorly armed men. But, at this point, Murillo and some of his coconspirators grew concerned with the direction that the new Junta government was taking and attempted to negotiate with Goyeneche. The result was that Murillo and most of the more radical elements of the regime were seized by the royal troops while the rebellion continued. On the arrival of the Cuzco troops, the rebel army fled to the Yungas, where, in November 1809, a major battle was fought at Irupana. The rebel army was defeated, and there followed the capture of all the former leaders, including Murillo. These men were tried immediately, and in January 1810 Murillo and eight of his fellow conspirators were executed, while over one hundred persons were exiled.

At the same time, the Viceroy in Buenos Aires appointed a new president of Upper Peru, Marshal Nieto, who also arrived with troops from Buenos Aires at about the time the Cuzco army arrived in the north, and in early December he took Chuquisaca. Nieto immediately arrested the rebel audiencia judges. By this action and by the execution of the rebels of La Paz, the independence movement of Upper Peru was formally brought to an end, and the first attempt at American independence crushed.

All opposition did not end in Charcas, nor did this repression destroy Creole enthusiasm for independence. While the generation of 1809 urban leadership was effectively destroyed, a host of guerrilla leaders now emerged and established themselves in six important rural areas in little rebel-controlled *republiquetas*. While the cities remained in royalist hands, the guerrillas controlled an important part of the countryside and were effective allies in the various republican invasions, which would come from the outside. From 1809 until 1816, these impromptu forces would obtain their support from all social classes in Bolivia, including the Indian peasant masses.

Despite the rise of a rural guerrilla movement, and the spread of the rebellion into the lower classes, however, the initiative for independence had passed out of the hands of the Upper Peruvians. Having been the first region formally to declare for independence, Upper Peru would paradoxically become the last region in South America to gain it. Moreover, it now became the battleground for more powerful forces to the north and the south, and lost its initiative in all the subsequent events to leaders and armies outside its borders.

Thus, the history of Upper Peruvian independence is now determined by events occurring thousands of miles from the altiplano cities. The most important of these developments was the successful establishment of an independent government in the viceregal capital of Buenos Aires. After having crushed a British army of invasion in the Rio de la Plata region in 1806, the Creole leadership of Buenos Aires soon found itself contesting the power of its viceroy, and finally carried out a full-scale rebellion in May 1810. The euphoric Buenos Aires regime soon felt the need to spread its power throughout the old territory of the viceroyalty and viewed Upper Peru as a prime area for liberation. For their part, the liberals and guerrillas of Upper Peru viewed the developments in Buenos Aires as an extraordinary opportunity for reestablishing an independent local regime.

The initial response of the royalists led by Paula Sanz in Potosí and Nieto as president of the Audiencia was to break formal ties with the old viceroyalty and return Upper Peru to the jurisdiction of the Lima Viceroyalty. But this action could not prevent the spread of revolution. By September 1810, Cochabamba rose in support of the Buenos Aires regime, and in the next month an Argentine army had reached the region under the command of Castelli. Receiving tremendous popular support, the Argentine army was easily able to seize city after city, getting an enthusiastic welcome everywhere. By November Potosí was taken, and Castelli seized Paula Sanz and Nieto and executed them both. In the meantime, the Cuzco President Goyeneche was forced to retreat, and soon Oruro and Santa Cruz rebelled against his armies and joined forces with Castelli, with the former defeating a royalist army. By April 1811, Castelli and his Argentine army had been welcomed in Oruro and La Paz, and the entire Upper Peruvian region was once again a free and independent zone.

But Castelli proved both an inept administrator and a poor general, and the popular support for his regime began to disappear. It became evident that the Argentines were not interested in allowing an independent republic to be established, nor in promoting Upper Peruvian interests at the expense of Rio de la Plata needs. Thus, a defeat of Castelli's armies at Guaqui on Lake Titicaca in June 1811 turned into a full-scale rout that led to considerable urban bloodshed and civilian attacks by Upper Peruvians against the rampaging and retreating Argentine forces.

The defeat of the Argentines and the retaking of all of Upper Peru by the Cuzco royalists under Goyeneche did not end the rebellion within Upper Peru itself. In November, Cochabamba again rebelled against the Crown and attempted to invade the altiplano. It took until May 1812 for Goyeneche to crush the rebellion, this time with considerable slaughter on both sides. Moreover, the desperate royalists were now turning to Indian support, and more and more caciques were enlisted on both sides to provide Indian troops for the fighting. In turn, the Indians began to obtain arms from all sides, with the result that the level of violence and social conflict escalated considerably by late 1811 and early 1812. Once reaching this state of mobilization, the forces unleashed by the independence movement proved difficult to contain, so the level of physical destruction and social dislocation became quite massive.

With Upper Peru now in the control of the royalists, Goyeneche decided to push the struggle into northern Argentina and attempt to retake the Rio de la Plata region. But in February 1813 at the Battle of Salta, Manuel Belgrano led a successful northern Argentine army against the royalists. Thus began the invasion of Upper Peru by a second Argentine army, which had as little success as the earlier adventure. Although Belgrano temporarily seized Potosí in the middle of the year, by the last months of 1813 royalist forces under the leadership of Joaquin de la Pezuela had defeated the Argentines and retaken all of Upper Peru.

With the defeat of this second army and the subsequent invasion of northern Argentina by Pezuela, the leaders of the Rio de la Plata were convinced that Upper Peru could not be their main objective and eventually supported San Martin's decision to concentrate on a flanking attack on Chile as the best means to move against the center of royalist power at Lima. But this decision did not mean that Upper Peru would remain a quiet zone; for there now occurred within Upper Peru a series of small revolts and Indian uprisings, including an antiroyalist Indian revolt in mid-1814, which saw the conquest and sacking of La Paz by Indians from the Cuzco region. Meanwhile, the potential threat of a royalist Upper Peru was of concern to the Argentine republicans, so a small third Argentine army was organized and sent to Upper Peru in January 1815.

Again, the invading Argentines found support from interior republicans. Upper Peruvian rebels seized Potosí and Chuquisaca from the royalists in April, and by May the Argentines once again were in control of these towns. But the Argentines could not take Oruro or Cochabamba and so in November 1815 suffered their worst defeat of the war, with their forces being totally destroyed. In the new year, the initiative shifted to the royalists, and Pezuela now undertook a massive attack on all the rebel forces in Upper Peru. The end was a resounding victory for the royalists. Whereas it is estimated that some 102 patriot caudillos operated in the rural areas from 1810 to 1816, after this date only some nine were left. Such famous rebel leaders as Manuel Padilla and Ignacio Warnes were executed, and even the intrepid Miguel Lanza was temporarily taken prisoner. Others such as Juana Azurduy de Padilla and Juan Antonio Alvarez de Arenales were forced into hiding. Of the formerly important zones under rebel control, only the republiqueta in Ayopaya (on the Cochabamba-Oruro-La Paz Cordillera frontier) survived, and it was totally isolated and neutralized.

Thus, by 1816, both all external and internal efforts to achieve independence had come to a disastrous end. Henceforth, Upper Peru would be isolated from the main events of the great struggles for continental liberation, while its final achievement of independence would come from the very elite that had supported the royalist activities throughout the period. By 1816, many of the cities of Upper Peru had been sacked several times, and each retreating Argentine army had emptied the Royal Mint at Potosí. What was not destroyed in urban conflicts was destroyed in the rural rebellions. Haciendas were razed, isolated mines were destroyed, and the economy of the region was left in ruins. Moreover, the arming of Indian forces by both sides temporarily destroyed the Creole control of the countryside and created violent social tensions and urban fears, which led to further economic uncertainty and disorder.

Although 1816 marked the nadir in the wars of independence everywhere in South America, change was occurring. In that year, Bolivar successfully reestablished his revolutionary movement in Venezuela, while the Argentines felt strong enough to proclaim their total independence from Spain. With a few representatives from Upper Peru, the republican forces gathered in Tucumán and in July of that year declared the United Provinces of the Rio de la Plata as an independent nation. By 1817, the counteroffensive against royalist power had begun, and San Martin crossed the Andes into Chile and liberated the colony in the battle of Maipú in April 1818.

In early 1817, the Argentines even sent a quick expeditionary force to Upper Peru, its fourth and last such invasion, but this army remained in the southern cities and had little influence over most of the region. Its only notable success was the capture of a young royalist officer, a native of La Paz, by the name of Andrés Santa Cruz, who was sent back to Argentina. Although Santa Cruz soon escaped, and rejoined the royalist armies at Lima, his experiences among the Argentines and his frustrations with the vacillating policies of the Crown led him to join forces with the rebels. In January 1821, he offered his services to General San Martin and his Chilean-Argentine army of invasion. After seeing considerable service in Peruvian battles, San Martin sent Santa Cruz with an expeditionary force to assist the Colombian troops under Sucre who were then in heated battle against the royalists in the Audiencia of Quito area. The result was that Santa Cruz and his troops now became fully allied with Sucre and broke their allegiance to San Martin.

All of this rebel activity in Peru and Ecuador was in preparation for a new invasion of Upper Peru by republican forces. Both the forces of San Martin and Bolivar no longer viewed the Charcas region as the main avenue to the taking of Lima, nor after so many years of warfare was it seen as a major financial center whose capture could lead to extraordinary wealth for the rebel cause. In 1820, San Martin had landed troops in southern Peru, and by 1823 Sucre in alliance with Santa Cruz had arrived in the northern Peruvian region. At this point, Santa Cruz was able to convince the rebel leaders that a major army of conquest could take Upper Peru. After a quick march from the coast, Santa Cruz led a successful invasion and captured his native city of La Paz in August. The royalist forces sent to oppose him were defeated in the battle of Zepita, and he was able to take Oruro as well. Meanwhile, the rebels under General Lanza seized Cochabamba. It looked as if liberation from royal control was finally at hand. But developments in Lower Peru left Santa Cruz's lines of communication exposed, and the existence of powerful royalist armies in central Charcas posed too great a threat. Thus, within a few short months of arriving, Santa Cruz was forced to evacuate La Paz, as the royalist armies successfully reestablished control over the entire region.

The retreat of the republicans and the defeat of Lanza left the royalists in undisputed control of Upper Peru until January 1825. But Upper Peru as a royalist stronghold would prove to be a rather strange place indeed. For the commanding general of the royalist forces in the region, Pedro Olañeta, a native of Charcas, was an archreactionary who was deeply disturbed by the 1820 liberal revolution in Spain. Although fully supported by the Lima Viceroyalty, Olañeta and his aide and nephew, Dr. Casimiro Olañeta, were convinced that the Spanish liberals threatened royal authority. Thus, in January 1824, the Charcas general declared his unwillingness to send troops or supplies to aid his fellow officers in their desperate battles against the invading armies of Bolivar. For some twelve months the Lima regime cajoled, pleaded, and finally sent in regular forces to threaten Olañeta. But he refused to concede anything, while also refusing – despite the constant communications of his nephew with the various rebel armies – to join forces with the republicans.

Thus, from January 1824, to January 1825, Upper Peru, although officially royalist, did not participate in any of the events affecting royalist power in the region and in fact succeeded in defeating several forces sent by the royalists to force their cohesion. At the same time, Olañeta refused to become a rebel. The end result was the total isolation of the regime and the weakening of the defense of Lower Peru. In December 1824, the final fate of the region was sealed when the Spanish armies were destroyed at the battle of Ayacucho by Sucre. Although Olañeta and his forces were included in the capitulation agreement after the battle, the latter refused to relinquish command or to endorse Bolivar. The result of this confusing state of affairs was that Sucre was finally forced to lead an army into Upper Peru to encourage the Olañeta troops to desert. In January 1825, the old general was killed in a battle with his own mutinous troops. With this death, the wars of independence both for Spanish South America and for Upper Peru itself finally drew to a close after almost sixteen years of bitter civil war, of serious loss of life, and of severe economic and social dislocation.

The liberation of Upper Peru in December and January of 1825 did not immediately resolve the question of the ultimate fate of the region. Just as the initiative for the war against the royalist forces had passed out of the hands of the local patriots after 1816, so, too, did control over their future destiny. It was in fact Bolivar and Sucre who would determine the destiny of the provinces of Upper Peru, since it was they who controlled both the army of liberation and the Peruvian Congress. Initially, the idea that Upper Peru should be an independent republic was anathema to Bolivar and his plans for a continent-wide republic. Such an act could only lead to the weakening of South America in the world order. But these initial ideas of unity were soon challenged by the reality of a growing conflict between his Gran Colombian state and the Peruvian regime that he had established. By 1825, Bolivar was already temporizing and was beginning to fear the growth of too powerful a Peruvian republic, which in turn could threaten the existence and importance of his own base in Gran Colombia. Finally, the unqualifiedly hostile reception of Argentina to all his plans made the idea of a buffer state between Peru and Argentina a reasonable proposition.

Bolivar in the end allowed Sucre to decide the situation for himself. Transferring the authority to Sucre was in turn a positive step toward Upper Peruvian autonomy. Sucre himself was not as concerned as Bolivar was with continental visions and at the same time was more influenced by local Upper Peruvian intellectuals, who were very much imbued with the idea of creating an autonomous state. The leader among these independent-minded figures was Olañeta's nephew, Casimiro Olañeta. Both he, and all the republican leaders who survived, had gone through a common experience during the war, which made them hostile to an amalgamation with Argentina. Both sides were disgusted with the conduct of the four Argentine expeditionary armies that had invaded Upper Peru. Although the local republiqueta leaders had all loyally supported Buenos Aires, the Argentines had clearly shown their indifference to the needs of the local population and their willingness to sacrifice the entire region to their own exigencies. At the same time, the royalists had now had almost fifteen years of government under the Lima Viceroyalty and were no longer tied to the Buenos Aires networks as they had been prior to 1810.

In contrast, there was some sympathy expressed toward an amalgamation with Peru. The southern highlands of Peru formed a natural region with the altiplano south of Lake Titicaca, sharing both a common Quechua and Aymara background, as well as a similar ecology and an almost identical economic base. Equally, the commercial ties for all the Upper Peruvian cities, although greatly weakened by the constant shift of viceregal centers, were still essentially with Lima, which was seen as the most important zonal city binding together all of the regional networks.

The Peruvians, however, were in an uneasy relationship with Bolivar and his Colombian armies at this time, while the Lima elite was not prepared to push coherently for the incorporation of Upper Peru into its own national borders. They were more concerned with defining the jurisdictions of Puno and the Atacama coastal borders, especially the region of Tarapaca, than with binding the cities of the old Audiencia of Charcas into a unified state. The Peruvians also saw Upper Peru as a crucial buffer against the aggressiveness of the Rio de la Plata regimes and were thus on the whole relatively indifferent to the fate of Upper Peru so long as it did not become part of Argentina.

In this context of conflicting needs and demands by the external power centers, the local elite took the initiative in their own hands and pushed Sucre into formally declaring for an independent republic. With Lima uninterested if not hostile, and with their own long history of autonomous regional government, the Upper Peruvians were more than willing to assume responsibility for their own fate and make – de jure – what in fact had existed for some time, an independent regional government.

On February 9, 1825, when Sucre and his army arrived in La Paz (accompanied by Dr. Casimiro Olañeta as Sucre's adviser), he decreed the calling together of a constituent assembly of all the provinces of Upper Peru, which were to send delegates in April of that year to determine the future of the region. This decree was the final decision made by the external powers to allow the Upper Peruvians to create their own government. While Bolivar was initially furious with Sucre's decree, he did not disallow it and proceeded to accept Sucre's initiative. After some delays, forty-eight delegates finally gathered together in Chuquisaca in July 1825 to decide the question, and with an overwhelming majority in its favor, the Assembly declared for formal independence. On August 6, 1825, a declaration of independence was issued, and the new state, in recognition of the ultimate necessity to obtain the leader's final approval, was named after Bolivar himself.

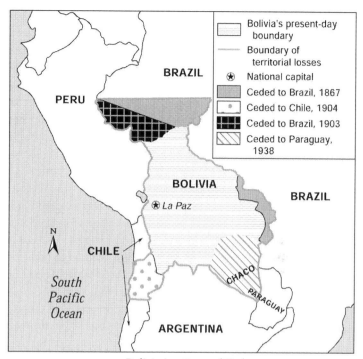

Legend:

- ☐ Bolivia's present-day boundary
- ⋯ Boundary of territorial losses
- ✪ National capital
- ▦ Ceded to Brazil, 1867
- ▫ Ceded to Chile, 1904
- ▰ Ceded to Brazil, 1903
- ▨ Ceded to Paraguay, 1938

4-1 Bolivia in 1825 and Today

It was just at this time that Bolivar, fulfilling an old pledge, was entering Upper Peru on a triumphal tour. The Chuquisaca Congress sent a delegation to him in La Paz requesting support for their actions and for the controversial decisions taken by Antonio Sucre. At first claiming that the Peruvian Congress still had to determine the ultimate fate of the region, Bolivar finally relented after his triumphal tour of the Upper Peruvian cities. In the end, he ignored his own previous decrees and accepted the independence of the new republic. He even became its temporary president for a few months.

By the last months of 1825 an independent republic of Bolivia was created out of the old Audiencia of Charcas (see Map 4-1). To the rest of the world, Bolivia was still a mythical region of Indian peasants and wealthy mines that represented a treasure house of riches. But unfortunately the truth was otherwise. On entering its republican life, Bolivia was a war-weary and economically depressed region that was to experience an economic stagnation that lasted for close to half a century. From approximately 1803 to the late 1840s the Bolivian economy experienced a progressive decapitalization of its mining industry, a crisis in its international economy, and the greatest decline in its urban population since the last great depression of the seventeenth century. If anything, the early nineteenth-century depression was to be far worse than the previous great depression, leaving the Bolivian economy by the 1840s more rural-dominated and more subsistence-oriented than at any time in its past.

The very declaration of an independence had a negative influence on the national economy and was to deepen and prolong the crisis begun in the last years of the colonial era. Whereas recent historians have tended to downplay the impact of political independence on Latin American society and politics, in contradistinction to nineteenth-century liberal historians who saw it as a great turning point in national history, a reading of the economic crisis again shows just how important the events of 1825 proved to be. Twentieth-century historians are right to point out the persistence of traditional elites under republican disguises and to stress the continuity of social and political institutions until well into the nineteenth century, urging the 1880s as a period of fundamental change from the colonial structures. But it is also important to realize that the destruction of the colonial customs union that was the Spanish-American empire also had a profound impact on the national and international economy of the new republics, Bolivia included.

The creation of all the new republics in South America led to a new era of mercantilism, as most of the new states rushed to set up tariff barriers against each other, if not always against the dominant English traders. For Bolivia, this meant that its traditional markets in northern Argentina were reduced, and in turn led to a long-term economic decline of the northeastern Argentine provinces. The end of intimate ties to Lima created a serious credit crisis, which the few arriving foreign capitalists could not easily alleviate. Transportation costs, which had always been a serious constraint on Bolivia's international trade, now became even more prohibitive as Peru,

Chile, and Argentina charged Bolivia for the use of their ports. The creation of a Bolivian port at Cobija in the Atacama desert was little compensation for these new trade barriers, since even at its height only a third of Bolivia's foreign trade passed through this harbor and the overland transportation facilities were all controlled by foreigners.

Thus, independence can be said to have seriously restricted most of Upper Peru's traditional economic ties and further pushed the economy toward subsistence. As its own revenues from international trade declined, the Bolivian governments in the early nineteenth century were forced to rely increasingly on regressive tribute taxes, the manipulation of currency, and the forced monopolization of minting and silver exports. While an expanding foreign trade was the common source for the increasing revenues of the more advanced states of the region, Bolivian taxation became increasingly regressive and a constraint on trade and production.

The destruction of mines and smelters in the independence wars, the government monopolization of silver exports, the increase in transportation costs as a result of new tariff barriers, and the end of royal credit and mercury sales subsidization by the imperial government all led to a severe crisis in the mining industry. Whereas in 1803 there were forty *ingenios* (or silver refining mills) and several hundred mines in operation in Potosí, by 1825 there were only fifteen ingenios and fifty or so mines still functioning. Silver production, which in the last decade of the eighteenth century was averaging 385,000 marks per annum, had dropped to 300,000 marks by the first decade of the nineteenth century, and declined further to an average of 200,000 marks in the 1810s, and finally to an all-time low of some 150,000 marks per annum in the 1820s. While production rose slightly in the 1830s, it was not until the 1850s that production again reached the two-hundred-thousand level.

There also was a decline in producing units. In an official census finally carried out in 1846, it was estimated that even at this late date there were some ten thousand abandoned mines in the republic. Nor were these mines abandoned for lack of silver ore. Rather, the wars, the destruction of capital and equipment, and the migration of technicians led to a simple process of abandonment. These still quite rich mines could be opened only with tremendous inputs of capital, and required the use of steam engines to remove the water from the flooded mines, a universal problem.

With its export sector in a long-term depression, Bolivia's urban Spanish-speaking populations declined as well. Potosí and Oruro, the two major mine centers, were so seriously affected that their combined urban population was estimated in 1827 by the British investigator J. B. Pentland to have fallen to below fifteen thousand persons (nine thousand for Potosí and forty-six hundred for Oruro). Other mining-dependent cities were little better off, with Chuquisaca falling to twelve thousand persons.

But Bolivia also was inhabited by an estimated eight hundred thousand Indian peasants in 1827. And just as the collapse of the export sector in the seventeenth-century crisis had been a positive aid to the more local regional agricultural markets and free Indian communities, the same would occur again in the early nineteenth-century crisis. Thus, in contrast to the decline of the mining centers and their satellite towns, the two key marketing towns of Cochabamba and La Paz continued to remain stable and/or grew in numbers. In 1827, the city of La Paz was unquestionably the most populous in the new nation and held some forty thousand persons, while Cochabamba was a close second with thirty thousand. Both were primarily farm center communities and both serviced hinterlands with large Indian peasant populations.

The fact that these cities grew, while the southern mine centers declined, demonstrates well the paradoxical problem of Bolivian growth prior to the twentieth century. The decline of the export sector reduced the level of Spanish exploitation and raised the income of the Indian peasants. The Indians were able to increase their internal trade because of their higher income and the cities that serviced them prospered. Just how important the Indian populations had become was revealed in the pattern of government revenues, which became apparent in the new republic. Whereas the first republican assembly was forced to adopt Bolivar's Peruvian decrees outlawing the tribute tax collected by the royal government from all Indian males aged eighteen to fifty, the Bolivian government soon found that it could no longer afford the luxury of doing without it, and within one year it had reimposed the colonial tribute on all its Indians. This tribute tax, again collected at the same rate as in the colonial period, now accounted for some 60 percent of government income, whereas in the late eighteenth century it accounted for less than 25 percent of Crown revenues. With a stagnant international trade, declining silver production, and a bureaucracy incapable of collecting land or business taxes from the whites and cholos, the government came to depend on the Indian head tax as its most lucrative source of income and was to maintain that tax until the end of the century.

While such a tax was an obvious burden on the Indian population, it nevertheless committed the Bolivian government to protecting the free communities from white and cholo threats. The Bolivian congresses gave ongoing legitimacy to the community governments and their land titles, in contrast to official Bolivarian legislation that had challenged their very right to existence. In fact, it was not until the 1860s, when the importance of the tribute tax seriously declined in the totality of government revenues, that the central government finally adopted the contemporary liberal ideology on land tenure and began to challenge the legality of the corporate landholding structure of the communities.

Just how disastrous an economic situation in Bolivia existed in the early republican years is revealed by the failure of the first reformist government to revive successfully a viable national and international economy. The regime of Antonio Joséde Sucre, established in early 1825 and lasting until April 1828, was in fact a model of its kind in Latin America and compared quite favorably with the reformist and liberal regimes of Rivadavia in Buenos Aires and Santander in Colombia, from which it copied many of its own reforms. Sucre was a classic eighteenth-century liberal with excellent ideas concerning the creation of a viable economic and social order. He also was an ardent republican and attempted to provide the institutions for a representative and relatively open regime. He even tried to undertake a serious reform in the relationships between the Indian masses and the Spanish-speaking state, in favor of the former.

Faced with the need to redevelop the war torn economy of Upper Peru, Sucre began a thoroughgoing reorganization of the mining industry. It was decided in August 1825 to nationalize all the abandoned mines. Sucre then turned to foreign capitalists to provide the desperately needed capital and invited both Argentine and, more important, British entrepreneurs to open the mines. This led in 1824 and 1825 to feverish activity, with several British engineers and representatives traveling to Bolivia to survey the mines. A speculative boom also developed on the London capital market with the creation of some twenty-six mining "Associations" or companies established to develop South American mines. The most important of these new companies as far as Bolivia was concerned was the "Potosí, La Paz, and Peruvian Mining Association," which was supposedly capitalized at £1 million but actually raised only 5 percent of that amount. The collapse of the London market in December 1825 led to a collapse of almost all of these speculative ventures, so that very little machinery, capital, or engineering staff ever reached Bolivia from England. What few miners did get through, from either Argentina or London, soon found that the costs of reopening the mines were prohibitive without the introduction of steam-driven pumping machinery and a substantial lowering of costs. Of these cost items, initially the most difficult to overcome was that of labor. In July 1825, Bolivar had abolished the mita in all of the Peruvian area, and the new republican government found itself incapable of reestablishing the institution. Thus, Potosí had to enter the free market for all its labor needs and was forced to offer high wages to attract peasants from agriculture. Such new costs were just too heavy a burden for the fragile industry to bear at this time.

While Sucre successfully resurrected both the *Casa de Moneda* (the Royal Mint) and the *Banco de San Carlos* (Minerals Purchasing Bank) on a sound footing and proceeded to get coin mintage up to reasonable levels, he could do little to reopen the abandoned mines and so ultimately was left with only local Bolivian miners using simple extractive methods from still accessible veins as the providers of the silver ores produced for the Bank and Mint. The introduction of usable steam engines to drain the flooded mines – the crucial technological innovation needed by the silver industry – was still decades away, which meant that Sucre was unable to increase actual production.

Even more revolutionary than his mining efforts were Sucre's attempts to introduce a progressive tax system to bolster the new republican regime. He pushed through the successful abolition of the mita and temporarily rescinded the tribute tax. The hated royal monopolies were also attacked, and the tobacco industry freed from all restrictions. The famous sales tax (or *alcabala*) was abolished by Sucre, and special taxes such as those on coca production were reduced. All these disparate taxes, which either were regressive personal taxes against the poorest element in the society or were restrictive on trade and production, were now replaced by a single direct tax on urban and rural property and individual incomes. This *contribución directa* was truly a revolutionary reform and promised to modernize the tax structure of the state by establishing the most progressive tax structure then available.

But within one year of their implementation, the new direct taxes on wealth (as expressed in both land and income) were abandoned. The state bureaucracy was incapable of administering such a tax, which required a careful assessment of all the resources of the citizenry. No cadastral surveys were available, and no censuses, aside from the old Indian tribute lists, existed; nor did the regime have the ability to carry out these vital registrations. With the liberation from the Spanish empire, Bolivia also had lost the best part of its technically trained and well-educated governmental bureaucracy. It was a problem typical of all newly liberated ex-colonial areas: the Bolivians were left with the shell of the state and with few trained individuals capable of managing the needs of the government. Moreover, with revenue declining, the new state also found itself incapable of paying salaries that would attract the few able people that remained within Bolivia to its service. Thus, Sucre's ambitious plans for a progressive tax system foundered on the inability of the state to carry them to fruition. Moreover, the continued decline of foreign trade, which remained heavily taxed, deprived the state of a potentially important and expanding source of revenue. By the end of 1826, the administration was forced to abandon the direct tax and return to traditional sales, tribute, and other regressive taxes to support the finances of the state.

The failure of his fiscal reforms to generate capital helped push Sucre toward a confrontation with the church. Anticlerical like most members of his generation, Sucre and Bolivar both sought to destroy the role of the church in the new republic. In this, Sucre was assisted by a rather reactionary hierarchy within Bolivia that had supported the royalist cause to the end. The church thus found itself with a weakened and discredited leadership when Sucre began his assault and so was unable to put up an effective resistance.

In fact, the Sucre attack on the church was one of the most radical in Latin America in the nineteenth century and unqualifiedly his most successful governmental action. He began by assuming control over the collection of the Church tithes, which probably amounted to some two hundred thousand pesos per annum. He then finished the earlier royal reforms of consolidating the credit structure of the church and confiscated all the *capellanías* and pious works, which were either mortgages paying interest or annual payments from private properties granted to the church to subsidize masses and benefices of clergy. He then attacked the monasteries and convents, by ordering the closing of all monasteries that housed fewer than twelve persons and succeeded in reducing the monasteries in Bolivia from forty to twelve in number. Those that remained had their private estates confiscated and administered by the government, which then paid the remaining monastery residents their salaries. By this stroke, some three million pesos in urban and rural property were confiscated. A similar attack was made against the convents, and their holdings also were now taken from them, and their numbers equally reduced. It was estimated that another 3.8 million pesos were thus confiscated from the female religious houses. With all these actions, Sucre probably brought under state control properties worth something on the order of eight to ten million pesos.

The confiscation of church wealth significantly reduced the importance of this institution in republican life. But in the end it did little for the regime financially, for in the depressed urban and rural markets the state could find few buyers for these many properties. The state was forced to rent out most of these lands and houses and collected no more than the church had on most of these properties. Yet, it now had to assume the responsibility for the salaries of the clergy and the maintenance of the remaining monks and nuns, a group probably numbering some five hundred persons. It also had to pay its own administrators, and so the final returns to the state on confiscated church properties were quite small. It was able to use some of these properties to secure internal loans, but, given the state of the national economy, the internal capital market was not large enough or secure enough to provide a major source of income for the state. Most of the income generated from the former church properties went to pay for the establishment of social services and educational establishments in the urban centers of Bolivia. The six major cities (La Paz, Cochabamba, Santa Cruz, Oruro, Potosí, Chuquisaca, and Tarija) all obtained free primary schools and orphanages. But most of these institutions survived for only a short time and had little real impact on the economic or social structure of the society.

Thus, the church reform of Sucre was not the unqualified financial bonanza that it was expected to be. But, in political terms, the Sucre church reforms were a total success. Bolivia took over complete royal patronage powers, absorbed all the lands of the church, reduced the monastic orders to an insignificant grouping, abolished the ties between laity and clergy by eliminating the religious brotherhoods (or *cofradias*), and even went so far as to take the church silver from all the temples. All this was accomplished with no protests from the urban elites or the peasant masses. As a result, the church became a dependent and passive actor in the affairs of the state for the rest of the century. Furthermore, Bolivia was spared the horrors of the religious conflicts that were experienced by many of the republics of America and showed a religious toleration unusual by Latin American standards.

In the late nineteenth-century revival of Roman power throughout the world Bolivia, too, would see the renaissance of an important church. The reappearance of the Jesuits and the coming of the new orders, such as the Silesians, would revive the educational and religious powers of the church. But its economic role was never restored, and the political power of the Bolivian church remained muted and of little interest for either the traditional elite or the revolutionary masses.

Although a popular leader and an able military commander, Sucre finally found himself faced with an ungovernable situation. Revenues of the state were declining or stagnant in his two-and-a-half years of government. The burdens of a Colombian army of occupation of some eight thousand men also weighed heavily both on the treasury and on national political life. The process of fragmentation of the generation of victorious republican generals was having its effect in all the liberated territories, and Bolivia proved no exception. The disillusioned Sucre soon found himself opposing former comrades in arms. An assassination attempt and an aborted coup in Chuquisaca in August 1828 thoroughly destroyed Sucre's interest in remaining head of state. Recovering from his wounds, he resigned the government and went into voluntary exile, returning to his native Caracas.

The end of the Sucre government did not bring an end to the liberal and reformist regimes or usher in an age of anarchy as occurred in some of the other republics when their original leaders were overthrown. In fact, it was men who served with Sucre and were his loyal supporters who would now lead the successive governments for the next generation. The liberal generals who subsequently followed Sucre would face the same problems as the first president, but they also held to the same goal of establishing a liberal and prosperous state.

The most important of these early leaders was Andrés Santa Cruz. A native of La Paz with a Spanish father and Quechua mother, Santa Cruz had entered royal military service at the beginning of the wars of independence, and after a long and successful career he joined the republican side in 1821, first fighting in the armies of San Martin and after 1822 in those of Bolivar. In that year, he was elevated to a generalship by Bolivar and won a major victory in mid-1823 near the Bolivia border at the battle of Zepita, the most famous of his many conflicts.

Closely tied through his military father to the Cuzco upper classes, and long associated with the major Peruvian political and military developments, Santa Cruz was intimately involved in Peruvian affairs and was initially more interested in Peruvian than Bolivian politics. Elected by his native La Paz to the Constituent Assembly in 1825, he declined the honor and remained simply prefect of Chuquisaca during the time of the Constituent Assembly, and later in the Sucre regime he was named head of the La Paz district. But in September 1826, Bolivar recalled him to Lima and made him president of the Peruvian republic, a post he held for only a year. But the overthrow of Sucre, which in part was due to the efforts of his friend the Cuzco General Agustín Gamarra, led to the decision to call Santa Cruz to the presidency of Bolivia. This was a move supported even by Sucre.

From the time the offer was made until his arrival, Bolivia was ruled by a series of temporary rulers, one of whom, General Blanco, unsuccessfully tried to seize the government for himself. But in May 1829, Santa Cruz returned to Bolivia and was sworn into office. The ten-year rule of Santa Cruz was to be a fundamental one in republican history, and the institutions that he founded were to provide the basic framework for the organization of civil life of the republic for the next two centuries. From 1829 to 1839, when he was overthrown by Chilean military intervention, Santa Cruz would prove to be one of the most able administrators Bolivia would ever know.

The primary accomplishment of the Santa Cruz regime was the creation of a stable political, economic, and social order. After almost a quarter of a century of uninterrupted wars and invasions, he was able to guarantee Bolivia something like ten years of peace. Given this stability, he was able to create a more viable state financial structure and to extract the most resources out of the economy. He also could apply those resources to pay for a semiprofessional army and to guarantee an active and responsible civil administration.

In economic terms, Santa Cruz was a determined mercantilist. On establishing his government he proceeded to set up important protective tariffs, even going to the extreme of totally prohibiting the importation of *tocuyo* cloths, the basic textile used in the country. He also decided that he would attempt to force all imports to go through Cobija, the only port left to Bolivia after the various treaties of territorial reorganization with Chile. Imports coming from the more natural ports of Arica and Tacna, now firmly in Peruvian hands, were heavily taxed, and incentives of lower taxes, a free port, and subsidies were provided for trade going to Cobija. It was estimated that at its most active, about one-third of Bolivia's international trade now passed through the city. Cobija went from a population of a few hundred to over a thousand, complete with its docks and warehouses. Also, a wagon road was built from Cobija to Potosí, while other internal routes were opened up to ease the crucial transportation costs.

Santa Cruz turned his attention to the usual areas of concern in mining. Again, typical of his manner of rationalizing the economic structure, he reduced mining taxes considerably. In 1829 the colonial minting tax was eliminated, and all other taxes reduced to a uniform 5 percent tax. The traditional 3 percent gold tax was eliminated altogether in 1830, and there appears to have been some increase in gold production, although silver production remained relatively stable throughout the period.

But despite these economic policies and the security of a well managed and peaceful state, the economy did not respond in any spectacular way. Tocuyo cloth production, despite protection, was estimated to have declined to one-quarter of its colonial levels, and by the end of the period the regime was forced to lift its prohibition on importations to meet the demands of the local market. Moreover, despite all the reduction of taxes, the lack of capital for mining prevented the expansion of production, and, for the decades of the 1820s and 1830s, production remained stagnant for silver, the prime export of the republic.

Despite the considerable improvement in public credit and taxation, actual government revenues stagnated in the first three decades of the republic. The figure of 1.5 million pesos per annum income seemed to have been one that no government could increase until the 1850s. Moreover, that figure hid long-term structural changes in the economy as well. As the Bolivian economist José María Dalence was to point out in 1846, every source of government revenue extracted from the economy declined steadily in the 1820s, 1830s, and 1840s. It was only the increase in rural population and the subsequent increase in the tribute tax that kept total income at a steady level. Thus, the relative importance of the tribute income in total republican revenues had gone from 45 percent in 1832 to 54 percent in 1846, while customs receipts from both the internal and external tariffs, the second most important tax item, accounted for just 22 percent of income.

The long-term stagnation of the mining sector was to prove fatal for sustained growth in the national economy, and greatly limited the availability of any serious government funds for the investment in basic infrastructure or the provisioning of credit for industrial growth. Despite his best efforts, Santa Cruz, like all the early republican presidents, found expenditures constantly outrunning income. While in the early years he did reduce military expenditures somewhat, the army still consumed the single largest share of government income. In a normal year, army costs represented between 40 and 50 percent of total expenditures, with the costs of maintaining the clergy the next most important item in the budget. Add the costs of sustaining the bureaucracy, and there remained few funds left for investment. As Santa Cruz was to show, only additional taxes applied on internal trade could generate funds needed for capital expenditures.

This long-term squeeze on government budgets, which were almost uniformly in deficit in this period, led to the decision of Santa Cruz to issue a new debased silver currency. In 1830, by secret decree, a new silver currency was minted at Potosí, which contained 18.05 grams of silver rather than the traditional 24.45 grams (in the old colonial *peso á 8*). While the decision to create the new devalued silver peso (*moneda feble*) was probably thought of as a temporary expedient to generate a windfall profit, it ultimately became a long-term liability for the economy, and its increasing production relative to the older "hard peso" is a good indication of the increasing crisis of the state financial structure. Whereas the regime in the 1830s issued only 3.5 million pesos of the debased silver currency as opposed to 16.5 million of the traditional one, by the 1840s the ratio had been reduced to nine million and eleven million, respectively. By the 1850s, the new currency was overwhelmingly dominant, with twenty one million pesos of it being minted as opposed to only 2.5 million of the old.

Given the fact that the regime attempted to collect taxes in the old peso and pay in the new one, a general uncertainty was created within the national economy that increased with the years. Thus, the long-term stagnation of the economy led to a long-term crisis in government financing, which in turn led to money manipulation that further accentuated economic uncertainty. Even the quite impressive growth of Cobija and its commerce under Santa Cruz quickly declined after 1836, when the creation of the Peruvian-Bolivian confederation once again made the port of Arica the legitimate port of Bolivia. The reduction of the discriminatory taxes against Arica allowed it to achieve its natural domination and virtually liquidate Cobija as a viable alternative.

While the long-range economic reforms of Santa Cruz may not have reversed the stagnation of the national economy, his political and administrative reforms and the political peace that he did achieve were to prove of vital importance. Commissioning parliamentary studies and organizing special commissions, he finally enacted a major civil and commercial code modeled along the lines of the Napoleonic decrees. He also systematized local administration and successfully reestablished the rural census-taking procedures that had been the basis for the success of the colonial tribute collection. While he approved a democratic constitution with a limited presidency, he also quickly obtained dictatorial powers, carried out complete press censorship, and readily exiled his opponents. It should be stressed, however, that by the standards of his day Santa Cruz was extraordinarily tolerant of his opponents and kept bloodshed to a minimum in political conflicts. Moreover, the tranquility of his rule from 1829 to 1835 was such that he received overwhelming popular support from the elite elements of the society.

While Santa Cruz was a dominant figure for Bolivia, Bolivia was not the exclusive concern of Santa Cruz. From his earliest involvement in the life of Cuzco to his presidential term in the mid-1820s in Lima, Santa Cruz was deeply involved in Peruvian developments. He was as committed a participant in the politics of southern Peru and Lima as he was in the intrigues of Potosí or Chuquisaca. At no point on taking up the presidential reins in Bolivia did he give up his political ambitions in Peru. And the more chaotic the political situation in Peru became, the more appealing did the figure of Santa Cruz become for the Peruvians, especially those of the southern region.

By the mid-1830s, the constant turmoil brought on by the intensive activities of the southern Peruvian leader Gamarra, who actively intervened in Bolivian politics as well, along with the enfeebling of the crisis-ridden Salaverry regime in Lima, gave Santa Cruz the excuse for his followers in both states to attempt to establish a new regime in Peru. In June 1835, a Bolivian army invaded Peru, invited by one of the factions in the local civil wars. By August, the Bolivians had defeated the army of Gamarra, and, after a long series of battles, Salaverry was finally defeated and executed in January 1836.

At this point, Santa Cruz decided to reorganize Peru itself into two autonomous states, Northern Peru and Southern Peru, and join them with Bolivia in what became the *Confederación Peruboliviano*. After he had himself named as protector, he maneuvered so that all regional groups supported his unity idea, and the Confederation government was established in October 1836. For all his astute political activity, however, Santa Cruz held a real power base only in Bolivia and Southern Peru, and in this latter area he was faced by the constant opposition of Gamarra.

Whatever its problems, there is little question that the Confederation brought both peace to Peru and respect for its power along the entire Pacific region. Although the population of Peru at this time was only slightly larger than Bolivia's – on the order of 1.5 million persons – the resources of the Peruvian state were much greater. Unlike Bolivia, Peru had a multiplicity of powerful regional economies with strong native manufactures, plus a large variety of relatively easily exploitable resources that could be quickly developed for export into the world market. In contrast to the stable but stagnant Bolivian economy, the wealth of Peru could be more easily developed, so the potential for major growth was readily at hand. What was essentially needed to awaken fully this sleeping giant was a stable political system and a controlled and responsible bureaucracy.

Such a situation was ideal for Santa Cruz, whose fame was based on his excellent administrative skills. Immediately, he established civil and commercial codes for the new state, statistics were collected, customs reorganized, protective tariffs introduced, and the bureaucracy reorganized and refinanced. The army also was quickly provided with funds and support and so became a major ally of the regime.

Unfortunately for Santa Cruz, his potential to make Peru a major power also was recognized by the Chileans. They saw their own expansion as being one of northern movement along the disputed territory of the Pacific and were competing actively with Peru for the same European markets. Thus, a revitalized Peru under Santa Cruz could not be accepted. As a result, Chile gave active support to dissident Peruvian politicians, to the extent of both arming them and transporting them back to Peru. They also "disguised" their own troops as Peruvian rebels and then made a major bid to defeat Santa Cruz through constant incursions.

The end result of these Chilean-inspired invasions and subsidized revolts was a weakening of the Confederation government. While

Santa Cruz won several important battles, the long-drawn-out conflicts finally took their toll. By 1838, the Chileans put a regular army into Peru, and in a major battle near Lima in January 1839 both the Confederation government and the political career of the remarkable Santa Cruz were brought to an end by Chilean arms.

Forced into exile in Ecuador, Santa Cruz by necessity had to abandon the Bolivian government as well, so his local representative, General José Miguel de Velasco, assumed control over the new independent state. But the Velasco regime proved a difficult one. The former ally turned himself into a bitter foe of Santa Cruz and confiscated all his personal goods. But he soon found himself in conflict with another one of Santa Cruz's generals, José Ballivián, who carried out several revolts against the new government. Velasco was able to carry out some reforms, rewriting the constitution to provide for a more controlled presidency and even renamed the city of Chuquisaca after Sucre, but he was unable to calm the political situation. Finally, after some two years in office, a pro-Santa Cruz revolt brought down the regime in June 1841.

The overthrow of a Bolivian government was not considered a local event in the context of contemporary international politics. Since the fall of Santa Cruz, the Lima government had been under the control of Gamarra, his oldest enemy. Peru, Chile, and even Argentina had closely monitored local Bolivian developments, and, when it became clear that Santa Cruz had finally won, Gamarra announced his intention to invade the republic to prevent the feared Santa Cruz from returning to power. In July, a Peruvian army began to cross the frontier, and by October it had taken La Paz without a major battle. It was now made clear to all that Gamarra hoped to annex a good part of Bolivia to Peru. Other neighbors of the republic saw this as a potential opportunity. Argentina supported an army under Velasco in the south, while Ballivián seemed to be wandering between various camps, first supporting Gamarra and then finally deciding to seize the government for himself and oppose the Peruvian invasion.

In all the intrigues and maneuvering, it was Ballivián who finally emerged as the leading figure. With three separate internal rebellions going on at the same time and with an invading army threatening the very existence of the state, all the factions finally decided to cease supporting the return of Santa Cruz and switched to Ballivián as the most capable general. In many ways, this turned out to be a vital decision in the international affairs of the new republic.

Ballivián met Gamarra in battle at the town of Ingavi in November 1841 and defeated the invading forces of Peru. As a result of this action, the Gamarra government fell in Peru, Bolivia was relieved of its economic obligations to Peru, which had been imposed as a result of the fall of the confederation, and the close connection between Peruvian and Bolivian politics was definitely broken. After Ingavi, Peru never again thought to involve itself in Bolivian affairs, and no Bolivian political leader ever again became a potential contender in Peruvian politics. The end of the Santa Cruz threat also meant that Chile and Argentina now both gave up their intense involvement in Bolivian internal affairs and allowed Bolivian politics to return to primarily national concerns and national issues. The end of the Santa Cruz era marked as well the end of Bolivia as a major power of contention in the Southern Hemisphere of Latin America. It also ended the most brilliant epoch in terms of extraordinary leadership that the new republic was to obtain. While the economic stagnation of the republic had ultimately limited their scope of action, the regimes of both Sucre and Santa Cruz represented the best of the revolutionary ideology of the great liberation movements. Both men showed an essential humanity and toleration in their political dealings, which ultimately would stand in sharp contrast to the next group of leaders who would govern the republic.

Chapter 5

The Crisis of the State, 1841–1880

José Ballivián was born in La Paz in 1805, and came from an upper-class family, his uncle being Sebastián de Segurola, the royal official who led the suppression of the Tupac Amaru rebellion. But he himself was relatively uneducated, having entered into a military career at the age of twelve. An important leader in the independence armies, he was to rise to the highest ranks in the armies of Santa Cruz. Although much involved in the complex political intrigues before coming to power, the Ballivián era from 1841 to the end of 1847 was a calm period of rule for Bolivia and is considered the last stable regime of the early caudillo period. Under Ballivián, Congress was active, and many able civilians came into the central government. Slowly, population and government income began to rise as the nation no longer was involved in major international conflicts.

Fundamental to the new regime was a change in its view of Bolivia within the Pacific power relations. After attempting to invade Peru and failing, Ballivián abandoned Peruvian pretensions and settled down to governing Bolivia. At this point, he faced an inflated army that absorbed almost half of the national budget and had one general for every hundred soldiers. Establishing special land grants and pension acts, Ballivián attempted to dismantle the Bolivian war machine and reduce its weight in national politics. The number of troops and officers was reduced, and even some "military colonies" were established in the eastern lowlands. Nevertheless, the costs of pensioning off this army created a new and heavy burden of public indebtedness and the overall expenditures for the army changed little.

In other areas, the regime was a bit more successful. Although the national budget continued its traditional deficit, revenues were pushed up from their 1.5 million peso figure of the 1820s and 1830s to something close to two million pesos by the late 1840s. Although modest, this still was an increase. Nevertheless, even here, the long-term structural restraints were still evident. Indian tribute income still provided 40 percent of total income, and customs revenues still fluctuated quite widely from year to year. Now, however, the state had organized some important internal tariffs and taxes that were paying more steady incomes. The tax on coca production, an item consumed exclusively by Indians, was now producing an annual average of two hundred thousand pesos, and the newly revived export of Peruvian bark (*cascarilla*) for the manufacture of quinine was yielding an equal amount and providing an important secondary export along with silver.

The government also turned its attention toward the eastern lowlands. The department of the Beni was formally established, military colonies were organized, and even various European colonizing companies were promoted, although with little success. There also was considerable discussion of opening up new river and canal routes in the eastern lowlands in order to develop an Atlantic outlet for Bolivian production. Just as the government was beginning to look eastward for the first time, it also finally recognized the changed reality of Bolivian population and resources by calling for an independent bishopric for Cochabamba, now the second largest city in the republic. In 1843, Congress decreed the establishment of this fourth major ecclesiastical district, which was finally approved by the Vatican in 1847. Thus, Bolivia now had bishoprics in La Paz, Santa Cruz, and Cochabamba and an archbishopric district in La Plata (Sucre).

Finally, in 1846, came Bolivia's first national census, carried out under the able statesman José María Dalence. It was discovered that the population had risen steadily to some 1.4 million persons, with an additional estimated seven hundred thousand ungoverned Indians scattered through the eastern lowland territories. But despite the growth of the population in the almost quarter-century of republican life, there had been little change within the social and economic organization of the society. La Paz was still the largest city but now held just forty-three thousand persons, while in Cochabamba – the second largest center – resided only thirty thousand persons. Counting the population of all eleven cities and thirty-five *villas* (or towns) of the republic (those living in towns of approximately five hundred persons and above) still produced an urban population of only 11 percent, a figure not much different from the estimates of Pentland in the mid-1820s.

As could be expected from the lack of government investments and the general stagnation of urban life, the educational level of the society was extraordinarily low. Only twenty-two thousand children were attending school in 1847, or 10 percent of the number of schoolage children in the republic. This would seem to imply that little change in literacy could be expected in the future, for Dalence generously estimated that there was a maximum of only one hundred thousand persons literate in Spanish in the republic, which meant just 7 percent of the population. Without a major increase in school attendance, it was evident that the next generation would be little more literate than the one of 1846.

Nor had the economy changed greatly, despite the relative peace now ensured by the Santa Cruz and Ballivián periods. Although silver mining had dropped to 156,000 marks per annum in the 1820s, it increased only moderately in the 1830s to 188,000 marks, and to just 192,000 marks in the 1840s, or exactly one-half of the peak production of 385,000 marks in the 1790s. Moreover, Dalence estimated that there were still ten thousand abandoned silver mines in the republic, two-thirds of which retained silver but were now under water and could not be developed without pumping machinery. There were, in fact, only 282 active mine owners in the republic in 1846 who employed only some nine thousand miners, most of whom were part-time specialists who worked in agriculture as well.

As for the national industry, Bolivia had a large artisan society that satisfied most of the needs of its poorest populations. Woolen textiles for home or local consumption was a major industry, along with food processing. The one area that the government attempted throughout the early years to develop – cheap cotton textiles – just did not survive. Despite sporadic prohibitions and high tariffs against cheap English cottons, the tocuyo cotton cloth industry, centered in Cochabamba, never regained its eighteenth-century importance. Whereas in the colonial period it was estimated that the tocuyo cloth industry of Cochabamba had several hundred *obrajes* (factories) producing cloth, these numbered just one hundred by 1846, and their value had declined from an annual production estimated at two hundred thousand pesos to some sixty thousand pesos in the 1840s. The cheap cotton textile needs of the Bolivians were now filled by British cloths that dominated the market.

Bolivia remained an overwhelmingly rural society. Eighty-nine percent of the population lived outside the cities and hamlets, and they produced over two-thirds of the national product (estimated at 13.5 million pesos worth of goods, compared to 2.3 million pesos in minerals and 3.9 million in manufactured products in 1846). This population remained not only illiterate but also largely ignorant of even the national language. While no figures are available on languages spoken, it would not be an exaggeration to estimate that no more than 20 percent of the national population was either monolingually or bilingually conversant in Spanish. Quechua remained the predominant language of the republic, with Aymara running a close second. Spanish thus was a minority language in the republic, although it was the only language of national political and economic life.

Within rural society, the balance of control between haciendas and *comunidades* (free Indian communities) remained rather much as it had existed in the late colonial period. In 1846, there were over five thousand haciendas valued at twenty million pesos and some four thousand free communities valued at only six million pesos. But while the relative value and numbers seemed to favor the haciendas in the rural areas, in fact the majority of the work force lived on the free communities. Dalence estimated that there were only 5,135 heads of families who were hacendados, with some 138,104 heads of households living on the comunidades. Accepting Dalence's own estimates of four and one-half persons per family as a multiplier means that over 620,000 Indians lived on the communities, and they made up a total of 51 percent of the total rural population. The hacienda population of yanaconas (or landless laborers) probably numbered between 375,000 and 400,000, and the other 200,000 persons of the rural population were probably freeholders in the southern regions or landless migrating workers who rented lands from either the communities or the haciendas.

While the haciendas had obviously had the more commercially valuable properties, they nevertheless were in a relative state of stagnation, except for the two exceptional areas of the Yungas and the Cochabamba Valley. The former was the major source of coca production, which was on the increase along with the increase in the Indian population. As for Cochabamba, it had seemingly recovered from the economic shock of the late colonial crisis and was now the principal national producer of the two basic grains, wheat and corn, and had now returned to its preeminent position as the granary of Bolivia. Elsewhere, however, the haciendas remained relatively quiescent and posed no serious threat to the densely populated regions where the free communities predominated.

Within the free communities themselves there were, however, ongoing changes and much internal stratification. The elimination of the mita obligation had clearly favored the originarios, or original members of the communities, with the greatest access to lands. With the onerous labor obligations removed, their numbers seem to have grown or at least stabilized and in the 1840s were estimated to represent 35 percent of all heads of households on the free communities. The agregados with land (or later arrivals with lesser landholdings in the communities) represented 42 percent of the communities' population, and a new and important group of forasteros without any land now accounted for 23 percent of all Indian families. Evidently, the slow growth of population was beginning to create a landless class of Indians on the free communities themselves.

While there were some changes going on within the dominant rural world, the stagnation of the mining industry and the failure of national manufactures to meet local demand meant that for the first quarter-century of its existence Bolivia was in the unusual position of being in a constant deficit in its balance of trade. In each year from 1825 until well into the 1850s, Bolivia showed a deficit in its legal trade account, which only could be met by the illegal exportation of silver and by a very active contraband trade. Thus, the government Minerals Purchasing Bank was having a harder and harder time collecting all the silver being produced in the country, while government losses on illegally exported items seem to have been quite high.

Finally, government deficits were a constant phenomenon, as expenditures, especially of a military nature, far outstripped the resources of the state treasury.

Thus, by mid-century, Bolivia was, if anything, in worse condition than it had been at the beginning of its republican life, and it appeared that things would only deteriorate further. This expectation would seemingly be reinforced with the fall of Ballivián and the beginning of Bolivia's most chaotic period of caudillo rule from 1848 to 1880. But, paradoxically, it was precisely this period of greatest political turmoil that was to prove the great age of expansion of the Bolivian economy. It was in the 1850s and 1860s that the successful implantation of steam engines into the altiplano mine industry began. It also was largely merchants and hacendados from the area of Cochabamba and some of the more advanced grain-producing regions who now provided the capital with which to open the major mines. Gaining their capital from interior commercial operations, these new merchant-miners were able to begin to invest seriously in new mine technology.

Along with the slow development of altiplano mining, the 1860s and 1870s would see the very rapid growth of mining on the Pacific littoral of Bolivia. The silver mines of Caracoles in the 1870s, as well as the older mines on the altiplano, would now come into full production. In turn, the growth of modern mine companies attracted international capital with the resources to expand new mining ventures even further.

All of this renewed economic activity would occur in the midst of the most politically violent and chaotic period of republican political history. But the chaos of political violence seems to have had little impact on the slow but steady growth of a modern export sector. If anything, the regimes that came in the 1860s and 1870s responded well to the demands of the new mining elite and met its most immediate concerns, which were primarily related to ending government monopoly positions in the purchasing and trading of metals.

But the cause of this paradoxical growth still remains to be fully determined. To begin with, it is evident that a series of events external to Bolivia played a decisive role in awakening the mining giant. The increasing productivity and declining costs of the steam engine in Europe and North America in the first half of the nineteenth century meant that the steam engine of the 1850s and 1860s was a far cheaper and more readily available and reliable item than it had been in the 1820s. Thus, the costs of opening up a flooded mine were considerably reduced. Moreover, the growth of Peruvian and Chilean mining in this period provided a general regional background of capital and technical expertise that could be readily exported to the incipient Bolivian industry and also provided a ready market for Bolivian exports. Finally, the decline of international mercury prices reduced a major cost item for silver extraction.

But these factors explain only the general international conditions that provided a much larger pool of engineers, machines, and mercury at much lower cost than previously for the altiplano miners. The initial capital placed in Bolivian highland mining came from Bolivians themselves. And the key question remains: Where did this capital come from, given the relative stagnation of the economy for the first quarter-century of republican existence? From an analysis of the early mining companies in Potosí and Oruro, it is evident that a disproportionate share of the capital stock came out of the merchant and landed aristocracy of the Cochabamba Valley. It would thus appear that the steady but unspectacular growth of the national population, despite some rather severe epidemics in the 1850s, created an expanding internal market for agricultural production, especially for corn and wheat, which was the core of Cochabamba agriculture. From this growing internal market, the Cochabamba elite was able to extract surplus capital. Cochabamba seems to have had, too, a class of incipient entrepreneurs who were more than willing to undertake the risks of heavy capital investments in the traditionally quite unpredictable mine industry. The fact that the Cochabamba region was the heartland of the most advanced cholo population in the republic and also had the most active rentier class of freehold peasants, the bulk of whom were bilingual in Spanish and Quechua, also helps to explain some of the evident entrepreneurial skill available.

Starting in the 1830s, it had become popular to establish national joint stock companies to begin mining operations. Usually selling a large number of shares at low costs per share, these companies on average would produce something on the order of ten thousand pesos of working capital. Among the numerous companies formed in this pioneer epoch, the most important was the Huanchaca Mining Company founded in 1832, which worked the Porco mines in the province of Potosí. Like all such ventures, these early companies barely met costs and spent many years building drainage and new mineral shafts so as to get the mines working, using the most readily accessible surface silver deposits to pay for ongoing costs. Many of the companies went bankrupt before they could complete the operations, and by 1856 the Huanchaca Mining Company was typical of these in having spent some 180,000 pesos on basic infrastructure and having as yet to produce a profit for any of its shareholders. The same year the merchant Aniceto Arze bought into the company for forty thousand pesos and quickly began to provide the crucial capital needed to get the company going. Similarly, in the mid-1850s, the Aramayo family bought out the bankrupt Real Socavón Mining Company of Potosí. Finally, in 1855 the merchant Gregorio Pacheco took over the Guadalupe mines from one of his debtors in the Chicas district of Potosí province.

Thus, within a few years of each other, the three major silver mining dynasties were implanted in the mining districts of Potosí. With new infusions of capital and leadership, the reorganized companies began to prosper. By the 1860s, the three leaders were well into rationalizing their operations and undertaking long-term structural changes in the industry through the introduction of modern machinery, pumping operations, and shaft reconstructions. By the 1870s, foreign capital began to arrive in ever-increasing amounts, and by the second half of the decade the Bolivian silver-mining industry can be said to have reached international levels of capitalization and technological development and efficiency. Bolivia was once again one of the world's leading producers of refined silver, and a thriving and vital export industry had revitalized both the internal economy as well as Bolivia's international commerce.

It was this increasing economic tempo of the 1850s that in many ways explains the rather strange configurations of governments that arose on the political scene. With the fall of the Ballivián regime, another *paceño* of his generation (born in La Paz in 1811), General Manuel Isidoro Belzu, emerged as the new political leader. Of humble origins, although apparently of Spanish extraction and, like Ballivián, primarily and exclusively a military officer from his youth, Belzu had been an important officer in the Santa Cruz armies. Once Ballivián had taken over, he had played a key military role in the new regime. Shifting alliances constantly, as had Ballivián before him, he emerged as the strongest opposition general demanding a place in the government.

After the fall of Ballivián in December 1847, Belzu emerged as the most powerful figure and took the presidency formally in 1848. He held power until 1855 when he voluntarily retired – the first Bolivian president to do so since the time of Sucre. But the continued chaos of government finance and the progressive weakening of loyalties and the emergence of contending personalities left the political scene filled with unpaid and unsatisfied generals, all of whom wished to be president. Without an established political party system to channel demands or aspirations or control appetites, national politics was a gruesome free-for-all in which any small-time regional leader could play. The result was that Belzu had to face something on the order of thirty to forty different revolts in his six years in government. In the end, the countless battles, assassination attempts, and intrigues exhausted even this indomitable warrior, so he voluntarily resigned his position.

Below the level of intrigue, however, certain very important changes were occurring that Belzu accurately reflected. The Belzu regime has been taken as an aberration by many Bolivian historians, with the epithets of "demagogue" and "socialist" being freely applied to him. There is no question that Belzu expressed a frank hostility to the upper aristocracy of Chuquisaca and the other provincial elites, or that he expressed himself in favor of some type of scheme to confiscate the wealth of the rich. He also was quite an imaginative populist who liked to declare himself a representative of the cholos and lower classes of the cities, and expressed himself in terms of Christian socialism and attacked the legitimacy of private property and class structures. Often, he distributed monies to the urban poor in quite classic demagogic gestures. But he essentially maintained the traditional social structure and was the last of the early nineteenth-century presidents to firmly support a traditional mercantilist position.

The profuse legislation that Belzu enacted in the economic area involved protective tariffs against English manufactures, promotion of national artisanal industries, tax incentives to national products, the creation of state monopolies, and even laws prohibiting foreigners from operating in national commerce. These were efforts that were directly opposed by the merchants and their new mining allies, all of whom very much favored free trade and an open economy. Just as the free trade movement was beginning to gain important economic adherents, the traditional classes struggled to prevent the dismantling of the old mercantilist scheme. Belzu proved hostile to the new silver miners, even going so far as to set up several more minerals purchasing banks and a monopoly bank for the purchase of quinine bark. For this, he was bitterly attacked by the new mining and commercial elites, while at the same time he received wide popular support.

Just how extensive popular support was for Belzu became apparent very early in his regime. In March 1849, an early attempt by some generals to overthrow his government led to popular uprisings in the cities of La Paz and Cochabamba – the most advanced and populated in the republic – in support of the regime. For several days in both cities, lower-class mobs took over and led a rather systematic attack against the local elites. Moreover, popular support was so powerful that an almost successful assassination attempt on Belzu in September 1850, followed by a long convalescence, did not lead to an overthrow of his regime.

Just as the upper classes were opposed to Belzu for his popular support and his strong mercantilist ideas, foreign states were embroiled with him as he tried to prevent the penetration of foreign goods into the national market and restrict the role of foreign merchants. This conflict even led to the expulsion of the British diplomatic representative and resulted in the often-told but untrue tale that Queen Victoria eliminated Bolivia from the map in retaliation.

The increasing economic power of the free trade opposition and the declining power of the artisans and local manufacturers did eventually erode the support of Belzu and fully financed his opposition. Tired of putting down another rebellion of his troops fomented by his opponents, Belzu declared his intention to retire and ran his docile son-in-law General Córdova for president. This controlled election in 1855, which saw some 13,500 electors voting, led to the establishment of what proved to be a transitory but moderate government before the final victory of the free-trade and proforeign capital advocates.

Córdova lasted two years and was replaced by Bolivia's first essentially civilian president, José María Linares, in 1857. The Linares regime, for all its problems, would clearly mark the shift of power to the newer elements in the economy and the end of the government's monopoly role in the mining industry. Whereas Belzu and Córdova had been indifferent to the demands of the mining industry, Linares made this the primary concern of his government. Although born in 1810 in Potosí, and thus very much a member of the generation of all the presidents since Santa Cruz, Linares was unique in that he never followed a military career. A son of an upper-class Spanish family, the well-educated Linares had quickly risen in politics and civil government and had played a role in secondary education in the capital of Chuquisaca. He initially had been a loyal supporter of Santa Cruz and had served as prefect, legislator, and central government administrator during the years of the Confederation. Eventually opposing the Confederation, he also rejected the Ballivián regime and went to live in Europe and practiced law in Spain.

Returning to Bolivia in the later Belzu years, he was constantly involved in plotting against the old general and even ran against Córdova in the elections of 1855, winning some four thousand votes. But his defeat at the hands of the government, which fully controlled the elections, committed him to a violent overthrow of the regime. The resulting Linares government, which lasted from 1857 to his own ouster in 1861, showed itself much more receptive to the ideas of free trade. The tariffs protecting the native cloth industry were lowered, the quinine monopoly was ended, and all ores but silver were now permitted free entrance to the marketplace if they were refined in Bolivia. The regime, however, did not go as far toward free trade as the miners wished, and in fact it tightened rules on mercury sales, making the industry a temporary state monopoly and increasing the control over mining. Nevertheless, the Linares government encouraged the miners to form a powerful government supported *camada*, or interest group, to push for their demands.

Just how important these new mine owners had become was evident in the early years of the new regime. Whereas total government revenues still hovered between 1.5 and 2 million pesos per annum, the major mine companies – such as the Aramayo-owned Real Socavón Mining Company of Potosí, for example – had invested 281,000 pesos between its organization in 1854 and 1861. Pacheco's companies from 1856 to 1861 had invested 333,000 pesos, with a like sum being spent on the Huanchaca Mining Company. The use of steam engines, railed carts, and modem refining machinery was already common in the mining zones, and by the mid-1860s these companies were going overseas for their capital needs. Thus, the investment in just the three largest of these companies was close to the total income generated by the national treasury in any one year.

Along with the steady growth of the traditional mining zones, the littoral province of Atacama along the Pacific coast was finally beginning to take on some significance. In 1857, the first nitrate deposits in the Mejillones region had been discovered. This led to the slow but steady growth of the port of Antofogasta, which was soon rivaling that of Cobija as the principal Pacific port of the state. This growth, however, was all under the control of British and Chilean capitalists, who worked out rather favorable contracts with the Bolivian government, which essentially added little real income to the central treasury.

In the budget of 1860, for example, the tribute tax was still double the income of any other source of national revenue and accounted for 36 percent of the budget. Furthermore, the once quite lucrative income from quinine exports had totally disappeared. A major source of government revenues and of exports in the 1840s and early 1850s, the monopoly of Bolivian quinine production was broken by Colombia in 1855 and thereafter production declined to relative insignificance. Finally, despite Linares's attempts to control the military and reduce the army to just fifteen hundred men, the armed forces still absorbed 41 percent of the national expenditures.

Although incapable of revising government incomes and expenditures, Linares made a successful effort to refund the internal debt and to restore some semblance of normality to the government minting of silver. He also attempted to reorganize the national administration and to provide for more efficient local government. He appears to have been able to get some successful funding provided for local education. Thus, while the Linares administration did not overwhelmingly change the public economy, it did initiate some long-term changes in the direction that was to mark the ultimate victory of the free trade ideology. He also began a thoroughgoing reorganization of public credit that was to prove a most important precedent for the regimes of the 1870s and 1880s.

The very strict reformism and harsh rule of Linares, who even established a formal dictatorship after September 1858, eventually created overwhelming opposition to his regime. While his most ardent supporters – among them, Tomás Friás and Adolfo Ballivián – formed themselves into a powerful supportive group that later would take on the sobriquet of the *rojos*, his opponents mobilized large-scale support for his overthrow. In 1860, the regime had massacred Indian rebels at the shrine of Copacabana on Lake Titicaca, and at the same time was forced to head off a major revolt attempt. These actions weakened the dictator, so Linares was forced into exile in January 1861 by three of his most important ministerial appointments.

A new congress was elected in which many of the rojos were represented. Nevertheless, General José María Achá, one of the three conspirators, was selected president of the republic by Congress, and Linares and his supporters were excluded from power. The new regime in many ways continued the basic policy decisions of the Linares period, in fact carrying out a further freeing of the economy. The mercury monopoly created by Linares was abolished and the fiscal reorganization continued, although the strong centralized budgeting arrangements carried out by Linares were abandoned.

The new regime was to have the unique distinction of being the most violent of the nineteenth-century governments in terms of the repression of its opponents. In 1861, in a typical episode of political maneuverings, some seventy supporters of Belzu, including ex-President Córdova, were taken into custody in La Paz by the local commander Colonel Yañez. Using the threat of a Belzu uprising as his excuse, Yañez ordered the execution of these leading politicians – the single most bloody reprisal in republican history to that date. Thereafter, the regime was faced, as usual, with constant political unrest, with the future presidential contenders testing themselves out in a series of power plays and military revolts. What is impressive about all these revolt attempts is the slight impact they had on the general economic and social structure of the state. Whereas the Bolivian army under Sucre and Santa Cruz had numbered between five thousand and ten thousand troops, the Bolivian army was reduced to a force of between fifteen hundred and two thousand men in the post-Confederation period, and especially after the end of the Peruvian threat at Ingavi in 1841. This was an army that supposedly controlled a society that numbered some 1.8 million persons in the 1850s.

Thus, the constant revolts usually involved only a few hundred men on each side and, in effect, produced little serious disruption of the economic or social life of the society. Moreover, so long as the military regimes reflected the increasing power of the new mining oligarchy, they were more or less ignored by the new miner capitalists. Deeply involved in establishing their companies on a viable economic base, they had little time for politics if their basic needs were satisfied by the government. And until the military caudillos finally fell into a serious war with these miners' closest allies and supporters, the Chileans, they felt no need to intervene.

Given the indifference of the new and old economic elites, the civilian politicians found themselves incapable of controlling the generals or the troops. Linares had been their best hope, with the result that the constitutionalist, or rojos, faction continued to offer a strong appeal for those committed to a powerful civilian-dominated regime. But the majority of factions, from those of Santa Cruz to those of the followers of Belzu, continued to find a convenient general or colonel to lead their cause and declare for their candidate. Until these other political and oligarchic factions would agree to press their claims in a different arena, the pattern of military revolts followed a precise and well-worn pattern.

Whereas the Achá regime conformed to the typical model, and also reflected the new economic interests, there was a new factor that was beginning to make itself felt in the Bolivian political and economic scene. In 1863, the Achá regime was forced to deal with the first major aggressive step of Chile in the Atacama mining region. In that year, a dispute between a Chilean- and British-financed mining company was taken to the Bolivian courts for arbitration. In this conflict, the Chilean government refused to recognize Bolivian jurisdiction and in 1863 extended its territorial claims to include the Mejillones nitrate fields. While Achá sent Friás to negotiate, and Congress in 1863 voted for war, the Bolivian government found itself impotent against its southern neighbor and was forced to accept Chilean demands for rights to these extraordinarily rich fields.

As the term of Achá drew to a close, the general attempted to establish free elections. The two most powerful civilian movements proved to be those of the rojos constitutionalists and the Belzu populists. But before the elections could be held, a close relative of Acha's, General Mariano Melgarejo, seized the government in December 1864. Thus began one of the longest and most bitterly contested dictatorships in Bolivian history – a regime that has caused great debate in Bolivian history. Like Achá before him, Melgarejo was of Cochabamba background and had participated in a series of military occupations, revolts, and political machinations. He differed from his predecessors mainly in age, having been born in 1820, and in his total lack of class support. Unlike all of his predecessors except Belzu, he was totally alienated from the upper classes. He was illegitimate and had made his successful career through military prowess alone. At the same time, he had none of the revolutionary ideology of Belzu and so made no serious attempt to reach the popular classes.

Yet, despite the term *"caudillo barbaro,"* as Bolivian historians have labeled him, Melgarejo in many ways represented the coming to full power of the mining elite of the country and the triumph of its policy of free trade. The liberal economic policies of the regime represented a coherent continuation of programs that had been set in motion as early as the Linares period. Moreover, despite his alleged "drunkenness" and dissolute living style, Melgarejo received important support from the new mining elite for much of his term in office. His regime also would see the first serious attack on the land question since the early days of the republic, in a confrontational attack on the legal rights of the free communities. Both his opposition to Indian corporate landholding and his liberalization of the economy reflected demands of the mining elite, which he fully supported. His regime fully reflects the reemergence of a powerful silver-mining export industry in Bolivia.

The Melgarejo period must be seen in the context of the international economy to be fully understood. The years 1864 to 1873 were an extremely prosperous time, and ushered in the great era of capital exports from Europe to the developing world. The same period saw the great boom in the Pacific coastal exports industry – first guano and then nitrates – and the entrance of English, North American, and continental European capital into the local mining industries in alliance with Chilean and Peruvian capitalists. All of this feverish investment activity also greatly affected the whole southern Atacama region known as Mejillones, which, although disputed constantly by Chile, was still under nominal Bolivian control. Here were major deposits of guano and nitrate, and in addition important deposits of silver would soon be discovered in the nearby Carracoles region.

What few Bolivian capital resources existed were totally tied up in developing a modern silver industry in the traditional altiplano mining centers. Therefore, all of these new zones acted as magnets for Bolivia's neighbors. For the altiplano miners, this foreign capital interest in coastal mining was welcome, because it spread over into interest in supporting highlands mining growth. For the always penurious Bolivian government, the income of which had remained virtually stable for almost fifty years, this interest in its coastal resources was an unexpected cornucopia which could lead only to unheard-of personal wealth. Whereas most of the previous rulers of Bolivia tended to die in poverty in exile abroad, the current leaders suddenly found themselves courted by foreign governments and foreign capitalists, and proved to be unwilling and unable to resist the temptations.

Bolivian historians and writers have justifiably condemned the Melgarejo government for consistently selling the nation to the highest bidder. But could other regimes have successfully resisted these blandishments after some fifty years of stagnant fiscal revenues and an officer corps that proved insatiable in its demands for power? Moreover, one can seriously question whether the new mining elite was at all concerned with the huge concessions granted to Chilean capitalists or other aspects of government policy that essentially ended all attempts at mercantilist control either in terms of the mining industry or in protecting national industries.

Whether Melgarejo and his generals were any better or worse than others is not the issue, but they certainly were more active. For the first time since the British speculations of 1825 and 1826, there was a rush of foreign capitalists into Bolivia with schemes to make everyone rich. Classic North American entrepreneurs such as Henry Meiggs and Colonel George E. Church were on the scene, along with venerable Chilean houses such as Concho y Torres, and such classic British companies as Gibbs & Co. The primary source of potential wealth was the Mejellones nitrate and guano fields. In a treaty of 1866, Chile and Bolivia had agreed to share the resources of the Mejillones region and had redrawn the frontier to give Chile direct control over everything below the 24th Parallel. This was a real source of income, and foreigners, mostly British and Chileans, entered into long-term export contracts and special railroad concession arrangements.

Because the Melgarejo regime was faced with a deficit budget from its first days in office, it was ready to give extremely generous long-term contracts for immediate but relatively small amounts of funding. Many of these contracts were worth several millions of pesos, taken on the worst terms for Bolivia and tying up invaluable resources for long periods of time with onerous commitments. Many of these contracts, in fact, would become quite binding on the government and would eventually provide the crucial background to the commercial conflicts that led to the War of the Pacific. But the government was essentially indifferent to all these long-term problems. In the first days of the new regime, Melgarejo resorted to forced loans to generate income for the treasury, and he never really caught up to his expanding expenses. Thus, anyone offering a few hundred thousand pesos of income could obtain millions in long-term concessions. Moreover, it would seem that for the altiplano politicians that the whole coastal boom market was an unreal world over which they had little control and over which they were willing to concede virtually anything these industrious foreigners wanted. It is also well worth noting that, despite complex guano and nitrate export contracts, Pacific coastal railroad schemes, Amazonian river boat and Belgian colonizing companies, and other real and imaginary speculative proposals, there was no attempt to allow foreign operators to enter into the highland mining industries. These remained firmly in the hands of national investors.

With its new wealth from coastal mining and speculative foreign capital, even nearby governments were willing to get involved with the overly generous Melgarejo regime. Thus, Bolivia signed commercial and territorial treaties in the late 1860s with every one of its neighbors. In 1865, a special treaty with Peru went into effect whereby Bolivia, for obtaining free port rights at Arica, virtually became part of the customs union with Peru. Bolivia ended up by charging Peruvian customs taxes at Cobija and in turn was granted a fixed income of 450,000 pesos per annum from the customs houses of Arica and Tacna. By this treaty, Peruvian manufacturers entered Bolivia without restrictions. In turn, this fixed income coming from Peru was quickly mortgaged to foreign interests for short-term loans by the Melgarejo regime.

Next came the Chilean treaty of 1866, which not only resolved the Mejellones and previous occupations in favor of Chile but also provided that the local Pacific ports could export mineral products free of Bolivian taxes and that Chilean goods could come into such ports also free of the usual tariffs. By these two acts alone, the whole mercantilistic program of protective tariffs was completely destroyed and Bolivia was now in a virtually free-trade arrangement with Chile and Peru. Bolivia then negotiated away its part of the joint guano output from these treaty areas, and did so with foreign firms on disastrous terms and in a manner that could only incite continued Chilean pressure. Finally, Melgarejo offered the Chilean diplomatic representative, whom he had grown to like during the treaty negotiations, the post of minister of finance in his own government. When this offer was rejected, Melgarejo then made him his own diplomatic representative before the Chilean regime!

Next came two treaties with Argentina and Brazil in 1868, which provided for free fluvial rights to the Atlantic for Bolivian shipping in return for further special concessions in relationship to the importation of the products of both of these nations. Moreover, in the Brazilian treaty a territorial "adjustment" of some forty thousand square miles was made in favor of Brazil. Thus, all the treaties – despite their excessive concessions of income and even territory, as in the Chilean and Brazilian cases – went far toward totally dismantling the carefully constructed edifice of protective tariffs that had been the hallmark of Bolivian political economy up to that date. All of this was directly related to the new altiplano mining elite's great desire to allow free trade to become the operating principle of the national economy.

In the internal economic sphere, Melgarejo also attempted some fundamental reforms. While the regime went to great excesses in minting devalued currency, it carried out the basic reform of the old colonial currency and gave up the peso for the new decimal-based currency of the *boliviano* in 1869. More important, it attempted to destroy the landowning rights of the free communities. This extraordinary decree of 1866 was the first really sustained attack on Indian communal property rights since the Bolivarian decrees of 1824 and 1825, which were left in suspense by the Sucre decision to return to the tribute as a basic form of taxation. With the sudden wealth being generated by the Pacific mineral and guano deposits, the relative importance of the tribute income in the total revenues of the state began to decline. Whereas the actual amount of tribute remained stable – at eight hundred thousand to nine hundred thousand pesos per annum – its relative importance was slowly declining, as income from mineral exports and mining taxes was beginning to become as important. In addition, the slow revival of the mining industry was having its impact on the growth of urban markets and the consequent increase in the tempo of commercial agriculture to supply those markets. Thus, the 1860s saw the first stirrings of revived interest in the rural haciendas and the beginnings of a sustained attack on the property holdings of the communities.

By the terms of the confiscation decree, it was declared that all community properties were really state-owned lands and that Indians residing on them were now required to purchase individual land titles at the sum of no less than twenty-five pesos and no greater than one hundred pesos. The Indian who did not purchase his title within sixty days of the decree would be deprived of his lands, and the state would then auction the lands off to other purchasers. It was provided that holders of the state debt obligations could use these in payment for land. If no one purchased the lands in public auction, then the Indians who worked them would be allowed to retain these lands as renters and would be forced to pay a rental tax to the state. Even if the Indian should be able to purchase his lands, ultimate possession still resided with the state, so that the lands would have to be repurchased all over again after five years.

At the end of the Melgarejo's period in 1870, over 1.25 million pesos-worth of land had been "sold" to whites and mestizos, the majority of which was paid for in debt obligations from the state. The outcry of the anti-Melgarejo forces and the fact that Indian protest was so violent and bloody had their impact on terminating this initiative before the community lands could be effectively confiscated, and the succeeding government actually restored most of the lands taken. But it was the fact that Melgarejo had anticipated the market too soon that really explains the "failure" of his confiscation scheme. For, in fact, the demand for community lands would grow enormously so that by the end of the next decade the Bolivian government would carry the entire confiscation program of Melgarejo through to fruition.

Melgarejo also completed his assault on the mercantilistic ideology of his predecessors by emasculating the entire silver monopoly arrangements that had been the key issue of contention between the new silver miners and the government. During his regime, the largest silver-mining companies such as the Huanchaca enterprise of Aniceto Arce received exemptions and were allowed freely to export their silver to the international market. Thus, from the late 1860s onward, the percentage of mined silver being purchased by the *Banco de Rescate* (Minerals Purchasing Bank) went into sharp decline, and the effective control of the government in setting prices for national silver production was ended. By these actions, Melgarejo satisfied the most important demand of the new mining elite.

The political overthrow of Melgarejo, when it came in 1870, brought no serious change to any of the policies that had been initiated in his six years of office. Although the new regime of General Agustín Morales (1870–72) desperately renegotiated some of the more extravagant contracts and temporarily restored the Indian lands, it actually furthered the general policies initiated under Melgarejo. With the opening up of the Pacific coastal Caracoles silver mines in 1870 – which in two years had a total invested capital of $U.S.10 million – and the continued boom of the Mejillones region, there was now even more money available to the central government. This meant it could afford to undertake the essential reforms that the extremely hungry Melgarejo government was unwilling to make. In 1871 and 1872, the government finally abolished the monopoly on silver purchases for all companies and declared a free trade in this mineral. It also terminated all minting of the famous debased currencies, which went back to the days of Santa Cruz. The semiprivate *Banco Nacional de Bolivia*, created in 1871, was given charge of redeeming these debased monies and reorganizing the national currency.

Nor was the new government adverse to continuing many of the essentially corrupt loan arrangements that Melgarejo had begun. The Church contract for a steamship company on the eastern rivers eventually raised £2 million, of which the government got practically nothing and under which no boats were ever delivered to Bolivia. The first successful railroad concession was granted to Meiggs and other foreign capitalists, also in 1872, and at least there was some success in this. The Nitrates and Railroad Company of Antofagasta was established that year with a heavy Bolivian subsidy and began the construction of a railroad from Antofagasta and the Mejillones fields through to the new Caracoles silver mines. Thus was begun the era of railroad construction in the republic, although as yet no railroad was successfully begun to the highlands from the coast – a move that was the next major demand of the new altiplano silver miners.

The overthrow of the Melgarejo regime essentially brought the old Linares civilian constitutionalists – or rojos – back to power. Whereas General Morales won a very controlled election in May 1872 with some fourteen thousand votes cast, his apparent derangement and eventual assassination prevented this potentially despotic ruler from seriously threatening the domination of the rojos in the government. In a new election in May 1873, their primary leader – Adolfo Ballivián, the son of the former president – was selected in a rather free electoral campaign in which some 16,674 votes were registered. An urbane, well-educated, and traveled figure, Ballivián successfully led his followers to power and was replaced on his death by illness in 1874 by Dr. Tomás Frías, the second leader of the party and head of congress. Thus, from late 1870 until 1876, the central government was essentially under the control of the old Linares party leaders and reflected the most advanced elements of the civilian leadership of the period.

But the inability of the rojos to control the army and their corruption in international contracts and negotiations – differing little from the Melgarejo modalities – meant that the civilian regimes (the first such regimes since the Linares dictatorship itself, and only the second episode of nonmilitary rule since the founding of the republic) could not successfully maintain themselves in office. These civilians, although embracing free trade policies, were still not directly related to the national mining elite. The mineowners were now in the midst of their greatest phase of organization and paid little direct attention to politics. The lack of elite support and the ongoing corruption weakened the civilians and made them vulnerable to the traditional military machinations.

General Hilarión Daza emerged under the civilians as the chief military figure in the republic, heading the elite Colorado battalion, which had been formed in the time of Melgarejo. In the same mold as Melgarejo and Morales, Daza overthrew the government in 1876. On seizing power, Daza as usual found himself badly in need of funds and plundered the national treasury to pay his restless officers and maintain himself in power. Thus, the fiscal reforms carried out by the civilians at the beginning of the decade were undone in the last half of the 1870s by Daza. The collapse of the central treasury in turn led to the wild extravaganzas of more fictitious loans, special entrepreneurial concessions, and further raids on the national treasury by foreign and national speculators. All this made for a potentially explosive environment as the conflicting concessions policies and changing taxation rules created a tense situation among foreign companies operating with Chilean support on Bolivia's coastal territory. It also encouraged the Chilean belief that the Atacama territories were theirs for the taking.

Thus, the short-lived civilian rule after the overthrow of Melgarejo brought little serious change to government policy or to national political organization. But the satisfaction of all the basic demands of the altiplano mining elite by Melgarejo and his successors allowed that elite to enter into its most expansive phase of operations and reorganization. The period from 1873 to 1895 is considered the great age of nineteenth-century altiplano silver mining. By the end of the decade of the 1870s, Huanchaca alone was generating more income than the central government itself. Moreover, all the other major firms now received major inputs of European and Chilean capital. The growth of Bolivian silver output in this period was phenomenal, as can be seen from the production statistics. The mines, which in the period of the 1860s had still averaged only 344,000 marks per annum, moved toward an average of 956,000 marks in the 1870s, then jumped to 1.1 million marks in the 1880s, and reached some 1.6 million marks per annum in the 1890s. The peak of nineteenth-century silver output occurred in 1895, when some 2.6 million marks were estimated to have been produced.

The Bolivian mineowners put no effort into guaranteeing control by the civilian elite of the government, for the return of military rule under Daza seemed in no way to threaten their fundamental interests. In fact, Daza supported them by continuing all their pet projects, promoting their Chilean interests, and even ruling with a civilian parliament that wrote the very important constitution of 1879, which provided a fundamental liberal charter for the national government and stressed private property rights.

But the political indifference of the altiplano elite would not last, for the very weaknesses of the military regime would carry Bolivia into a full-scale war with Chile, which in turn would create serious political and economic problems once again for Bolivia's mineowners. The Pacific War of 1879 appears from the Bolivian perspective almost as a Greek tragedy. Although Bolivia had protested Chilean expansion from the beginning, it had allowed de facto control of its Atacama territories to pass into the hands of both Chilean capitalists and Chilean workers and settlers from the earliest period of guano discoveries in the 1840s and 1850s. Ever since 1863, the pressures internally and externally were building to their inevitable climax. The increasing tempo of guano exports led to the Chilean military occupation of that year and the treaty of 1866, which gave legitimacy to Santiago's most extreme claims. Then nitrates were discovered in the jointly held area near Mejillones, and a new period of intensive penetration began, quickly followed by the establishment of the port of Antofagasta in 1868, with the consequent abandonment of Cobija. The silver strikes at Caracoles in 1870 were followed by the British-Chilean Nitrates and Railroad Company in 1872. This mining concern soon controlled the nitrate fields and succeeded in dominating the more interior desert mining camps at Caracoles as well, once its railroad had been completed. With the Bolivian coastal territories populations being made up mostly of

Chilean citizens, the province was for all intents and purposes a colony of Chile.

Bolivian authorities had allowed this unusual state of affairs to develop because of their need for funds and the inability of national capitalists to develop these previously empty deserts. But the military leaders became increasingly desperate once they had emptied the treasury and found that their source of new income could come only from these same coastal centers. On the altiplano, the power of the Oruro and Potosí miners prevented the military from increasing their exactions, lest they succumb to a direct political confrontation that would lead to their immediate overthrow. The coastal territories, by contrast, were distant and indifferent to the actual politics of the highland cities, so that the generals felt less inhibited in trying to rearrange concessions or renegotiate taxes.

It was in this context that in 1878 the Bolivian government initiated a new minimal tax on nitrates exported by the Nitrates and Railroad Company of Antofagasta. The English director, with the full backing of the Chileans, refused to pay this "unjust" and "illegal" tax. When Bolivian authorities attempted to arrest the disobedient director, he escaped to Chile. After the government announced it would confiscate company property to pay indemnity, the Chileans made their long-planned and carefully prepared move. In February 1879, Chilean troops made a successful landing at Antofagasta in support of the local Chileans, two days later seized Caracoles, and in March finally fought a major engagement with the Bolivians at the Calama oasis. In April came a formal declaration of war, and the involvement of Peru on the Bolivian side. But by this time, the entire coastal territories, including Cobija, had been seized by the powerful Chilean navy. Thus, within two months of the beginning of the conflict, the entire Bolivian littoral territories had been seized by Chile.

The War of the Pacific was just beginning, for the Chileans were intent on seizing not only the Bolivian territories but also most of the Peruvian coastal mining regions. Using as an excuse a so-called secret treaty of mutual support signed between Bolivia and Peru in 1873, the Chileans in fact had prepared for a long naval war with Peru. Chile deliberately provoked Peru into aiding Bolivia and then proceeded to concentrate all its efforts at destroying the military power

of Peru. Within hours of the formal declaration, it was blockading
southern Peruvian ports.

By the time Bolivia was able to mobilize an army of four thousand troops and get them to the coast, the Chileans were already
attacking Peru's ports of Iquique and Tacna, and the Bolivian forces
in joint operations with the Peruvians were destroyed piecemeal by
the Chilean forces. By the end of the year, Daza was at the head of
the Bolivian troops on the Peruvian coast, but he proved an even
worse general than a politician. Despite all the efforts of the troops,
the miserable quality of Bolivian generalship led to inevitable defeat,
as the Chileans by now had complete control of the seas and could
strike at will along the coast.

Although the Bolivian government thought that a highland invasion was imminent after the defeat of its major armies by the end of
1879, in fact the Chileans had no intention of crossing the Andes.
They were totally indifferent to the Bolivian highlands, and recognized that a campaign in Bolivia's heartland would be a bitter and
very costly affair resulting in few gains. Thus, the Bolivians now
became largely minor partners of the Peruvians and essentially passive spectators of the massive warfare going on in Peru. The shock
of the war, the total unpreparedness of their troops, and the disastrous campaigns of Daza as a military leader led to widespread
popular discontent. In December 1879, both the citizens of La Paz
and the troops on the Peruvian coast rose in rebellion against the
government and drove Daza from the presidency.

After intense negotiations, the rebel leaders finally agreed to ap-
point Narcisco Campero as the new president. He was the one general who had not participated in any of the rebellious activities and
who was unqualifiedly the best-trained officer in the Bolivian army.
With great reluctance, Campero took office in January 1880 and
agreed to lead the nation in its continued struggle with Chile. An
engineer trained at St. Cyr in France and at other leading European
military centers, Campero was totally committed to the elimination
of the worst aspects of militaristic rule and to the establishment
of a stable civilian regime. He quickly put down the worst of the
old officers, brought in the able liberal General Eliodoro Camacho
to support his efforts, and then immediately called into session a
special congress to give him support.

The fact that the Congress of 1880 contained among its members not only every leading political leader of the country but also mine-owners such as Gregorio Pacheco and Aniceto Arce indicated that the indifference of the highland mining elite to national politics had ended. The Pacific War had disrupted their traditionally close links with Chilean capital, interrupted their exports, and forced them to recognize that their long-term interests now required the establishment of a stable and financially sound government. Equally, the industry would soon find its expansion dependent on the creation of a modern communications infrastructure now perceived as a basic necessity for future mining growth. Only a politically stable and economically viable regime, it was thought, could provide the funding for roads and railroads, now that the chimerical wealth of the Pacific coast was lost forever. The discrediting of the old military leaders, the disaster of the state financial structure that had led directly to the costly war, and the loss of all the wealth-producing coastal centers combined to force the miners and the altiplano elite to participate directly in politics. The Pacific War disaster destroyed the power of the army and also gave the civilian politicians the justification they needed for finally and effectively bringing the national political structure into some kind of coherent relationship with the changing nature of the export and urban economies. The result was the ending of the era of military caudillo rule and the beginnings of a modern parliamentary structure with limited political participation that was dominated by civilians. Thus, some fifty-five years after establishing an autonomous republican government, Bolivia finally was to enter the age of classic nineteenth-century civilian rule.

Chapter 6

The Ages of Silver and Tin, 1880–1932

The year 1880 marked a major turning point in Bolivian history. To contemporaries, the most dramatic event of this year was the utter defeat of Bolivian arms at the hands of the Chilean invaders and the loss of its entire coastal territory in the War of the Pacific. Less dramatic but equally important was the establishment of a new government to replace the previous caudillo regime. Although the replacement of governments by military coups was a common feature of political life in the republic since its creation fifty-five years previously, the new regime did in fact mark a fundamental change in national political development. It represented the first viable republican government of a civilian oligarchic nature, which would become the norm of political life until 1934. Although the loss of its direct access to the sea would remain the most intransigent of Bolivia's international problems from 1880 to the present day, the establishment of a modern political party system and a civilian-dominated government would cause long-term political, economic, and eventually even social and cultural changes within Bolivian society, changes that were profoundly to shape its historical evolution.

The fundamental stabilization and maturation of Bolivian politics after 1880 was not the result of the war with Chile but rather derived from basic changes within the Bolivian economy that had begun at least thirty years previously. Starting approximately at mid-century, the silver mining industry had broken almost half a century of depression and had begun to reorganize on a massive scale. That reorganization involved the introduction of capital into mining in the form of modern machinery, the consolidation of many mining companies, and the liberation of production and minting from governmental control. All these developments took considerable time, since most of the capital was internally generated, and a new generation of technicians had to be created to develop the industry. By the 1860s and 1870s, Bolivian mines were reaching world standards in terms of both output and technology. This in turn led to greater needs for capital and an opening up of highland Bolivian mining to Chilean and European capital.

Having initially organized themselves politically to break the government silver monopoly over foreign sales and forced local purchases, the new mining elite began to operate as a coherent pressure group to obtain a government ever more pliable to its interests. These interests were primarily focused on creating stable governments, which could help finance the vital railroad linkages so desperately needed by the mineowners. Coming into full production just as a long-term secular price decline in silver was beginning on the world market, the new elite was constantly forced to lower costs and increase productivity. This involved the increasing use of machinery and electricity and, above all, the mechanization of transportation.

While mechanization of the mines and their electrification would be the exclusive concern of Bolivian mineowners, the problems of transport were beyond even their resources. Yet, this was a cost item that had become a major obstacle to continued Bolivian expansion. For this reason, government subsidies and international financing were imperative, and only a stable government responsive to their needs could provide the mineowners with what they wanted. For them, the war was a terrible shock, which they desired to terminate as quickly as possible and turn into an advantage for Bolivia. Closely tied to their new Chilean capitalist links, they saw the war as a fatal break with their sources of new funding as well as a serious disruption in international trade. They also blamed the incompetence of the preceding military regimes as the primary cause of the war. The end result was that the miners formed a powerful peace party and threw their weight to the enlightened General Campero, who had helped overthrow the Daza military regime in December 1879.

Thereafter they sought a rapid end to the conflict with Chile and indemnification for all lost territories to be used exclusively for railroad construction. To accomplish these ends they created a formal political party known as the *Partido Conservador*. Constructed along the lines of such movements elsewhere on the continent, Bolivia's Conservative Party was in fact not formed in the traditional mold. While formally they defended church interests, the primary concern of the Conservatives was with the creation of a powerful parliamentary regime, a civilian presidency, and a government dedicated to massive support for the construction of a communications infrastructure. Given the role of the Bolivian Church as a weak and eventually apolitical institution, a powerful and coherent anticlerical movement never developed in Bolivia. Thus, the Conservatives, unlike most of their contemporary American counterparts, engaged in few attacks on liberal anticlerical reforms and concentrated all their energies on the political and economic modernization of Bolivia.

The development of a modern export sector had a major effect on the nation's social as well as economic and political structure. The growth of the mines in Oruro and Potosí created new demands for foodstuffs and labor, and, as a result, the population of some two million Bolivians was deeply affected by the changes. A dynamism entered the area of commercial agriculture, and the opening up of railroad links created new markets for hitherto isolated areas.

All of this growth meant that the hacienda system, which like mining had been restricted for almost half a century, was able to recover and expand. At the same time, the decline in the importance of the Indian head tax, at one time the government's major source of revenue, meant that the national government no longer had a vested interest in protecting the free communities in their lands. While the land titles of the free communities had been challenged as early as the Melgarejo period in the 1860s, Indian resistance had nullified this attack, and the communities had effectively retained their control over the lands. But by the 1870s, the whites and cholos were increasing their pressure, and the new urban and mining camp markets provided the economic incentive for the landed elite to undertake a new full-scale attack. Accepting the self-serving thesis that the communities were an anachronistic system of land tenure and a barrier to social integration and modern economic growth, the elite used classic nineteenth-century liberal ideas of the need for a free peasantry holding title directly to the land. They forced on the communities in the 1880s a system of direct land purchase in which the titles to the land were held by individuals and not by the corporate group. The creation of an individualistic Indian "peasantry" holding de jure title gave the hacendados the power to break up the de facto control of the communities by purchasing a few small parcels and thus destroying the cohesion of the community. The rest was simple, with fraud and force being as common as simple purchase, and soon there was a major expansion of haciendas throughout the highlands and the adjacent subpuna valleys at the expense of traditional Indian landholdings.

The Melgarejo attack of the 1860s on the communities had been based on these same "liberal" ideas. But the 1870s and the 1880s were a period in which new capital was made available to make the attack an effective one. Thus, 1880 to 1930 saw Bolivia's second great epoch of hacienda construction. Still holding half the lands and about half the rural population in 1880, the communities were reduced to less than a third of both by 1930. The power of the free Indian communities was definitively broken. Only the marginality of the lands they still retained and the stagnation of the national economy after the 1930s prevented their complete liquidation.

This progressive decline of the community meant the loss not only of land title but also of social cohesion. While many of the haciendas had recreated the political and social organization of the free community governments, the hacienda ayllus often were powerless to protect their members from expulsion from the estates. Moreover, the need for laborers on the estates was less than the requirements had been for the former free communities. The result was an increased breakdown of Indian social norms, migration to cities, and an expansion in the urban and rural mestizo populations. The only thing preventing a total destruction of Indian culture was the continued growth of the Indian peasant populations throughout the nineteenth century. Though a series of epidemics at midcentury had slowed that growth, the disappearance of such communicable diseases as cholera by the last quarter of the century allowed for the continued strong rates of growth. In addition, the absence of public education in the countryside prior to the 1930s meant that the languages of the rural areas for all classes and groups remained the indigenous ones.

Bolivia remained predominantly a rural and Indian peasant nation well into the twentieth century, despite the growth of a modern export sector, the dramatic expansion of the haciendas, and even the growth of modern urban centers. It was estimated in the 1846 census that indigenous people represented 52 percent of the national population and they still accounted for 51 percent of the national total by 1900. Even by a generous definition of urban, Bolivia in 1900 still claimed 73 percent of its population as rural. Finally, not only was Spanish a minority language in the republic but the illiteracy rate even among Spanish speakers was extraordinarily high. With the population of seven years or older as the base, it was estimated in 1846 that only 10 percent had received some schooling, a figure that had increased to only 16 percent by 1900. If anything, these figures probably overstate the actual literacy rates of the period.

Thus, the republican governments established after 1825 were constructed on the base of a small percentage of the national population and for all intents and purposes were representative of only the Spanish-speaking literates of the republic, at best only a quarter of the national population. Given the literacy requirements for voting and the financial restrictions for holding office, the Bolivian regime was in every sense of the word a limited-participation political system with the electoral base ranging from thirty thousand to forty thousand persons in the period to 1900.

In terms of the Indian peasant masses there was nothing democratic or participatory about the republican governments that existed after 1880. In this respect, the regimes if anything were more exploitative than the previous caudillo rule, if only because the economic expansion of the white elite was always at the cost of the Indians, either as miners or as landed agriculturalists. Nor was there any dispute about this among the elite, who were deeply concerned about keeping the Indian masses out of politics and denying them access to arms or any other effective means of protest. The army, especially after its professionalization and modernization, became an indispensable tool to maintain Indian submissiveness and was called on to suppress periodic Indian uprisings.

The elite divided into political parties and even resorted to arms to overthrow governments. But such acts of conflict and violence were quite circumscribed and largely urban and intraclass affairs. Appeals from the elite to nonelite and non-Spanish-speaking groups were extremely rare. Political life for the period 1880–1934 was largely carried out within strictly defined rules. Only once, in 1899, would Indian peasants be allowed to participate even temporarily in a national political conflict, and this intervention ended in total suppression of the Indian leaders. For the Indian rural masses, political expression was confined to traditional village elders or temporary leaders of revolts who led them in their conservative "caste wars." These were uprisings confined to small communities and were exclusively defensive in nature, protesting either increases in exploitation or attacks on land rights. Until well into the twentieth century, politics was the exclusive concern of only 10 to 20 percent of the national population even as participant observers, let alone formal actors.

This impact of economic change on the political and social life of the nation also had its counterpart in national culture. Cultural life under the early republic was a much debased aspect of national existence. Social and intellectual isolation as a result of independence had its impact on elite thought and activity, just as the collapse of great centers of wealth reduced the patronage for popular art that had so flourished in the colonial period.

Although new universities had been established in the early decades of the century, the Universidad de San Francisco Xavier in Sucre continued to be the dominant intellectual center of the nation. But students from Chile and the Rio de la Plata no longer came to study, while the fields of activity remained the traditional ones of theology and law. In addition, the loss of metropolitan cadres, combined with the general decline in Bolivia's international trade and contacts, meant the loss of immediate European stimulation. Now Bolivia received European currents filtered through the experience of its American neighbors. In the first decades of the century, Bolivia reverted to a level of intellectual activity much less intense and cosmopolitan than at any other time in its history.

There were, of course, some exceptions to this general pattern, but these were isolated individuals who were educated abroad and wrote their works outside Bolivia or worked within the country in a

totally isolated environment. Also, a few distinguished foreign intellectuals such as José Joaquin de Mora, Bartolome Mitre, and Ramón
Sotomayor Valdez wrote significant poems, novels, histories, or
other literary works during their residence in Bolivia. There was,
of course, an active pamphlet literature produced in this period
that focused on immediate political or economic issues, but few
of these works showed outstanding originality or had more than
an ephemeral impact. The only exception to this general picture of
pre-1880 literate culture was José María Dalence, whose statistical
work on national society clearly earns for him the title of the father
of the social sciences in Bolivia. His efforts at the systematic reconstruction of the social and economic structure of the nation in
the 1840s were unique, and the intelligence and sophistication of
his work mark him as a social analyst conversant with the latest
European developments.

In the fields of literature and the arts, little was accomplished. The
first novel that was written by a Bolivian did not appear until the
1860s, and the first ephemeral literary journals until the end of that
decade and the beginning of the 1870s. The poetry and drama of
the time are considered by national critics to be of the poorest quality. The only exception was Nathaniel Aguirre, considered one of
Bolivia's most important novelists of the modern period. Although
Nathaniel Aguirre did begin his formal education and early writing
before 1880, his major work appeared afterward.

After 1880 intellectual life revived under the combined impact of
stable civilian government, increased national wealth, the professionalization of the occupations, and the establishment of modern
curricula in the schools. Individual writers found kindred groups,
while individuals of good families now had ample opportunity to
write and live abroad and participate in the latest Latin American
or European cultures. Thus, the Bolivian poet Ricardo Jaimes Freye
joined Rubén Darío in Buenos Aires and was a powerful voice
in the modernist movement that swept through Latin American
and Spanish letters. Such national writers as Gabriel René Moreno,
Bolivia's leading historian, found employment in the libraries and
archives of Chile, and novelists and essayists such as Alcides
Arguedas, living in Paris, became known throughout the Americas
for their new realistic approach to letters. Given the increased tempo

in the writing of poetry, literature, and the humanities in general, Bolivians came to term the writers who came of age in this period as the "generation of the 1880s." This was the first literary generation to appear in republican letters and provided an important base on which all later cultural developments could occur. The period from 1880 to 1920 was in many ways a golden age for national literature.

In the sciences, however, the traditional structures of the national universities prevented any serious development. Although Bolivia was as technologically advanced in mining as any nation in the world by the 1880s, all its machines and technologists were imported. Foreign engineers from the best schools in Europe and North America established the latest in plants and mines, but few native engineers were produced, and no significant discoveries even in metallurgy occurred in Bolivia. The problem in what Bolivians called the "exact sciences" was the total lack of an infrastructure. Low budgets and part-time teachers prevented the establishment of scientific laboratories or systematic research. Whereas novelists, humanists, and social scientists could develop out of the traditional professions of law, theology, and medicine, this was not possible for the sciences or technology. Although Bolivians trained and working abroad did participate in the development of modern science in the advanced countries, until the present day Bolivia has remained an importer of science and technology.

In the plastic arts, the economic stagnation and the concurrent decline of the Catholic Church in the first decades of the nineteenth century served to bring to an end the great age of creative artistic activity of the colonial period. Sucre's elimination of tithes and confiscation of church incomes and properties had brought church construction to a halt. With the church and wealthy pious citizens no longer available for patronage, the demand for paintings and carvings also declined. The nineteenth-century church also became less tolerant of folk Catholicism, more timid in its acceptance of native mestizo and Indian art styles, and archly conservative in its overall artistic taste. Thus, when church revenues again became significant after the victory of the Conservatives and church construction resumed, the clerics and the white elite rejected Bolivia's rich colonial artistic heritage and slavishly adopted the most reactionary of European models. The result was the stagnation of Bolivian plastic arts for most of the nineteenth century, and the elimination of the Indian and cholo artisans from significant participation in the cultural life of the nation.

The growth of the export sector of Bolivia in the second half of the nineteenth century, and especially after 1880, thus had both its positive and negative aspects in terms of the nation's political, social, and cultural life. International trade now left Bolivia with consistent surpluses for the first time in its republican history and provided the national government with stable and significant financial resources. But the growth had some disturbing effects on the national economy as well. Not only did the growth of the silver industry revive the urban centers, stimulate the hacienda economy, and reorganize the internal economic space of the society, but also it made the Bolivian economy more vulnerable to international economic forces. Both the importers of manufactured goods, who paid for their purchases with hard currency earned in mineral exports, and the government, which had become totally dependent on taxes on international trade, were now intimately involved with the fortunes of the export sector. This sector in turn became ever more vulnerable to fluctuations in international demand the more successful it became. Thus, the government, the mineowners, and the national elite were subject to international constraints, which created problems of stability over which they had little control.

Bolivia, in an economist's terms, was a classic example of an open economy. Because the bulk of internal purchasing power came from the leading mining sector, it was extremely vulnerable to changes in prices of its primary exports. Moreover, even in the mining sector, until late in the twentieth century, it was an economy dominated by one metal. To 1900, this metal was silver, and from that period until the late twentieth century it was tin. Thus, world price changes had a direct and immediate impact on the local economy. Powerful regional elites could be eliminated overnight by abrupt changes in international prices, with a consequent disruption of the very foundations of the governing elite. Bolivians learned to live with this uncertainty and tried to respond as quickly as possible to new price incentives. But the limitations of natural resources guaranteed that their response had its limits and that long-term economic progress was not inevitable for the nation as a whole.

It was this uncertainty that explains much of the behavior of the mineowners who were predominant political leaders in the post-1880 period. Faced by falling world prices and limits to their own capital, they seized control of the government and directed its undivided efforts at lowering the costs of transportation, the most expensive element in the mining process. This meant that the miners wanted a stable civilian government whose fiscal resources could be devoted to railroad construction. In this aim, the miners and their allies were successful, though in the end the total collapse of the world silver market would lead to their own downfall.

Formal political parties were necessary to the political system that the mining elite desired. These were created in the debates over the War of the Pacific. The mineowners took a pacifist pro-Chilean position from the early days of the war and grouped themselves around two key figures, Mariano Baptista, a lawyer for the mine companies, and Aniceto Arce, the largest single mineowner and producer in the nation. The anti-Chilean and antipeace group gathered their forces behind the popular Colonel Eliodoro Camacho, leader of the anti-Daza revolt and a leading Liberal theoretician.

The testing of the viability of these parties occurred in the elections of 1884. General Narciso Campero, who had directed the diminished Bolivian war effort after overthrowing Daza, completed his legal term in office, established a viable Congress, and even put into effect in 1880 the constitution written in 1878. Overseeing a completely free election, the Campero regime was able to provide the stability for the creation of two coherent parties. The eventual winner of the election, after the necessity of a congressional second count, was the maverick mineowner Gregorio Pacheco, Bolivia's second leading silver producer. With Mariano Baptista as his vice president, Pacheco initiated the era of what Bolivians have called the age of the "Conservative Oligarchy," which lasted from 1884 to 1899. During this period the two parties fully defined themselves, while the government concentrated on achieving a settlement with Chile and promoting major railroad construction.

Although Pacheco promised to remain neutral in the elections of 1888, in fact the Conservative regime threw its support behind Aniceto Arce. As a result, the election of 1888 became a violent affair, with the embittered Liberals finally abstaining altogether. Thus, there was a return to the use of violence in politics by the end of the 1880s. This resort to violence was made inevitable by the refusal of all subsequent governments to relinquish the presidency to the opposition party. Once in office and close to the only major source of income outside of mining and the haciendas, politicians refused to give up their spoils by any electoral or democratic means. Voting in all elections was open and readily controlled by central government appointees in the local districts, so presidential elections and congressional seats were easily secured. Each governing party guaranteed its majority in Congress but did permit a substantial representation of all the opposition parties as an easily supportable escape valve, which did not seriously threaten its own control over office. The presidency, however, was to be controlled at all costs, including the use of fraud. This meant that throughout the period of both Conservative and Liberal eras political violence was endemic. But it should be stressed that this violence was usually dominated by civilians of a particular party, was quite clearly limited to an urban and elite environment, and involved little bloodshed.

Given the fact that the democratic processes seemed to be in play at all times, violence also tended to be confined to periods following illegitimate electoral defeat when an opposition party, and most of the voting public, felt that the government had violated their rights. Revolts tended to be timed to changes in presidential periods, and while the tradition of *golpes* (coups d'etat) remained a permanent part of the political landscape, they did not necessarily represent the breakdown of powerful civilian rule, or the emergence of social anarchy. Although later commentators on Bolivia were to count the high number of revolts that occurred in this period and assume total disruption, in fact, the period from 1880 to 1936 was one of remarkable continuity and stability despite the periodic resort to limited violence.

The regime of Aniceto Arce (1888–92) represented the most spectacular period of Conservative rule. Arce crushed a major Liberal uprising. He then carried through a major road construction program and initiated the vital railroad link from the Chilean port of Antofagasta to the city of La Paz, thus giving Bolivia access to the sea by rail for the first time in its history. Arce also founded a military academy and systematically professionalized the army. He adopted the now common practice of allowing Liberals representation in Congress but denied them access to the presidency. The result was another fraudulent election in 1892, with Mariano Baptista, the ideologue of the Conservative Party, emerging as president. Like his predecessors, Baptista (1892–96) concentrated on railroad construction. He also signed a preliminary peace treaty with Chile and concentrated on developing Bolivia's natural rubber resources in the Acre territories. In turn, Baptista passed his government along to the last of the Conservative oligarchs, the mineowner Sergio Fernández Alonso (1896–9). By this time, however, the power of the Conservative regime, which was firmly entrenched in southern silver mining areas and the city of Sucre, was being progressively eroded by the collapse of silver prices on the world market. In turn, the Liberals found their strength progressively increasing, as they became more intimately associated with the rising urban professional classes of La Paz and with non-silver-mining groups, above all the new tin miners, intent on displacing the older oligarchy.

The rise of tin production as the primary industry of Bolivia after 1900 had its origins in developments of the Conservative era. The great age of the modern silver mining industry had seen Bolivia obtaining the latest in mining technology, from the use of power tools and electricity to the employment of modern engineers. At the same time, the silver magnates and their Conservative regimes had constructed a vital rail network connecting the mine regions to the Pacific coast.

When silver collapsed on the international market, it was possible to transfer the technology and communications to other metals. In this case a fortuitous expansion of world demand for tin in canning and a hundred other new industrial uses, along with the exhaustion of the traditional European tin mines, allowed Bolivia to capitalize on its resources and quickly and effectively respond to international demand. Tin had been an important byproduct of silver mining from the earliest times. But the costs of shipping it in bulk to European smelters had always been prohibitive, primarily because of Bolivia's primitive communications systems. The availability of cheap railroad transportation for the first time in national history meant that it suddenly became profitable for Bolivia to ship this mineral. Equally, the fact that tin occurred in exactly the same mining areas as silver, and often in the very same mines, meant that there was relatively little dislocation in terms of traditional mining enclaves or transportation networks. The transition from silver to tin was a relatively easy one for the Bolivian economy and society to make. It was less easy for the traditional elite. First of all, the growth of tin mining had a boomlike quality as production rose from quite minimal levels to massive exports in a period of less than ten years. Moreover, while the general mining zones were the same, there was a subtle but important shift of emphasis to the north, with the mines in northern Potosí and southern Oruro having the dominant role in production. Finally, the shift was so sudden and the capital invested in fixed assets so heavy that many of the traditional silver miners found it difficult to change over to tin. The result of all this was that much of the traditional silver magnate elite did not make the transition, a plethora of foreign companies entered the market, and a new group of Bolivian entrepreneurs emerged for the first time on the national scene.

All these changes created an important rupture in the national political scene. The old elite, entrenched in Potosí and its supporting town of Sucre, found itself more and more incapable of suppressing the growing popularity of the opposition Liberals. At the same time the enormous growth of La Paz, which now became the key servicing center for the new tin mining industry, even further accentuated its dominance in national economic and social life. This led to a combined Liberal and regionalist revolt in 1899, whereby the largely Liberal elite of La Paz called for local federalist rule and the overthrow of the Conservatives.

The revolt of 1899 (which lasted from December of 1898 until April of 1899) initially found the La Paz rebels isolated, with few arms and threatened by a well-equipped national army led by President Alonso. Thus, the Liberals went beyond the traditional rules of elite conflict and encouraged the Indian peasant masses to participate. Under the leadership of a principal Aymara leader, Pablo Zárate "Willke" of Sicasica, an Indian army was raised among the peasants of the Department of La Paz. This poorly armed peasant force served as a defensive screen for the Liberal forces, suffering major casualties, and allowed the Liberals time to build an effective fighting force. But the Indians had their own agenda as well, and in two communities, that of Mohoza and of Peñas, they seized disputed lands and began slaughtering local whites. The Indian mobilization spread from La Paz to Oruro, Cochabamba, and Potosí, and involved the most comprehensive Indian military activity since the time of Tupac Amaru. But once the Liberals had defeated the army of Alonso, they not only abandoned federalism, as La Paz became the de facto capital of the nation, but also they sent troops to disarm the Indians and imprisoned their leaders, thus violently suppressing the Indian mobilization.

The new century thus began with the emergence of a new political party and the creation of a new mining industry. In many ways, the Liberal regime that followed the Conservative one differed in few fundamental aspects. Both were committed to major government subsidization of transport, support for the mining industry, and development and modernization of its urban centers. Both regimes actively sought the destruction of the Indian communities and the expansion of the hacienda system, while all governments proved to be indifferent to the church question, a prominent issue in most other Latin American states in this period.

During the Liberal era, the old patterns of political participation persisted. Although congressional elections would remain relatively free, those for the presidency would be controlled, with a corresponding resort to limited violence as the only means for "out" politicians to obtain the executive office. An open press, civil liberties for whites and mestizos, and a thriving intellectual life for the elite all were maintained in the new Liberal era. But a new type of political leadership now emerged. Reflecting the complexities of the new mining era, the tin miners were far too involved in their own affairs to participate directly in national life. Meanwhile, the systematic support for education and professionalization on the part of the Conservatives finally had created a class of lawyers of sufficient number and experience to run the affairs of the government.

Thus was born what later political analysts would call the *rosca*, by which was meant a government of professional politicians operating primarily in the interests of the leading tin barons of the nation. The economic power groups were now no longer required to intervene directly in the political process to obtain their own ends. This proved essential for the local tin leaders, since it allowed them fully to concentrate on the intense and competitive struggle for domination in the Bolivian tin mines. Given the fact that there were no restrictions on foreign investments in the mines and that Bolivia was open to all types of entrepreneurs and engineers from abroad at the very beginning of its tin expansion, it is a surprise to note that Bolivians themselves emerged as the dominant mine-owners after three decades of very intense competition. At the beginning, European, North American, and even Chilean capitalists competed with local Bolivian capitalists for control of the tin mine sector. Hundreds of companies were established, many of them often working the same local mountain of tin. Yet, despite the competition of all these powerful and well-endowed opponents, the local capitalists became the dominant group in control of the industry by the 1920s.

Of the three major leaders to emerge, the most powerful unquestionably was Simon I. Patiño. Born in the Cochabamba Valley in 1860, Patiño appears to have come from an artisan and part-cholo background. He received a local secondary education and then apprenticed himself to various mining and mine equipment importing firms in the 1880s and early 1890s when the silver industry still predominated. In 1894, he purchased his first share in a tin mine in Oruro, in the canton of Uncía on the border of the province of Potosí. By 1897, Patiño had purchased full control of the mine and in 1900 struck one of the richest tin veins ever found in Bolivia. By 1905, his "La Salvadora" mine had become the single largest tin mine in Bolivia, and Patiño had assembled there a full complement of foreign technicians and the latest in refining equipment. From this initial investment, Patiño rapidly expanded his holdings both vertically and horizontally. In 1910, he bought out his neighbor, the British-owned Uncía Mining Company, and in 1924 he completed his domination of the two mining centers of Uncía and Llallagua by buying the Chilean Llallagua Company and thus achieving his permanent position of controlling almost 50 percent of national production with a labor force of over ten thousand workers.

Meanwhile Patiño turned his attention to the vertical integration of his mining operations, and, in a move rare in Latin American capitalist circles, moved to control his European refiners. After joining forces with his North American consumers, he eventually took control over the world's largest smelter of Bolivian tin, Williams, Harvey & Co., Ltd., of Liverpool, in 1916. By the early 1920s, Patiño lived permanently abroad and could by then be more accurately described as a European capitalist, given his vast non-Bolivian holdings. Nevertheless, he remained Bolivia's dominant miner, its chief private banker, and finally its most powerful capitalist until his death in the 1940s.

Of the two other leading miners who emerged to divide evenly the other half of total production, one was also Bolivian, belonging to the old silver mining family of the Aramayos, and the other was a European Jewish engineer by the name of Mauricio Hochschild. Both the Aramayo and Hochschild companies had heavy inputs of European capital, but both were – unlike the Patiño firms – largely run from Bolivia itself. While Hochschild had some investments in Chile, his primary residence virtually to the end of his career was in Bolivia, and this was his principal area of investment. For the Aramayo family as well, Bolivia was to be their primary area of activity. Thus, by the 1930s, the big three miners who dominated tin production, and a good percent of the lead, zinc, wolfram, and other local mines, were based primarily in Bolivia, or, like the Patiño companies, wholly owned by Bolivian nationals. Given the totally open nature of the Bolivian mining industry to all foreign entrepreneurs from the middle of the nineteenth century onward, such national control was truly an unusual development in the history of Latin American mining.

The withdrawal of Patiño and the other new tin magnates from direct involvement in national affairs left Bolivian politics in the hands of an elite of rising urban professional upper-middle-class individuals and representatives of the provincial landed elite (men of modest landholdings who controlled relatively few peasants, but with solid social backgrounds). Almost all of these men were trained in the law and, while committed to a liberal conception of parliamentary government and constitutional law, believed strongly in a caste system and rule by a white oligarchy.

This belief in caste was given support by the surprising stability of the social structure of Bolivia, despite all the very rapid changes that had occurred. Thus in the census of 1900, only 13 percent of the population were listed as "white." Equally, while the census implied a major growth in urban population since 1846, this was based on a rather generous definition of urban as any community over two hundred persons. The use of the more realistic definition of urban as towns over twenty thousand population, however, shows how little significant change had occurred. Thus, from 1846 to 1900, the percentage of the population living in such towns had increased from 6 percent to only 7 percent. Even La Paz, the largest urban center of the nation, had only grown to some fifty five thousand persons in 1900, or just twelve thousand more than half a century before. Although new mines had created several new towns in southern Oruro and northern Potosí, the booming mining industry in 1900, with its thirteen thousand workers, still absorbed only 1 percent of the economically active population. Thus, despite the growth of a new export sector, the expansion of new elite white and cholo classes, and the massive breakdown of Indian land ownership in the rural areas, Bolivia remained surprisingly traditional in its social makeup. The Liberals therefore felt little compulsion to concern themselves with the serious class and caste problems that divided this multiethnic society.

The Liberals were even more aggressive against the free communities than their Conservative predecessors had been, and they disarmed the Indians who had supported them in the 1899 revolt. They also justified themselves to the same economic elites by continuing powerful government support for the mining sector. This involved advocacy of free trade, minimal taxation on mining and the landed and monied elites, and government subsidization of railroad construction. Even in terms of their political ideology, the Liberals showed themselves to be no more liberal than their predecessors. Like the Conservatives before them, this new breed of political leaders also refused to relinquish presidential office to opponents. Despite the tremendous growth of the national economy, the government still represented an important source of employment, with the president the major guarantor of that employment. Thus the traditional patterns of open parliamentary elections, fraudulent presidential elections, and limited civilian-led coups to replace long-term party rule continued to be the norm.

Once in office, the Liberals adopted virtually all the positions of the previously despised Conservatives. Federalist ideology was totally abandoned and a centralist regime fully established in La Paz. In their desperation to complete the railroad network and to modernize the cities, they willingly abandoned national territories and traditional international positions, a policy that left Bolivia totally deprived of its access to the sea and rather heavily indebted as well.

The first of these major international developments was the Acre dispute. In the heart of the Amazonian rubber boom area, the Acre territories adjoined the Brazilian border and were largely populated by Brazilian migrants. When the last Conservative regime succeeded in establishing a customs house on the Acre River at Puerto Alonso and collected significant tax revenues on the rubber being shipped through to Brazil, the local tappers revolted. The Liberal regime sent in troops to the distant eastern lowlands to crush the revolt, but covert Brazilian support gave the rebels enough strength to overcome the Bolivians. The result was total defeat for Bolivian arms and the annexation of the Acre territory to Brazil in the Treaty of Petropolis in 1903 for the sum of £2.5 million sterling.

While the Liberal government had made a concentrated stand on the Acre territory, it was much less aggressive on the Chilean front. Here it went well beyond the most extreme concessions ever proposed by its Conservative predecessors in an attempt to obtain funds and terminate a longstanding and politically sensitive issue that it felt was distracting national resources. Reversing their previous irredentist stand that demanded an unqualified return of the seized territory, the Liberals signed a formal peace treaty with Chile in 1904. Bolivia agreed to cede all seized littoral lands and gave up its demands for a Pacific port. In turn, Chile agreed to construct a railroad from Arica to La Paz, provide a formal indemnification of £300,000, guarantee internal Bolivian railroad construction loans, and give up its special most-favored-nation arrangements on trade with Bolivia. Although the treaty formally resolved the Pacific territorial problem, in fact, the issue has remained an unresolved question of Andean international relations from the 1880s to the present day.

The Acre and Chilean accords gave the Liberals relative peace on the international front and extensive financial support to continue railroad construction. Internally, as well, the accords temporarily removed the major international issue of political dispute. The elimination of this divisive issue, the adoption of the basic economic program of the Conservatives, and the decline of the Sucre elite resulted in the almost exclusive domination of the Liberals in national government. So strong was the liberal movement, in fact, that there would be no coup attempts from 1899 until 1920, a record in the history of the political evolution of the nation.

The first Liberal regime was led by José Manuel Pando (1899–1904), the leader of the party in its years of opposition. While Pando kept to some of the positions of his earlier years, the men who followed were far more pragmatic and interested exclusively in power. These new men were dominated by Ismael Montes, the second president of the Liberal period, who would end by serving for two terms in office (1904–9, 1913–17). A lawyer by training, Montes represented the new breed of middle-class urban politicians. A forceful personality with a shrewd instinct for politics, he was able effectively to prevent the rise of an opposition party of "outs" until after World War I. In this effort he was aided by the tremendous boom in the economy brought about by the rising exportation of tin. This provided the funds for a major expansion of the state bureaucracy, which in turn he used to buy out all potential opposition.

The national elite was also effectively compensated by the new Liberal regime through a massive commitment to public works construction. With a positive and rather sizable balance of trade surplus, Montes was able to secure private international bank funding for governmental loans. In 1906, a huge United States private bank loan enabled Bolivia to complete its international rail connections with spurs to the major interior cities of Cochabamba and Sucre as well as the international links to the mining centers of Potosí and Oruro. A new railroad was constructed to Guaqui on Lake Titicaca, thus linking up with the Peruvian rail network. There also was major urban construction, sanitation, and lighting projects, and a buoyant economic scene until the crisis of 1913–14 on the eve of World War I.

Montes was thus able to dominate the selection of his successor, Eliodoro Villazón, and then to secure his own formal reelection in 1913. But the second Montes administration was not the unqualified triumph the first had been. Liberal administration attempts to establish a national bank created bitter pressure from a key element of the elite. Next, the sudden pre–World War I crisis in international trade caused tin production and exports to decline by a third between 1913 and 1914. Finally, adverse weather conditions caused a severe agricultural crisis in that same period. With money tight, and government revenues declining, the free-wheeling Montes found himself with an intransigent opposition that he could not buy off. Moreover, having been in power too long, he was unwilling to use tact or subtlety to calm this growing opposition. The result was the almost inevitable splintering of the Liberal Party into two formally constituted groups. The new party that emerged was given the name of Republicans and formally established in 1914.

Thus, Bolivia once again returned to a more normal two-party arrangement. But as both Montes and the founder of the new party, Daniel Salamanca, recognized, this new political grouping was a carbon copy of the Liberals. It drew its strength from the same classes; it unquestionably supported all demands of the mining establishment; and it was as racist and oligarchic as its opponents. Montes called them liberal "apostates," while Salamanca claimed his party's aim was only to guarantee free elections and the restrictions on presidential power. The final result of the return of effective two-party politics was a return to the policies of closed and fraudulent presidential elections and an ultimate resort to violence and coups on the part of the opposition.

The recovery of the post–World War I period enabled Montes to carry through his banking and financial reforms with little Republican opposition and even to win popular support among the some eighty thousand now voting in the republic in congressional and presidential elections. In 1917 he passed his government on to a more moderate successor, who proved unable to keep the Republicans under control. With strong support from disgruntled elements in the business community, the Republicans made considerable headway, and, when the last Liberal president, Gutiérrez Guerra, attempted to control the elections of 1920, the Republican Party rose in a successful revolt and ended Liberal rule.

The advent of Republican rule, which lasted until 1934, brought a subtle but important shift to the local political system. From a simple two-party arrangement, national politics evolved toward multi-party groupings. At the same time the standards of belief, based on nineteenth-century liberal ideology and supported by a strong element of racism, would slowly begin to change. Finally, the extraordinarily open nature of the national economy would mean that Bolivia was one of the first nations in the world to feel the full effects of the great crisis in the world economy known as the Great Depression.

The economic growth that had been the hallmark of both Conservative and Liberal governments initially had been confined to certain elite groups. By the second decade of the twentieth century, this growth was beginning to have an impact on the mestizo and Indian majority, but often in a conflictive manner. The expansion of the haciendas led to increasing land conflict with the community Indians, which would lead to a series of major revolts in the 1920s; but even more immediate for the elite was the organization of the first modern labor unions in Bolivia. Although organizational activities went back to the nineteenth century, Bolivia was several decades behind its neighbors in labor agitation and organization. It was not until 1912 that the first May Day celebration was held and not until 1916 and 1917 that even local urban labor confederations were established. Important national and/or urban strikes did not begin until 1920.

In the decade of the 1920s, the elite became aware, for the first time, of the existence of alternative demands and of potentially threatening groups outside the elite political arena. As political life became more complex in the Republican party era, minor parties would emerge that for the first time seriously discussed the problems and potentials of class conflict. Also the 1920s witnessed the first stirrings of European Marxist thought as it arrived in Bolivia, filtered through Argentine, Chilean, and Peruvian writers.

Almost immediately after seizing power, the Republican Party divided into two opposing branches, one led by the urban middle-class intellectual, Bautista Saavedra, and the other by the Cochabamba hacendado, Daniel Salamanca. It was Saavedra and his followers who were able to seize the initiative and take control of the government and the party in 1921. But Salamanca and his forces established a new "Genuine Republican" Party and proceeded actively to agitate against the new regime.

The increasing political tension of the 1920s combined with the deepening political crises and the beginnings of the Great Depression to unleash political violence and social conflict more intense than anything experienced in the previous decades. Saavedra had hardly been installed in office when a massive Indian uprising in the Jesús de Machaca district near Lake Titicaca led to the killing of hundreds of Indians and dozens of local whites and cholos. Saavedra unhesitatingly used full force to suppress the revolt and attacked the community governments, or ayllus, as reactionary institutions that had to be forcibly suppressed. Thus, he took a classic nineteenth-century Liberal position on the Indian question.

Saavedra, however, proved more open in his views on organized labor. He saw the unions as a potential political ally, especially as his own bases in the upper and middle classes were eroded by Genuine Republican and Liberal opposition. He appealed to these new political actors by initiating the first modern labor and social legislation in Bolivian history. He also expressed a willingness to support limited strike activity and unionization drives, a first for a national president. But faced by increasing strike activities, including serious agitation in the mines and the first general strike, which occurred in 1922, Saavedra found himself quickly withdrawing his tentative support. In fact, troops were used in a bloody suppression of miners at Uncía in late 1923, one of the first of many such mining massacres. Thus, while his labor legislation and pro-labor speeches represented some awareness on the part of the white elite that class conflict existed in Bolivia, the constant retrenchment of the regime on this issue revealed that Saavedra held this position more as a result of political expediency than because he and his followers had advanced well beyond the beliefs of nineteenth-century liberal and positivist thought.

But the 1920s were a period when other members of the elite began to adopt nontraditional positions. In 1920, the first local socialist parties were established. By late 1921, a national Socialist Party was founded that, although a small group of intellectuals with minimal labor support, nevertheless began to discuss such basic issues as Indian servitude (*pongueaje*), the legal recognition of the Indian community governments, and the rights of labor and of women. While these ideas were new and revolutionary in the

Bolivian context, they were already part of the well-established and more radical Marxist political tradition of all of Bolivia's neighbors, including Peru. The famous splintering of the Latin American Marxian socialist parties and the rise of the communist movements in South America in the 1920s, for example, found no echo in Bolivia. Bolivia did not produce its first even moderate Marxist party until the end of the 1920s, while its first formal communist party was established only in the 1950s.

Much of this early agitation was associated with a short but very intense depression that began the decade of the 1920s. Once mine production resumed by late 1922, labor agitation began to subside. Moreover, Saavedra found that the nascent organized labor movement, although finally establishing its first national federations and producing its first general strike, was too weak a support for his regime. The lower middle classes, finding themselves favored for the first time by mild social legislation, supported Saavedra. But, given his strong personality, it was inevitable that the Liberals and Genuine Republicans would join forces to oppose his regime, so he found it more and more difficult to govern.

After his first tentative moves toward alliances with labor and the lower middle classes, Saavedra turned toward foreign private capital markets to promote major development projects, the source of popularity of previous governments. He negotiated a U.S.$ 33 million private banking loan in New York for railroad, public works, and Banco de la Nación financing. These were the classic concerns of Liberals and Conservatives before him. But debt servicing for Bolivia was already high, while the terms of the loan, which included direct United States control over Bolivian taxation services, were totally unacceptable to most Bolivians. There was little question, in fact, that Bolivian negotiators had been corrupted and that, despite its excellent credit rating, the nation had been forced to pay very high interest rates. The opposition to the so-called Nicolaus loan was immediate and intense.

To add to his problems, Saavedra in the arbitrary manner of Montes also tried to resolve the great debate surrounding the petroleum concessions in the Bolivian eastern lowlands region. In 1920, the Republicans had opened up the reserve areas to foreigners after Bolivian entrepreneurs proved incapable of developing productive wells. In 1920 and 1921, North American entrepreneurs secured concessions, but these smaller companies were really fronts for the Standard Oil Company of New Jersey, which in 1921 was permitted by the government to purchase these concessions, add new ones, and establish the Standard Oil Company of Bolivia. Given all the special treatment accorded to Standard Oil, and the intense opposition of the elite to Saavedra, it was inevitable that there would be an outcry.

Thus, to all the usual issues of corruption, favoritism, and presidential domination, Salamanca and his more conservative followers added a totally new theme, that of economic nationalism. Opposition to exploitation of natural resources by foreign companies started in Bolivia virtually from the first concession ever granted in petroleum. While no outcry was ever raised over mining, and Guggenheim and other North American companies actively participated in the economy, petroleum became a special subject, and the attack against Standard Oil became part of the rhetoric of both the traditional right and the nascent left movements in Bolivia.

By the end of his term, Saavedra was desperately attempting to appease all factions. On the one hand, he helped the mineowners crush the Uncía strike in June 1923, and, on the other, he carried out a major overhaul of the mining tax structure in late 1923 and succeeded in doubling the government's taxes on tin production. In a rage, Patiño in early 1924 removed his mining company headquarters from Bolivia to the United States, incorporated Patiño Mines and Enterprises in Delaware, and even lent the government £600,000 for railroad construction, in return for a guarantee from Saavedra not to raise taxes further for five years.

All of this activity of Saavedra was to no avail, and despite every attempt to control his successor and even prorogue his term, Saavedra was forced to turn his regime over to his own party candidate, Hernando Siles, whom he opposed. The subsequent Siles period was one of active political evolution and a continued splintering of the traditional parties. Faced by Saavedra's control of the Republican Party, Siles created his own Nationalist Party grouping. He supported the University Reform movement, a major innovation of university governance and curriculum, and in 1928 radical students established the first FUB (National Federation of University

Students of Bolivia). Both the socialists and the FUB, though still small groupings of intellectuals, were now suggesting radical transformations of society, with both calling for agrarian reform and the end of rural labor feudalism. They urged socialization of the natural resources and changes in the definition of private property and gave strong support to the nascent labor movement.

At the same time, the economic scene began to deteriorate at an alarming degree. In the period 1926–9, the government faced increasing budget deficits and growing difficulties in meeting its international debt obligations. This was occurring just as the price of tin on the international market had peaked and had begun its long secular decline into the catastrophe of the Great Depression. In an attempt to meet this crisis, whose extent was as yet unknown, the government resorted to both traditional and some fairly radical measures. In 1927 and 1928, with the backing of specially created taxes, new United States private bank loans were secured. In the same year the government adopted the reforms proposed by the United States Kemmerer mission and finally established a government-controlled Central Bank to oversee all aspects of the national money supply. In addition, the temporary flareup on the disputed Chaco border with Paraguay in late 1928 both presaged more bitter conflicts and gave Siles the excuse to use a formal state of siege to control his internal enemies. The border incident was a bloody affair, forcing Siles to call up the reserves and order an open reprisal. But he did not want a full-scale war to develop and negotiated an Act of Conciliation with Paraguay in early 1929.

The surge of patriotism, the imposition of states of siege, and the political and economic reforms carried out by Siles had little effect on national politics. Siles proved to be too much in the traditional mold to permit the free play of democratic forces. His regime galvanized the Liberals, the Genuine Republicans, and the Saavedrista Republicans into a temporary united front. Meanwhile, in 1929, Bolivia reached its all-time record output of forty-seven thousand tons of tin exported but at a price that was below that of the early years of the decade. Quoted at $917 a ton in 1927, it had dropped to $794 a ton in 1929, and would eventually bottom out at $385 per ton in 1932. Government revenues followed tin price declines. By 1929, some 37 percent of the government budget was going for foreign debt servicing and another 20 percent for military expenditures, leaving little for bare government necessities, let alone for public works or national welfare.

Siles tried to continue in office beyond his presidential term. In mid-1930, he announced formal plans to prorogue his government by having parliament formally elect him for a new term. He then handed the government over to a military junta to oversee his formal reelection. But opposition to this move was universal. For the first time in national politics university students made their power felt by rioting against the government. In response the army rose in rebellion, and the junta leadership was forced to flee. In the midst of the disorders there was even an invasion of Marxist radicals at the southern frontier town of Villazón, which found some echo in the urban labor movement. Thus, the fall of Siles involved more complex opposition forces than had been manifested before then. Although the traditional and conservative forces would ultimately gain victory over the popular 1930 revolt, it was nevertheless the first break in the unified political ideology of the white oligarchy and would eventually lead to an erosion of basic traditional beliefs.

Daniel Salamanca eventually emerged as the presidential candidate of the coalition of an all-party alliance. A politician of the classic mold, Salamanca was even less attuned to the new developments on the student and labor fronts than either Saavedra or Siles. He was a rural landowner from Cochabamba, a famous parliamentary orator, and otherwise an extremely intemperate and unbending nineteenth-century style Liberal. His only immediate programs were moral government and free elections, meaningless slogans that he violated as rapidly as his predecessors had.

But the oligarchic republican government based on limited political participation that had been established by the Conservatives in the 1880s was beginning to come apart by 1930. There now emerged a subtle but clearly important shift in political ideology of the governing classes. The university student reform had brought radical Marxist thought into the homes of the white elite for the first time in national politics. The labor movements began to get national attention with ever more severe strike activity, leading to military intervention in the mines and open warfare. Even the Indian peasantry had been unusually restive with two quite massive uprisings, the one at Jesús de Machaca in 1921 and one at Chayanta in Potosí in 1927.

In many ways, the Depression would give a reprieve to the Salamanca government. Massive layoffs of workers forced many miners back into the countryside and into subsistence farming again, while the Depression wiped out most of the gains of the weakly organized labor movement. Indian peasants grew more passive as the great hacienda expansion age drew to a close with the end of heavy capital investments in rural landholdings. But the university youth would not quietly disappear, and the increasing impact of the Depression created a new awareness that Salamanca was incapable of responding to, except in total fear and repression. By the standards of the other countries of South America, Bolivian radicalism remained weak and relatively unsophisticated and a good generation or two behind developments in bordering countries. But the consistent refusal of Salamanca and his followers to offer a hearing to these ideas, unlike the Republicans of the 1920s, meant that the marginal radical and reformist groups would find themselves forced into an even more violent confrontation with the traditional political system. Nevertheless, these groups were still only a small sector of the elite society and might never have become the threat they did had not Bolivia undergone the greatest military disaster of its history under the leadership of Daniel Salamanca. The Chaco War in the midst of the Great Depression was to provide the crucial disruptive force by which the traditional system of the 1880–1934 period would finally be destroyed.

First of all the Tin industry went into severe decline. By 1929 Bolivia, with three other tin-producing regions – Nigeria, Malaya, and Indonesia – provided close to 80 percent of world production. But Bolivia had the lowest-grade ore, the highest transportation costs, and was therefore the highest-cost tin producer. It thus felt the declining prices first and also found it impossible to force the other major producers to cut production voluntarily, since at negative prices for Bolivians, the others could still obtain some profit margins. In July 1929, at the urging of Patiño, a voluntary Tin Producers Association was formed by the private companies working in the four major centers of production. They agreed to production cutbacks, which all three major Bolivian companies eagerly carried out in late

1929 and early 1930. But the non-Bolivian companies did not follow suit, so by mid-1930 the voluntary scheme was considered a failure.

With free market conditions intolerable and voluntary restrictions impossible to achieve, the producers decided in late 1930 to take the drastic measure of demanding government participation in the production control scheme. This was a major and abrupt change from the private mineowners' belligerent stand against any kind of governmental intervention in private enterprise. For the first time, the Bolivian government would be assigned not only minimal taxing privileges but also full control over production quotas, which would lead in the following decades to full marketing control over foreign sales. Clearly this was an act of desperation by which the main producers hoped to retain direct control over governmental decisions that affected them. But equally, it made possible the first really powerful intervention of the government in mining affairs since the mid-nineteenth century. Although there would be rough agreements over quotas, the much reduced production schedules for all the firms meant that any one of them could easily and quickly increase production if their market quotas were changed by governmental decree. This introduced a special tension into the relationship between the big three and brought their competitive conflicts into the very halls of government. The big miners were now to pay considerably more direct attention to the local political scene than they had in some time, so they began to support differing factions in the elite itself.

Since there were only three major governments involved – Bolivia, the Netherlands, and Great Britain – it turned out that a forced quota production system could be successfully carried out, and on March 1, 1931 the International Tin Control Scheme went into effect, just a few days before the inauguration of the new Salamanca government. Bolivian production was drastically reduced, creating a massive internal economic crisis for the republic. Although the scheme of restricting production eventually reduced the world's unsold stock of tin and finally stabilized the price, it would not be before 1933 that Bolivian production would slowly begin to return to even moderate production levels.

All of these international changes and the resulting shock to the local economy were closely followed by the Bolivian elite. The Junta government experimented with public works schemes and fully supported all Patiño's curtailment of production plans. It also cut budget outlays to the barest minimum and paid serious attention to the various national recovery projects being tried out elsewhere in the world. Of all the groups engaging in this debate about the national economy, the Liberals offered the most concrete proposals. Although their approach was an orthodox one, they suggested serious government intervention. But Salamanca seemed oblivious to the whole issue. Constantly asked what his economic ideas were, he replied evasively about the need for moral government. Such vacuous ideas might have been fine in times of growth with a stable social order but were meaningless in the contemporary context. As a result, his Genuine Republicans suffered total defeat in the congressional elections of 1931 and the Liberals had an absolute majority of votes. The rigid Salamanca suddenly found himself faced by a hostile Congress completely outside his control, with an economy he little understood, and a society suffering a severe malaise for which he could provide no solutions. He would also alienate the traditional elite parties by making his government a partisan one, despite the all-party support that had brought it to power.

He not only rejected Liberal support, but also he announced to a rather startled public that the primary problem facing the country was not the economic crisis but radicalism and communism. This obsession with the "red" threat was something entirely new on the part of a traditional politician. At the same time, Salamanca took an openly hostile stand against organized labor and forced the dissolution of the legal Telegraph Workers Union during a strike, and suppressed a sympathetic general strike of the La Paz labor federation. But the economy would not go away as an issue and the government refused to pay its employees in anything except promissory notes, and in late July Salamanca announced that Bolivia was defaulting on its external debt.

Despite his extreme retrenchment in normal government services, Salamanca proposed the most ambitious and expensive scheme for military penetration of the Chaco ever envisioned by a Bolivian president. Because large areas of the Chaco were still unexplored and unoccupied by either Bolivia or Paraguay, this new, more aggressive stance proposed by Salamanca meant a major shift in national policy from a largely defensive to offensive position. As the internal economic and political scene became ever more tense, Salamanca gave more of his attention to the Chaco border question, which he saw as easily soluble with firm righteous stands, while the economic situation became ever more complex and seemingly insoluble.

On July 1, 1931, Salamanca used a typical border incident to break diplomatic relations with Paraguay, a move many felt was overly aggressive. Then, in his presidential address in August, he acknowledged the continued decline in government revenues, stressing that virtually all government services had been cut, but then went on to announce an expansion of the military budget. He also proposed an open policy of total suppression of union or strike activity among the organized working classes of the nation.

In June, Salamanca brought Demetrio Canelas, an Oruro party leader, into the Ministry of Finance. Canelas broke with the conservative policy of the previous months and pressed Salamanca on the need for more radical economic measures to combat the crisis. His primary proposal was for an inflationary monetary solution which was then being adopted by many countries of the world. He wanted Bolivia to get off the gold standard, adopt inconvertible paper money, and increase the money supply. The Liberals at first opposed these changes, especially as they controlled the Central Bank as well as Congress. But they were forced to accept them when Great Britain itself announced in September that it was going off the gold standard. As part of the sterling block, Bolivia was forced to do the same. But prices immediately started rising, and the government position became extremely unpopular. In response, the Liberals put new pressure on the government, and, after a series of aggressive parliamentary interpellations of ministers, forced the Salamanca government to come to terms. Those terms included a formal biparty pact and an agreement to give the Liberals veto power over all economic decisions.

Frustrated in his initiatives in the economic sphere, Salamanca then attempted to implement his ideas on authoritarian government. Claiming that there was a communist menace that few other traditional party leaders seemed aware of, he proposed at the end of 1931 to enact a law of "Social Defense." This was a bill granting extraordinary powers to the president to deal with political opposition on the left. The reaction to this proposal was intense. In January 1932 mass demonstrations by labor, the small leftist parties, the students, and the *saavedristas* finally forced the government to withdraw the projected law. At the same time, Salamanca failed in his attempt to float an international loan to ease government deficits and in March 1932 was forced to accept three Liberal-appointed ministers in his cabinet and the ouster of Canelas.

Salamanca, embittered about the national political scene, turned even more aggressive on the international front. He built up the army systematically at the expense of every other government service. He also pushed the army into an ever more expansive exploration and settlement program in the Chaco. So clearly aggressive were Bolivia's intentions that throughout the early months of the year, radical groups began calling for an end to the warlike preparations. But on this issue there was a split between the fringe radicals and student groups and the more traditional parties. The saavedristas, who now called themselves the Republican Socialist Party and who had joined the left against the Social Defense Act, fully supported Salamanca's Chaco adventure, while the Liberals also gave Salamanca undivided support in his buildup of the army.

Thus Salamanca found himself with strong traditional backing and decided to push this backing to the absolute limit. In May and June, a major linkup between two army divisions led to a typical minor clash over an important watering spot in the Chaco. Bolivian troops ousted an already entrenched Paraguayan force. Later claiming that a preexistent Paraguayan position did not exist, the Bolivian army refused to relinquish the new post and began a major and rapid buildup in the area to oppose the expected counterattack by the Paraguayans. In the last days of June, the expected counteroffensive occurred and was beaten back by the Bolivians. Up to this point, this incident was no different from dozens of others, and the number of troops involved was quite small and the conflict quite limited. Standard procedure now called for formal negotiation, but at this point Salamanca decided to break with precedent and push for all-out war. By late July, full-scale warfare had begun.

This decision had a great deal to do with Salamanca's bitter political frustrations in national politics and his perception that increasing economic crisis would lead to social anarchy. The fact that in May the International Tin Control organization adopted the radical procedure of prohibiting all tin production for the months of July and August and of reducing production thereafter to one-third of 1929 output meant that the most extreme cutbacks were proposed just on the eve of Salamanca's decisions concerning the Chaco. In response to the two-month closing and the extremely unbalanced trade situation that resulted, the government was forced to take complete control over all gold dealings of its citizens and forced mineowners to hand over 65 percent of their letters of exchange on foreign currencies to the Central Bank. There is little question that this most extreme shutdown of the national export economy was of crucial importance in the decisions taken by the government in the following weeks.

There is no doubt, from all the documentation that has emerged since the war, that Salamanca and the Bolivian government deliberately escalated a typical border incident into a full-scale war to the surprise of even the Paraguayans. It is also evident that, when the final decisions were made, it was Salamanca who, against the written advice of his general staff, forced the conflict beyond any peaceful settlement into what would become Bolivia's most costly war in its republican history.

In popular belief, however, it was almost immediately accepted as truth that the Chaco War was the result of a basic conflict over oil lands between Standard Oil of New Jersey, with its support of Bolivian claims, and Royal Dutch Shell, which was entrenched in Paraguay. There is no doubt that toward the end of this long and bloody conflict, when victorious Paraguayan troops were reaching the end of the Chaco region and approaching the Andean foothills, oil became an important concern in their war aims. But until late 1935 the war was fought hundreds of miles from the nearest fields. Moreover, it was evident after the war that Standard Oil of New Jersey had illegally sold Bolivian oil to Argentina and thence to Paraguay, while claiming it could produce nothing for Bolivia from these same fields. The cause of the war, rather, must be found first in the complex political conflict within Bolivia and the strains caused by the Great Depression on a fragile political system; and its continuation can be understood only in terms of Argentine support for

Paraguayan aims. The ability of Argentina to prevent peace moves until the end, along with continued Paraguayan successes, meant that once the war began Bolivia had little ability to stop its onslaught. That the causes of the war were other than those claimed at the time does not in fact reduce the vital importance of the general belief in the Chaco War as an oil conflict. In the postwar period fundamental political and economic decisions, including the confiscation of Standard Oil in 1937 and the creation of a state oil monopoly company, were the direct result of this belief. Much of the bitterness of the postwar political scene, as well, was very much defined by this conception.

More important than the cause, however, were the consequences of the conflict. The Chaco War, in effect, destroyed the political system that had been in existence in Bolivia since 1880. The end of the war saw the collapse of both civilian government and the traditional political parties. Ideas that had previously been the coinage of only a small group of radical intellectuals now became the concern of much of the politically aware youth and ex-combatants. So distinctive was this change that Bolivians themselves would refer to the groups that came to maturity in the Chaco war as the "Chaco generatio." The Indian question, the labor question, the land question, and the economic dependency on private miners became the new themes of national debate rather than the old issues of civil government, honest elections, and railroad construction. These discussions led to the creation of new parties and revolutionary movements in the late 1930s and 1940s and finally to the social revolution of 1952.

The Chaco War also marked an important turning point in the economic history of the nation. The Great Depression and the resulting Chaco conflict marked the end of the expansion and even the capitalization of the mining industry. Thereafter, production and productivity began to decline in an industry that saw virtually no change in its structure or patterns of investment until 1952. In the rural areas as well, the relative stagnation of the national economy brought an end to the great hacienda expansion boom, which had lasted from the 1880s until the late 1920s. By the end of this period landless peons had probably doubled, and the number of free community Indians was now considerably less than the number of peasants without land. Thus a fundamental restructuring of the rural economy had occurred in the period 1880–1932, but it ended before the complete destruction of the free communities and provided an endless source of conflict in the post–Chaco period as the haciendas went on the defensive.

All the growth that had occurred as a result of the great tin expansion had little impact in modernizing the society as a whole. It was still estimated that by 1940 over two-thirds of Bolivians were primarily outside the market economy, and even as late as 1950 the number of urban artisans in the national economy equaled the number of factory workers. Although two-thirds of the economically active population were engaged in agriculture, Bolivia was still a net importer of foodstuffs, including traditional highland root crops. Thus, while the tin boom did affect the third of the nation that was urban and Spanish-speaking, its multiplier effects had little impact on the rural population, except possibly to lower their standard of living as a result of the corresponding expansion of the latifundia system.

Bolivia entered the Chaco War as a highly traditional, underdeveloped, and export-dominated economy and emerged from that conflict with the same characteristics. But it changed from being one of the least mobilized societies in Latin America, in terms of radical ideology and union organization, to one of the most advanced. The war shattered the traditional belief systems and led to a fundamental rethinking of the nature of Bolivian society. The result of that change in largely elite thought was the creation of a revolutionary political movement that embraced some of the most radical ideas to emerge on the continent. The war also would create the climate for the development of one of the most powerful, independent, and radical labor movements in the Americas. From these perspectives, the Chaco War, like the War of the Pacific before it, would prove to be one of the major turning points in Bolivian historical development.

Chapter 7

Disintegration of the Established Order, 1932–1952

The Chaco War began on 18 July 1932, when Salamanca announced to the startled nation that the Paraguayan forces had seized a Bolivian fort in the Chaco. That this fort was in reality a Paraguayan one that had been seized by the Bolivians at the end of May was ignored. Salamanca ordered a major offensive that night and carried out a state of siege. At this point, the Bolivian General Staff refused to endorse Salamanca's war plans. It claimed that the army was unprepared for a major assault, and considered the escalation of the conflict to be out of all proportion to the incident. So intense was the debate between the general staff and the president that Salamanca was finally forced to acknowledge full responsibility for all his decisions relating to the initiation of the conflict in a formal written document. Having thus absolved itself from any responsibility for the assault and subsequent actions, the general staff declared these actions were against the national interests, but agreed to carry out Salamanca's decisions.

Despite Paraguayan and international protests of the legitimacy of Bolivian claims, local leaders supported Bolivia's position and attacked Paraguay as the initiator of the bellicose situation. Manifestos of nationalist support were signed by everyone from Alcides Arguedas on the right to Franz Tamayo and Carlos Montenegro on the left. There were also major patriotic demonstrations in all the urban centers as the economic crisis was momentarily forgotten. To guarantee unanimity, the government used a state of siege to round up labor and political radicals, either jailing or exiling such men as Ricardo Anaya, José Aguirre Gainsborg, and Porfirio Díaz Machicao, among others. Those of the left not jailed or exiled were immediately conscripted into the army and sent to the front lines. Thus, in one quick gesture, Salamanca had seemingly exterminated the left, but the disastrous war effort would bring it back stronger than ever.

Despite Bolivia's mobilization, the Paraguayans assumed that they were dealing with a typical border incident. After retaking their fort in July, they returned to Washington and expected to continue negotiations on a nonaggression treaty. But Salamanca refused to budge, and three major forts of undisputed Paraguayan ownership were seized. These three forts – Boquerón, Corrales, and Toledo – were vital to Paraguay's defensive line. Their seizure necessitated a full-scale response, which the Bolivian general staff had recognized as inevitable and leading only to total war. But Salamanca thought that this one bold act had destroyed all Paraguayan initiative and he now called a halt to military operations early in August. There now developed a bitter debate between the generals and Salamanca as to what had really transpired on the first contacts between the troops, who was to blame for the mobilization, and what were the ultimate war aims of the Bolivians. The language of accusation and recrimination was as violent as it would ever become and clearly indicated an extreme pessimism about the whole affair, which seemed to imply an ultimate and disastrous defeat for Bolivian arms. And all this occurred in the first month of the war before Bolivia had lost a single major battle!

From such a beginning, the war quickly deteriorated into a corrupt, bloody, and bottomless defeat and disaster for Bolivia. Realizing that Salamanca meant to hold their forts indefinitely, the Paraguayans ordered a general mobilization and initiated a major counteroffensive. By September, the Bolivian advance was totally stopped and the battle of Boquerón was begun. Some six hundred Bolivian troops were successfully encircled by Paraguayan troops in their old fort. With only fifteen hundred troops in all on the Chaco front, the Bolivians were unable to do anything about the encirclement. At the end of a month the troops were forced to surrender, and a shocked nation received the news in the first days of October.

The effect of the fall of Boquerón was immediate and dramatic. Already literate public opinion was subjected to rumors of Bolivian duplicity; was disturbed by the deliberate political use Salamanca was making of the war; and was made increasingly uneasy by the tense social situation as military conscription began to be felt in all levels of society. The news of the Boquerón defeat thus led to major rioting. On October 4, some twenty thousand antigovernment rioters demanded the resignation of Salamanca and the return of the German General Hans Kundt, former adviser to the Bolivian army, whom the salamanca Republicans had expelled in 1930. Four days later Congress also demanded the return of Kundt to lead the troops. Two major field officers, David Toro and Carlos Quintanilla, even demanded the dismissal of Salamanca himself. Although the rebellion was eventually stopped, the omnipotent power of Salamanca, which had lasted in its new form all of four months, was over, and the president was forced again to ask the Liberals to join him in a coalition government.

Before such a multiparty government could be formed, however, another Bolivian fortress was taken. By late October, the Paraguayans had not only recaptured all their old forts but had now carried the offensive into Bolivian territory, outflanking and finally seizing the Bolivian fortress of Arze. The Arze battle was a total rout of Bolivian forces. The result of this major defeat was a breakdown in government and out-party negotiations. The Liberals and opposition Republicans attacked Salamanca, and he in turn encouraged mob violence against their newspapers. In November, Salamanca also outlawed all unions and labor federations. But by December he had no more options left, and was forced to recall General Kundt from Europe, thus reducing his own role in the military to that of civilian adviser.

Although Kundt was an excellent organizer and rapidly rebuilt the shattered Bolivian army, he was a poor tactician and strategist. Having created a powerful force, he then spent six months wrecking it in a headlong assault on the impregnable Paraguayan fortress of Nanawa, in a campaign that lasted from January to July 1933. Not only did the Paraguayans hold this fortress, but they destroyed the forces attacking them and proceeded to outflank the Bolivians in other regions, inflecting a further series of defeats. By midyear in 1933, the Paraguayans not only were destroying division after division but also were making tremendous territorial inroads into the Bolivian-held part of the Chaco. By the end of the year Kundt was dismissed and General Enrique Peñaranda given charge of the army, with David Toro as his key adviser. But the change only deepened national pessimism. Under Kundt, seventy-seven thousand men had been mobilized, of whom fourteen thousand died in action, ten thousand were made prisoners, six thousand deserted, and thirty-two thousand were evacuated because of sickness and wounds. This left seven thousand troops in the field, with eight thousand in rearguard support services – a pitiful and demoralized remnant of a once-powerful and well-equipped army.

Under Peñaranda, a third army of some fifty-five thousand men was organized, and for six months a relative stalemate occurred. But in August 1934, the able Paraguayan leader General Estigarribia finally found a weak spot in Bolivian defenses and broke the Bolivian Chaco line. From this point on, the Paraguayans made a mad dash to the Andean foothills, and the war turned into an open struggle for oil, as the Paraguayans were finally within striking distance of the Bolivian deposits. In the four months from August to November, the Paraguayans captured more territory than they had ever claimed in their most extreme prewar demands.

By late November Salamanca had engineered the election of his loyal supporter Franz Tamayo and was intent on completing his last acts in office by destroying military opposition to himself. Specifically, he traveled to the Chaco to force Peñaranda and Toro to give up control over the army. What occurred instead was that on November 25, 1934, the army arrested Salamanca at their headquarters at Villa Montes and forced him to resign. The government was then handed over to the vice president and Liberal Party leader Tejada Sorzano.

The immediate consequences of this military revolt were extremely favorable for the Bolivian war effort. Tejada Sorzano was both an excellent administrator and an able politician. He quickly organized an all-party cabinet, which even included Salamanca's supporters, got the tin baron Aramayo to take over the Ministry of Finance, and then gave unqualified support to the army command. Bolivia's war finances were greatly strengthened, the internal conflicts on the home front were ended, with even the attack on the far left was stopped, and a united front was created. On the military side, Bolivia was now finally close to its own supply lines, fighting in well-known and settled territories, and facing an enemy that was now dangerously overextended and badly underfinanced.

With the fall of Salamanca the war slowly ground to a halt. The Paraguayans invaded Tarija and Santa Cruz and even seized some of the oil fields in early 1935. But without Villa Montes this advance could not be maintained, and a major battle for this southern Bolivian stronghold ensued. At this point there emerged Bolivia's most effective military leader of the war, Major Germán Busch, who took over the planning for the defense of the southern command area. Not only did he defeat the Paraguayans at Villa Montes, but he was able to mount a major counteroffensive, which cleared all the Paraguayans from Tarija and Santa Cruz and led to the recapture of all of the oil centers previously seized.

At this point both sides proved ready for peace. Paraguayan resources were exhausted, and the defeat at Villa Montes meant that they could never take the Andean foothills region. At the same time, it was evident that continued warfare might cause some losses to their Chaco gains, as the new military leadership on the Bolivian side seemed to have revived Bolivian military abilities. For the Bolivians, the recapture of all the non-Chaco territories was enough of a victory. Although the government, unlike the Paraguayan regime, was well endowed financially, from mining taxes on the reviving tin industry and could have continued the war for some time, the entire nation wanted peace. The bitterness of the Salamanca years and the general belief that the war was fought for Standard Oil and was most likely initiated by Bolivia itself had destroyed national faith in the war effort. A peace conference was organized in Buenos Aires in May 1935, and on June 14 of that year a formal peace treaty was signed.

Thus ended, almost to the month, three years of the most bitter conflict in Bolivia's history. Although Bolivia lost more valuable territory in its war against Chile in the nineteenth century, the fighting then had been minimal and the impact on the population itself slight. In the Chaco conflict, the losses were major. Over sixty-five thousand were killed, deserted, or died in captivity, or roughly 25 percent of the combatants on the Bolivian side. These losses were out of a total population of just about two million persons, a ratio equal to what the European nations had suffered in World War I. Moreover, the very validity of national institutions had been deeply challenged by the war. The army itself had been organized by caste. The whites were the officers, the cholos the subofficials, and the Indian peasants the troops. The only group to violate these divisions were the workers and radicals seized by Salamanca who were sent to the front lines. Thus, the very caste system of the national society was fully maintained on the front lines, which created a severe gulf between commanders and troops and further encouraged the notorious corruption of white officers. For the few whites who did serve in the front line, the experience was a bitter one and committed many of them to a radical stance toward the racial divisions of their society. For the Indians it meant the continuation of the standard patterns of exploitation. Many troops deserted, and there were even several major frontline mutinies. But when the war ended the Aymara and Quechua troops, desperate to return home, went back to their farms and were reintegrated into the communities as quickly as possible.

But for the cholos and nonmilitary whites, there was a different story. Many of these formerly committed individuals found themselves alienated from the traditional system. They had been appalled by the corruption and incompetence of the high command and shocked by the revelations of Bolivian duplicity in the war. To these youths of the "Chaco generation," their sacrifice had been in vain. They emerged from the war bitter at the army leadership that had led them into the disaster and frustrated with the political system that had created the whole Chaco imbroglio. The most immediate release for this sense of bitterness and frustration was a great outpouring of social realist novels that began to appear as early as the first months of the war and continued to dominate national literature well into the next decade. Bitter proletarian novels became the Chaco genre, and in novel after novel, the cruelty of the war, the waste of lives, the hunger and thirst, the incompetence, treason, and cowardice of the officer caste became common themes.

The Chaco novel did not arise phoenixlike out of the ashes of the Chaco defeat, but had its origins in the realistic and bitter novels of the generation of 1880. At the peak of Liberal peace and euphoria in the first decades of the century, writers such as Armando Chirveches, Alcides Arguedas, and Jaime Mendoza had published novels with themes of political corruption of elite politics and the exploitation and oppression of the mineworkers and the Indian peasants. Nor were such class themes the only ones explored by this generation, for Adela Zamudo in both poetry and the short story explained the problems of sexual discrimination. Building on this heritage, the writers of the 1930s were able to express themselves in an idiom already well appreciated by the literate elite. The Chaco novel brought to them an intimate experience of the Chaco disaster. As much as any single form of political ideology or revolutionary propaganda, the realism of the Chaco War novel had a profound impact on the youth and intellectuals who made up the core of elite thought.

But the novelists were not the only voices raised in bitter protest. The disaster also created a new radical political movement that offered a host of challenging ideas to the national elite. Although Salamanca had done everything possible to destroy this movement, the disaster of the Chaco War gave the left an important role to play. The prewar radical left maintained a remarkably active frontline antiwar and antitraditional-society propaganda, which in fact proved so successful that they were able to encourage desertion of troops and to become a major ideological force in the postwar era.

This radical reinterpretation of the Bolivian reality was a fundamental attack on the racist consensus of Bolivian society and on the oligarchic nature of its political and economic life. The war was blamed on the multinational corporations, specifically Standard Oil of New Jersey. It was also considered to be the death gasp of the old order that, to defend its power, had taken the nation into an international conflict. For this group of radical thinkers, among whom the most prominent in this early period was Tristan Marof, the Indigenista and Marxist ideology of the Peruvian José Mariategui provided a framework for the reappraisal of Bolivian society. This conception of Andean reality held that the problem of the Indian was really a problem of exploitation and land; that the Spanish and their followers had robbed the Indians of their lands and attempted to destroy their culture in order to exploit them; and that the passivity and backwardness of the Indians was in fact exclusively due to their exploitation. The only way to break this exploitation was to destroy the haciendas and return the lands to their Indian workers. Many of these writers also argued that so long as private individuals controlled the minerals, which were the major source of national wealth, the nation would not benefit from these nonrenewable resources. It was held that the state itself was run by the *rosca*, a derogatory term that implied a group of politicians and lawyers who ran the state apparatus for the miners and *hacendados*. The nondemocratic oligarchic regimes that governed Bolivia were there by necessity, since this was the only way the economic mandarins could fully exploit the nation. While Marof and others offered different solutions, all talked about worker, miner, and Indian peasant alliances whose ultimate aim would be *"Tierras al Indio"* (lands to the Indians) and *"Minas al Estado"* (mines to be owned by the State).

While few initially accepted all of the arguments proposed by the radical left, the enunciation of the primary problems of national society created the framework in which all future debate would occur. The theme of the nationalization of the mines was now firmly implanted in the political consciousness of the whites and cholos, and even the issue of the Indian and their just claims was now accepted as legitimate.

That these ideas found a responsive chord can be seen in the subtle shift in the nature of postwar politics. Indian uprisings, for example, became less classic caste wars and more social protest movements in which pan-Indian rights were the prime issue. The increasing class consciousness on the part of Indian peasants was matched by a more radical Marxist commitment of both labor organizers and young radicals. So intense was the activity of desertion committees and antiwar groups that from their Argentine exile many of these movements finally coalesced into more permanent political movements. Thus in 1934, at a special Congress in Cordoba, Argentina, was born the first of the major postwar radical parties, the *Partido Obrero Revolucionario* (POR; or Revolutionary Workers' Party), under the leadership of Tristan Marof and José Aguirre Gainsborg. Although a small grouping of radical exiles, this was the first party of the Chaco generation to be created, and in later decades it would form the vanguard of the revolutionary movement.

Although the POR would soon be riven by internal disputes over Trotskyism, its ideological impact was impressive. The utter defeat of Bolivian arms, despite greater manpower, wealth, and resources, was a shock to most literate persons. But even worse was the much publicized corruption and incompetence of the officer class, which led to the wholesale slaughter or capture of troops through starvation and incompetence. There was surprisingly little hatred for the Paraguayans but much hostility shown by all Bolivians toward their own leaders. It was this aroused and bitter public that at the end of the war demanded an accounting from all who had led them to this defeat. And when that accounting was not forthcoming, they sought to change the social, economic, and political order of the society in which they lived.

With the signing of peace in June 1935, all these political tensions came to fruition in the collapse of the traditional party arrangements. While the army had asked Tejada Sorzano to prorogue his presidential term until the arrangement of a definitive peace, the older parties had opposed the moves, and the saavedrista expected to return to rule. But there were now a host of new parties, which took on exotic names and symbols, but represented the youth and veterans who had formerly made up key supportive elements of the older parties. Suddenly the word "traditional" became an epithet for all the prewar oligarchic parties, and everything from Italian corporatist to indigenista and Marxist ideologies became the currency of those who had formerly supported the old order. Not only were the supporters of the recently deceased Salamanca blamed for all the ills of the war, but so, too, were the Liberals and various Republican parties.

A bitter veterans' movement also emerged as a powerful political force demanding accountings for the defeat. A vitally revived labor movement demanded basic rights, and a nervous officer corps insisted on protection of their threatened caste. These three major power groups feared and opposed a return to traditional politics. The parties themselves could no longer mobilize the popular elite support to defuse these opponents, for that support had now fragmented into a host of new reformist, fascist, and radical groupings. Even among the traditional parties themselves, there were important changes. While the Liberals held firm to classic positions and supported Tejada Sorzano, the old Siles Nationalist Party, the most reformist of the old groupings, was dissolved, thus cutting any formal link between the new left and labor and the traditional politicians. The Saavedra Republicans announced a "socialist" program at approximately the same time and even changed their formal name to the Republican Socialist Party. But the socialist title brought little change to the group, and it was ignored by the postwar forces.

After the peace treaty, the able Tejada Sorzano government attempted to appease all of these new movements. It formally supported the veterans and in October it initiated a legal action against Standard Oil, which would ultimately lead to its confiscation. By the end of the year it agreed to a constitutional convention and even proposed to set up new ministries of welfare and labor to initiate social reform legislation. But none of these gestures seemed to satisfy the reformist groups. A reviving labor organization, in a tight labor market due to a booming postwar economy, finally provided the catalyst for the overthrow of the regime. The returning labor radicals succeeded in reorganizing all the old provincial confederations and in May 1936, led by the radical printers union, a General Strike was declared. So powerful was the movement that Tejada Sorzano, fearing revolutionary violence, returned the police to their barracks and the general staff declared its neutrality. The General Strike was a total success, and unionists even temporarily took over police powers in the cities. Demanding 100 percent wage increases, the workers declared the strike for an indefinite period. The obvious weakness of the central government in the face of this massive labor turnout was the excuse that the restive officer corps needed to mature its plans, and on May 17, 1936 the old order was brought to an end when Colonels David Toro and Germán Busch declared a *golpe de estado* and took over the government.

The military coup of 1936 ushered in a period of governments led by the younger Chaco War officers. But the military would reflect the divisions within national political life as a whole, shifting from moderate to radical and then to conservative as the national political forces realigned themselves. For the young colonels who were to lead the Bolivian government in the next dozen years, it was a combination of identity with the "generation of the Chaco" and its demands for reform, as well as a clear fear of a reprisal that motivated their intervention. Veteran and congressional demands for a war crimes tribunal proved a crucial motivating factor behind the army's own decision to intervene.

Initially, the rebel colonels asked David Toro to lead them, with Germán Busch as the power behind the throne. Much like Saavedra in his sensitivity to changing national currents, Toro responded to the new political mood of the nation by declaring that his government would be one of "military socialism." As politically unsophisticated about Marxism as was Saavedra when he renamed his party the Republican Socialists, Toro meant by this term an essentially populist and reformist administration. Reaching to the left, he created Bolivia's first Ministry of Labor and appointed the head of the radical printers union as its incumbent. While this brought a small coterie of Marxist and anarchosyndicalists into the government, the main civilian groups that came to be associated with the new regime were more closely tied to a modified fascist position. The group that most clearly articulated the "national socialist" ideology was a small Socialist Party that had been created a few months before the Toro takeover. It was best represented by political ideologues such as Carlos Montenegro and Augusto Céspedes, both of whom would prove crucial in the formation of later mass movement nationalist parties. In the first months of the new regime this group began publishing *La Calle*, which became the organ for German fascist propaganda and took a virulent antisemitic position. The fact that Hochschild, one of the three tin barons, was Jewish, provided the nationalists with a combined theme of attacking the mineowners and also mouthing their thesis of an international conspiracy. The national socialists were influential enough to get Toro to propose a corporate model for the national legislature and a forced unionization under state control. But the Labor Ministry radicals were adamant against these proposals and, while supporting labor's organizing needs, demanded that the government leave union control in the hands of the workers. Their opposition and Toro's own essential indifference were sufficient to terminate these plans.

While the new radical political groupings and the traditional parties constantly maneuvered to gain control over the direction of the Toro government, the restive officers became disenchanted with all the discussions, debates, and lack of unanimity among the civilians.

The rather creative period of political ferment came to an abrupt end in late June when Busch announced the end of the military-civilian alliance, the exiling of the troublesome Saavedra, and the creation of an all-military regime. The powerless Toro was forced to accept these decisions and in the next few months governed with the aim both of pleasing Busch and the younger officers and of carrying out some moderate reforms that would generate national and popular support for his regime.

All this ferment had created an unease not only among the native officers but also among the traditional elite. With the liberals unable to retain power, tho Salamanca Republicans in disarray, and the Saavedra forces flirting with the new radical movements, the oligarchy felt called upon to reorganize its formal defenses. In May, the tin miner Carlos Aramayo founded a new Centralist Party, the aim of which was to defend the interests of the elite. Although initially getting powerful support from the Miners Association, it would eventually collapse as a major force. But by its very creation it signaled to the older parties that their brief relaxation in the face of the post-Chaco fermentation was not to be tolerated. It was a clear oligarchic statement that politics as played under the old rules was insufficiently class-oriented and detracted from the basic role these parties should henceforth fulfill. While the radical movements might still be in their reformist and relatively ineffectual stage, their potential threat was clear, and the mineowners wanted a more powerful response to this potential threat. The aim of the Centralists was to force the traditional parties to forget their old conflicts and to unite in a coherent coalition class-based party. This would be the aim of the mining elite from 1936 until 1952 as they sought to recreate the old stability through either legal or extralegal maneuverings. The fact that the Centralist Party shortly disappeared from the scene, as coalition talks got under way among the Liberals and various Republicans, meant that the lesson had been learned by the traditional parties.

To satisfy the conflicting demands facing him, Toro in his usual way tried to compromise with all factions. He appeased the far right, by getting the radicals out of the Ministry of Labor, and responded to the reform groups by proposing a constitutional convention and a new national charter. But Busch and his coterie of younger officers grew impatient with these discussions and in the early days of 1937 Busch offered his resignation as a vote of no confidence in the Toro regime. For all intents and purposes, this was a formal announcement of an impending golpe.

In response to the Busch threat, Toro sought to create a popular issue that would give him desperately needed support. Ten days after the Busch pronouncement he speeded up the legal process against Standard Oil and on March 13, 1937 announced the formal confiscation of the Standard Oil Company of Bolivia. All of the holdings, equipment, and material of the company were automatically turned over to the newly formed state oil monopoly *Yacimientos Petroliferos Fiscales de Bolivia* (YPFB) without compensation. This was an historic action both nationally and internationally. It was the first such confiscation of a major North American multinational company in Latin America and preceded the larger Mexican confiscations by a full year. At the same time, it thrust the government directly into the market, making it a major producer of primary products. By this act, the Bolivian government deliberately broke with its more traditional laissez-faire position and took an active role in the economy. The existence of minerals purchasing banks in the nineteenth century and the tin rationing plan in the early 1930s were precedents. But this was to be the beginning of a major evolution, which by the 1950s would see something like half of the gross national product under control of state corporations.

Next, Toro attempted to organize a new Socialist Party and even received some tentative support from the national trade union confederation. But this feverish activity did not quell Busch's growing feeling that Toro was not to be trusted and that he himself was now experienced enough to govern the country in his own name and with the support of the junior officers. In early July after fifteen months of some of the most chaotic and creative political activity in national history, the Toro regime came to an end when Busch announced that it no longer had the support of the army. Given the wide popularity enjoyed by the reformist Toro regime, it appeared to most observers that the unknown Busch would bring about the restoration of traditional party rule under stronger miner control. But in fact the new regime would prove to be a continuation of the period of reform and party reconstruction of the Toro era.

Although initially Busch showed some interest in reviving a coalition of the traditional parties, in fact the opposite occurred. Busch refused to allow the old parties to join the government and continued to issue new reformist legislation. No one party was ever to be associated with the regime, and so the new party activity continued unabated, leading at the end of the decade to the establishment of powerful new national reformist parties. The traditional parties for their part found that the failure either to join the government or find voice in a normal parliament meant four bitter years of erosion, such that by 1940 they would be skeletons of their former selves.

It should be stressed that the reforms advocated and enacted by Toro and Busch were relatively mild welfare and prosyndicalist proposals that involved no serious redirection of national resources or confiscation of private property except in the unique case of Standard Oil. In fact, the army, if anything, was more heavily subsidized in the postwar Toro-Busch era than it had been during the Chaco War itself. Although now reduced to a five-thousand-man standing body, the military still absorbed 32 percent of the national budget in 1937. In addition, the more Busch moved toward the left, the more the leading generals of the older class of officers moved to the right, and the appointment of Carlos Quintanilla as head of the general staff involved a distinct loss of power for the radical younger officers.

But for all its reformist and indecisive nature, the era of military socialism laid the groundwork for more far-reaching change. Nowhere was this potential better expressed than in the new constitutional convention of 1938, the first since the enactment of the liberal charter of 1880. This typical constitution of the nineteenth century provided for a relatively limited style of constitutional regime in which the rights of the individual were protected against the intervention of the State and the central government's powers were strictly limited.

This tendency to limit government intervention changed in Latin America with the Mexican Constitution of 1917. The radical reformers in all the region now demanded that the state take a positive role in the education and welfare of all citizens as had the Mexican charter even if it reduced the property rights of the individual. Known as "social constitutionalism," this trend soon dominated the political thought of radical Latin American theorists as they sought to create blueprints for radical change and give a constitutional legitimacy to the new developments. Such a change in Bolivian constitutional theory was evident in discussions of the immediate postwar period and became a common denominator among the new political forces appearing among the Chaco generation. In the elections for the Constitutional Convention of May 1938, the Busch regime supported the new groups favored by Toro and even permitted the veterans' movement and the central labor federation to run their own slate of candidates. This, plus the weakened state of the relatively disorganized older parties, meant that the composition of the 1938 Convention was extremely radical.

The new convention revised the 1880 charter along the lines of social constitutionalism. The convention debates also provided a legitimizing forum for the dissemination of the most radical ideology current in the nation. Although the more radical proposals of agrarian reform, legalization of the ayllu, and nationalization of the mines were ultimately rejected by the Convention, the Constitution itself severely limited individual property rights. Property was no longer to be held an inalienable private right of individuals but instead was to be considered a social right whose legitimacy was defined by social utility. At the same time, the state was made responsible for the economic well-being of the individual, for the protection of women, children, and the family, and for providing free and universal education. The essential aim of the Convention in all of these articles was to commit the state to the full responsibility for the health, education, and welfare of all its citizens. The classic liberal laissez-faire government with a minimum of intervention was now replaced by the concept of an active state intervening in all areas of a citizen's private life in order to provide for the collective good.

Such active reformism left Busch rather bewildered. Shifting constantly from right to left, he seemed incapable of defining his own political position, just when the moderate leftist and even traditional parties were clearly defining their own positions in the postwar period. For the moderates and radicals, the Constitutional Convention provided a forum for both ideological education and the establishment of more coherent political groupings. The Liberals rejected their more reformist wing and gave their party over to the writer Alcides Arguedas, now a rather reactionary intellectual opposed to all the Chaco generation reforms. In March 1938, the death of Saavedra, the last of the great prewar caudillos, allowed all the Republican parties to rejoin in one united front. The two traditional parties then worked out an agreement known as the *Concordancia*. This "alliance" was another step toward forcing the prewar parties to act as a consistent class defense grouping to stem the onslaught of the new movements. In turn, the Convention provided for many of the new parties to establish a firmer base.

But none of these political clarifications satisfied Busch, nor could he even make up his mind to accept the reforms of the 1938 Constitution despite the relatively wide popular support the new social reforms were enjoying. He found no satisfaction even in the new political calm that had emerged. In April 1939, he declared that henceforth his government would be run as a dictatorship. By this act all political parties were prohibited from functioning, congressional elections was canceled, and the 1938 Constitution was suspended. The new dictatorship now issued a flow of new legislation, most of which was concerned with morality in government. But among these rather naive acts, a new labor code was decreed in May 1939. Although having its gestation in the reforms proposed by the Ministry of Labor created under Toro, the final enactment of a modern labor code was a major piece of national legislation, and the *Codigo Busch*, as it was called, was considered – along with the Constitution of 1938 – the most lasting piece of governmental activity carried out under Busch.

Busch also fought back a rather bitter attack mounted by the tin barons against their dependence on the Central Bank for foreign sales. In 1936 Toro had established a Minerals Purchasing Bank to help small and medium-sized miners and to regularize mineral sales through government purchases. Even more important, he had required the big miners to turn over their foreign earnings to the Central Bank to be converted at special exchange rates into Bolivian currency. By maintaining a lower than open market exchange rate the government was thus able to quadruple its direct and indirect taxes from the mining industry. Busch not only defended the position of Toro on this but further strengthened the requirement and lowered the special rates, thus increasing the government's share of profits from the mines to 25 percent of the value of total tin exports. Although the miners had hoped finally to return to a free market with Busch, his actions went in the opposite direction. Moreover from 1936 to 1952 the Central Bank, under radical and conservative regimes alike, maintained complete control over all foreign sales of Bolivian tin, manipulating the exchange rate to generate government income in the form of indirect taxes.

Despite all the genuine advances carried out by the new regime, Busch seemed to remain totally dissatisfied with the political ambience. He was badly disturbed by the scandal over the sale of visas to Jews in Europe, despite his decision to provide such visas free for the European Jews to settle in the Chaco and eastern lowlands. He thought Hochschild was violating the rules on foreign exchange and had him arrested, and then was forced to release him a few days later. He kept organizing and then disbanding his own governmental party, only to renegotiate contacts with the traditional parties. And while he ruled by decree, hoping miraculously to change the destiny of Bolivia, a sentiment he often expressed in public, he also soon realized that most of his moderate reforms were having no dramatic impact.

From his last public speeches and acts it was evident that Busch was a driven and highly disturbed individual who seemed totally dissatisfied with anything that he carried out. In August 1939, he committed suicide; this act both stunned the nation and generated the kind of veneration and support Busch felt he lacked in his own lifetime. His suicide, plus the immediate change of politics that occurred upon his death, made Busch a martyr to the revolutionary left. It also became a popular belief that the tin barons and their rosca of supporters had somehow assassinated the Chaco War hero. While most scholars accept the evidence of a suicide, the death of Busch, like the role of Standard Oil in causing the Chaco War, became another powerful political myth in the armory of the radical and reformist left, legitimating their demands for change.

The death of Busch brought an end to the charismatic leadership of the Chaco War officers and permitted the conservative oligarchy to terminate the experiment in military radicalism. Working through the leadership of General Quintanilla, who headed the army under Busch, the right had successfully removed key radical officers from power; and thus when Busch died the army was more than ready to turn the government over to the traditional parties. For many on the right, the death of Busch seemed to provide a golden opportunity to eliminate all the change that had occurred as a result of the postwar ferment.

But the traditional parties were to discover that a return to prewar conditions was impossible. The period from 1936 to 1939 had been one of remarkable growth for the radical left, but even more so for the previously nonexistent moderate left. It was a time of educating the Spanish speaking minority in contemporary radical and reformist ideology, a campaign that also reached some peasants and poorer urban cholos. At times encouraged by Toro and Busch and at other times neglected and even persecuted, the moderate left grew unchecked throughout the postwar years, especially among the middle and literate working class. For the far left, the vital groups of labor and university students, the heart of all leftist movements in Latin America, were radicalized and achieved new organizational strength and power. Moreover, having penetrated these groups, the radical left even began to have a hearing among the middle class as well.

Thus, the era of military socialism marked the end of the traditional political system that had been created after 1880 and saw the transition from a classic intraclass republican regime, with limited participation, to one based on class politics, with a major struggle developing over the participation of the lower classes in national political life. Although the moderate and far left were still relatively weak and few stable parties had yet been created, the right found it impossible to stop their development. In the post-Busch period, the struggle would become sharp and bitter as each side turned away from the civilian political structure and resorted to violence to support its ideological and class positions.

On the death of Busch, however, it appeared to the conservatives that the situation might be restored to the prewar norms. They immediately put pressure on Quintanilla to move toward open elections and a return to civilian rule. While Quintanilla clearly had ambitions to run his own government, he faced strong opposition to a continuation in office. On the other hand, the Concordancia parties demanded an end to military rule and on the other the restive junior officers were giving their loyalties to General Bilbao Rioja, a hero of the war period and a supporter of the Busch-Toro line. After a month in office, Quintanilla returned to the 1938 Constitution and called for congressional and presidential elections. He also exiled Bilbao Rioja, thus ending the alliance between the Chaco officers and the new left groups. It appeared as if the left was leaderless and the right would take over again.

But the elections of 1940 were to prove a shock to the old elite. All the traditional parties gathered around the banner of General Enrique Peñaranda as their official candidate for the presidency and supported a unity slate of Liberals and Republicans for the congressional elections. The far left organized behind a Cochabamba professor of law and sociology, José Antonio Arze. Arze was a member of the small fringe of radical Marxists who not only had opposed the Chaco War but also had fought the reformism of Toro and had been exiled by him in 1936. From his exile in Chile Arze organized a Marxian socialist coalition of groups called the *Frente de Izquierda Boliviana* (or Bolivian Leftist Front). In the election, Arze obtained ten thousand votes out of the fifty-eight thousand cast in the election, although he was an unknown national figure, without formal party organization, with no newspaper support, and without the support of the moderate left who voted for Peñaranda. Despite all these obstacles, Arze was able to convince ten thousand voters of the old regime – that is, the literate and urban whites and cholos – that a revolutionary Marxist program was the only viable one for Bolivia. The shock of the Arze candidacy destroyed the complacency of the right and put an end to its hopes to return to the pre-1932 system.

That complacency was even further disturbed in the congressional elections. The left, in both its moderate and radical wings, took control of the new Congress. The Peñaranda era of the early 1940s, rather than being a return to earlier norms, proved to be a new period of political definition and organization. Essentially a liberal politician, Peñaranda returned the country to the traditional parliamentary system and also strongly supported the allied powers in the international conflict then being carried out in Europe. By these two efforts he provided the forum for debate and the national and international issues by which the left could organize and define its various positions and thus create more coherent and stable parties out of the several trends of radical and reformist thought that had risen in the previous decade.

The single most important group to emerge in the new Congress was the moderate-left, middle-class intellectuals who formed part of the Toro and Busch administrations and were influenced by fascist ideology. These so-called national socialists had supported Peñaranda's candidacy for the presidency but were bitter over his growing warmth to the United States. This pro-Allies policy also meant a conversion of the Bolivian tin industry into an ally and dependent of the United States war industries, further angering these economic nationalists. Admirers of Germany and Italy on the international scene, the national socialists were committed within Bolivia to the nationalization of basic industries, above all the tin mines. Given their positions, it was in their interest to foster a powerful and radical mine labor movement. Under the direction of Carlos Montenegro, Augusto Céspedes – both then in charge of the newspaper *La Calle* – and Víctor Paz Estenssoro, who headed their congressional wing, a new party began to emerge in the Peñaranda era, which took the name of the *Movimiento Nacionalista Revolucionario* (MNR; or Nationalist Revolutionary Movement).

To the left of the MNR emerged a party from Arze's followers in the old Front group. Led by Antonio Arze and Ricardo Anaya, these Marxist intellectuals formally established a radical party called the *Partido de la Izquierda Revolucionario* (PIR; or the Party of the Revolutionary Left) in the middle of 1940. The PIR called for the nationalization of the mines and the liberation of the Indians and also took a very strong pro-Soviet position on international affairs. Although still not officially a communist party, the PIR was extremely sympathetic to the cause of the Allies because of the participation of Russia in World War II.

The MNR and PIR emerged along with the older Trotskyite POR as the three parties of the left that opposed the traditional parties variously known as the Concordancia or Democratic Alliance. All three left parties believed in the nationalization of the tin mines. All three supported the labor movement, especially the miners. But beyond this point there were fundamental differences. Both the POR and PIR went much further than the MNR and spoke of the Indian problem, demanding an end to personal service obligations and the latifundias. They also demanded that peasants be organized into coalitions with workers and the middle class to form a revolutionary vanguard. In this concern for the Indian peasantry the MNR program was silent if not essentially hostile, reflecting its white middle-class origins.

In the debate over international issues, which for the first time began to take on an importance in national politics, the POR remained indifferent to the great world conflict and was able to concentrate exclusively on national issues. The MNR and PIR, however, took on committed positions, with the MNR being profascist and the PIR pro-Allied. Given the context of Bolivian mining politics, this meant that the MNR, like the POR, was in a far more independent position in relation to national issues than the PIR, which was always concerned that Bolivian mine production continue to support the Allied cause. This prowar effort position, and their susceptibility to appeals from the right for an antifascist alliance, seriously hampered the PIR in national politics.

Initially the PIR was the dominant party of the left, with the MNR a distant second, and the POR a fringe minority. Since the left had a powerful voice in Congress, the labor movement readily responded to the changed climate among the elite. Feverish unionization activity occurred among the miners, with constant walkouts and strikes, and all labor groups pushed for increased wages and better working conditions. The workers found major support for these efforts in Congress, and men like Víctor Paz Estenssoro became exponents of syndicalization rights. The traditional parties bitterly opposed the support of labor and the left's attack on the administration, but Peñaranda refused to censure the three left parties. The parliament of the 1940s was the most radical and free in Bolivia up to this time.

Although liberal on political questions, the Peñaranda government was conservative on economic and labor issues. Desperate to obtain United States government loans, technical assistance, and long-term commitments for tin sales at reasonable prices, the government was faced by the implacable opposition of Standard Oil. Demanding compensation and/or a return of their facilities, Standard Oil was able to control United States foreign policy toward

Bolivia. Despite the desire of the United States State Department to terminate the close ties between Bolivia and Germany – which included everything from military missions and support for the national air lines (*Lloyd Aereo Boliviano*) to the subsidization of the MNR paper *La Calle*; and its unquestioned need to obtain mineral contracts, the State Department for a long time seemed incapable of overcoming the demands of the oil companies.

But the need for Bolivian cooperation became so vital that by late 1941, the United States was indirectly applying lend-lease formulas to Bolivia, sending technical missions and finally arranging government-controlled long-term mineral purchasing agreements. In this context, the Standard Oil Company finally agreed to negotiate. The eventual settlement involved "compensation" for Standard Oil for the confiscation, in terms of the Bolivians purchasing all the surveys and oil maps still in the possession of the multinational company. In fact this was a victory for Bolivian diplomacy, as its confiscation was not challenged and even the legality of its position was accepted. But it provoked a storm of protest from the left and the nation as a whole, which still held Standard Oil responsible for the Chaco War.

So violent did the protests become that the government accepted falsified documents supplied by the United States, which accused the MNR of a fascist plot paid for by the Germans. *La Calle* was closed, the German minister expelled. The MNR deputies in Congress were not exiled, and the ensuing debate was a passionate one. It revealed that the PIR and other radical groups essentially distrusted the fascism of the MNR, even though they believed that the putsch plot was a United States fabrication. While supporting the reformist and nationalist elements in the MNR program, they bitterly opposed the other aspects of the MNR ideology.

In December 1941, the United States entered World War II, and in January 1942 Bolivia joined the Allied forces and broke relations with both Germany and Japan. While the MNR retained its fascist sympathies, it was now no longer as closely associated with Germany, since that link was formally broken. This enabled the party to concentrate more fully on the national scene, which was becoming a hotbed of strike and union activity and to moderate its hostility toward the far-left parties.

That all of this radical agitation was having its impact was evident in two major events that occurred during the later part of the Peñaranda period. The first was the congressional elections of 1942 and the second was the successful organization of a national mineworkers union in the context of a major mine massacre. In the congressional elections of May 1942, the traditional parties gained just 14,163 votes, as opposed to 23,401 votes for all the new nontraditional parties. The erosion of support from the literate and largely white electorate for the traditional parties could not be stopped. In every election up to the presidential election of 1951, the essentially middle- and upper-class white electorate, by ever-increasing majorities, showed its opposition to the prewar system of politics and moved further toward a more radical position.

With the progressive radicalization of the middle-class whites, there came a more profound radicalization of the laboring classes, and especially of their most powerful and revolutionary vanguard, the mine workers. As early as 1940, the various local mine unions had attempted to organize a national confederation. Despite government attempts to break these organizations under pretext of the war effort, the miners' unions received powerful congressional support from all the left parties. In November and December 1942 a series of major strikes took place in Oruro and Potosí for higher wages and recognition. The longest and most bitter of these strikes involved the Catavi mines owned by Patiño. In late December, troops opened fire on the miners and their families, and hundreds of unarmed workers were slaughtered. The Catavi massacre became a powerful rallying cry of the left and the mineworkers, and was the event that welded the two groups together into a powerful political vanguard.

The government decided to make the Marxist PIR the scapegoat for the massacre and closed its newspapers and imprisoned its leaders. But it was the MNR that most capitalized on what was still an apolitical mineworkers' movement. Under the leadership of Paz Estenssoro, the party mounted a major congressional attack on the Peñaranda government in support of the miners, and coincidentally on the whole relationship between the mineowners, the government, and the United States. In the ensuing debates, the government stopped a censure move but in so doing destroyed the coalitions that remained between the moderates and the increasingly radical left.

The old moderate socialists grouping left over from the Toro and Busch period was destroyed in the debates over Catavi, and even many traditional politicians deserted their parties. The result was that the government found itself with the support of only the most reactionary Liberals and Republicans. The potential support of the PIR, which because of Russia's entrance into the war on the Allied side was now more sympathetic to the government, was rejected by the Peñaranda regime. Thus, the PIR was forced by the government itself to join the MNR and POR in opposition.

By the end of 1943, it was clear that the regime had lost political control. It also had begun to lose control over the army. Several small revolts had occurred and news began to circulate of the organization of secret military lodges. The most important of these clubs was the *RADEPA,* which had been organized in the Paraguayan prisoner-of-war camps among the junior officers. With the exiling of Bilbao Rioja, RADEPA emerged as the single most politically aware group in the army. But unlike their predecessors, this group and its various offshoots were far more inclined toward the fascist than the reformist-socialist line. In late December 1943, these officers allied themselves with the MNR and carried out a successful coup against Peñaranda, thus bringing into partial power the first MNR government in Bolivian history.

The new regime that emerged was a military junta led by the unknown Major Gualberto Villarroel, who was neither a war hero nor a major figure in the military-socialist era. Nevertheless, his position within the RADEPA was vital, and he was committed to the vague reformist and fascist model that the group espoused. Accepting three members of the MNR in his cabinet, Villarroel attempted to ally his minority officer group with the new radical movements. In organizing the new government, the MNR put up Paz Estenssoro as its leader rather than the extreme fascist wing represented by Carlos Montenegro and Augusto Céspedes. However much the junta felt sympathies for the Axis cause, by 1944 the realities of the situation required them to moderate their expectations. When the United States and the majority of Latin American governments refused to recognize the junta, the regime was forced to divest itself of the more extreme MNR leaders and then to call for their complete removal by the early months of 1944. But this temporary break with the

MNR in no way destroyed the ties between the two groups, and the ideological line of the regime became defined by MNR concerns.

These concerns now involved a commitment to the Indian masses and support for the mineworkers' movement, especially the labor wing of the POR. The MNR worked closely with the mine leader and the *porista*, Juan Lechín. This support, along with assistance from the railroad workers, finally led to the organization of a national miners federation, some sixty thousand strong, at Huanuni in June 1944. The *Federación Sindical de Trabajadores Mineros de Bolivia* (or Federated Union of Mine Workers of Bolivia) took over the leadership of the labor movement, as its most powerful union, and gave important support to the MNR and the junta, despite general labor opposition to the regime and labor's traditional support for the PIR.

The regime assembled over one thousand Indian leaders from both the Quechua- and Aymara-speaking peasantry in the first national Indian Congress in La Paz in May 1945. At this convention Villarroel promised to provide educational facilities in the free communities, and decreed the abolition of the hated labor service obligations of the Indians known as *pongueaje*. A truly revolutionary act, this decree was never put into force. Nevertheless, the congress provided a minimum position for the Indian radicals, and gave many traditional Indian leaders their first cross-community contracts, thus paving the way for the later mobilization of the peasants.

In the area of democratic rights and civil liberties, the Villarroel regime would prove to be one of the most vicious in national history. When the PIR took a major portion of the votes in the constitutional convention elections of 1944, the government assassinated its leaders and jailed its followers. In turn, a short-lived revolt in Oruro in late 1945 gave it the excuse it needed to pick up leading traditional politicians and execute them. This resort to violence against middle-class intellectuals and politicians was new to Bolivian politics and deeply divided the nation, rendering most of the reform activities of the regime useless as most members of the elite viewed the regime as one of gangsterism and fascism. Ultimately it was the use of violence and the regime's hostility to the Marxist and the traditional political leaders that finally destroyed it and temporarily reduced the MNR to a minor power in the national scene.

Throughout 1944 and 1945, the continued repression of both the far left and far right finally forced the two groups into an antifascist democratic coalition. By early 1946 this coalition had control of most of the nonmine labor movement, the university students, and most of the national political elite. Despite continued government repression, the coalition gained ground and in June and July 1946, a teachers' strike enabled them to mobilize popular opinion against the regime. On July 14, 1946, a popular protest march turned into a popular revolt. Thus, without the defection of any army or police officials, the civilians carried out an overthrow of the regime. Villarroel himself was dragged from the presidential palace and hanged from a lamp post in the central plaza.

It thus seemed that the MNR and RADEPA had been discredited and that the future lay with the PIR, which in fact was the key radical element in the popular July revolt. But within three years of the revolt and exiling of the MNR leadership, the MNR again emerged as the most popular party on the left and the single most powerful political movement in the nation. This reversal of fortune owed as much to the astuteness of the MNR as to the gross incompetence of the PIR leadership. For what the MNR quickly realized, and the PIR forgot, was that the Chaco generation still lived and that the demands for change were as powerful as ever. It was to prove to their credit that the MNR learned from its disastrous experience with the military fascists and was able to reemerge in the period of the so-called sexenio (the six years from 1946 to 1952), as a radical and popular party of change. It rid itself once and for all of its fascist elements. In this it was helped by Lechín and his miners, who were committed to revolutionary transformation and demanded that the party support their program. At the same time, Paz Estenssoro and such new leaders as Hernán Siles Zuazo concentrated on reestablishing their solid middle-class base, with a strong program of economic stabilization on the one hand and economic nationalization on the other. So successful would they become that in the subsequent revolutionary mythology the murder of Villarroel by the popular crowds in July 1946 would be converted into a major reactionary act and Villarroel would become another martyr, along with Busch and the miners of Catavi, in the revolutionary pantheon of the nation.

In all these developments, the actions of the PIR were crucial, for in the overthrow of the MNR and Villarroel the PIR decided that only full cooperation with the traditional parties could serve their cause, and in this they were mistaken. For just as the MNR did not forget the changes wrought by the Chaco conflict, neither did the traditional parties. Wedded to their now class-defense position, the Concordancia was intent on destroying the new political forces unleashed by the various reformist and radical regimes. They were thus delighted both to use the PIR to cover their own actions and to have it blamed for all their antilabor moves, especially those directed against the mine workers. The traditional parties, once securing power, were determined to stop all change and attempted to return to the prewar system. But this was a quixotic hope. They ended by destroying not only the PIR but also themselves. At the conclusion of the sexenio, the traditional politicians were forced to abandon constitutional government entirely and rely on the military as the only defense against popular demands for change.

Just how revolutionary those demands were became clear in the months after the revolt. At the fourth national miners' Congress at Pulacayo in November 1946, the FSTMB adopted the thesis of the permanent revolution and called for a violent armed struggle of the working class. The so-called Thesis of Pulacayo was a revolutionary document that rejected all reformist positions. Although it accepted the July revolt as a popular one, it challenged the antifascism of the Democratic Alliance parties and spoke of the true fascism of the oligarchy. It demanded a worker-peasant alliance and a government under worker control. Even in its very specific demands, usually the moderate part of worker declarations, the FSTMB called for the immediate arming of workers, for worker participation in mine management, and for the promotion of revolutionary as opposed to economic strikes. This in fact was the most powerful statement of the POR wing of the miners, and it not only committed the miners to revolutionary action, but also forced the MNR to adopt a far more revolutionary stand.

In response to this plan the government decided to repress the union and used the PIR ministers to direct the attacks on the workers. The PIR for its part, once having tasted power under the temporary post-Villarroel government, refused to relinquish it when the

Republicans won the election of 1947 and continued in a coalition cabinet. This was to prove a fatal mistake, for the Republicans under Enrique Hertzog and Mamerto Urriolagotia belonged to the most reactionary wing of the traditional parties and were determined to destroy the FSTMB. In early 1947, it was a PIR minister who ordered the troops into the mines. The resulting massacre and termination of a strike in Catavi led to the end of the PIR as the representative party of the left.

The MNR for its part never lost its middle-class following, even with most of the leaders, including Víctor Paz Estenssoro, in exile. In the 1947 elections, they had been reduced to their minimum popular support but still gained thirteen thousand votes as opposed to the forty-four thousand of the victorious Republicans. Then, as the PIR was destroyed and the traditional parties showed increasing hostility even to the moderate postwar reformism of the Toro-Busch model, the MNR succeeded in expanding its support. By the midterm congressional elections of May 1949, it emerged as the second most powerful party after the Republicans, despite strong government opposition. So unexpected was their comeback that Hertzog resigned the presidency and turned the government over to his vice president Urriolagotia.

But both the Republicans and the PIR refused to leave the government. Shortly after the congressional elections, more strikes began at Catavi, leading to the exiling of Lechín, Mario Torres, and the other leaders of the FSTMB. News of their exile led to an armed workers' uprising in Catavi and to a massive army intervention. By this act, it appeared that the army had completely purged itself of all reformist elements and was totally committed to the repressive policies of the Republican regime. Fearing a worker and MNR revolutionary movement, they united behind their conservative upper-officer caste.

But the post–World War II decline in international prices for tin triggered a severe fiscal crisis in government. Prices began to rise rapidly on the domestic market. The Republican government could not deal with the economic stagnation and inflation, so it lost its following even among previously supportive groups. Key elements of the elite showed themselves indifferent to the final showdown between the government and the MNR. As for the MNR, the violent suppression of the workers and the use of fraud to reduce their electoral victories committed the party to an armed overthrow of the regime. In September 1949 the MNR under Siles Zuazo organized a civilian revolt and for two months fought the army in all the provincial cities, even setting up a temporary headquarters in Santa Cruz. Although the revolt was crushed with much bloodshed, it marked an important change in the style of national politics. It was an entirely civilian operation and the army maintained unity against the rebels and supported the regime. Despite the former close alliance between the MNR and the army, the officer corps stood firm against the party and fought it to defeat. The revolt was unique as well in its coalition of worker and middle-class support. It also indicated to the party that, despite all its old fascist and military ties, it would have to make the revolution by destroying the army itself.

Despite continued repression, the MNR's strength only increased from day to day. An indication of its increasing dominance over the worker movement came in May 1950, when the factory workers of La Paz turned a strike into another MNR-labor armed insurrection. Planes and artillery were used on the workers' quarters of La Paz to destroy the revolt. But the significance of the event was in the MNR's takeover of the urban labor movement, hitherto a stronghold of the PIR. Now the party had the support of virtually all of organized labor, whatever its local political complexion, as well as most of the middle class.

Although the more radical members finally forced the PIR to abandon the government, they could not make it take a more revolutionary stand. In early 1950, the youth of the party deserted its ranks and formed the Bolivian Communist Party, and the party dwindled into insignificance. Meanwhile, the MNR made one last attempt at gaining power by democratic means. In the May 1951 presidential elections, it ran a slate of Víctor Paz Estenssoro, who still remained in exile, and Hernán Siles Zuazo. To the dismay of the right, the MNR won the election with a straight majority, gaining thirty-nine thousand votes out of fifty-four thousand cast. The Republicans gained only thirteen thousand, and the PIR ended with just five thousand votes, even less than the Liberals.

Before the MNR could take the presidency, however, the army decided to intervene. In days after the election, Urriolagotia resigned and handed over the presidency to the chief of the general staff, who in turn appointed General Hugo Ballivián president. The new government immediately annulled the elections and outlawed the MNR as a communist organization, the new rhetoric reflecting the developing Cold War ideology in the international context. But the military found only the Republicans and a small right-wing proclerical fascist party, the *Falange Socialista Boliviano*, willing to give it support. Even the generals realized the inevitable outcome of the coming struggle, and many leading officers took diplomatic positions abroad at this crucial movement in the conflict.

To all observers it became evident that the MNR would now attempt to take by force what it had been denied at the polls. Never loath to use violence, the MNR went into full-scale military opposition, convinced that only a policy of civil war would give them the government. The officer corps remained totally loyal to the junta. Thus, Paz and the leaders of the party finally agreed to an arming of all civilians and the commitment to a popular armed uprising. Even in the civil war of 1949 the party had not opened the armories to the public but had used only its own members in the fighting, fearing that a total civil war would lead to the destruction of all order in Bolivia. But now they were committed to that position as the only one that could lead to victory.

In this context of this intense plotting and violence, the military regime blocked sale of tin to the United States over the issue of prices, which led to a severe depression in the national economy. In late 1951, the government supported the tin miners' complaints about the low price for the long-term purchase of tin and agreed to stop sales and stop production for a few months to force the United States to come to terms. While this tactic would eventually prove successful, it only exacerbated the political and economic tensions in the country.

After numerous attempts, the final revolt got under way on April 9, 1952, In three days of intensive fighting, during which the armories were opened to the public and the miners marched on La Paz, the army was finally defeated. At the cost of much destruction and the loss of over six hundred lives, the MNR returned to power. But the 1952 party was a vastly different one from the profascist group overthrown in 1946. It was now a party of radical middle-class elements and revolutionary workers and represented a new type of populist movement. It also had come to power at the cost of the traditional political parties and the main institutions of order and authority, the army and the police. By accepting the workers' participation and ideology and by arming the populace, it had committed itself to a destruction of the old order.

Having achieved power against the opposition of the army and the traditional parties, the MNR leaders felt under no obligation to offer a moderate program or compromise with any traditional institution, political or military. The urban white and cholo classes, and the rural Indian masses were in possession of arms, and the army and the national police force completely disorganized. The aims of the party were known to all, the arms were in the hands of a militant populace, and the exiled leaders returning from abroad were not to be restrained. Thus began Latin America's most dynamic social and economic revolution since the Mexican Revolution of 1910.

Chapter 8

From the National Revolution to the Cold War, 1952–1982

Bolivia in 1950 was still a predominantly rural society, the majority of whose population was only marginally integrated into the national economy. Of all economically active persons registered in the census of 1950, fully 72 percent were engaged in agriculture and allied industries. Yet this workforce only produced some 33 percent of the gross national product, a discrepancy that clearly indicates the serious economic retardation of this sector. But since 1900, Bolivian society had experienced marked changes in its social composition. The urban population (those living in cities or towns of five thousand or more) had risen from 14 percent to 23 percent of the national population, and in each of the departments of the country, the major urban centers had grown faster than the department as a whole. The level of literacy and the number of children attending school also increased in the same period, especially after the major investments in education carried out by the post-Chaco regimes. Between 1900 and 1950 literates rose from 17 percent of the population to 31 percent, and the pre-university student population went from some 23,000 to 139,000, or from 1 to 5 percent of the total population. At the top, however, much less change had occurred, and while the number of university students by 1951 had reached twelve thousand, only 132 persons in the entire country had graduated with postsecondary degrees in that year.

Largely rural and agricultural, Bolivia could not even feed its national population by the middle of the twentieth century. Through the constant expansion of the hacienda system, land distribution had become one of the most unjust in Latin America. The 6 percent of the landowners who owned one thousand hectares or more of land controlled fully 92 percent of all cultivated land in the republic. Moreover, these large estates themselves were underutilized, with the average estate of one thousand or more hectares cultivating but 1.5 percent of its lands. At the opposite extreme were the 60 percent of the landowners who owned five hectares or less, true minifundias, which accounted for just 0.2 percent of all the land and were forced on average to put 54 percent of their lands into cultivation. The extreme inequality in the division of lands was essential in the control of rural labor. Controlling access to the best lands in all the zones of the republic, the hacendados obtained their labor force by offering usufruct estate lands in exchange for labor. The Indians were required to supply seeds, tools, and in some cases even animals for this work, which left the owner with few capital inputs to supply. The Indians were even required to transport the final crop. The hacendado also required personal service to himself, his family, and his overseers. *Pongueaje* (personal service obligation) had been part of the work requirements of estate Indians since colonial times. But it did not make these obligations any less onerous. The one thing universally hated by all Indian peasants was the *pongo* service. It required attendance on the hacendado family even in a distant urban residence and took up large amounts of time and effort, all at the peasant's own cost.

This system did not involve debt peonage or other means of force, and Indians tended to move in and out of the latifundia with no restrictions, but the increasing pressures on land in the free community area, especially after the last great age of hacienda expansion, compelled the peasants to adapt themselves to the system. Although the urban centers were expanding, they were not doing so fast enough to absorb the growing rural population. Equally, the subdivisions of plots in the free communities was rapidly reaching crisis proportions, so more and more sons were forced to work either on the haciendas to obtain land to feed themselves and their families or as a cheap labor force in the mines and towns.

With labor inexpensive, with seeds and even tools sometimes free or at minimal cost, and with protected agricultural markets, the incentives for hacendados to invest in their holdings were minimal.

In fact, absentee ownership was the dominant form in all the rural areas, and the majority of hacendados had urban professions. The result of this system was the use of rudimentary technology and poor quality seed with extremely low yields of foodstuffs. The agricultural sector was so backward that it was unable to meet the needs of the expanding population in the urban centers and of the nation as a whole. Whereas 10 percent of the imports in the 1920s was food, the figure was 19 percent in the 1950–2 period, and a good proportion of the imported food was traditional Andean root crops that were produced only in Bolivia and Peru. Inefficient, unproductive, and unjust, the Bolivian agricultural system also kept a large percentage of the national workforce out of the market by holding down their income in exploitive work and service obligations. This in turn restricted the market for manufactures to the small urban minority and the relatively few active agricultural centers such as the Cochabamba Valley.

Given the limited nature of this internal market, it is not surprising that Bolivia had a small industrial sector, which in 1950 accounted for but 4 percent of the economically active population. Industry essentially consisted of some textile factories and food-processing plants. By 1950 it was estimated that there had been little change in the capital structure of this sector and that the majority of the factories were overaged and underproductive by world standards. The same lack of new capital inputs that affected agriculture and industry was even more evident in mining. From the late 1930s onward there was apparently little new investment in the mining sector, just when most of the mines began to run out of richer veins. Thus aging plants and declining quality of minerals inexorably forced the costs of mining up to levels that were becoming uneconomic and noncompetitive except in periods of wartime shortage on the world markets. By 1950 Bolivia was the world's highest-cost producer of tin, and in some years the industry was barely covering its costs. The margins of profit were thin, making the industry even more sensitive to minor fluctuations in world prices. Moreover, even when prices took a sudden upturn, the low quality of ore available and the low productivity of the mines meant that Bolivia found it extremely difficult to increase production. By 1952 it was still the case that the best year of tin output was 1929, when the nation had exported forty-seven thousand tons of tin. In fact, that figure remains a record until the present day.

Given the relative stagnation and backwardness of the national economy, the MNR would find it relatively easy to carry out profound changes. The haciendas, owned as they were by a largely absentee class, and with little capital invested, could be seized without major opposition. Given peasant mobilization after April 1952, they could not be held without full support from the police powers of the State. The takeover of the aging mining sector by the state also would not be vigorously opposed by the tin barons so long as adequate compensation could be provided. In short, the strength of the economic elite was relatively drained at the time of the revolution, much as their political power had been weakened.

The new MNR leaders also found themselves without an army opposition. The three days of fighting between the civilians and miners on one side and the army on the other had seen the collapse of the military. This was the truly shocking event of April 1952, for in one moment the entire police power of the State was overwhelmed. The wholesale distribution of arms to the populace at large, the creation of urban and rural militias, and the neutralization of the national police changed Bolivian political, economic, and social reality beyond even the wildest expectations of the MNR leadership. Thus, no matter how limited the aims of the more moderate MNR leadership may have been even in April 1952, the reality of the collapse of the state and the arming of the popular masses and their leaders meant that a serious social revolution would be the end result. The "reluctant revolutionaries," as some have called them, were thus slowly and inexorably forced to propose a total reorganization of Bolivian society.

One of the first acts of the new regime was to establish universal suffrage by eliminating the literacy requirements. In one stroke, the Indian peasant masses were enfranchised, and the voting population jumped from some two hundred thousand to just under one million persons. Next the national military academy was temporarily closed and some five hundred officers purged from the ranks. While the army itself was given the task of its own reorganization, it was so reduced in power and numbers that many persons believed for a time that it had ceased to exist. Initially the MNR civilian militias were better armed than the police and the army and took over all the internal duties that these two forces usually managed. The MNR also set about reorganizing its forces so as to strengthen its own power base. The regime fully supported the miners when they set up a new national labor federation, the COB (Bolivian Workers Central), in the late days of April. While the COB proclaimed itself politically neutral and allowed the POR, PIR, and the new PCB to have representation, it in fact became a powerful ally of the regime and ended up by naming three labor ministers to the new cabinet. Lechín, who was head of the FSTMB, also became head of the COB and in turn was given the Ministry of Mines and Petroleum. The COB and FSTMB represented the radical revolutionary wing of the party, and they were not slow in enunciating a revolutionary program. One of the COB's first acts was to demand the nationalization of the mines without compensation, the liquidation of the army and its replacement by the militias, and Agrarian Reform with the abolition of the latifundia system and all forms of peasant work obligations.

The MNR leadership under President Víctor Paz Estenssoro and Hernán Siles Zuazo slowly responded to the political and paramilitary pressure of the workers but tried to restrain their reforms as much as possible. It took until July for the regime to declare the export and sale of all minerals a state monopoly, which would now be handled by the Banco Minero. Although a logical step according even to prereform patterns, it had taken several months of intensive debate to get even this far. But those in the party who wished to stop at this point were faced by increasing worker demands for uncompensated confiscation. So powerful did this pressure become that the leadership finally agreed to full-scale nationalization. In early October the government set up a semi-autonomous state enterprise to run any state-owned mines, which was given the name of *Corporación Minera de Bolivia* (COMIBOL). Then on October 31, they nationalized the big three companies of Patiño, Hochschild, and Aramayo. By this act they turned over some two-thirds of the tin mining industry to COMIBOL and state control.

While the labor radicals demanded confiscation without indemnification, the MNR was concerned about the response of the United States government. Since the MNR had done everything to smooth those relations, including ending the tin boycott on largely United States government terms, it did not wish to antagonize a potentially dangerous ally. Given that the Cold War was in full development and that the United States was actively intervening in Guatemala to suppress a radical government, the MNR hoped to avoid the label of a communist-inspired regime. Since the United States had in fact initially mistaken the MNR for a fascist and Peronist-oriented party, recalling its old role under Villarroel, it had been mildly supportive of the new regime. The MNR thus promised compensation to the big three, but it made no gestures toward nationalizing any other mines, including the several medium-sized non-tin-producing mines owned by American companies. But the regime was forced to accept COB and FSTMB direction and worker "co-government" in the administration of COMIBOL. Workers obtained two out of the seven seats on its Board and were given veto power on COMIBOL decisions which affected workers. This shifted power toward the workers, who pushed both for increased hiring and for the establishment of well-subsidized *pulperías*, or company stores.

Meanwhile in the last half of 1952 and the beginning of 1953 rural society began to collapse, despite all the efforts of the regime to control the situation. With the army ineffectual, arms quickly reaching the countryside, and young political radicals spreading the word of change, a systematic peasant attack began on the entire latifundia system. Similar to the peasant movement known as the "Great Fear" in the French Revolution, the period from late 1952 until early 1953 saw the destruction of work records in the rural areas, the killing and/or expulsion of overseers and landowners, and the forcible seizure of land. Peasants, using traditional community organizations, began to organize *sindicatos* (unions) with the encouragement of the COB, and to receive arms, and create militias. Although the countryside had been relatively indifferent and little affected by the great conflicts of April 1952, it was the scene of tremendous violence and destruction by the end of that year.

However reluctant the new regime may have been to attack the hacienda problem seriously, the massive mobilization of the peasants, now the majority of the electorate, and the systematic destruction of the land tenure system forced the regime to act. In January 1953, it established an Agrarian Reform Commission that included members of the POR and PIR, and by August 3 a radical Agrarian Reform decree was enacted. It confiscated all hacienda lands and provided compensation for the landlords in the form of twenty-five-year indemnification bonds and granted these ex-hacienda lands to the Indian workers through their *sindicatos* and *comunidades*, with the proviso that such lands could not be individually sold. The bonds eventually were considered worthless and in fact, this was confiscation without compensation. The government tried to salvage whatever modern capital-intensive sector remained in the rural area by excluding capital intensive farms from being seized. In the highland Indian areas, almost all the lands were seized, and the Indians quickly stopped paying compensation, with the lands, in effect, being confiscated. The only exceptions were the relatively unpopulated Santa Cruz region and such southern medium-sized hacienda regions as Monteagudo, which had some modest capital-intensive agriculture and no resident Indian populations, and the smallholding vineyard region of the Cinti Valley. Everywhere else, the hacienda was abolished, the hacendado class destroyed, and land now shifted predominately into the hands of the Indian peasants.

At the same time, the tutelage of the Indian sindical organizations by urban labor and mineworkers soon ended, and peasant leaders emerged as major powers in the rural areas. Although there were numerous competing groups and regional associations among the Indians, the most important centers of peasant political leadership became the community of Achacachi in the Lake Titicaca district and the pueblo of Ucureña in the Cochabamba Valley. The former became the center of Aymara peasant organization and the latter that of the Quechua speakers. While often working at odds with each other, and being suborned by the regimes in power, the peasants nevertheless retained control over their own sindicatos and have been vital sources of national political strength from 1952 until the present day. Satisfied on the land question, the Indians initially became a relatively conservative political force in the nation and grew indifferent to their former urban worker colleagues. For the next two generations their primary concern was the delivery of modern facilities of health and education to their comunidades, and the guaranteeing of their land titles.

The genius of Paz Estenssoro was to realize the importance of this totally new and quite conservative force on the national scene. As his power declined among his former supporters in the middle class, and his dependence on the radical COB and workers' groups grew, he realized that he would have to create a new power base for the center and right wings of his party among the peasantry. So successful was this drive that for the next quarter-century the peasantry became the bastion of the conservative elements of the central government. And once created, this alliance would survive the initial destruction of the MNR and even the return of rightist military regimes.

The collapse of the state, the nationalization of the mines, the destruction of the hacienda system, and the massive shift of government resources into social welfare programs all created havoc in the national economy and in government income. The takeover of the mines drained massive sums from the state coffers, and agrarian reform reduced agricultural deliveries to the cities drastically, thus necessitating massive food imports to prevent starvation. The only way to resolve all of these problems was to increase national currency. The result was one of the world's most spectacular records of inflation from 1952 to 1956. In that time the cost of living increased twentyfold, with annual inflation rates of over 900 percent.

By this decision to finance the revolution through the dramatic devaluation of national currency, the MNR in effect was making the middle classes pay for part of the revolution. Fixed rents were wiped out, and urban real estate values disappeared overnight. Suddenly the middle class found its most fundamental interests attacked. The elimination of a large part of their incomes created immediate hostility to the regime. Formerly the heart of the party and its staunchest supporters, the urban middle class deserted the MNR on a major scale. Rejecting the PIR and PCB as viable alternatives, they shifted their allegiance to the previously minor Bolivian *Falangista* Party (the FSB).

A conservative Catholic party with fascist leanings, the FSB was established in Chilean exile at the Catholic University in Santiago in the 1930s. Like the POR a relatively minor party in its early phases, the FSB had powerful Church support and was committed to a moderate nationalist position. But given its appeals, it competed with the center and right groups who were supporting the MNR in the pre-1952 period, while its clerical leaning alienated the majority of followers, given the weak position of the church in national society. But when the MNR attacked the income of the middle class after 1952 and in effect forcibly shifted its savings toward the more popular classes, the clericalism of the FSB was forgotten and it emerged as the most powerful party in the urban centers. The new strength of the FSB was revealed in the mid-term elections in the first Paz regime and even more so in the presidential elections of 1956, in which the FSB effectively dominated the cities, seizing most of the MNR's traditional pre-1952 supporters.

But the MNR coalition of urban radicals, organized workers, and the peasantry replaced the former middle class backing and enabled the party to gain victories at the polls. But despite its loss of the middle class, the MNR refused to move any further toward a socialist revolution. It constantly stressed its legitimacy and relationship to the old order and, while nationalizing the big three mine companies, did everything in its power to attract new foreign capital and to protect private property. In the Agrarian Reform, it did sacrifice property in a major way, but it still attempted to retain the Santa Cruz area as a prime zone for the expansion of private investment. Finally, while the creation of COMIBOL and YPFB made the government the single largest producer in the national economy and created a "state capitalism" model for the economy, the government development corporation, CBF, expended large sums in providing working capital for the private industrial sector.

Faced with a bankrupt economy, an inability of the regime to feed its people, and a lack of capital to undertake all the ambitious welfare and reform programs proposed, the party also decided to seek financial assistance from the United States. As early as June 1953, under intense United States pressure, and the refusal of Patiño's Williams Harvey Company smelters in England to refine Bolivian tin, the government agreed to compensate Patiño, Hochschild, and Aramayo. The following month it signed a minerals purchasing contract with the United States, which also announced both a doubling of its previous aid program and the immediate shipment of $5 million worth of food under U.S. Public Law 480. Bolivia was the first Latin American country to receive such a food exports grant. By the end of a decade of massive aid Bolivia had achieved the extraordinary distinction of having obtained $100 million in United States aid, making it at that time the largest single recipient of United States foreign aid in Latin America and the highest per capita in the world. So dependent on this aid did Bolivia become that, by 1958, one-third of its budget was paid for directly by United States funds.

For the United States, the Bolivian aid decision was an extremely paradoxical one, since it occurred under the very conservative and Cold War regime of Secretary of State John Foster Dulles and President Dwight Eisenhower. Hostile to all revolutionary regimes, the United States Republican administration would seem to have been the least likely government to be receptive to Bolivian requests for aid. But the recent emergence of radical regimes in Guatemala and Guyana had created an unusual fear in the United States of losing control over the Western Hemisphere, and it was convinced that Bolivia would quickly follow suit. Faced with the first challenge in the Cold War to its absolute hegemony over its Latin American sphere of influence, the Eisenhower administration felt that supporting the MNR "fascists" was the only way to prevent the revolution from falling into communist hands. Bolivia had actually been a model region for the first of the major Latin American aid programs, that of Point-Four aid under the Truman administration, and it had achieved major results. Thus, the local United States embassy favored continued aid to Bolivia and accepted the Paz Estenssoro line that he and his regime were the only factors preventing a communist takeover. Finally, given the small amount of United States investment in the Bolivian mining companies and/or in agricultural lands, none of the confiscation decrees had seriously affected United States companies, so that the State Department was under no pressure to oppose the regime.

The massive aid that poured into Bolivia proved vital in providing economic stability for Bolivia. Public Law 480 food shipments gave Bolivia the crucial foodstuffs needed to pass through the period of severe agricultural dislocation occasioned by the Agrarian Reform. This aid undoubtedly gave the government the equanimity to deal with the peasants that it might otherwise not have had if there was real starvation in the cities. It also provided funds to establish a modern road system so vital to the integration of the national society. United States aid was also crucial in the development of the Santa Cruz region, which is so important to the Bolivian economy. Massive inputs of capital into health and education were also instrumental in developing Bolivia's backward social services into a more modern system. Finally, the very crucial and unusual funding of direct government operations, helped provide the social peace that might not have existed had the regime gone unaided. Given the money needed to keep the regime afloat and the population fed and clothed, the absence of that funding would surely have led to a more bloody social history than Bolivia experienced after 1952.

But this aid was not without its costs, for the United States government as usual demanded support for private United States companies operating overseas. This meant that, along with its unceasing demands for the reduction of the power of COB and the end to worker co-government in the mines, were concessions such as repayment on defaulted bonds from the 1920s to new investment and petroleum codes favorable to United States interests. Despite its massive support to the government, the United States resisted all efforts by the Bolivians to fund YPFB. It was made clear to Bolivia that new investments in petroleum would only come with a new petroleum code that permitted direct United States private investments once again in Bolivian oil. In October 1953, a new petroleum code was drawn up with United States assistance, and by the end of the decade some ten United States companies were operating in Bolivia, the most important being Gulf Oil Company, which began operations in 1955. Moreover, when Brazil's state-owned oil company Petrobras proposed to the Bolivian government that it be granted concessions under both preexistent treaties as well as the new quite liberal code, the Bolivian government refused all overtures.

In most cases, these pro-U.S. capital or international pro-U.S. voting decisions were relatively costless to the regime. But the decision to force Bolivia to accept monetary stabilization was another matter entirely, along with direct U.S. intervention in national politics. By the last years of the Paz regime, the MNR had developed two rough groupings, a center-right middle-class wing represented by Siles Zuazo and a left and labor coalition led by Lechín and the COB. While favoring one side or the other, Paz essentially played the role of neutral leader above the factions. The moderates accepted the various social reforms but put pressure on the regime to maintain its middle-class base. It was also the moderate wing of the party that demanded a modernization of the economy, even at the expense of some of the social aims of the revolution. Given the completion of the initial destructive phase of the revolution and the continued sluggishness of the national economy, it was probably inevitable that the moderate conservative elements would come to dominate. Although the two groups split ideologically, there was no question that they worked closely together. Thus, when Paz finished his term, it was agreed that Siles succeed to the presidency and that Lechín would seek the third presidential term when Siles stepped down. To seal the agreement, Siles accepted the Labor Minister in charge of peasant affairs, Nuflo Chavez Ortiz, as his vice presidential running mate.

In the June elections of 1956, it was evident that the MNR had little trouble mobilizing its powerful peasant and worker coalition so that it obtained a comfortable majority with some 790,000 votes. But the erosion of the middle classes was also evident in the 130,000 votes, largely urban and white, which the FSB captured, making it the second largest party. It was an attempt to recapture this restive middle-class base, as well as to further its ideas of development, that the Siles regime decided to accept the dictates of the International Monetary Fund in terms of national fiscal policy. Given the increasingly difficult situation of the national economy and the inability of the regime to survive without direct United States subsidies, it was inevitable that some concessions had to be made. The Siles regime had only three options: generate the capital it needed by completely socializing the economy, which it was ideologically unwilling to do; continue with the inflationary program until a total collapse occurred and/or a Falangista revolt ended the regime; or accept the United States terms and extract the largest aid possible for doing so at the minimum cost to its social programs. It opted for the last solution.

The United States worked out its "Stabilization Plan" by late 1956, and Bolivia accepted it under IMF auspices in January 1957. The plan required that Bolivia balance its budget, end the food subsidization of the miners, hold down wage increases, create a single exchange rate, and adopt a host of other measures restricting government initiative and expenditures. The stabilization plan was an extreme one by the standards of the day, envisioning the creation of a stable currency with almost zero inflationary growth within the space of one or two years. The plan was successful. The currency was stabilized, deficits in government spending were cut, and COMIBOL achieved a more balanced budget. By the early 1960s, in fact, Bolivia was finally able to give up direct United States budget subsidies. Also a great deal of foreign private, and above all government, capital now entered Bolivia in the form of loans and investments. Productivity in the mines did increase, and the economic stability needed for internal savings and investment finally began to be achieved.

But the costs were high. The United States insisted that the program be carried out regardless of political consequences. The left went into strong opposition to the Siles regime. Vice-President Nuflo Chavez resigned, and despite major mining strikes led by Lechín, the subsidized pulperías in the mines were closed. Now the U.S. Embassy felt confident that it could isolate and destroy Juan Lechín, who became in the eyes of the United States the arch enemy. Just as Siles never used force against the miners and achieved almost all the concessions from COB through hunger strikes of his own and threats of resignation, he never seriously rejected the left of the party. Holding that stabilization and retrenchment were the only policies that could guarantee the victories of the left and suppress the rising right wing and the Falange, he nevertheless accepted the idea that Lechín and the COB would succeed him in 1960. But continuing United States pressure, now influenced by a series of Cold War liberals who were United States ambassadors under the Democratic regimes, was adamant against Lechín and the left. Hoping to diminish this hostility Lechín and Siles agreed on a compromise platform for the third presidential term. Paz was again to lead the party, and Lechín would be his vice president. Lechín traveled to Washington and even went to Formosa to meet with Chinese Nationalist leaders and thus symbolically accept the worst Cold War positions of the United States. He also agreed to end worker co-government in the mines when it became the price for the arrangement of a major infusion of German and United States government investments in COMIBOL in the so-called Triangular Plan.

Unlike Siles, however, Víctor Paz Estenssoro in his second term (1960–4) showed himself implacably opposed to the continued power of COB and the mineworkers. He rearmed the army, justifying this constantly to the United States as a means of preventing communist subversion. He allowed the United States army to infiltrate the Bolivian command structure, and to push its ideas of "internal subversion" and counterinsurgency in its training of the local army. Paz also prevented the militias from rearming and did everything possible to shift the balance of military power back to the army and away from the civilian and worker militias. But at this point Siles and Lechín joined forces and broke with the party, thus temporarily destroying the MNR. Finding himself with only the army and the peasants as his major supporters, Paz put up a leading general, René Barrientos, as his candidate for vice president and attempted to run for a third term.

The election of 1964 gave Paz the presidency, but with the left and center of the MNR in opposition and the Falange still an implacable enemy, it was inevitable that the army would be encouraged to return to power. Thus in November 1964, a few short months after the presidential elections, the army ousted Paz in a relatively bloodless coup and put the government in the hands of a junta headed by Vice President Barrientos. Thus the army was back in national politics, and it would remain the dominant force in the national government from 1964 until 1982. Thus the revolutionary phase of the National Revolution had come to an end and a long thermadorian reaction was to ensue.

For the next eighteen years various groups and institutions within national society would struggle to dominate the forces that had been unleashed in the period of the National Revolution. The army, the peasants, organized labor, and both traditional and new political parties all sought power. In this long, bitter, and violent struggle there emerged a more sophisticated political system and a more complex society, but at a high cost to all. Although leaders of the MNR opposition assumed that the overthrow of Paz Estenssoro was a temporary transition, the reality was that a new political era had emerged in 1964. Younger military officers who had come to power under the MNR were to create a complex alliance with the peasants and were hostile to democratic politics and organized labor.

These officers justified the legitimacy of military authoritarian governments as the only solution to modernization – an ideology prevalent throughout the Americas in this period. Many of these regimes also would find support among the newer elements of the wealthiest classes and powerful regional elites which saw the military as more likely to favor their interests than the old MNR.

But the institutional change, often chaotic personnel advancements and ideological conflict within the army itself, as contrasted to more traditional and firmly hierarchical military organizations in Chile, Argentina, and Brazil, created an officer class that was far more unpredictable than many others in Latin America. Thus the era of military regimes was one of radical shifts of viewpoint, abrupt changes of regime, and constant emergence of new and unexpected personalities. But despite all the very rapid and often seemingly random changes, there existed a series of basic arrangements that were only rarely modified. These coalitions were based on the army's acceptance of the basic social and economic reforms of the National Revolution and above all a firm commitment to Agrarian Reform and mobilization of the peasantry. It was their recognition and active acceptance of the peasantry that would mark these new military regimes as semipopulist ones essentially based on an often unexpressed, but nevertheless fully functioning, alliance of peasants and the military. All these features were clearly expressed in the first of these military regimes, that of René Barrientos, which established most of the basic norms that would dominate these military governments in the years to come.

The Barrientos regime quickly showed its implacable hostility to organized labor and the left. It sought its urban support in a new governmental party coalition from among the Christian Democrats and elements of the Falange. But from the beginning it gave unstinting support to the revolutionary reforms that affected the peasants, such as Agrarian Reform and universal suffrage. One of the first acts of the new regime – one supported by every subsequent regime of the left and right – was to declare its unswerving support for Agrarian Reform and quickly increased the distribution of land titles. Full assistance was also given for welfare programs, rural education, and the peasant sindicatos, which both retained their arms and received protection. In fact, the Barrientos regime became the most popular one after that of Victor Paz Estenssoro in the countryside. A native speaker of Quechua, Barrientos, dominated the peasant unions, and was known for his largess in buying individual aid and peasant support. The result was an urban antilabor and conservative military regime allied with the Indian peasantry. It was, in short, a powerful coalition that only the rampant corruption and instability of the army itself rendered unworkable.

The Barrientos regime succeeded in dismantling the mine union (FSTMB), discharged some six thousand miners from COMIBOL, and even massacred striking miners on the night of San Juan in June 1967 at the Catavi-Siglo XX mines. Barrientos temporarily succeeded in decapitating the union movement, but he did not eradicate its potential power. Bolivian labor had become radicalized in the 1940s and successfully resisted the repeated interventions and suppressions that a succession of military regimes attempted after 1964. Nevertheless, the almost constant use of troops at the mines succeeded in isolating and temporarily controlling the once-all-powerful labor movement for the first time since 1952.

A combination of rising tin prices on the international market, inputs of foreign capital, and forced retrenchment of the work force and wages created the first profit for COMIBOL in 1966. Thereafter began a long-term trend in production and prices that was to make COMIBOL an important source of government revenue. Basic changes now occurred in the private mine sector as well. Fully encouraged by all the MNR governments through special subsidization and other assistance, the medium and small mine sectors also increased production, with the middle-rank mines becoming especially important and rising to about a third of total output in the tin sector by the end of the decade. Thus not only was COMIBOL itself expanding but the entire industry was becoming more complex with a new group of middlesize mineowners emerging as a powerful force in the private sector. In 1965 a liberalized investment code for foreign capital was issued: United States Steel was allowed to rent the Matilda zinc mine from COMIBOL, and Gulf Oil was given further concessions. All of these economic developments aided Barrientos in his political positions. In the 1966 presidential election, he was able to put together a powerful coalition party of peasants, the new wealthy groups, the conservative Falange politicians, and members of the government bureaucracy. Despite his landslide victory and the seeming disintegration of the formal left opposition, however, worker hostility toward the regime did not abate, and for the first time since 1952, the La Paz government began to experience a problem with armed rebellion.

While many small, largely urban intellectual-based guerrilla groups began to operate during the Barrientos period, the most important instance of rebellion came from a source totally external to the national scene. In 1966, Argentine revolutionary Ché Guevara arrived in Bolivia. Establishing a base camp in the province of Santa Cruz, Ché was apparently more interested in setting up a central guerrilla headquarters for operations in Argentina and Brazil than in Bolivia itself. Although he was in touch with the Bolivian Communist Party, he made no attempt to contact or work with the miners. Yet, at this very moment the mining camps were centers of siege by the army, and violence and conflict were an almost daily occurrence. Rather, Ché seemed intent on quietly establishing an extremely isolated training center for his small band in preparation for other adventures.

But in March 1967, a year after his arrival, Ché and his group at Nancahuazu had their first clash with the Bolivian army. With strong support from the United States, Barrientos and his Chief of Staff, General Ovando, crushed the rebels. By April, Regis Debray, the French journalist accompanying Ché, had been captured, and by October the rebels had been taken and Ché executed. Thus Barrientos was able to survive the armed opposition of the left and yet retain a vast popular support among the peasantry and the middle class. There is little question that when he died in an air accident in April 1969 he was still in full control of the nation. Despite the corruption of the regime, the defection of his close friend and Interior Minister, Colonel Arguedas, and other problems, Barrientos proved to be such a consummate politician that he could surely have won a second term in open elections.

The military caste that supported Barrientos was incapable of maintaining his ideological and political position. They remained divided and corrupt. Despite their common background and experience, their political tastes differed widely, so that there was no guarantee that their past histories would prove any guide to their future political positions. All of this became evident in the regimes that replaced Barrientos. From 1969 until 1982, one military regime after another would emerge, with their politics stretching all the way from extreme left through reformist to reactionary right. Government policies depended completely on the personalities and ideas of the individual officers who seized power and in no way reflected a coherent position of the army itself. Whereas in most of the major states of South America in this period the army was presenting a corporate personality and common policy toward the civilian world, in Bolivia this did not occur.

General Ovando, Barrientos's partner in the 1965 coup and head of the general staff, eventually seized power in September 1969. Ovando was of the moderate reformist MNR tradition and, in fact, tried slowly to push the regime toward a modus vivendi with the left. In October 1969 he nationalized the Gulf Oil Company of Bolivia, and by early 1970 had once again legalized COB and the FSTMB and permitted Lechín to return to power, and troops were withdrawn from the mines for the first time since 1964. He also tried to mobilize the old left in a new revitalized MNR. In the end, however, Ovando could neither mobilize the popular support that Barrientos had achieved nor organize a coherent political party system to support his regime. At the same time, the army become unhappy with Ovando who had been in power as chief of the general staff and/or as president for some eight years. Frustrated ambitions of the military thus played their part. The result was the decision in October 1970 to replace Ovando with General Juan José Torres, his former chief of staff. Thus began one of the most extraordinary governments in Bolivian history. From October 1970 to August 1971, when he was overthrown, Torres would prove to be the most radical and left-leaning general ever to have governed Bolivia.

Although he had been a Falangista in his youth, active in the campaign against Che, and supported the army's actions in the period up to his own takeover, Torres emerged as an idealistic left politician who wanted to extend Ovando's "democratic opening" to include even more radical mobilization of workers and left politicians. One of his first acts on taking office was to accept Russian and Eastern European financial aid for COMIBOL. Such support had been offered several times in the past, but the MNR and previous military governments had procrastinated in accepting it under pressure from the United States. Torres also signed contracts for the construction of a tin smelter, thereby liberating Bolivia for the first time from its dependence on European and North American smelters to process its ores. In the end the Russians were to provide almost as much financial assistance to COMIBOL as the United States, each giving in the neighborhood of a quarter of a billion dollars.

Torres also annulled a special COMIBOL contract with a United States mining company for extracting tin from Catavi wastes and rescinded the contract with U.S. Steel for running the Matilda Zinc mine. While this type of anti-U.S. company sentiment was not without its precedents, Torres went one step further and expelled the Peace Corps on the grounds that it was fomenting abortion policies among the peasantry. Although these anti-North American actions were popularly supported, they produced a strong reaction from the United States, which now found itself almost totally estranged from Bolivia for the first time since 1952.

The fact that Torres could take his opposition to this extreme largely reflected the changed conditions of the Bolivian economy. By the beginning of the 1970s, Bolivia was beginning to reap the economic benefits of the economic and social investments carried out by the MNR from 1952 onward. The development of a modern road system, the growth of commercial agriculture in the Santa Cruz region, and the heavy investments in COMIBOL and especially in YPFB – combined with rising mineral prices on the international market – produced major growth in the national economy. Added to this were spectacular advances in literacy and public education and the freeing of human resources through the abolition of all the pre-1952 restrictions on the rural population, which thus increased the value of human capital in the country. The Bolivian government became far less dependent on direct United States assistance to maintain the level of government investments or even to provide expanded development funding. Between international financial sources and the beginnings of a major private investment in minerals developments and commercial agriculture, Bolivia found itself relatively free of its dependence on North American largess.

Torres's efforts to create a united left on the national front were less effective. Torn by the divisions of the Communist Party into

Moscovite and Chinese wings, and the subdivision of the PIR into numerous factions, the COB, Lechín, and their supporters failed to unite on policies and actually feared the increasing radicalization of their erstwhile middle-class radical allies. At the same time their experiences under Barrientos made them wary of allaying with the powerful peasant sindicatos. But in early 1970 the COB did establish a political assembly, which sought to bring some unity to the old MNR left. This formed the basis for a so-called Popular Assembly organized in June 1970 for the purpose of replacing parliament. But this assembly neither obtained the legitimacy of a popular vote nor did it obtain the powers of a Bolivian legislature, despite the fact that it was housed in the Congress building. Ultimately made up of some 218 delegates, the Assembly counted only twenty-three representatives of the peasant confederations, as against 123 delegates from the labor unions, of which the FSTMB alone had thirty-eight. It also contained all the major left groupings, plus a new powerful party, the MIR (*Movimiento de la Izquierda Revolucionaria* or Left Revolutionary Movement), which had just been formed out of the left wing of the Christian Democratic movement and the university sector of the old MNR. But the radical left and labor were unable to secure the full cooperation of the relatively unstable Torres. Although the Assembly frightened the right and the center with symbolic acts of defiance, it enacted no significant legislation. Moreover, the government refused to supply arms to the workers or in any way challenge the power and supremacy of the army.

The agitation of the Popular Assembly created civilian support for a military coup. In January 1970 Colonel Hugo Banzer, then head of the *Colegio Militar*, attempted such an overthrow, but the army remained loyal. In the subsequent months the Assembly supported a worker takeover of the newspaper *El Diario* and worker seizures of small mines and some Santa Cruz haciendas organized by the pro-Chinese Communist Party. Thus, when Banzer attempted a second coup in August 1971, the left was unable to stop him. Supported by Paz Estenssoro's old right and center MNR party and by the FSB, Banzer received major financing from a Santa Cruz regional elite that was disturbed by the threats of extending agrarian reform to the new zones of commercial agriculture. The overthrow of Torres was not without resistance. Although Torres refused to open up the arsenals to the workers, students and workers did oppose the military, while loyalist troops attempted to defend the president. The result was that the Banzer coup of 1971 was the bloodiest overthrow since the April 1952 rebellion.

Banzer began to govern just as changes in the international price structure for minerals were finally having a profound impact on the national economy. Between 1970 and 1974, the current value of Bolivian exports almost tripled (from $226 million to $650 million). Given the preceding twenty years of investment and structural change, this new wealth was easily absorbed, and an economic boom occurred. Not only were there major new investments in medium-sized mining and the expansion of non-tin mineral exports, but the Santa Cruz region now yielded significant surplus production and, for the first time, the nation became an exporter of agricultural products, above all sugar and cotton. Urban construction boomed, and there was even some development in the manufacturing sector.

At the same time, the twenty years of significant investments in education were finally having an impact. Now a group of technical experts arose within the government and its autonomous production agencies that gave the regime a new source of power and expertise. Added to the appearance of this new professional and service sector was the rise of new regional elites. In this respect, the dramatic growth of the city of Santa Cruz is striking, for it moved from fourth-largest city in the republic in the 1940s to second in the 1970s, and became as well a modern advanced urban metropolis connected to the rest of Bolivia by all-weather paved roads and tied to the outside world by daily international flights. The expansion of Santa Cruz brought a profound change to national and regional power groups. Given the significant investments in oil and agriculture in the Santa Cruz region and the growth of its population, it was inevitable that their largely white and cholo populations would demand a greater voice in national decision making. For the first time in national history there existed an important source of economic and political power outside the traditional highland and intramountain valley regions.

The Banzer regime was consistent with its predecessors in pushing Agrarian Reform and encouraging active lowland colonization. It granted more land and benefited more peasant families than any previous regime, military or civilian. Thus of the thirty-one million hectares granted to the 434,000 landless peasant families between 1953 and 1980, some 81 percent of the land went to 62 percent of all families in the military interregnum period from 1964 to 1980, with the Banzer regime alone granting over half the total lands and benefiting half of all the landless families. But despite this strengthening of a fundamental aspect of the military-peasant pact, Banzer was the first of the generals to reduce the importance of the peasants in national political life largely because of changing demands coming from the peasant sector. The growth of population in the rural areas and the consequent fragmentation of holdings, plus the emergence of a new consciousness of peasants as farm producers for urban markets, were beginning to have an effect on the rural populations. No longer content with titles, they now wanted credit and price supports and other government assistance in improving their leverage in the marketplace. Thus it was no accident that the first peasant-military confrontation and massacre since 1952, which occurred in the Cochabamba Valley in January 1974, concerned peasant protests over government-maintained food prices.

The Banzer administration also adopted the antidemocratic ideas then dominating the continent. The Brazilian model became an example to the Bolivian military. It was held that democratic rule ultimately led to social chaos, and only through "depoliticizing" these masses could economic development proceed in a rational manner. Through careful tutelage and "controlled" participation rapid "modernization" could occur. Military intervention was no longer seen as a temporary affair, but rather as a long-term alternative to democratic politics. Almost immediately on taking office, Banzer declared the COB and the FSTMB as illegal, and all of the parties to the left of the traditional MNR were formally denied recognition. This resulted in the jailing of many persons and the exiling of the leadership of the MIR, PRIN – which was then the name of the old Siles-Lechín wing of the MNR – as well as the deliberate use of assassination and torture.

Banzer immediately moved to resolve the conflict with the United States that had erupted under Torres. A new and more liberalized investment code was enacted, and considerable aid was again sought, and obtained, for the building of army materiel and personnel. But the new relationship with Russia and Eastern Europe had become too important for even the Banzer regime to reject, and so the socialist states continued to provide long-term aid for the development of tin and other smelters. The Banzer government also made an abrupt shift in the traditional alliance with Argentina in favor of a new and close relationship with Brazil. Reflecting long-term Santa Cruz interests in opening up their economy and products to Brazilian markets, the Banzer regime signed an important series of international economic pacts that favored Brazilian participation over Argentina in the development of Bolivia's natural resources, above all with the gas and iron ore resources of the Santa Cruz region.

Banzer attempted to create a national political party and forced his two allies, the Falange and the Paz Estenssoro wing of the MNR, to ally themselves with his "Frente" before participating in the government. This attempt at creating a populist right-wing military government would ultimately prove uninviting to Banzer and, by late 1974, he announced an abrupt shift in his entire regime by carrying out an "auto-golpe," as it was called, and establishing an all-military nonparty government based on support of the technocrats and nonaligned ex-politicians. Dismissing the MNR from his regime and then exiling Paz Estenssoro, he announced that all parties, even those of the center and the right, were henceforth abolished and that the army would now rule without any democratic concessions whatsoever.

The decision to break sharply with tradition was clearly based on two important developments, one international and the other local. The first and most important factor was the overthrow of the Allende administration in Chile in September 1973 and the coming to power of the Pinochet regime. It was clear to Banzer that the model of a nondemocratic authoritarian and antiparty regime was becoming the norm in the region. The second factor was the extraordinary growth affecting the national economy, which created popular support for the regime despite its antidemocratic activities. Between 1973 and 1974 the price of tin on the world market almost doubled, which in turn resulted in a doubling of the total value of national exports and the creation of the largest trade surplus in national history. Also rising oil prices suddenly turned Bolivia's relatively

small oil output into a bonanza export, which in 1974 accounted
for 25 percent of the total value of exports. Of more long-term significance, since oil exports ceased by the end of the decade, was
the beginning of the export of the very abundant supplies of natural gas, which were exported for the first time in 1972 and by
1974 accounted for 4 percent of all exports, a figure that would rise
steadily throughout the rest of the century. Also the first exports of
smelted and processed tin started in 1971; by 1974 they accounted
for 9 percent of the value of all exports. All this meant that traditional tin ore exports and other unrefined minerals had dropped
from approximately 90 percent of the total value of exports in the
decade of the 1960s to just under 50 percent by the middle years of
the 1970s. Finally, the first exports of agricultural products began in
1970, with sugar and then cotton, and grew substantially in the following years, accounting for 6 percent of the total value of exports
by 1974. While this was still a relatively small item in the total of
goods being exported, it was the second-fastest-growing export in
the country in the years 1970 to 1976, at an annual average growth
rate of 49 percent, just behind the phenomenal growth of natural
gas exports, which were increasing at 50 percent per annum.

The boom of the early 1970s seemed to represent long-term
change in the nature of Bolivian exports and economic growth,
not just the classic short-term boom cycle resulting from the sudden shifts of international prices. Santa Cruz was now permanently
exporting its agricultural produce and, when sugar prices fell, the
shift to cotton showed that a basic infrastructure now existed that
could survive changes in world demand. At the same time, it was
evident that Bolivia's natural gas exports to its neighbors, primarily
Argentina and then Brazil, represented a market that would expand
steadily in the coming years. Finally, long-term price growth for non-
tin minerals and the export of finished tin metal seemed to imply
a long-term and quite prosperous economic future for the country. Bolivia's trading partners also were changing. Bolivia no longer
found itself dependent on any one trading partner as it had in the
past. The Latin American Free Trade Area now took a third of its
exports, Europe another 20 percent, and the United States only a
third, with the Asian nations taking the rest. Moreover, the mix of
imports also was quite varied, with the LAFTA countries and Asia

taking on greater importance and Western Europe and the United States lesser weight. The extraordinary increase in the favorable balance of trade led to an massive building boom. The major cities of La Paz and Santa Cruz became dotted with modern skyscrapers, and the whole urban architecture of these two cities changed. The airport system was overhauled and an international airport was constructed in Santa Cruz. Even more crucially, the paved road network was extended from La Paz to Oruro and to the Lake. A paved road broke through to the Chapare frontier in the province of Cochabamba, thus opening up the modern illegal trade in cocaine. Chapare, which had produced no more than 5 percent to 10 percent of total coca production in the nation prior to the new road, was producing over 70 percent of the national crop by the end of the decade, almost all of this production going into international market.

But the boom faded, and Banzer could not control the profoundly mobilized Bolivian society. Overspending on national budgets and rising corruption forced him to devalue the national currency by 40 percent, the first devaluation since the 1956 stabilization act. The resulting inflation created unrest and the clampdown on wages proved to be only stopgap measures. Despite the maintenance of troops at the mine heads and the supposed liquidation of the FSTMB and COB, strike activity and worker violence continued. By early 1976 there were national strikes, and Banzer had to close the universities. Not only was the regime unable to suppress the unions, but it also lost most of the middle-class nationalist vote when it admitted defeat on the Chilean negotiations for an outlet to the sea. Despite Banzer's desperate attempts to extract a solution at any cost, including even the proposal to exchange Bolivian territory for a port, nothing could be extracted from Pinochet, and by the end of 1976 all negotiations were abandoned. Finally, the middle and upper class that provided the civilian base of support for such military regimes in the rest of Latin America, in Bolivia were far more willing to trust their interests to a democratic party system than to an unknown military regime. Given the corruption and indiscipline of the officer corps, the civilian elite could not trust the outcome of an anti-Banzer coup, since there was no way of knowing if the next leader would be a Torres, a Barrientos, or a Banzer.

By early 1977 Banzer promised presidential elections in 1980, and by November, just three years after their promulgation, all the authoritarian decrees were removed. But so hostile had the army become that he was forced to announce that he would not become a candidate and by the end of the year he announced that elections would be held in 1978. But even this was not enough, for demands were soon made for a total amnesty for the 348 syndical and political leaders in exile. When Banzer refused, there began in late December 1977 a hunger strike by wives of mine union leaders in the Cathedral of La Paz. The church fully supported the move, and by early January over one thousand persons had joined the hunger strike from all over the country. The strikers demanded total amnesty and syndical freedom as well. So overwhelming was the strike that Banzer was forced to capitulate and was even made to sign a formal agreement with the human rights groups supporting the movement.

The returning exiles seized the unions from the government in-teventors, and within days the FSTMB and the COB were recreated with the same leadership that had existed prior to the 1971 coup. Strikes, labor agitation, and feverish political activity led Banzer to give up any pretense of attempting to maintain himself in office. He announced that General Pereda Asbun would be his successor and the new regime would reestablish democracy. Opposing the army candidate was Hernán Siles Zuazo and a new grouping of left and center political parties. Leaving the Paz-dominated MNR party in 1972, Siles had established his own MNRI, or left MNR, in Chilean exile. The MNRI banded together with the MIR and other groups to form a loose electoral coalition called the UDP (Democratic and Popular Unity) just before the July elections. To the shock of the military the election showed that the peasants were no longer voting as a bloc. So many peasants supported the popular Siles slate, along with the masses in the cities, that the regime found the election going against them and the military decided to undertake a coup.

But the Pereda government lasted only a few months and in November came a new junta under General David Padilla that not only proposed free elections but also announced that the government would not present a formal candidate or support any of the civilian contenders. Thus began one of the most politically creative periods in recent Bolivian history. In the space of four years and in three presidential elections, the older patterns of national voting shifted in important ways, ushering in a new and more complex political system in Bolivia which predominates until today. Instead of one massive popular party based on peasant support, in 1978 and continuing to the present day, there emerged a host of competing parties that were supported by complex combinations of urban and rural voters. Bolivia had in fact created a modern electorate.

This new diversity in the national electorate reflected changes in both the society and the economy. As the 1976 census revealed, Bolivia had finally felt the full effects of the introduction of modern social welfare in terms of health and education. The introduction of minimal medical care to virtually the entire population meant that the death rates in Bolivia had finally dropped and stabilized at lower levels. With falling death rates and high birthrates (at approximately forty-four per thousand), population began growing at a rapid rate. Thus, despite an overall mortality rate of eighteen per thousand and an extraordinarily high infant mortality rate of 202 per 1,000 live births in the late 1970s, Bolivia after 1950 had a population growth of 2.6 percent per annum, with the total population increasing naturally from 2.7 million persons in 1950 to 4.6 million by 1976.

Moreover, this growing population was far more urban and far better educated than had been preceding generations. Whereas in 1950 the total of persons living in towns and cities of any size was just 34 percent, by 1976 this figure had risen to 50 percent (with 42 percent of the population living in cities of two thousand persons or more). Only 31 percent of the schoolage population or above were considered literate in 1950. By 1976 the figure had climbed to 67 percent, with over 80 percent of the children in the ten-to-fourteen age category now listed as attending school. Finally, the percentage of Spanish speakers had risen to such an extent that by 1976 Spanish for the first time become the majority language of Bolivia. Of the 4.6 million persons listed, 1.6 million were now considered monolingual speakers of Spanish and another 1.7 million were bilingual in the language, representing together 72 percent of the population. Monolingual Indian speakers, despite the growth of the rural population at unprecedented rates, had now declined. Quechua monolinguals had fallen from 988,000 to 612,000 and

Aymara monolingual speakers from 664,000 to 310,000 between the two census years. It was the growth of bilingual speakers, which explains the majority position achieved by Spanish in 1976, proof of the impact of the schools on the rural areas. Not only had the cholo population expanded enormously, as these figures imply, but even more important, rural Indian peasants were now using Spanish on a large scale along with their traditional Indian languages.

Thus the Bolivian electorate of 1979 was better educated, more literate, and more Spanish-speaking than any other population in Bolivian history. Both Víctor Paz Estenssoro and his revived MNR, as well as Siles and his UDP alliance, found support among the peasants and the workers. Moreover, the new professional classes established new parties and alliances to express their particular needs. Suddenly the new and older parties found themselves in a balanced series of groupings on the right, the center, and the left. Even the formerly despised Banzer succeeded in organizing his own party, with some important regional support, and would convert himself into one of the leading national civilian politicians, a rare case of a transition in Latin American politics in any country.

These very complex political divisions explain why the elections of July 1979 saw Siles and Paz Estenssoro leading the opposition groupings, and why another old politician from the MNR days, Walter Guevara Arze, would emerge as the compromise candidate, once the two leaders fought out the election to a draw. Until the new and younger leaders could determine their strengths in open elections, they preferred to support the heroes of an earlier age. The election of 1979 was extraordinary. One of the most honest elections in national history, it brought over 1.6 million Bolivians to the polls, with most of the alliances and parties showing strengths in all regions, and with Santa Cruz in fact ending in the anti-Banzer camp.

Although Paz Estenssoro won the election by a plurality, the parties could not agree on a candidate, especially as Banzer and his new party were still considered nonnegotiable partners by the other groups. To forestall a bitter fight, Congress eventually decided to rerun the elections the following year and appointed Walter Guevara Arze, president of the Senate and an old friend of both Siles and Paz Estenssoro, as the caretaker president until the new elections.

The first civilian regime since 1964, the administration of Walter Guevara Arze lasted only a few months and was temporarily overthrown by a military junta in November 1979. But the political opposition within the nation was so intense, with violence and general strikes leaving over 200 dead, that the military was forced out within a few weeks. A compromise civilian, Lydia Gueiler Tejada, was put into office. She was the first woman president in national history and one of the few in all of American history. The selection of Gueiler also demonstrated the tremendous popular support for the return of a civilian regime. No party in November 1979 supported the coup, and accusations that Víctor Paz Estenssoro had supported the coup was sufficient to break the electoral deadlock that had occurred in the previous two elections, and in a third national election in as many years Hernán Siles Zuazo and the UDP achieved a plurality victory in June 1980.

The temporary return to civilian rule under Gueiler cost too many concessions, however, to the hardline military officers led by General Luis Garcia Meza. They refused to allow Siles to assume office, so that in July 1980 the army seized the government, despite opposition from all civilian parties and groups. But the return to an early Banzer-style authoritarian military regime had destroyed neither the powerful unions nor the civilian party system. Although declared illegal as in times past, these organizations continued to maintain a powerful following among the civilian population. Throughout the two years of junta domination, there was massive civil opposition, which included everything from illegal strikes and marches to hunger demonstrations, which destroyed any possible civilian base for these regimes. The level of corruption in the army achieved new heights with its direct involvement in the newly emerging international cocaine trade. Finally the authoritarianism of the officer class reached the point were they carried out the assassination of nine leaders of the MIR in La Paz in January 1981 and organized paramilitary death squads along the model of contemporary Argentina. So extreme was the Meza government, which lasted until August 1981, and those temporary juntas that followed it, that they employed internationally known fascists such as the Italian Pier Luigi Pagliai and the German Klaus Barbier of World War II fame.

Unrelenting civilian opposition, highly publicized corruption of the army, and the unresolved economic problems of the late 1970s came to haunt the junta governments and finally destroyed even their support among the officer corps. These economic problems derived from the dependence of the nation on the profitability and performance of autonomous government agencies. After seven years of Banzer rule these administrations were in total chaos. Although Bolivian exports had risen from $200 million at the beginning of the Banzer regime to over $700 million by the end, and government investment in development projects had reached an extraordinary 48 percent of the national budget, the bulk of these funds had been badly misspent. Above all, the three major autonomous agencies – YPFB, COMIBOL, and SNAF (the national smelting agency) – had overbuilt capacities and underfinanced new explorations. The result was economic disaster. Production was down everywhere and the public debt generated by these firms was staggering, and financing this public sector debt was taking an extraordinarily 30 percent of foreign exchange earnings by 1980. Finally came falling international prices for primary exports. Whereas in the early years of the decade growth rates were as high as 6 percent per annum, by 1977–8 there was no growth whatsoever. Beginning in 1978 the gross domestic product (GDP) actually declined and in the following year there was negative growth, the first time that this had occurred since the late 1950s. This crisis in national production continued uninterrupted into the next decade, with the worst annual decline (of −6.6 percent) occurring between 1982 and 1983. Bolivia was entering into one of its longest depressions in national history, a crisis that would last into the decade of the 1990s. In the context of this political and economic crisis, the violent and exploitative military regimes became an anachronism the country could ill afford. Nor could a violent military, however repressive, control so mobilized a society.

Chapter 9

Creating a Multiethnic Democracy, 1982–2002

The forced resignation of the last military junta in September 1982, and the decision to recall the congress that was elected in 1980, finally brought an end to the era of military authoritarian regimes. This reconstituted congress immediately elected Hernán Siles Zuazo to the presidency in August 1982. In one stroke, the democratic political system was revived. On the left was Siles Zuazo, the leader of the reconstituted progressive wing of the MNR, who was allied with traditional labor leaders of the COB, newer peasant leaders, various parties of the left, and the important MIR group of radical intellectuals led by Jaime Paz Zamora, who became his vice president. To the right and center were the parties that had run in the original 1979 and 1980 elections, all now well developed political forces that would dominate the national political scene for the next decade. In the center was the historic MNR – led by Víctor Paz Estenssoro – which incorporated both the older center and right of the party and a group of older Indian leaders who, although they had become independent of the MNR, still gave strong support to Paz Estenssoro. Finally there was the ADN (Acción Democrática Nacionalista), the party that was founded by Banzer at the end of his military rule, and that he then expanded in April 1979 to include elements of the old Falange as well as the reconstituted PIR. To the surprise of many, this party proved more forceful than expected and not only legitimated Hugo Banzer as a powerful civilian leader but also gained the support of the new economic elites, such as the private mining entrepreneurs and large-scale farmers of Santa Cruz, as well as many of the highly trained technocrats who had emerged in the twenty-five years since the National Revolution. Banzer managed to distance himself from the military juntas of the 1979–82 period and consistently supported the democratic processes, thus becoming a pillar of the civilian political system. The military interregnum had delayed the emergence of a younger civilian political leadership and thus provided one last chance for the old leaders of the period of the National Revolution to rule. While the leadership in the first part of the 1980s was from the 1950s, by the second part of the decade a new circle of younger politicians began to take over the national political scene.

With surprising decisiveness, Siles moved to dismantle the ferocious paramilitary apparatus that the last military juntas had constructed with the aid of Argentine officials and foreign fascists. In rapid succession, the gestapo leader, Klaus Barbie, was exported to France, and the terrorist, Pier Luigi Pagliari, was turned over to the Italian government. Argentines were expelled, and the government quickly moved to eliminate the more authoritarian leaders from the army. Thus the initial national and world reactions to the government were quite enthusiastic.

But the economy inherited by the Siles Zuazo regime was in tatters, and the situation would only worsen during the rest of the decade. Although he was an able opposition leader with a reputation for probity, Siles was an incompetent administrator and poor political negotiator. Within months of his election, he alienated the MIR and his other major supporters, and he proved incapable of controlling a seriously failing economy. The combination of these factors would destroy the credibility of his regime – although they would not destroy the legitimacy of civilian rule.

The end of the OPEC price inflation in the late 1970s and the decline of mineral and petroleum production all combined with the state mismanagement of the junta period to create a bankrupt public sector and a deeply depressed private economy. Between 1980 and 1984, the value of agricultural output declined by 11 percent; the value of exports by 25 percent and between 1981 and 1984, GDP per capita in current U.S. dollars declined by 1 percent per annum. Agricultural production itself was badly affected by a severe drought in 1983. The foreign debt contracted in the days of high world mineral prices and low interest payments reached some $3 billion by 1983, which, although low by Latin American standards, was high for Bolivia. This sum represented 80 percent of the total GDP, and in 1984, the servicing of this debt was equivalent to 36 percent of the value of all exports. Even more significantly, tin production went into a severe and permanent decline. Although annual production was still averaging above thirty thousand metric tons in the 1970s, and in the upper twenty thousands in the first four years of the decade, in 1984 it dropped below twenty thousand and kept declining, never again reaching twenty thousand tons. Brazil became Latin America's largest tin producer in 1983, and thereafter Bolivia has accounted for less than 10 percent of world production. In 1986 private mine owners (grouped into middle- and small-size miner and worker cooperatives) out-produced COMIBOL for the first time. The era of tin in Bolivian history could be said to have officially ended by the second half of the 1980s, and by 1990 zinc had become Bolivia's most valuable mineral export.

Although international demand for cocaine would begin to generate an important new market for Bolivian products, even this highly profitable export could not compensate for the general decline in the mining economy and the disappearance of foreign loan funds. At the same time, the government proved incapable of controlling costs despite the decline of state revenues. The inevitable solution for the Siles government was to print more money. Between 1980 and 1984, the total stock of money in circulation increased by over 1,000 percent. Prices were quickly affected, and by May 1984, Bolivia was officially entering hyperinflation with rates of price increases of over 50 percent per month. Whereas growth in the decade of the 1970s had averaged 4.7 percent per annum and inflation just 15.9 percent, in the decade of the 1980s growth was declining at an average 2.3 percent. Inflation jumped to three digits in 1983, and to an incredible annual 2,177 percent in 1984. In the first six months of 1985, it rose to 8,170 percent on a per annum basis.

In such a context of total fiscal crisis, it was inevitable that Siles Zuazo would soon find himself with little popular support and with most of his political allies deserting the government. In January 1983, Paz Zamora resigned the vice presidency, and the MIR withdrew from the government. Siles also lost the support of Lechín, the COB, and many of his old allies from the MNR. Despite self-imposed hunger strikes (recalling his successful 1957 tactic) and even a temporary abduction by the military that was stopped by massive civilian opposition, Siles was unable to govern effectively or pass any serious stabilization policies. Given this impasse, Siles was persuaded that he should abandon the presidency early on the grounds that his mandate really dated from 1980. He thus agreed to hold presidential elections in July 1985.

The election of 1985 provided an opportunity for the older parties, particularly the so-called historic MNR and the ADN, to establish their presence as powerful entities. But it also gave many of the newer groups, which had formed parts of the democratic and left alliances behind Siles, the opportunity to emerge as independent entities. On the established left, the MIR of Paz Zamora and the Partido Socialista-1 of Marcelo Quiroga Santa Cruz, founded in the 1970s, emerged as the two most important parties. Even more significant in terms of future developments, however, was the appearance of the Movimiento Revolucionario Tupac Katari, which represented a straight indigenous rights party and would gain 2 percent of the popular vote. Indigenous leadership had been alienated by the COB for many years, and people on the left associated it with the military–peasant alliance, but in fact an autonomous new Indian leadership had been developing. As early as the late 1960s, younger leaders arose among the traditional rural *sindicatos*, especially among the previously more quiescent Aymaras. The 1974 Cochabamba blockade and subsequent peasant massacre by the military had given an impetus to these new men. In 1976 the Tupac Katari movement was organized among Aymara peasant leaders in the La Paz region. By the end of the 1970s, the movement took over most of the official government peasant unions and organized its own CSUTCB (Unified Syndical Confederation of Peasant Workers of Bolivia). By 1981 the *kataristas* had seized control of the Aymara peasant unions and obtained representation in the COB. In that year, for the first time the COB appointed a peasant leader and a member of this movement, Jenaro Flores, as its leader. This shift in the COB was permanent as the peasant leaders, government workers and urban trade unionists now replaced the previously all-powerful mine workers as key groups in the national confederation of workers. The new indigenous leaders demanded changes in what they perceived to be their unequal treatment from the state in terms of agricultural prices, provisions for credit, education, health, and even respect for their traditional cultures. They proposed a series of changes in relation to the nature of Bolivian identity and the role of the indigenous peoples in modern society and stressed ethnic problems as much as class issues. Although there quickly emerged rival organizations to contest the right to express this new political power of the previously subservient indigenous peasant and urban mestizo groups, this new indigenous movement grew increasingly more powerful and independent in the following years. It would finally find its most coherent and powerful expression in a new mass political party that would emerge in the late 1990s, and this newly mobilized indigenous majority would finally destroy the traditional party system in the first decade of the next century.

Initially, it appeared that the traditional parties were able to harness this new political movement and direct it from above with classic non-indigenous or mestizo elite political leaders. From the early 1980s there emerged a complex political system in which no single party dominated. In every election from 1985 on, the electorate usually divided into three rough groupings of left, center, and right – with each political alignment made up of a complex of parties. To resolve this impasse, an informal second turn voting for the presidency occurred - though in this case it was conducted by the newly elected congress. In no election after the last Siles regime did any presidential candidate obtain a majority in the polls until 2005. Thus every presidential election involved complex post-electoral negotiations, usually between the MNR, the MIR, and the ADN. This system gave a lot of power to smaller parties and splinter groups, many of which joined with the party that took the presidency in coalition arrangements. These fragmented elections also forced all parties to respond to the indigenous and mestizo populations, who made up the majority of the voters. Though poor and with a significant ratio of illiterates, these peasants tended to produce high voter turnouts because of their political mobilization and powerful *sindicatos* and communal organizations. This also led

to new Aymara- and Quechua-speaking political leaders who organized either populist or straight ethnic parties that tried to mobilize
this vote.

The election of 1985 clearly defined the new electoral system
that was in place after the military interregnum. Some 1.4 million
voters went to the polls, and gave Hugo Banzer a plurality victory. But the new congress was dominated by the center-left parties,
and they chose seventy-seven-year-old Víctor Paz Estenssoro for his
fourth term in the presidency. While his previous administration of
the early 1960s had laid the foundations for the military–peasant
alliance, and he appeared to be involved in the military *golpe* of the
early 1980s, Paz Estenssoro remained a powerful figure among the
peasant masses that associated his name with the still strongly supported Agrarian Reform of 1953. To the surprise of both enemies
and friends, this seeming relic of a past era proved to be the most
dynamic and able civilian politician to rule in the last decades of
the twentieth century. Abandoning traditional positions, accepting
radical reforms, and ruthless and quick in his political responses, he
soon dominated national life in a manner that recalled his very first
presidential term. Without question, his single most important act
was his so-called New Economic Plan of mid-1985. Adopting many
of the proposals of the ADN, and even arranging an informal pact
with them, Paz Estenssoro imposed an economic program that was
both traditional in its structure and unusual in its context. While
contemporary governments in Argentina and Brazil faced with the
same problems of a runaway inflation and an international debt
crisis were still applying what their economists would come to call
a "heterodox shock", Paz Estenssoro turned toward a traditional
"orthodox shock" This meant that currency would be devalued,
prices and exchange rates would be free of government control,
and government expenditures severely reduced. This was in many
respects a classic example of the group of policies known as the
Washington Consensus.

To the surprise of all, Paz Estenssoro adopted the principles of
economic liberalism and rejected the economic nationalist and state
capitalist ideologies which he had been instrumental in implanting
earlier in Bolivia. The reasons for this rejection were twofold. First,
there was the impact of hyperinflation for the second time in modern

Bolivian history, a crisis that sent the national economy into a severe decline and second, there was the total collapse of the expensive state mining system that had been constructed on the basis of a tin industry that was now rapidly declining. That these two irreducible events occurred in a society more developed and more complex than the one Paz Estenssoro inherited some thirty-three years later led him to believe that a radical solution had to be adopted. With the help of North American advisers, Paz Estenssoro in a matter of a few months carried out a classical orthodox economic shock, which was a textbook model of conservative economic policy.

By the terms of Decree 21060 of August 29, 1985, the national currency was devalued; a uniform and free-floating exchange rate was established; all price and wage controls were eliminated; public sector prices were substantially raised; government expenditures were severely restricted; and the real wages for government employees were reduced. Payments on Bolivia's foreign debt were temporarily halted – the only heterodox action of the program. With prices rising and investments halted, the economy went into a severe recession. An attempted general strike was stopped by a state of siege, and the general popularity of the end to hyperinflation gave Paz Estenssoro the support he needed to force through the reform. Along with the fiscal shock came major tax reforms that went back to many of the recommendations of the tax advisory group known as the Musgrave Commission of the 1970s. A value-added tax was soon imposed, and the state coffers once again began to accumulate surplus funds.

Paz Estenssoro went on to attack the state bureaucracy. With gas replacing tin as the primary export and Bolivia producing ever-smaller quantities of high-cost tin, the very purpose of COMIBOL made little sense. Paz Estenssoro, who had initially founded this institution, began dismantling this once-powerful state agency. The reform of COMIBOL also meant the emasculation of its labor unions. Between 1985 and 1986, COMIBOL was reduced from twenty-seven thousand workers to only seven thousand five hundred workers. Even YPFB was forced to dismiss four thousand workers and was reduced to a workforce of five thousand in the same period. All these changes led to a major decline in the power of the FSTMB and organized labor in general, which no longer was able to play the powerful political and economic roles it had assumed in Bolivian society since the 1940s. One indication of these changes was the retirement of Juan Lechín as head of the FSTMB in 1986 and his removal from power in the COB in the following year. For the first time since 1944, one of the three great leaders of the MNR held no office in the organized labor movement. The much-weakened FSTMB was taken over by Trotskyite leaders. At the same time, the CSUTCB, led by Jenaro Flores, became the single most important group within the COB.

The continuing crisis of the world tin market helped Paz Estenssoro greatly at this crucial moment. In October 1985, the International Tin Council, a thirty-two-nation- supported organization that purchased tin for price support purposes, went bankrupt and the international tin market collapsed. For almost half a year, no tin was traded on the London minerals market, and even the world's leading tin producer, Malaysia, was forced to close one hundred tin mines and lay off four thousand workers. By world standards Bolivia was one of the world's highest cost tin producers and had one of the lowest grades of tin ores. Given these high mining costs and the inefficiencies of the Bolivian smelters, which had finally gone into production in the early 1970s, Bolivia's refined tin – just like its unprocessed ores – could then not find a market. Hunger marches, general strikes, road blockages, and protests brought little support for the miners from other members of society. When Paz Estenssoro broke up their demonstrations and jailed their leaders, there was little serious opposition.

But the political and fiscal successes of the so-called New Economic Plan were achieved at the cost of economic growth and led to increased social misery. Unemployment soared to over 20 percent, and the traditional mining centers of Oruro and Potosí went into severe economic decline. U.S. aid was fundamental in alleviating the worst aspects of the government austerity plan, but it was the rise of an illegal and parallel coca economy that provided Bolivia with some crucial resources to lessen the impact of this harsh shock treatment. Although the coca leaf was native to Bolivia and was a major domestic crop produced in the Yungas valleys of the Department of La Paz from pre-colonial times, it slowly emerged as a major export crop in the 1970s with the rising world demand for cocaine – its principal derivative – and with the opening up of new coca-producing lands in the tropical eastern lowlands.

The construction of the first modern roads in the 1950s to the Amazonian foothills region of the Chapare, a lowland tropical district in the eastern end of the province of Cochabamba, brought highland migrants to these undeveloped lands in large numbers, and coca was one of the traditional crops produced. With higher alkaloid content than Yungas-produced leaf, the Chapare product was not highly prized for local consumption by the indigenous Andean populations, and initially, the Cochabamba migrants who farmed the area were not major coca producers. But the Chapare leaf proved ideal for producing cocaine. The changing drug consumption fashions of the populations of the advanced world economies, and above all, those of the United States, moved toward cocaine as the drug of choice in the 1970s. This proved to be a boon for Bolivian producers, who accounted for more than a third of world production. With Chapare leaf more highly desired on the international market than on the national market, and with its location far from traditional urban centers, the Chapare region from the mid 1970s became the dominant center for coca leaves being used for illegal cocaine exports. Not only was coca native to the region, and a highly labor-intensive product, but it was primarily produced on small farms, with an estimated two-thirds of production coming from plots of six hectares or less. These peasant-owned plots were grouped into colonies and organized into large unions, or *sindicatos*, which were an effective voice for the small landowners. Thus for the first time in modern Bolivian history, a primary export product was dominated by small peasant producers. Given the labor-intensive nature of the crop and the powerful peasant syndical movement, international traders were content to leave the cultivation of the leaf in the hands of small farmers and confined themselves to processing and marketing the output of peasant producers. Although Bolivian merchants would produce cocaine base (or paste) by the mid-1980s, final crystallization and commercialization of the product on the world market remained in the hands of Colombian middlemen. The Chapare, the neighboring region of the Beni, and the cities of Santa Cruz and Cochabamba became the centers of this new export trade, while the Yungas continued to produce coca leaf for its traditional internal consumer markets.

While there are obviously problems with estimating the size and importance of this clandestine economy, which formed part of the so-called informal or unregistered market, it is evident that even by conservative calculations, coca exports were as important as, if not more important than, all legal exports by the mid-1980s. Physical output followed rising exports. Whereas only twelve thousand hectares were devoted to coca leaf production in 1976, by 1985 the area of cultivation had grown to over sixty-six thousand hectares. Output in this same period went from just under fifteen thousand tons to approximately one hundred fifty-three thousand tons of leaf, with the Chapare region alone producing over one hundred thousand tons in 1986 on some forty thousand to forty-five thousand hectares. By this time, it was conservatively estimated that a quarter of a million farmers were cultivating the crop. Without question, coca leaf became, for a time, the single most important agricultural crop of the nation, although, even in the Chapare, peasant coca farmers also grew food crops.

But Bolivian cocaine exports began facing ever more stringent international controls in the form of increasing pressure from the United States, which replaced the "Cold War" with "the Drug War," and that made this a fundamental aspect of the relationship between the two countries from the 1980s until today. Equally important, however, was the competition from other producers. Not only did production expand in neighboring Peru, but Colombian farmers began to produce coca leaf for the first time. By the early 1990s, a combination of falling prices, increasing competition, and international control efforts had greatly reduced the importance of Bolivian production. By 1992 Bolivian coca plantings were down to 40,000 hectares. In contrast, Peru was using 113,000 hectares, and Colombian farmers were planting 89,000 hectares. As of 1999, only 14,000 hectares were in production, and just 70 metric tons of cocaine were produced, compared to the 300 to 400 metric tons that were produced in Colombia and the 175 to 240 metric tons that were produced in Peru. Given falling prices and production, the cocaine shipments were no longer a dominant element in national exports. By the late 1990s, government intervention also resulted in a major reduction of the illegal cocaine exports.

In the 1980s, there was little question that coca paste and cocaine exports were extremely important for the Bolivian economy, and the government did everything possible to encourage reinvestment of these clandestine profits in the national economy. These profits provided Bolivia with a major source of economic growth in the 1980s; especially as new growth sectors such as natural gas and commercial agriculture were just beginning to become important. Although the economy finally began growing again in the 1990s, the rates of growth were still relatively low. Nevertheless, by the last decade of the twentieth century, there occurred a profound reorganization of the national economy that had a great deal to do with government policies and investments. The two new areas of growth that eventually came to dominate exports were natural gas, developed by YPFB in conjunction with private and government-owned foreign firms, and commercial crop exports, especially soybeans. The construction of a natural gas pipeline from Santa Cruz to the Argentine frontier in 1972 was eventually followed by the joint construction of a similar pipeline by YPFB and Brazil's Petrobras from the Santa Cruz fields to the industrial metropolis of São Paulo. Finished in 1999, the new pipeline both created a new outlet for Bolivia gas and these exports to Brazil quickly surpassed natural gas exports to Argentina, with the total volume climbing from around 100 billion cubit feet in the late 1990s to over 500 billion cubic feet in 2008. If the previous two centuries in Bolivia could be known as those of silver and tin, the current century could easily be labeled the century of natural gas. By 2008 it was evident that a major shift in the mix of products Bolivia exported had occurred, with a dramatic decline in traditional minerals and their replacement by hydrocarbons, principally natural gas. There was also a major increase in non-traditional exports such as soybeans and other commercial agricultural crops (see Graph 9-1).

Although Santa Cruz had become an ever more important commercial agricultural area of large farms from the late 1950s on, it was the expansion of Brazil's western soybean frontier into Santa Cruz in the late 1990s that turned the Santa Cruz region

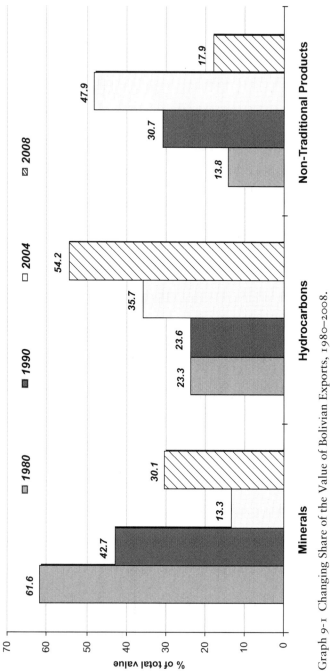
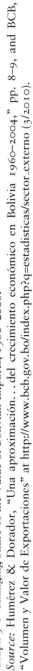

Graph 9-1 Changing Share of the Value of Bolivian Exports, 1980–2008.
Source: Humérez & Dorador, "Una aproximación…del crecimiento económico en Bolivia 1960–2004," pp. 8–9, and BCB, "Volumen y Valor de Exportaciones" at http://www.bcb.gov.bo/index.php?q=estadisticas/sector_externo (3/2010).

into a major international exporter of agricultural products. Soybeans have recently became one of Bolivia's more valuable exports, accounting for 5 percent of the value of all exports in 2008. Soybeans, along with sugar, sunflower seeds, and tropical woods made up one-tenth of the total exports. What is impressive about these agricultural crops is that the efficiency of the Bolivian producers is close to that of the Brazilian soybean farmers, who are among the most productive in the world. Unfortunately, little investment by the state or private investors has occurred in the traditional highland food producing regions, and thus potato farmers in the highlands produced crops per hectare that were only 12% of what US potato farmers were obtaining from their fields in 2008. The road construction and agricultural credits provided by the La Paz government from the mid-1950s onward, along with the funds generated by illegal cocaine exports, have finally created a modern agricultural sector in Bolivia but have had little effect on the productivity of the traditional peasant farmers.

Even the traditional minerals export area has seen basic change. Zinc has become the single most important traditional mineral and was twice as valuable an export in 2000 as was tin, despite the fact that Bolivia is still a minor world producer of the metal. Even silver exports are more valuable than the once mighty metal. But Bolivia continues to have major reserves of the tin and production, though less than Peru and Brazil, has settled down to a steady ten thousand to twenty thousand tons in the last two decades.

Bolivia has even exported some refined tin from its underutilized smelters. Although traditional minerals continue to lose their share of exports, the rapid growth of natural gas exports has meant that the overwhelming majority of Bolivia's exports are still made up of nonrenewable resources. Natural gas production, which was slow to develop, finally became Bolivia's principal export in 2001 and grew so rapidly that by 2008 gas alone accounted for 45 percent of the value of all exports, with zinc reduced to 11 percent and tin just 3 percent. There has also has been a steady growth of renewable and non-traditional exports, from woods and cashew nuts, to coffee, sugar, cotton, soybeans, and sunflower oils. Soybeans and vegetable oils by 2008 made up 8 percent of the value of exports. The growth of these new industries, which came into full production in the 1990s and the first decade of the twenty-first century, meant that the economy of Bolivia had begun to expand at rates not seen since the 1960s, achieving growth above general Latin American rates in the 1990s and again in the first decade of the new century.

Despite the rapid growth in exports, which has more than doubled in just a few years in the 2000s, Bolivia still ranked at the bottom of the countries of Latin America in the total value of its exports of goods and services in 2008, just above most of the Central American republics and Haiti but behind Honduras and Paraguay. Thus despite the growth of new sources of wealth from gas to soybeans, Bolivia remains a poor country. While per capita income has grown from $730 current dollars in 1990 to $1,723 in 2008 (see Graph 9-2), Bolivia is still ranked as the third poorest country in Latin America, just ahead of Haiti and Nicaragua. The country still receives large amounts of foreign aid, though this assistance has been declining over time. As late as 1999, 30 percent of central government income came from foreign aid, but this had fallen to just 3 percent in the budget of 2010 thanks to rising tax receipts, increasing royalty incomes, and migrant remittances.

Just as the economic structure of Bolivia continues to change and evolve, so, too, has the political structure of Bolivia changed in the past twenty years. Without question, the establishment of a multiparty system, the rise of a powerful legislature, the increasing importance of municipal and regional politics, and the use of multiparty pacts to govern the country had become new elements in the political evolution of Bolivia. The fight for basic civil rights at the end of the military interregnum had weakened the revolutionary left and the extreme right within national politics. At the same time, the base of the radical left has been transformed with the decline of both the old labor federation and the miner's union and the rise of new peasant organizations. In 1971 the *kataristas*, with their Aymara rights program, grew ever more powerful in local altiplano *sindicatos* and then came to dominate the new and powerful peasant confederation, the CSUTCB (*Confederación Sindical Unica de Trabajadores Campesinos de Bolivia*), which was founded in 1979. Soon the CSUTCB held a major stake in the COB and would eventually take over its leadership and reorient its demands away from exclusive class concerns toward both ethnic and class issues.

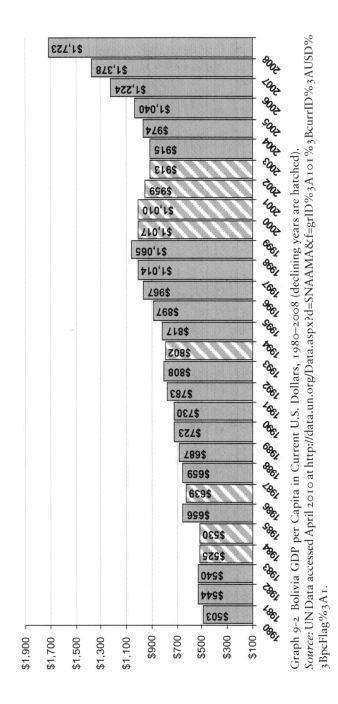

Graph 9-2 Bolivia GDP per Capita in Current U.S. Dollars, 1980–2008 (declining years are hatched).
Source: UN Data accessed April 2010 at http://data.un.org/Data.aspx?d=SNAAMA&f=grID%3A101%3BcurrID%3AUSD%3BpcFlag%3A1.

Although some unions remained with the radical left, most especially the trotskyite (POR), which controlled the primary teachers confederation, the majority adopted more moderate positions.

In turn, the inability of any of the three major parties – the old MNR, Banzer's ADN, and the new MIR – to obtain an absolute majority in either congress or the presidential elections forced the parties to work out multiparty pacts in order to govern and led to the most orderly transition of governments in the history of the nation. The establishment of an electoral court with significant power also led to the most fraud-free elections era in Bolivia's democratic history. All these changes created a climate of consensus and political negotiation between competing parties, which was new to the political scene. At the same time, the post-military regimes debated, and finally implemented, some of the most important changes in governmental institutions since the founding of the republic.

Many of these changes began with the Siles regime and continued with the presidency of Víctor Paz Estenssoro. The last Paz Estenssoro regime was also important in helping to usher in a new generation of political leaders. The most important of these younger leaders was the U.S.-educated Gonzalo Sánchez de Lozada, one of the new mine owners to emerge in the post-1952 period. Eventually rising to leadership of the senate and then to the position of Minister of Planning and head of the government's economic team, Sánchez Lozada proved to be a formidable opponent of the old Paz Estenssoro clique that had been deeply involved in the bloody Natasch Busch regime of 1980–1981.

Paz Estenssoro worked closely with his former rival, Hugo Banzer, and his ADN in putting through his economic plan. With the two parties dominating the congress, it was easy for the MNR government to control both the legislation being passed as well as the army and other forces of the state, which were relied on to control worker protest. But the cost was high for his own party. Although Sánchez Lozada eventually took control of the historic MNR and ran as its presidential candidate in the May elections of 1989, he was now faced by a powerful opposition led by Hugo Banzer and the growing power of the MIR, which had stood apart from the more aggressive anti-labor attacks of the MNR regime.

The election of 1989 marked the passage of an entire generation of political leaders who had dominated national life since the 1940s. The presidential candidates of all three parties were, for the first time, men who had come to political prominence after the Revolution of 1952. With Lechín out of the labor movement, Siles disgraced, and Paz Estenssoro too old to govern again, only Banzer remained from the earlier generation, and even he had only entered the political scene in the late 1960s. Although Banzer had won the 1985 elections in terms of total votes, this time he came in second to Sánchez Lozada. The big winner in the 1989 elections was the MIR, which had taken only 9 percent of the votes in 1985, but now claimed 20 percent of the total cast. Given the strong showing of the MIR, Banzer conceded the election and made a pact with the MIR to elect Jaime Paz Zamora as president of the republic. By this act, Banzer brought a member of the new post-revolutionary left to power for the first time.

This election also showed that a complex division of both parties and political preferences had been firmly established within the nation. The trends noted in the elections of 1980 and 1985 were present in 1989 in that three major parties dominated the political scene. But the potential for change was also seen in the rise of two new populist parties of importance, which were created just prior to the 1989 election: the CONDEPA (Consciousness of the Fatherland) party, which the media personality, Carlos Palenque, founded in 1988 based on wide support in La Paz and among the mestizo and Aymara speakers of the altiplano, and UCD (Unión Cívica Solidarid), created in 1989 by the beer industrialist, Max Fernandez, with strong support in Santa Cruz. Both parties did well in the elections, and CONDEPA would later be considered the origin of most of the mass indigenous-based parties that would emerge in the first decade of the next century. It was impressive that the three major parties – MNR, ADN, and MIR – all received significant votes from all classes and in all parts of the country. This election also saw the attempt of the *katarista* movement to directly enter politics, and although CONDEPA and UCD did well, the *kataristas* garnered only twenty-three thousand votes. The days of a single-party state, which was never complete even in the early days of the MNR-led National Revolution of 1952, as well as the rote voting in mass among the rural populations, were a thing of the past. Although some communities might still vote as a block, many peasants in the rural regions began to split their votes among multiple parties, which meant that a return to the days of a peasant–military alliance were gone.

Equally impressive about the 1989 campaign was the fact that none of the three leading parties challenged the New Economic Plan of Paz Estenssoro and the dismantling of the state capitalist system, which in fact may have been one of the long-term factors that would influence their decline. Even the MIR promised to respect the economic stability programs and refused to support the reconstruction of the old state enterprises, although this did cause it to lose its far left wing. Rather, the effort was to stress the issues of growth and development. The MIR proved no more radical in power than the older parties, especially as it worked closely with Banzer's conservative ADN party. They continued state retrenchment in the tin industry, and supported the opening up of the economy to foreign and private capital. They also withdrew government support from the COB and the FSTMB. But the MIR, despite its abandonment of the syndical movement, initially did not loose its base and continued to represent a portion of the left. Although a splinter MIR party would make some inroads in the 1990s, the MIR recovered most of its old support and even became a significant party in El Alto, the classic mestizo city, until the mid-2000s.

Although the MIR had governance problems when it came to power, this was a period of major intellectual debate about the nature of the state and about the traditional social and economic order. The viability of presidentialism, centralism, and other previously unquestioned ideas were challenged. The government also succeeded in sentencing and jailing the military dictator, General Luis Garcia Meza, for his violent overthrow of the civilian government in 1980 – one of the few democratic governments to have successfully imprisoned one of the leaders of the earlier military era. There was also the first manifestation at the national level of the poor conditions experienced by the eastern lowland (oriente) indigenous populations. In 1990, leading a dramatic march to La Paz from the Beni, some eight hundred men women and children from twelve Indian nations of the oriental lowlands demanded protection of their lands against invasion and exploitation by non-Indians. For the first time, the CSUTCB joined forces with these new indigenous groups representing the Chiquitanos, the Guaraní, and other previously ignored peoples. Also, municipal politics became a more important center of activity as many of the cities of the nation were taken over from the national parties by the newly emerging ones. Thus CONDEPA, under "Compadre" (Godfather) Palenque and his second-in-command, Remedios Loza, the so-called cholita Remedios, captured the city government of La Paz. Moreover, in 1989 Remedios Loza was the first *mujer de pollera* (traditionally dressed mestiza) to be elected to parliament, and she headed this important party after the death of Carlos Palenque in 1997.

The election of 1993 brought the MNR back to power, with a very substantial 34 percent of the vote gained by Gonzalo Sánchez de Lozada. But the MNR had to rely on the *kataristas* in the rural areas to win, and in recompense gave the vice presidency to one of their leaders, Víctor Hugo Cardenas. This appointment was a recognition by the elite of the new importance of the mestizos and indigenous urban and rural populations in national politics. Not only did the vice president's wife make it a custom to dress for political and social occasions in traditional indigenous dresses, but the new government reformed the Constitution of 1967 in 1994 by declaring in its first article that "Bolivia [was not only a] free, independent, sovereign" country, but that it was also "multiethnic and pluricultural", the first time this was formally recognized in republican history. A major set of laws was also approved that not only recognized the legal personality of the *comunidades indígenas* but also those of the peasant associations and *sindicatos campesinos*. The revised charter also guaranteed the *ayllus* and the *comunidades* their traditional land rights by unequivocally guaranteeing the existence of the *propiedades comunarias*, that is the communal property rights vested in communities rather than individuals, and even guaranteeing their right to use local traditional laws.

In support of this newly emerging vision of a multiethnic nation, the Sánchez de Lozada regime of 1993–1997 was to make fundamental changes in state organization and political participation. With the decrees of the Law of Popular Participation (1994) and the Law of Decentralization (1995), the MNR attempted to change the centralist nature of the state by giving far more economic and political autonomy to the municipalities. Whereas there had only been a few dozen municipalities in existence prior to the law, and these all located in major urban centers and departmental capitals, the government announced the creation of 311 municipal governments, each with its own mayor and town council, all electoral offices, and established them throughout the nation. This meant that there were rural as well as urban municipalities. By this act the government increased the number of local elected officials from 262 before the law to 2,900 afterward. At the same time, these new local regimes were to be overseen by legally appointed vigilance committees made up of registered local grassroots organizations. In the next three years, the government formally recognized 13,827 such territorial organizations, from urban neighborhood committees to peasant unions (the *sindicatos*). These committees were supposed to oversee local government and could bring formal impeachment proceedings for malfeasance in office against local officials.

Finally, these newly elected governments were given serious economic power for the first time. Municipalities now controlled their own budgets and 20 percent of state revenues were devolved to them, with the total funding they received based on population size. The government set up research organizations to assist the municipalities and large quantities of foreign aid flowed into this decentralization program. The new municipalities were also given some control over local education in an Education Reform Law of 1994, having authority over the noncore curriculum, all costs of infrastructure and school supplies.

So profound was this political/administrative change that it was estimated that almost two-thirds of the 1,624 municipal mayors and councilmen elected to office after the enactment of the Popular Participation Law were peasants or indigenous peoples. National politics began to change as the major parties were forced to enter local politics in a major way. In subsequent municipal elections, many local leaders from small and often radical parties were elected, thus undermining the old national parties. The fact that these new municipality governments had close to three thousand patronage jobs to distribute became important for even nationally based political parties. The government also decided to increase democratic representation by dividing the deputies into those elected from national party lists (plurinominal) and those running, like the U.S. system, under their own single ticket (uninominal), even if they belonged to a national party, which was another factor weakening the old traditional parties. Whatever the short-term problems faced by this program, there is little doubt that it started one of the most profound processes of political and administrative changes in Bolivian history.

But the Sánchez de Losada regime also significantly extended the neoliberal economic policies that had begun in the mid-1980s by undertaking a major privatization of state companies. In 1992 a privatization law had been passed and the government made a great effort to carry it to completion. Most of the small firms were sold off to private investors, but the large government firms were sold through capitalization schemes. This meant that the state retained 50 percent of the companies but sold the other 50 percent to private groups which also would administer the companies. These privatized companies included YPFB, which was in charge of oil and gas; ENDE, which was the national electricity company; ENFE, which controlled the railroads, ENTEL, which was in charge of all communications; and LAB, the national airline company. To soften the impact, the government devoted its share of the funds to BONOSOL, an entity which paid out pensions to retired workers who had not participated in any retirement plans.

Of all these nationalizations, the one that would have the most impact was the privatization of YPFB in 1996. The organization immediately went from almost six thousand workers to two thousand workers upon its capitalization, and it eventually gave up active exploration, production, and transportation of oil and gas in a period when it was transformed into what was called YPFB-Residual. Contracts were signed with numerous foreign companies, both private and governmental, and royalties for new discoveries of oil and gas were drastically reduced. It was these contracts and the passive role of YPFB that would generate enormous political conflict in the coming years.

As a result of privatization and decentralization, the MNR did poorly in the elections of 1997, dropping to 18 percent of the national vote, behind both the ADN (21 percent) and the still powerful MIR (20 percent). Given the previous alliances, it was no surprise that MIR threw its support behind the ADN in the post-election congress, which named Hugo Banzer president of the republic. Thus the former dictator and general returned to govern the country, this time for a five-year term, as mandated by the changes made in the 1994 constitutional revisions. Neither a populist in the mold of Perón nor a leader with powerful military support, Banzer was the unusual case of a military dictator turned politician who headed a respectable center-right party. Whatever were his administrative abilities, there is little question that Banzer represented a unique phenomenon in Latin American politics of the past century. But ill health in mid-2001 and a failing economy with negative growth rates forced Banzer to resign and he was replaced by Vice President Jorge Quiroga.

The election of June 2002 again saw the leading candidate gain less than a quarter of the 2.8 million votes cast, with the resulting parliamentary second round voting giving the presidency to Gonzalo Sánchez de Lozada for a second term. Thus a seemingly revitalized MNR under its new generation of leaders appeared destined to return to power as the dominant party. But the election proved to be a fundamental turning point in modern Bolivian political history. The system of political party rule since 1985 was about to end. In this period Bolivia's presidential system had been significantly modified by the increasing importance of parliamentary government. In turn, the bicameral legislature had been reorganized to make it more sensitive to direct voting by the population. Between the effective strengthening and extension of municipal government and the increasing power of the senate and congress, Bolivia moved away from its traditional centralist, presidentialist system of government. But the parties which had created this more decentralized system were about to disappear. Both Banzer's old ADN and the MIR declined as significant national parties in this election, and the candidate who came in second to the MNR with a quarter of the votes came from a new party and was an indigenous Aymara leader.

This fundamental change was the culmination of the rise of indigenous political parties that had been evolving since the 1970s with the rise of the Tupac Katari movement followed by the extraordinary growth of CONDEPA, the first truly indigenous party, in the late 1980s and early 1990s. The reforms of the state under *Participacion Popular* in the mid 1990s, brought ever more rural indigenous and mestizo leaders into office. Finally, a new center of indigenous political mobilization emerged far from the usual regions of the altiplano and the Cochabamba Valley. This new *cocalero* movement was a result of the U.S. war on drugs policy, which had led to massive U.S. intervention in Bolivian politics in the late 1980s and 1990s, and the often violent conflict between the government and the *cocaleros* and their *sindicatos* and federations. All these traditional and new movements help to explain the origins of the massive mobilization against the more extreme of the neo-liberal policies that had been carried out by the traditional parties since 1985.

While radical Aymara groups presented themselves in the elections of the 1990s, especially under the leadership of Felipe Quispe, who became the head of the CSUTCB in 1998, the most notable of these new movements was the one organized by the *cocaleros* of the Chapare region under the leadership of Evo Morales, who had taken over one of the important regional syndical federations, the FCT (Federación de Cocaleros del Trópico), in 1988. Morales and his followers created the Asamblea por la Soberanía de los Pueblos (ASP), which was the immediate antecedent to the Movimiento al Socialismo (MAS) party. Using the peasant *sindicatos* as a base, his new party was able to capture municipal governments not only in the coca zones but throughout the Department of Cochabamba, and Morales himself was overwhelmingly elected to the National Congress from Chapare in 1997. Four indigenous leaders were elected to congress that year, all from Cochabamba. Although expelled from Congress in 2002, Morales and his party shocked the traditional political establishment in the presidential elections that year by coming in second to the MNR. In fact, in the election of 2002 a third of congressional seats were taken by the two indigenous parties, the MAS of Morales and the Movimiento Indio *Pachakuti* (MIP) of Felipe Quispe, and the MAS even elected eight senators. These new Indian leaders now presented a series of demands relating to specific economic and social issues related to the urban poor and rural masses. They also proposed a change in the nature of Bolivia's political economy with a return to state control over natural resources, a new national identity and a new role for the indigenous peoples in modern Bolivian society.

This movement not only led to the development of new parties and pressure groups at the local and national levels, but it also created a new era of increasing political mobilization and mass violent protest in the streets and highways of Bolivia. This era began just before the presidential election with the "Water War" in January 2000 in the Cochabamba valley. The government attempt to privatize the region's public and communal waterworks and sell them to Bechtel, a North American multinational, created an ever increasing popular protest. After three months of massive mobilization of local groups, which included general strikes and an important participation of the Quechua-speaking agriculturalists, the government finally abandoned its effort to privatize the water system in the valley. Although the government's decision to abandon privatization calmed the protests, this was the first significant popular mobilization that combined immediate economic demands with large-scale debates about government policies and the demands of indigenous groups for greater political power.

The opening of the modern natural gas industry to foreign participation, even though many of these companies were in fact state enterprises of other nations, was the second issue around which a popular massive attack on the post-1985 privatization policies was organized. The second Sánchez Losada government was intent on using this new natural gas resource outside the control of YPFB and wished to sell Bolivian gas to overseas transatlantic markets. The decision to build a natural gas pipeline over the Andes to Chilean ports led to the Gas War of 2003 and the massive and often violent mobilization of the peasant and mestizos against the MNR and its leader. The use of Chilean territory for the proposed pipeline and the continued privatization of this crucial new natural resource, as outlined in the Hydrocarbons Law of 1996, were the key factors that created both a nationalist and left movement that made for a powerful frontal attack on government privatization policies related to natural resource. In September 2003 came urban protests in La Paz and Cochabamba and then a massacre of peasants in the crucial

Aymara altiplano center of Warisata. A blockade from El Alto of communications with La Paz on October 13th by anti-gas protestors led Sánchez Losada to send troops to the altiplano which resulted in a large number of deaths among the unarmed protestors. The result was an immediate escalation of road blockages, the closure of the city of La Paz by a mobilized population of the city of El Alto, and increasing police and protestor confrontations and violence. Whatever sympathy the elite classes felt for the MNR evaporated with the ongoing blockades and daily protests that were bringing the economy of the capital city to a halt. On October 17, 2002, Sánchez Losada resigned the presidency and left the country. Vice President Carlos Meza, a media personality and historian without a national party or group who supported him, became the new president of a much changed Bolivia. In recognition of the sudden and profound changes that were occurring in Bolivia, Mesa was sworn into office not in the traditional presidential palace in La Paz, but was inaugurated instead in the mestizo city of El Alto.

Chapter 10

The Emergence of a Mestizo and Indigenous Elite, 2002–2010

The shock of the election of 2002, followed by the massive, violent and ever more effective blockades by mestizos and indigenous groups created the background for the emergence of the first coherent and powerful mass political party led by mestizo and indigenous leaders. By the time of the presidential election of December 2005 most of the traditional parties had been replaced by a new non-indigenous party known as PODEMOS, while Morales and his MAS party emerged as the single most important party in the country. In December 2005, the MAS and the MIP, the other indigenous party, received 1.6 million votes out of the 2.9 million cast, or 56 percent of the total. Thus in just three short years all the traditional parties lost their importance and were replaced by new groupings of non-indigenous movements as well as a multiplicity of indigenous parties, the most important of which was the MAS, led by Evo Morales, which finally came to power in the 2005 election. For the first time in republican history a president was elected who defined himself as an indigenous person.

Not only were party politics changed after 2002, but new regional alliances were emerging in this more decentralized state. Slowly, and with some local variations, a new political division appeared in a fairly dramatic way between the core highland departments and a group of eastern and southern lowland departments (Beni, Pando, Santa Cruz, and Tarija), which formed what Bolivians began to call the *media luna* group (defined by its appearance on national maps as a half moon in their geographical relationship to the highland departments). The tensions between the militant indigenous leaders in La Paz and Cochabamba departments, and these peripheral regions rich in gas, oil and commercial agricultural farms controlled by non-indigenous groups, helped define a new political reality. This reality did not mean that all national parties were not represented in all zones or that regional tensions between urban and rural populations in each area was not another point of division. Moreover, these core and peripheral states would shift from election to election in the coming years and so the regional grouping were rather fluid and even the ethnic divisions were not entirely geographically defined. No region ever seriously contemplated political independence and every conflict ended in compromise between the two groups of regions. But the division however imprecise, defined a new political reality between a traditional elite and a new indigenous class that had come to power in the central government and which is well illustrated by the presidential election of 2005 which shows the departments won and lost by MAS (see Map 10-1).

The origins for this profound political change go back half a century to the National Revolution of 1952. There is little question that this event had a profound impact in both its intended and unintended consequences. The two most important acts of this early revolutionary period were land reform and the enfranchisement of all adult voters regardless of literacy for the first time in republican history. The August 1953 land reform decree effectively confiscated all highlands hacienda lands and granted these ex-hacienda lands to the Indian workers through their *sindicatos* and *comunidades*, with the proviso that such lands could not be individually sold. The only lands not confiscated by the state were the lightly populated Santa Cruz region and such southwestern medium-sized hacienda valley regions as Monteagudo, and the small-holding vineyard region of the Cinti Valley, which had some modest capital-intensive agriculture and no resident Indian populations. Everywhere else, the hacienda was abolished, the *hacendado* class destroyed, and land now shifted predominately into the hands of the Indian peasants. By 1993 some 831,000 land titles had been issued for 44 million hectares – or some 40 percent of the total land area of Bolivia – to 626,998 persons. To this land reform were added the two periods of hyperinflation in the mid 1950s and again in the early 1980s which

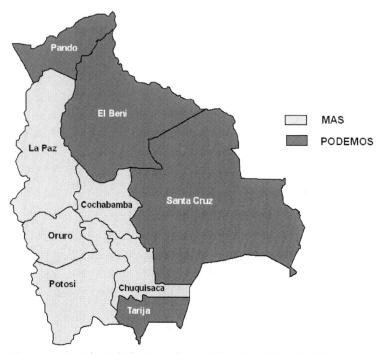

Map 10-1 Presidential Election of 2005, Victorious Party by Department.
Source: CNE, *Boletín Estradistica*, III:7, Noviembre 2007, Mapa 7, p. 1.

weakened and in many cases destroyed the traditional rural white elites that had ruled over the small villages and rural communities. These elites were replaced everywhere by a new mestizo class; that is, Indians who entered the labor market, adopted urban norms, bilingualism, and moved into small towns and cities throughout the nation. Mestizos now became the middlemen between the rural and metropolitan worlds evolving in Bolivia.

Crucial as well was the enfranchisement of the Indigenous population. In one of the first acts of the MNR regime of 1952, universal suffrage was established by eliminating the literacy requirements. In one stroke, the Indian peasant masses were enfranchised, and the voting population jumped from 126,000 in 1951 to 955,000 in 1956 and reached 1.3 million voters in the election of 1964. Though the Indian masses would take several generations to find their independent political voice, every successive government, whether military or civilian was required to make some gesture to satisfy their demands for schools, housing, electricity, sanitation, and general economic support. Though the government was less than efficient in delivering this support, and the group's demands often shifted over time, the change to national life was profound.

Equally important as its land provisions, the Agrarian Reform of 1953 also freed all Indian peasants and rural workers from all personal servitude (*pongueaje* and *colonato*) that had tied them to the land. This act alone led to far greater mobility for the poor than ever before in national history. Migration to ever more rapidly expanding urban centers provided new opportunities for education, employment, and well-being. At the same time, the establishment of a viable road network and the opening up of rural areas to national markets brought in new wealth to the countryside. Syndical and communal organizations guaranteed support for common projects and an ability to make effective demands for the delivery of better health and educational services. These organizations were so important in fact that they became the norm in the new lands being opened up to highland migration in the eastern lowlands districts.

With a new commitment to the health and welfare of its citizens, the post-1952 governments established or deepened important earlier initiatives in health and education, which eventually had a major social and demographic impact. While earlier efforts in sanitation and the delivery of health services had begun to lower overall mortality, the major investments in health carried out by the post-1952 governments led to a rapid decline in infant and child mortality and a significant decline in the crude death rates (see Graphs 10-1 and 10-2). Moreover, the relative importance of neonatal and post neonatal infant deaths was slowly changing. Whereas the post-neonatal deaths made up 55 percent of infant mortality in 1970, by 2010 they were only 47 percent of the total infant mortality rate. This was a key change since in advanced countries, postneonatal deaths make up only a third of the total infant mortality rate, which reflects the fact that most infant deaths occurred very early in the birth year and were primarily related to birth defects and not to differing social and economic conditions. In poorer societies the higher ratio of deaths after one month to one year (postneonatal)

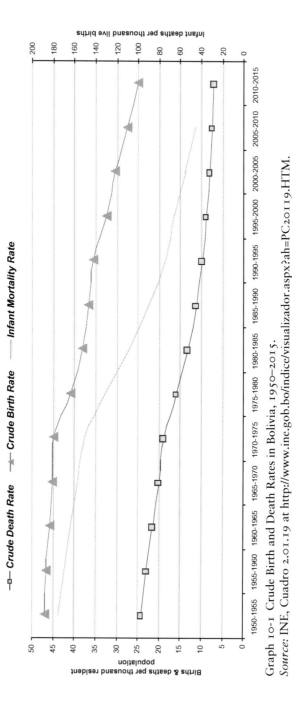

Graph 10-1 Crude Birth and Death Rates in Bolivia, 1950–2015.
Source: INE, Cuadro 2.01.19 at http://www.ine.gob.bo/indice/visualizador.aspx?ah=PC20119.HTM.

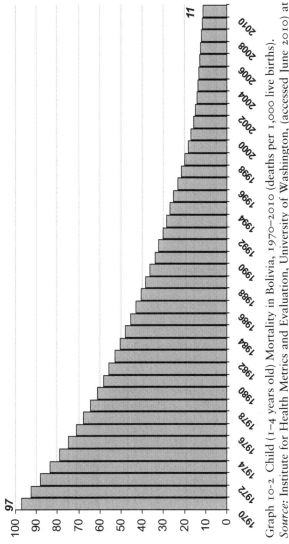

Graph 10-2 Child (1–4 years old) Mortality in Bolivia, 1970–2010 (deaths per 1,000 live births).
Source: Institute for Health Metrics and Evaluation, University of Washington, (accessed June 2010) at http://www.healthmetricsandevaluation.org/resources/news/2010/unexpected.decline.0510.html#one.

are more directly correlated with economic and social conditions. Thus the relative decline of importance of these post neonatal deaths is another important indicator of the improving mortality picture of infants and children, all of which would have a major impact on the life expectancy of Bolivians.

Given this ongoing decline in infant and child mortality, the indices having the most influence on life expectancy, it is not surprising that survival rates in Bolivia experienced very rapid and dramatic change since 1950 In 1950, the average life expectancy of males was only 38 years at birth and, for women, just 42 years. By the time of the first post-Revolution census of 1976, average life expectancy had increased by over 10 years for both men and women (reaching 48 years and 52 years, respectively), and the infant mortality rate had dropped to the 130s – still an extraordinarily high rate – but a major improvement compared to the 1950 rates. The economic crises and relative stagnation of the 1980s and early 1990s were not matched by any stagnation in the demographic indices. Much of this more rapid decline in recent years was due to a series of acts and decisions made in the 1990s. In the 1994 Popular Participation Law some 6 percent of monies devolved to the communities went to develop a basic health care program, which was supplemented by a fund devoted to supporting free access to medical care for childbirth. By 2005 infant mortality fell to 61 deaths per 1,000 live births, and maternal mortality declined to 229 deaths per thousand live births from a rate of 390 deaths as recently as 1994. Although these rates were still high by world and even Latin American standards, they represented a profound and lasting change in Bolivia. Life expectancy increased dramatically. By 2010 life expectancy had increased for both sexes an extraordinary 26 years on average in the sixty years since the census of 1950. Bolivian males now had a life expectancy of 64 years and women of 69 years of life, both rates which are expected to increase with each quinquenium, arriving at mid century to close to contemporary Latin American rates(see Graph 10-2). Although these increases are part of a worldwide trend and still leaves Bolivia with one of the lowest life expectancy rates in the Americas, the gap between rich and poor has decreased. Compared to Latin America rates as a whole, Bolivian life expectancy rates have progressively closed the gap, going from an 11-year difference for both sexes in 1950 to just 7 years difference in 2010–15 (see Graph 10-3).

The decline of child and infant mortality was due to government health programs, especially the massive immunization of children in recent decades. As late as 1980, immunization had been given to only 10–15 percent of the children under 3 years of age. By 2008 a more extensive program of standard immunizations was given to between 80% to 95% of all infants which involved all the major vaccinations including BCG, DPT-1, DPT-3, POL-3, MCV, and since 2000, HepB3 and Hib3. Moreover, the government immunization program is as effective in poor rural populations as it is in the urban ones. Thus in 2000 some 92 percent of children under 3 years of age had the polio vaccination in the urban areas and 86% of rural children had been so treated. There has also been a slow but steady increase in prenatal medical consultations and assistance at births, all of which effectively aided in bringing down infant and maternal mortality. Finally, the increasing availability of potable water and modern sewerage in Bolivian homes clearly helped decrease the high rates of intestinal disorders which were the biggest killers of children. Whereas two thirds of all Bolivian homes in 1976 had no potable water, this rate had declined to just over a third of the homes by 2003. Rates of intestinal disorders and malnutrition among infants and children have also declined significantly. But unfortunately diarrhea and respiratory diseases – classic indices of poverty – still remained the biggest killers of children.

Although there have been important regional, class, and ethnic differences in terms of mortality and fertility, there is little question that the directions of the trends are the same in all regions and among all groups. The question then arises as to how many of these changes were accounted for by the governments of the post–National Revolution era and how many can be accounted for by general hemispheric changes. In some ways, both influences can be seen in comparable world demographic statistics. What is impressive is that Bolivia had not changed its rank position – among the worst in the Americas – in terms of mortality or life expectancy compared to all the other nations of the Western Hemisphere, But the gap between the higher mortality of the Bolivian population and the

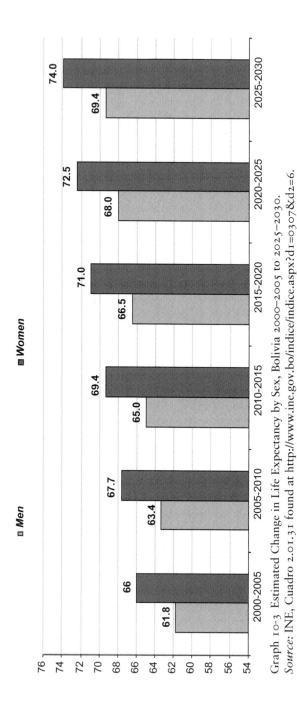

Graph 10-3 Estimated Change in Life Expectancy by Sex, Bolivia 2000–2005 to 2025–2030.
Source: INE, Cuadro 2.01.31 found at http://www.ine.gov.bo/indice/indice.aspx?d1=0307&d2=6.

general Latin American rates have declined consistently over time (see Graph 10-4).

The impact of this massive population growth and the corresponding increase in the educational level, and the availability of contraception finally led to a dramatic decline in fertility in the late 1970s and early 1980s. In Bolivia, as elsewhere in the developing world, unwanted pregnancies began to decline at an ever more rapid rate in the last half of the twentieth century, though for Bolivia this decline occurred fairly late by world standards. The high rate of 6.5 children being born to women in their fertile years was still the norm as late as the mid-1970s, but then births began to fall quickly and total fertility rates have dropped to 3.4 children by 2010 and have slowly begun to approach hemispheric norms. It is estimated by INE that Bolivian fertility will only fall below replacement levels by the period 2035-2040, some twenty years after this occurred for Latin America as a whole (see Graph 10-5).

Declining mortality and fertility have also had an obvious impact on population growth. As death rates initially fell significantly before birth rates declined, an explosive growth of population occurred. Whereas in the early 1980s, population growth was still below 2 percent per annum, but by the 1990s it reached 2.7 per annum and only dropped below 2% in 2009 and is estimated that this rate of growth will continue to decline for the rest of the century. But the high growth rate achieved in the 1990s meant that the national population was doubling every 25.7 years. Since the late 1980s, Bolivian population growth has been consistently higher than Latin American growth rates in general. The population had doubled from 3 million to 6.4 million between the censuses of 1950 and 1992, and added an estimated two million more by the census of 2001 and was estimated to have passed 10 million in 2010. This growth means that Bolivia contains one of the world's youngest populations. Although declining birth rates and increasing life expectancy are slowly changing the structure of the population, the median age of the national population went only from 18 years of age in 1992 to 21.9 years of age in 2010. Bolivia thus has one of the youngest populations in the Americas. A look at the age distributions by sex show significant reshaping of the classic pyramid shape of 1950 (see Graph 10-6) to the beginnings of a more jar like

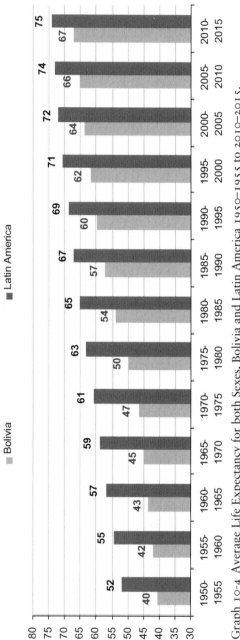

Graph 10-4 Average Life Expectancy for both Sexes, Bolivia and Latin America 1950–1955 to 2010–2015.
Source: CEPAL, Anuario Estadística... 2009, cuadro 1.1.

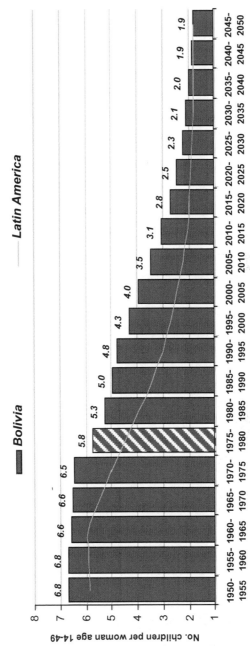

Graph 10-5 Total Fertility Rates in Bolivia and Latin America, 1950–1955 to 2045–2050.
Source: Same as Graph 10-4.

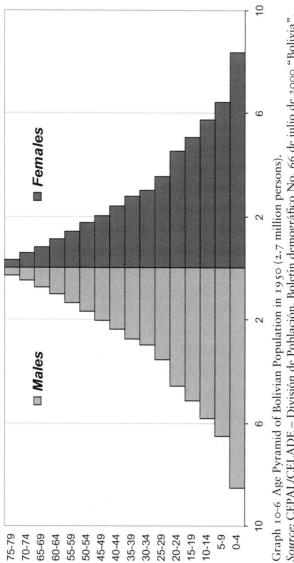

Graph 10-6 Age Pyramid of Bolivian Population in 1950 (2.7 million persons).
Source: CEPAL/CELADE – División de Población. Boletín demográfico No. 66 de julio de 2000 "Bolivia".

structure typical of advanced industrial societies with lower birth and death in 2010 (see Graph 10-7).

If the fertility and mortality of Bolivians has remained among the regions highest, indicating that Bolivia has changed slower than the other Latin American countries, this is not the case with literacy. Bolivia has exceeded its past ranking in terms of literacy and education to such an extent that it is no longer among the poorest nations of the hemisphere for these factors which are so important in the evolution of human capital. Although it has been suggested that increasing investments in education and rising student enrollments preceded the National Revolution, there is little question that the most rapid changes that have occurred in the past 50 years are in education and literacy. Although it was among the least-educated populations in the Western Hemisphere in 1950, by 2010 Bolivia had finally achieved a rate close to that of all its South American neighbors and well above most of the Central American republics and Haiti. In fact, the evolution of its educational and literacy indices compares favorably with that achieved by neighboring Brazil during this period.

By the end of the century the government was spending more on education than most countries in the region, or about 8 percent of its GDP. In 1950 the country was only educating a quarter of its children in primary schools, but this net matriculation ratio had risen to 84 percent by 2007. Bolivia does less well at the secondary school level, educating just 47 percent of boys and girls of this age group in 2007 – rates that would place it toward the bottom of most Latin American countries. In this same year, there were 1.9 million students in primary and kindergarten schools and another 537,000 in secondary grades. The net and gross rates of enrollment however show that there are often more students attending then the age group at risk, which suggests significant levels of retention and failure. But these rates have been slowly declining and both the retention rate and the drop out rate have fallen to under 10 percent in recent years for students at both the primary and secondary school levels. But whatever the current problems with the system, the trend is toward universal coverage, at least for the primary grades, and increasing rates of net enrollment in secondary schools. This has meant that the average number of years of schooling also has been climbing

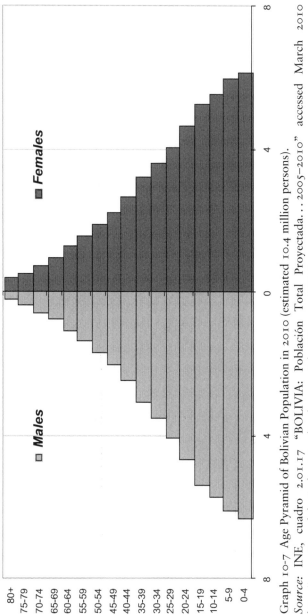

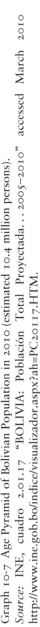

Graph 10-7 Age Pyramid of Bolivian Population in 2010 (estimated 10.4 million persons).
Source: INE, cuadro 2.01.17 "BOLIVIA: Población Total Proyectada... 2005–2010" accessed March 2010 http://www.ine.gob.bo/indice/visualizador.aspx?ah=PC20117.HTM.

steadily in this period from 4 years toward 9 years, and the ratio of those who have had no education who are 19 years of age or older in 2006 has fallen to 12 percent (7 percent for men and 17 percent for women). As could be expected, the more recent generations have a much higher number of years of school completed than the national average.

Unlike most social and economic indicators that consistently show that the non-indigenous part of the Bolivian population is richer and healthier than the indigenous sector, in primary education attendance, there is virtually no difference between the two groups. As of this century, 93 percent of both indigenous and non-indigenous children 6 to 11 years of age attend school, with only the rural rates showing a slight difference in favor of the non-indigenous children; that is, 90 percent versus 87 percent. As could be expected given the greater poverty of the indigenous and rural populations the rates shift at the secondary school level, which show that only 79 percent of the indigenous children 12–16 years old attend school and 83 percent of non-indigenous of this age group attend school for children 12-16 years of age. Equally in completion rates for primary school for teens 15–19 years of age, non-indigenous students have an 85 percent rate of completion compared to 75 percent for the indigenous students. Obviously, education attainment at the advanced level is not equal between the two groups or even between boys and girls. Nevertheless the government of Bolivia has gone a long way to providing access to education for the entire population, and secular trends indicate an ever increasing number of students enrolled in secondary education.

All of these developments in education have had a direct impact on literacy rates. Given Bolivia's complex language divisions, attaining such high literacy rates has been an extraordinary achievement. As of 1950 the majority of the population did not even speak Spanish let alone were literate in the language. Only 31 percent of the population over 15 years of age was considered literate in 1950, but by 1976 the figure had climbed to 67 percent, and by 2003 the figure was 87 percent. In fact, during this period Bolivia had moved from thirteenth place in terms of literacy to the eighth highest literacy rate in Latin America, and has a higher ratio of literates than neighboring Brazil.

That Bolivia now educates almost all of its children at the primary level has had a profound impact on all aspects of society, but especially on the national language spoken. Spanish finally became the nation's majority language only by the census of 1976. As of this date, over 83 percent of the population over the age of 6 years now spoke Spanish, though only 42 percent of the population was monolingual in that language. Equally 62 percent of the total population declared themselves to be indigenous. This meant that the indigenous population through education has now become primarily bilingual and literate in the national language. In the census of 2001, some 74 percent of the 3.7 million speakers of Indian languages were bilingual in Spanish. It is worth noting that the Aymara speakers were considerably more bilingual than the Quechua speakers, a fact which may help explain their greater political militancy. Among the 1.3 million speakers of Aymara, some 80 percent were bilingual, whereas among the 2 million Quechua speakers, only 69 percent were bilingual. Various investigators have noted that there is a continuum among literate speakers of an indigenous language, with a continual movement from monolingualism in an indigenous language to bilingualism, which was the norm until the early 1990s, and in this century the movement is increasingly from bilingualism to monolingualism in Spanish. This explains the origin of monolingual Spanish speakers who self-identify as indigenous people. Nevertheless, the size of the population that knows and speaks an indigenous language is still quite impressive. The more rapid population growth among the indigenous people initially meant that those speaking an indigenous language went from an estimated 1.8 million persons 1950 to 4 million persons in 1992. But this number declined to 3.7 million in the census of 2001. Despite the growth of the rural population at unprecedented rates, the number of monolingual Indian speakers continued to decline. Quechua monolinguals had fallen to 632,000, and Aymara monolingual speakers to 263,000, by 2001. Moreover these monolinguals in 2001 were essentially all rural dwellers, the majority of whom lived dispersed in the countryside (only 10 percent and 17 percent, respectively of these two groups lived in towns or cities over 2,000 population). At the same time, the number of bilinguals has slowly begun to decline as more indigenous peoples drop their native language despite the introduction of bilingual education in the 1990s. The majority position achieved by Spanish as of 1976 was proof of the impact of the schools on the rural areas. Not only had the mestizo population greatly expanded, as these figures indicate, but even more importantly rural Indian peasants were now using Spanish on a large scale, along with their traditional indigenous languages.

Despite the loss of native languages, the number of persons who self-identified as indigenous has actually remained quite high. Although only 45 percent of the total population in 2001 either was monolingual or bilingual speakers of an indigenous language, it was estimated that 5.4 million persons (or two-thirds of the national population) were in fact indigenous people. Of this indigenous population who were 15 years or older, some 4.4 percent who spoke an indigenous language did not identify as indigenous persons, whereas 14 percent of the indigenous population who did not speak an indigenous language identified themselves as indigenous. In a national household survey conducted in 2005, it was reported that 53 percent of the population identified themselves as indigenous, but only 42 percent spoke an indigenous language. While some indigenous people move into the non-indigenous category, for the majority of indigenous peoples, indigenous identity remains very strong despite the decline of both monolingual and bilingual speakers of these native languages. Moreover, those who identify as being either Quechua or Aymara are in fact largely urban, even though very few monolingual speakers live in the urban areas. Finally, it was estimated in the national household survey of 2007 that 79 percent of the population who were native indigenous speakers were literate. In the urban area 87 percent of the group was literate, and in the rural areas 73 percent of the group was literate. The fact that self-identified indigenous peoples are primarily Spanish speakers and primarily literate even if they speak an indigenous language, both in the urban and rural areas, suggests an indigenous population highly integrated into the national society and polity despite their high levels of poverty.

The increasing urbanization of society had a profound effect on the changes in language and literacy that occurred, as well as the health and demographic outcomes of the Bolivian population. From being a primarily rural society as late as 1950, the nation moved toward a predominantly urban one in the past 60 years. In 1950, only 20 percent of the population lived in towns over 20,000 and by the census of 2001 more than half the population lived in urban centers. The city of Santa Cruz which in 1950 had a population of just 364,000 persons now has over 2 million persons. The three largest urban centers in 2010, Santa Cruz, the twin cities of La Paz–El Alto which contained just under 2 million, and the city of Cochabamba with its 1 million urban dwellers, contained 5.3 million residents, or just over half of the estimated 10.4 million Bolivians. This urbanization of the national population also brought with it increasing standard of living. Every index of health, welfare, and education consistently showed that there were better conditions for the urban populations than for the rural ones.

That said rates of poverty, however defined, have declined very slowly in the past few decades in Bolivia, especially in the urban areas. Although poverty levels have fallen rather sharply within the rural population through income transfers and other government measures, urban poverty has remained fairly constant. Thus extreme poverty between 1999 and 2007 dropped from 59 percent to 48 percent in the rural areas, but it remained at the same 21–22 percent level in the urban zones. Moreover in this period overall national poverty levels (extreme and normal poor) remained at roughly 60 percent for the entire period. As late as 2005, it was estimated that two out of every three Bolivians were poor and one out of every four was indigent. Although urban conditions were better than rural ones, poverty was still the norm for the majority of Bolivians. In the same year of 2005 when Bolivia had 31% of the population listed as being in extreme poverty (usually defined as not having sufficient food intake), only Honduras, Nicaragua, and Paraguay had the same or greater levels of indigence. By the definition of the government itself, some 60 percent of Bolivian homes in 2007 could not meet the minimum standards of housing, food, access to water, and sanitation. In the rural area this number reached 77 percent, and even in the urban area it was over half of the homes.

At these rates of poverty, it is not surprising that Bolivia still remains the second largest recipient of foreign aid from the developing world in all of Latin America. According to figures compiled by the OCED, Bolivia received just under half a million dollars per annum in aid in the 2004–2007 period and this represented an average of 2 percent of national GNP. Although second in total aid among the Latin American countries, this aid to Bolivia was much less of total GNP than in Haiti and Honduras.

Given the poverty, the recent decades of economic turmoil, and the rising levels of education, it is not surprising that significant out-migration has been occurring in Bolivia in the past two decades. First, many workers went to Argentina over many decades, then in the 1980s and 1990s there was a steady migration to the United States, which was followed by a massive hemorrhage of emigrants to Spain after 2000. There are now some 229,000 Bolivians residing in Spain (Padrón Municipal 2009), approximately 232,000 residing in Argentina (as of the census of 2001) and in 2000 another 53,000 resided in the United States (census) and 20,000 in Brazil (census). The other neighboring Latin American countries probably contained approximately 10,000 Bolivians in addition to the large number of seasonal migrants who worked in Argentina, and to a lesser extent, Chile and Brazil. Together these roughly half a million permanent overseas Bolivians have remitted a constant stream of savings to Bolivia in the past several decades. This volume peaked in 2007 at a figure representing 7.4 percent of the GDP – this, at a time when foreign aid had fallen to 1.5 percent of GDP. But with the recent world recession, these remittances have steadily fallen to just 5 percent of GDP in the most recent estimates.

Along with international migration, internal migration has also been important in the recent evolution of Bolivia. Urbanization in the second half of the twentieth century also brought about profound changes in the distribution of the national population. At the beginning of the twentieth century, the primary axis of the nation was La Paz–Oruro–Potosí, a north–south line, which was the dynamic heartland of the nation. Here was the center of mining, commerce, and agriculture, whereas Santa Cruz was an isolated and depressed region, and Cochabamba had a relatively enclosed and backward economy. With the progressive decline of mining, especially after the middle of the twentieth century, the commercial heartland has slowly moved in an easterly direction from La Paz and now encompasses the departments of La Paz, Cochabamba, and Santa Cruz, while the Oruro–Potosí–Sucre axis has gone into severe decline. Essentially the new NE–SW corridor connecting the three cities of La Paz–El Alto, Cochabamba, and Santa Cruz, and their respective provinces account for most of the economic activity of the nation. The three departments provided 93 percent of state taxes in 2009 and produced 71 percent of the GDP of Bolivia in 2000. The three provinces also have the most advanced and fastest growing cities. The old mining centers of Potosí and Oruro have stagnated, and their urban and rural populations are now the poorest in the country. The government recently estimated that over 80 percent of the populations resident in these two formerly wealthy mining provinces were poor and that more than 60 percent were living in extreme poverty. Even their urban populations were considerably poorer than the norm. Whereas the departments of Potosí, Chuquisaca, and Cochabamba accounted for 34 percent of the nation's population in 1950 – a figure quite similar to the figure in 1900 – by the census of 2001, these three provinces only accounted for 20 percent of the population. Santa Cruz, which had just 10 percent of the population in 1950 – again, almost identical to the figure in 1900 – by the census of 2001, contained a quarter of the residents of national population. Between them La Paz, Cochabamba, and Santa Cruz had gone from having just over 50 percent of the population in 1950 to over 70 percent in the census of 2001, and they contained an estimated 72 percent of the national population in 2010.

Although the rural population has declined dramatically as a share of the total population, Bolivian agriculture, except in new areas of cultivation, has remained surprisingly backward. As late as 1976, agriculture still absorbed 54 percent of the male workforce, and still accounted for 34 percent in 2007. Yet farmers were not more efficient and farming only accounted for 13 percent of the GDP in the same year. Most of that agriculture, especially in the highlands and eastern valleys, has remained traditional low-productivity foodstuff farming. There was, however, a radical transformation in lowland Bolivia in the past half century. In the past few decades, industrial crops have become a new industry in the Santa Cruz region. In 1980 industrial crops (above all, cotton, sugar, soybeans, and sunflower seeds) accounted for 12 percent of the land devoted to agriculture. By 2008 that ratio had risen to 47 percent of the total land use and was roughly equal to that of all grains and root crops being farmed in Bolivia. Such commercial crops as soybeans and sunflower seeds are produced in the Santa Cruz lowlands at output levels close to world standards. But highland food crops were less productive than similar crops produced in the neighboring Peruvian highlands. Much of this low productivity has to do with the fact that Bolivia spends less money on agricultural research and extension programs than any other country in Latin America. Traditional agriculture, which still absorbs the majority of the rural population, has remained undercapitalized and inefficient. Despite all of the recent agricultural transformations in Santa Cruz and some of the nearby valley regions, Bolivia is still one of the most backward agricultural nations in the Americas.

The picture of Bolivia that emerges from this analysis of over a half century of social and economic development is one of major social change, combined with persistent poverty and relative economic backwardness. Education and health have seen the most dramatic progress. But this persistent poverty and partial increase in living standards common to all the Americas has occurred within the context of a radically changing social system. If the slow growth of the economy has not promoted much social mobility, urban migration and the rise of rural peasant and urban mestizo political power have made a profound difference in the response of all Bolivian governments to demands for improved social conditions. What can only be called the *mestizaje* of Bolivian society has become an important phenomenon after a half century of social revolution and two periods of hyperinflation, which have destroyed a great deal of the traditional white economic power. The increasing life expectancy and the increasing years of education of the Bolivian popular classes helps explain their ability to significantly participate as autonomous actors on the national political scene. The new century clearly marked a great change in the relative balance of political, social, and even to some extent, economic power among the ethnic groups in the country. In the last decade, the political power of the mestizo population has found expression not only in traditional and radical parties and in the national government, but also in Bolivia's El Alto, which is the quintessential mestizo urban center. In 1988, the working-class suburb of El Alto, located on the outskirts of La Paz, was finally incorporated as an independent city and its administration was taken over by the new mestizo elite. This high-altitude town, which then held some 307,000 persons, was half the size of La Paz, but already was overwhelmingly bilingual, and very closely associated with the surrounding Aymara rural communities. It was the fourth largest city when it was created, but by the census of 2001 it had become Bolivia's third largest city, with 695,000 people, of whom 86 percent were counted as indigenous. By 2005 it contained some 872,000 residents and had finally replaced La Paz as the second largest city in the country. Though El Alto had higher poverty rates and worse living conditions than La Paz, its population still had a higher standard of living than the rural altiplano hinterland from which the migrants came, and thus has proved to be an extraordinarily important factor in increasing the social mobility of the mestizo class. El Alto is also a center for intense interactions between indigenous and non-indigenous peoples where Spanish has become the language of contact even for the dominant Aymara population.

At the same time, the integration of the regional economies with the central cities and the elimination of the old Spanish rural elites have created a more powerful mestizo regional elite. It is from this elite and the upwardly mobile urban mestizo population that has emerged a whole new generation of mestizo secondary and university-trained professionals. While some mestizos had obviously attended the university from the earliest times, they were a distinct minority and were forced to abandon their language, culture, and origins and adapt to the norms of "white" culture. The new breed of educated mestizos – far more numerous than ever before – now seem to have the option of retaining their ethnic ties, self-identifying as indigenous, and sometimes even speaking their original Indian languages along with Spanish. These urban mestizos thus proclaim their identity as both mestizo and Aymara, Quechua, or another indigenous people, and thus refuse to adopt a "white" identity. This has had profound social and political consequences for Bolivia and is a relatively unique development by Latin American standards. It also means that even as monolingual speakers of indigenous languages decline with ever higher levels of education, indigenous identity remains a powerful and mobilizing force in national politics.

From the election of 2002 to the presidential elections of December 2005, the indigenous and mestizo classes took to the roads and highways of Bolivia in an extraordinary period of popular mobilization. The eruption of the Gas War in 2003 was followed by the fall of the Sánchez Losada government in October, which was then followed by the tumultuous 6-month presidency of Carlos Mesa. His swearing in ceremony at El Alto was a recognition of the power of this new mobilization. Though Mesa was able to stop the bloodshed by withdrawing the police and military from active confrontations with the protestors, he was unable to fully stop the blockades. In turn, he was forced to resign when it was obvious that he could not control Congress. Eduardo Rodríguez Veltzé, the head of the Supreme Court, was appointed acting president in June of 2005, and he was able to finally achieve a level of political calm that had not existed for 2 years. Although most of the pre-election surveys gave Evo Morales a plurality of the potential votes for the presidency, there was a generalized belief that any return to post-election congressional negotiations would lead to the return of massive popular indigenous protests. At this point, most of the elite decided that it was preferable to give Evo Morales a total victory, and he was able to double his pre-election estimates and win the election with 56 percent of the vote, becoming the first president to receive more than 50 percent of the vote in the post-military era. Of the 2.9 million valid votes that were cast in the 2005 presidential election, Morales obtained 1.5 million and the MIP received 62,000. The MAS also won 12 out of the 27 senate seats, and 72 out of the 130 deputy positions.

The election of Evo Morales has proven to be a far more radical transformation than was initially assumed. It was expected that there would be a major introduction of indigenous and mestizo political leaders into positions of power in the La Paz government, and this occurred. Also, given the long conflict over coca production and Morales's connection to the Chapare producers' unions, it was expected that a change in the policy of coca eradication would occur along with an increased independence from the United States. All of this did occur, even to the extent of expelling the U.S. Ambassador. What was less expected was the total rejection of the privatization program that had dominated national government policy since the 1990s. Slowly and carefully the Morales government has renationalized gas and oil production, taken over all telecommunications, all the electricity companies, even from national cooperatives, proposed the elimination of private pension plans, re-created a state airlines company, nationalized two Swiss smelters, and systematically pushed for state control over mineral resources from iron ore to lithium. Slowly but steadily the state is becoming the dominant player in the national economy through state companies which have been created or revitalized, a program that only a few of the other Latin American nations have attempted, even as many of them rejected the more extreme policies of the neoliberal era of the 1990s. Since January 2006 when it came to power, the Morales government has nationalized a total of 12 major foreign companies and one national electricity cooperative.

The single most important act was the nationalization of the Bolivian gas and oil deposits being developed or exploited by a host of foreign companies, many of which were state enterprises of other nations – above all of the Brazilian oil company Petrobras. On 1 May 2006 the Morales government seized the gas holdings of all the major foreign companies. Bolivia's YPFB, which had been made a passive partner to the new oil and gas explorations and developments, was given active control over the fields and their facilities. All companies operating in Bolivia had 50 percent of their locally owned operations taken over by YPFB. The foreign companies would still run the facilities, but would be paid only 18 percent of the total receipts for their operating expenses. The state would take 32 percent of receipts, YPFB would take another 32 percent, and the remaining 18 percent went for royalties to the state – effectively bringing the state's share of total gas and oil sales up to 50 percent (82 percent, counting the YPFB share). In May of 2007, the government also withdrew from the World Bank, claiming it supported these multinationals. Next, in May 2008 came the nationalization of the Italian telecommunications company Telecom, which, since 1995, had been 50 percent partners with the government-owned

ENTEL and had administered the telecommunications monopoly in Bolivia. Then in May 2010 came the nationalization of all the electricity companies.

All these nationalizations and increased royalties initially increased government revenues to an impressive degree. Also Bolivia has been running a trade surplus since 2003 and thus has accumulated important reserves of foreign currency. But the continued nationalization of foreign companies has seriously affected the amount of foreign direct investment in Bolivia. This has been on the decline since the first half of the decade, and now represents less capital inflow than obtained from foreign aid funds and remittances of overseas workers. Also, the stock of foreign capital investment has gone from a high of 61 percent of GDP in 2000 to just 35 percent in 2008, and is still falling. Unfortunately, this dependence on foreign aid and remittances and the declining importance of foreign capital investment has the potential to have a long term negative impact on the national economy. With mineral and gas exports affected by world prices and declining reserves, it is unclear if export revenues from the nationalized companies and the few private producers will be sufficient to replace the lack of foreign investment in the long-term development of the country.

At the same time, the lack of significant investment, especially in labor-intensive manufactures, has led to Bolivia having one of the largest informal labor markets in the Americas. It is estimated that 80 percent of the labor force today is employed in low-productive and low-wage jobs in the informal sector or in subsistence agriculture. In 2007 it was estimated that 88 percent of the Bolivian population was not affiliated with any pension plan and that 82 percent could not count on the traditional *aguinaldo* (thirteenth-month salary), which was guaranteed to workers in the formal sector. In this same year, only 27 percent of all Bolivians had a tax identification number (NIT). Given the major shocks to the economy in the 1980s and again in the late 1990s and early 2000s, Bolivia has not been able to generate a significant number of jobs to change this dynamic. This lack of well-paying and productive jobs helps explain the extraordinarily high levels of poverty throughout the country.

Aside from its nationalizations, the Morales government also made major advances in providing access to land for the poorer groups within Bolivian society. Although the Agrarian Reform of 1953 had returned most of the highland and major valley lands back to their indigenous workers, the vast lowland areas were left untouched since they were mostly undeveloped. But the systematic opening of the Santa Cruz, Beni, and Pando regions to modern agricultural development and colonization in the post-1953 period led to the rise of a new zone of latifundia, as these lands were freely and often corruptibly distributed to favored elites on a massive scale. Especially under the military regimes, vast areas had been granted to private individuals. Already under the second Sánchez de Losada government it was recognized that this corrupt system had to be curtailed, not only in the name of justice for the indigenous groups in the lowlands, but also for the sake of the greater economic efficiency of the commercial agricultural regions which now needed these abandoned but privately owned lands. In 2002 a new land reform act was passed, which was designed to eliminate these large tracts of abandoned land and return some of them to the newly empowered lowland Indian groups, as well as to productive private farmers. This program was given a major boost by the new Morales government, which from 2006 though mid-2009 had distributed some 31 million hectares to 154,000 peasants and farmers (some five times the amount distributed during the pre-2006 period), with a higher ratio now going to indigenous peoples than before.

The new MAS government was also committed to a major realignment of Bolivia's international politics. Under the leadership of Evo Morales, Bolivia has moved away from the United States's sphere of influence as never before in the post–World War II period. This has led to an activist and independent foreign policy, with the government stressing its alliance with indigenous groups from Central America to Northern Europe. It has also led to a campaign for environmental protection on an international platform. This government has unquestionably played a far more active role in international affairs than any previous Bolivian government and has been more independent of the United States than any previous regime.

Less surprising than its nationalization program and foreign policy, was the push of MAS and Evo Morales for a new constitution that greatly expanded both the concepts of a plurinational state and a decentralized one – a major theme of his party and supporters well before 2005. Since the constitutional convention delegates were voted upon in a separate election, it was both a far more radical and representative body than the national congress. Almost half of the delegates were under 40, some 34 percent were women, and a significant 56 percent identified themselves as pertaining to an indigenous group. Given this representation, it was evident that the charter produced by this assembly would express most of the ideas favored by indigenous radical leaders for decades. In a bitterly fought debate, the new constitution was written in 2008, and approved by referendum in 2009. It then went into full effect by 2010, when for the first time in Bolivian history the departments elected their own governors and legislatures.

The Constitution of 2009 not only guaranteed all the traditional rights of the indigenous community governments and also reenforced decentralization through departmental, regional, communal, and municipal autonomies. But above all the charter was an excellent expression of the demands that the mestizo and indigenous leaders had been making for the previous 40 years for basic recognition by the state and the elite white society of their needs and desires. Above all it called for the recognition of their dignity and worth as full citizens, especially for those who traced their origins to preconquest times. Respect, dignity, and the recognition of individual and traditional community rights and beliefs were declared a fundamental aspect of state policy. Not only were the usual highland indigenous groups recognized and their importance stressed, but so too are the lowland Indian people and even the Afro-Bolivian community were singled out for support from the state.

The Constitution of 2009 also declared that Bolivia was a unitary state based on communal plurinational law that was democratic, decentralized and with autonomous regions (which in a very broad manner included self-governing departments, municipalities, regions, ethnic groups, and communities). Article 5 declared that the official state languages were Spanish and the 37 other indigenous languages spoken in Bolivia, and that the national and local governments were required to use two languages, one being Spanish and the other an indigenous one that would depend on local conditions. The constitution speaks of "interculturality" as fundamental to the maintenance of a unified state (Article 98), and throughout the charter there is a constant repetition of the theme of respect for individuals and communities, from their dress to their belief systems. In fact, after this constitution Bolivia would be officially called the Estado Plurinacional de Bolivia.

The civil rights of citizens granted in Article 21 went well beyond the usual items to include such things as "privacy, intimacy, honor, self-image and dignity" as well as cultural self identification. The new charter also prohibited any discrimination of citizens on the basis of their language, race, color, gender, religion or any other human characteristics. It also outlined the specifics of a very ambitions social welfare state, guaranteeing that the state would provide water, food, free health care, pensions, housing, and education to all of its citizens. It even proposed that the state should guarantee a healthy environment for all. In fact, the constitution had many articles providing for the protection of the environment, for guaranteeing biodiversity, and a host of other issues related to these modern concerns. In addition to providing all of the usual pro-family declarations, the constitution also specifically recognized stable free unions as having the same rights as legally married couples in terms of patrimony and personal relations (Article 63, II).

The communal land rights of the traditional indigenous communities were to be guaranteed by the state (Article 30), but also their traditional cosmology, medicine, rituals, symbols, and dress were to be respected and even promoted (Article 30, IX), and they were to be allowed to exercise their own unique political, judicial, and economic systems as defined by their own cosmology (Articles 30, 190–192). There was even an entire section of the constitution dedicated to the protection of traditional cultures as national patrimony (Articles 98–101). The state was also to guarantee intra- and intercultural and plurilingual education (Article 30). In a really unusual expansion of autonomy, the state would also allow indigenous communities of *originarios* to declare themselves self-governing entities independent of municipal or departmental governments with self-governing rights that were equal to those granted to these institutions. All indigenous peoples or communities that were being threatened with extinction, as well as the isolated and uncontacted indigenous groups, were to be protected, and the latter were even allowed to remain isolated if they wished.

This was clearly a "social constitution" as earlier defined by the Mexican Constitution of 1917 and by the Bolivian Constitution of 1938. The right of private property (individual and communal) was limited by its necessity to fulfill a social function, and could not prejudice the collective interest of the society (Article 56). Also, it specifically sanctioned the right of the state to directly participate in the economy to produce goods and services (Article 316). The constitution gave priority to national over foreign capital, and stated that all foreign investments be completely subject to Bolivian law without exception (Article 320). In addition to reasserting traditional subsoil rights to all minerals, the constitution had an entire chapter on hydrocarbons, which were to be under the exclusive control of the state and its representative YPFB (Articles 359–368). Finally, in a response to the placement of U.S. military groups in the country as part of anti-coca campaigns, it also specifically prohibited the establishment of foreign military bases on national soil (Article 10).

Along with obligatory voting of all adults 18 years of age and over, and the significant right of overseas Bolivians to vote in presidential elections, the constitution also permitted the indigenous communities to use their traditional norms for electing leaders, with the state only intervening if the vote was not "equal, universal, direct, secret, free and obligatory" (Article 26). The rights to strike and collectively bargain were also guaranteed. Finally, the decentralized political organization of the Bolivian state, which had begun in 1995, was finalized with the election of departmental governors and legislatures (Articles 277–279). The constitution also allowed for autonomous regions and even autonomous indigenous communities of *originarios* to be established, though their limits and powers seemed to have been left for post-constitutional enactment (Articles 289–296).

Along with revising the constitution, the Morales regime has greatly expanded earlier welfare programs and especially stressed income transfers based on the funds generated by the nationalizations. The government has made a major effort to expand the income redistribution programs that began under the second government of Sánchez de Losada. The BONOSOL pension program of the 1990s was converted into the Renta Dignidad, which provided minimum pensions to all Bolivians older than 65 years, regardless of whether they had contributed or not to the retirement plan. By early 2009 some 757,000 elderly Bolivians were receiving this pension. Another program, which was becoming common in Latin America, consisted of conditional cash payments given for school attendance called the *bono* Juancito Pinto (given to families that maintained their children in school). Finally, came a program called the *bono* Juana Azurduy, which provided funding for pregnant women to receive quarterly medical exams and postpartum support, and was designed to reduce the high incidence of infant mortality and maternal deaths. While the former programs were generated out of government funds, the Arzurduy program was supported by major funding from the Inter-American Development Bank. That these programs are significant can be seen both in terms of their coverage and in terms of their share of GDP. In 2010, the Renta Dignidad accounted for 1.5 percent of the GDP (quite a large figure for this type of conditional cash transfers), the *bono* Juancito Pinto accounted for 0.3 percent, and the *bono* Juana Azurduy accounted for another 0.2 percent. The Pinto program provided cash payments to 1.7 million students in the primary grades in 2009, and the new Azurudy cash transfers reached 340,000 mothers and amounted to US$25 million in 2009. But instead of the state providing funds out of the privatization programs, these funds now derive from the increased royalties, which the state has generated through the re-nationalization of various industries.

In many ways the Morales government has been fortunate in its timing. The increased demand by China for raw materials has kept international prices for basic mineral exports high and government revenues growing. The fact that the Brazilian government under Lula was sympathetic to the Morales regime meant that the nationalization of the gas fields could be accomplished with relatively little conflict and with Petrobras still committed to exporting gas to Brazil even if it was no longer willing to invest heavily in new explorations or new facilities. The international environment was also propitious. The United States had abandoned an active interventionist policy in Latin America since the beginning of the century because of its concentration on the Middle East. Finally, the existence of sympathetic governments in Venezuela and Ecuador, along with left of center governments in Argentina, Brazil and, for most of the period in Chile, has given Bolivia a great deal of space in the international area with little immediate negative consequences for nationalizing foreign companies, many of which were state-owned enterprises. Nor has it harmed Bolivia among its neighbors to take active anti–U.S. positions in the international arena.

But there have been costs. The MAS party and its leaders have become increasingly willing to attack fundamental democratic institutions in their commitment to their vision of a revolutionary society. It is still unclear how far the party and its leaders will go in this direction to justify their social and economic reforms. They have also provoked constant political tension internally. Finally, their return to their nationalization of natural resource exploitation and the reconstruction of state enterprises has occurred at a high economic cost. It has meant the loss of foreign direct investment, nor has a national capital market developed sufficiently to provide for sustained long-term economic growth. It has also occurred as the government has lost or expelled some of its technical experts and has weakened the bureaucracy just at the time it needs that bureaucracy to carry out these nationalizations in an efficient manner.

Recent calls for judging previous democratically elected presidents for economic policies they undertook are an example of a regime that feels threatened by the former elites and that is sometimes unwilling to negotiate with opposition forces. The attacks on the efficient and crucial National Electoral Court after the election of April 2010, when the vote did not reproduce the results desired by the governing party, was another disturbing expression of certain authoritarian tendencies within MAS. Finally, the rather consistent campaign to undermine elected opposition leaders at the national, departmental, and municipal levels suggests a government that is still having trouble practicing the norms of democratic politics.

The party itself has also begun to fray at the edges as indigenous and mestizo leaders prove to be more independent and more local in their political commitments. MAS has had problems controlling the cities and even some of its traditional centers of support. Thus in the departmental and municipal elections of April 2010, the opposition gained serious support in El Alto as well as capturing the city of La Paz. MAS also has some difficulties in the

altiplano with opposition leaders challenging national party candidates. The party also lost three departments – that is Santa Cruz,
Tarija and Beni – to the opposition. But despite all of these set-
backs, even in the "media luna" departments that it lost, the MAS
came in a respectable second. In these lowland departments, which
are the heartland of commercial agriculture and the centers of the
natural gas and oil deposits, MAS was now well established. Thus
despite the inevitable weakening of the movement at the beginning
of the second administration of Evo Morales, MAS remains a powerful national party led by newly empowered indigenous leaders.
Moreover, Morales himself is still considered a dynamic and charismatic leader and one who currently has the majority support of the
population.

POLITICAL CHRONOLOGY

2500 B.C.	Beginnings of Village agriculture.
1800 B.C.	Beginnings of Ceramics.
800 B.C.	Chavín, First Pan-Andean civilization.
100 B.C.	Regional States: Early Tiahuanaco.
600–1200 A.D.	Tiahuanaco State (Middle Formative).
1400s	Rise of Aymara kingdoms.
1460s	Inca Conquest of the Aymara kingdoms and creation of Kollasuyo.
1470	Aymara revolt against the Incas.
1532	Arrival of Spanish in Peru.
1537	Manco Inca rebellion.
1538	Beginning of Spanish settlement of Bolivian altiplano.
1545	Discovery of silver at Cerro Rico (Potosí).
1558	Creation of independent government for region as Audiencia de Charcas.
1560s	Final settlement of Bolivia's frontier regions.
1572–76	The visita of Viceroy Francisco Toledo to Upper Peru: beginnings of mita labor, mercury amalgamation of silver ores, and forced resettlement of Indian population.
1580s	Beginnings of the Shrine of Virgin of Copacabana on Lake Titicaca.
1584	Publication of the first Aymara grammar.
1624	Creation of a university at Chuquisaca.
1650s	Beginning of a century-long crisis in silver output at Potosí.
1695	Discovery of silver near Oruro.

1734	Tribute tax extended to forasteros and yanaconas.
1751	Creation of the Banco de San Carlos at Potosi' to purchase minerals.
1776	Establishment of the Viceroyalty of the Rio de la Plata at Buenos Aires and the transference of the Audiencia de Charcas from Peru to the new viceroyalty.
1780–82	Tupac Amaru rebellion in both Perus. Tupac Catari, Tomas Catari, and Andres Amaru leaders in Upper Peru part of rebellion. Creole, cholo, and Indian revolt in Oruro only multiethnic movement in rebellion.
1784	Administrative reorganization of the Audiencia de Charcas with creation of intendants.
1796	Spain goes to war against England; beginnings of a major crisis in international trade that severely affects Upper Peru.
1808	French invasion of Spain and collapse of Royal Government.
1809	Elite rebellion in Chuquisaca (May 25). Popular rebellion for Independence in La Paz (July 16).
1809–25	Wars of Independence in Upper Peru.
1810	Independence of Viceroyalty of Rio de la Plata (May 25) and return of reconquered Audiencia de Charcas to Lima control and old Viceroyalty of Peru.
1824	Battle of Ayacucho. Sucre and his Colombian army defeat last royalist army in Lower Peru in December.
1825	Liberation of Upper Peru and Declaration of Bolivian independence (6 August).
1825–28	First Republican government under Antonio José de Sucre and nationalization of the Roman Catholic Church.
1829–39	Governments dominated by Andrés de Santa Cruz. 1836–39 Bolivia forms part of Peru-Bolivia Confederation government, which is finally overthrown by invading Chilean troops. 1841 Battle of Ingavi brings to an end Peruvian and Bolivian involvement in each other's internal political affairs.
1841–47	Governments dominated by Jose Ballivian.
1847–55	Governments dominated by Manuel Isidoro Belzu.
1850s	Beginnings of modern silver mining industry.
1860s–1870s	Discovery of major mineral deposits of guano, silver, and nitrates in Bolivia's Atacama province by Chileans.

1864–70	Government of Mariano Melgarejo. Intense negotiations with foreign governments and foreign entrepreneurs.
1879	Chilean invasion of Bolivia's Pacific ports and beginnings of the War of the Pacific.
1880	Battle of Tacna (May 26) and end of Bolivian participation in War of Pacific with total defeat of Bolivian armies. Passage of a new constitution that would become fundamental charter of new civilian era and last until 1938.
1880–99	Civilian Governments of Conservative Party control. Dominance of silver mineowners in government and Congress.
1899	Federal Revolution of Liberal Party that overthrew Conservatives and Sucre Oligarchy. Capital city effectively becomes La Paz for all major governmental activities.
1899–1903	Separatist rebellions of rubber workers in Acre territory finally lead to cession of territory to Brazil.
1899–1920	Civilian Governments of Liberal Party control. Dominance of Liberal leader Ismael Montes.
1902	Tin passes silver as Bolivia's most valuable export and accounts for over 50 percent of the value of all exports.
1920–34	Civilian Governments of Republican Parties control. Period of peak of tin output in 1920s and of the Great Depression. Key leaders were Bautista Saavedra, Hernando Siles, and Daniel Salamanca.
1932–35	War with Paraguay over disputed Chaco territory. Most costly defeat in Bolivia's history.
1936–39	Military governments under David Toro and German Busch of left populist nature and known as "military socialism."
1937	Nationalization of Standard Oil of Bolivia and creation of YPFB, Bolivia's national oil company.
1939–43	Conservative civilian rule under Enrique Peñaranda.
1942	Foundation of the Movimiento Nacionalista Revolucionario (MNR) party.
1943–46	Radical military-MNR government under leadership of Gualberto Villarroel.
1944	Foundation of first successful national mineworkers' union: Federación Sindical de Trabajadores Mineros de Bolivia (FSTMB).
1945	Meeting of First National Congress of Peasants.

1946	"Thesis of Pulacayo"– radical declaration of FSTMB congress after Villarroel's overthrow.
1946–52	Civilian-military conservative regimes.
1952	National Revolution of MNR in April.
1952–64	Civilian governments under MNR leaders Víctor Paz Estenssorro and Hernán Siles Zuazo. Nationalization of the mines and creation of COMIBOL; land reform (1953), universal suffrage, and creation of national labor federation Centro Ohrero Boliciano (COB).
1967	Constitution with revisions in 1994.
1964–70	Populist military governments under René Barrientos and Alfredo Ovando.
1965–67	Che Guevara in Bolivia.
1970–71	Radical populist military government under Juan José Torres and establishment of "Popular Assembly" regime.
1971–78	Conservative military rule under Hugo Banzer.
1978–79	Transitional military regimes and political reorganization of civilian parties.
1979–80	National elections and the emergence of Siles Zuazo as leader of a left coalition of new and older parties. Temporary civilian governments under Walter Guevara Arze and Lydia Gueiler.
1980–82	Reactionary military rule with massive popular protest.
1982–85	Hernán Siles Zuazo made president in the return of civilian rule, but with problem of hyperinflation.
1985–89	Last administration of Víctor Paz Estenssoro and the implementation of a radical "orthodox shock" on August 29, 1985.
1989–93	Jaime Paz Zamora and MIR government.
1993–97	Gonzalo Sánchez de Lozada and MNR in power. Popular Participation and Decentralization laws, Privatization and first universal pension plan (Bonosol)
1997–2001	Hugo Banzer and ADN in power.
1995	Founding of the MAS (Movimiento al Socialismo) party.
1997	Evo Morales elected to congress.
2002–2006	Incomplete second term of Gonzalo Sánchez de Lozada, with Carlos Mesa (2003–2005) and Eduardo Rodríguez Veltzé (2005–2006) completing his term.

2006–2010	First administration of Evo Morales. Nationalization of natural gas and electricity. Reconstruction of YPFB and COMIBOL. Plan Dignidad and other conditional cash transfer programs created.
2009	New *plurinacional* constitution.
2010	Second administration of Evo Morales.

TABLES

Table 1. Population of Bolivia for the Principal Departments and Capital Cities According to the National Census, 1846–2001

Department	Capital	1846	1900	1950*	1976*	1992	2001	Sq. Miles
LA PAZ		412,867	426,930	854,079	1,465,078	1,900,786	2,350,466	51,731
	La Paz**	42,849	52,697	321,073	654,713	1,118,870	1,487,248	
COCHABAMBA		279,048	326,163	452,145	720,952	1,110,205	1,455,711	21,479
	Cochabamba	30,396	21,881	80,795	205,002	397,171	778,422	
ORURO		95,324	86,081	192,356	310,409	340,114	391,870	20,690
	Oruro	5,687	13,575	62,975	124,121	183,422	202,010	
POTOSI		243,269	325,615	509,087	657,743	645,889	709,013	45,643
	Potosí	16,711	20,910	45,758	77,334	112,078	133,268	
CHUQUISACA		156,041	196,434	260,479	358,516	453,756	531,522	19,893
	Sucre	19,235	20,907	40,128	62,207	131,769	194,888	
SANTA CRUZ		78,581	171,592	244,658	710,724	1,364,389	2,033,739	143,096
	St.Cruz	6,005	15,874	42,746	256,946	697,278	1,114,095	
TARIJA		63,800	67,887	103,441	187,204	291,407	391,226	14,526
	Tarija	5,129	6,980	16,869	39,087	66,900	135,651	
BENI		48,406	25,680	71,636	168,367	276,174	362,521	82,457
	Trinidad	3,194	2,556	10,759	27,583	57,328	75,285	
Pando		1,560	7,228	16,284	34,493	38,072	52,525	24,647
	Cobija***					10,001	20,987	
TOTAL COUNTRY		1,378,896	1,633,610	2,704,165	4,613,486	6,420,792	8,274,325	424,162

Notes: * The censuses of 1950 and 1976 have been corrected at the Departmental level in recent publications, see INE, cuadro 2.01.11 "Bolivia:Población por censo segun departamento... censos de 1950–1976–1992–2001".

** The figures for the city of La Paz include those for the newly established municipality of El Alto which was separated from La Paz. In the census of 1992 the city of La Paz held 713,378 persons, and El Alto some 405,492. The census of 2001 listed the population of El Alto at 694,749 and that of La Paz at 792,499.

*** The province of Pando has had no significant urban centers before 1992. In 1976 Cobija had only 1,726 persons.

304

Tables

Table 2. *Silver Production in Bolivia – 1550–1909 Output of Silver per Decade in Marks of Silver*

Decade	Average Annual Production	Maximum Year Ouput	Minimum Year Output
1550–59	278,055	379,244	207,776
1560–69	241,348	284,443	216,516
1570–79	278,093	613,344	114,878
1580–89	750,073	865,185	668,517
1590–99	803,272	887,447	723,591
1600–1609	762,391	844,153	624,666
1610–19	666,082	746,947	620,477
1620–29	590,900	646,543	536,473
1630–39	598,287	793,596	530,674
1640–49	520,859	619,543	463,799
1650–59	461,437	523,604	424,745
1660–69	362,425	398,459	321,889
1670–79	343,478	380,434	289,216
1680–89	370,646	409,338	326,904
1690–99	290,526	375,459	236,935
1700–1709	198,404	226,186	178,087
1710–19	152,696	198,682	114,310
1720–29	145,555	200,693	119,576
1730–39	140,186 e*	169,707	82,811
1740–49	92,119 e	111,947	81,081
1750–59	123,864 e	126,957	115,373
1760–69	142,114	158,883	117,323
1770–79	170,381	242,067	150,746
1780–89	378,170	416,676	335,848
1790–99	385,283	404,025	369,371
1800–1809	297,472	371,416	194,535
1810–09	208,032	338,034	67,347
1820–29	156,110	177,727	132,433
1830–39	188,319	228,154	169,035
1840–49	191,923	256,064	142,029
1850–59	201,482	224,313	189,573
1860–69	344,435 e	391,304	312,174
1870–79	955,629 e	1,150,770	391,304
1880–89	1,111,568 e	1,660,804	597,686
1890–99	1,655,762	2,630,907	1,202,927
1900–1909	799,791	1,288,452	385,522

Sources: Peter Bakewell, "Registered Silver Production in Potosí district, 1550–1735," *Jahrbuch für geschichte von Staat, Wirtschaft und Gesellschaft lateinamerikas* 12 (1975), Table 1, 92–97; Ernesto Rück,

Table 2 (*cont.*)
Guia General de Bolivia, Primer Año (Sucre, 1865), pp. 170–71 for 1755–1859; [Lamberto de Sierra], *"Manifesto" de la plata extraida del cerro de Potosí, 1556–1800* (Buenos Airres, 1971), pp. 35–37 for the years 1735–54: Adolf Soetbeer, *Edelmetall-produktion und werthverhältniss zwischen gold und silber seit der entdeckung Amerika's bis zur gegenwart* (Gotha, 1879), pp. 78–9 for 1860–75; *The Mining Industry, Its Statistics, Technology and Trade*, Vol. I (1892), p. 207 Vol. II (1893), p. 333 and Vol. VII (1898), p. 203 for 1876–1884; República de Bolivia, Oficina Nacional de Inmigración, Estadística y Propaganda *Geográfrica, Geografia de la república de Bolivia (La Paz, 1905)*, pp. 354–55 for 1895–1905; and Walter Gomez, *La Minería en el el desarrollo económico de Bolivia, 1900–1970* (La Paz, 1978), pp. 218–20 for 1905–9.
Notes: * The letter "e"signifies estimated production. All figures after 1859 have been converted from kilograms to marks using the conversion rate of 230 grams = 1 mark. Since no production data exists for the years 1734–55, I used the tax figures given in Serra. A multiplier of 5.2 was used to convert pesos corrientes to marks of silver – this number was the highest in a range of ratios between Rück's production figures and Serra's tax receipts for 1756–60.

Table 3. Tin Production in Bolivia, 1900–2008

Decade	Average Annual Production	Maximum Output Year	Minimum Output Year
1900–09	14,909	21,342	9,739
1910–19	24,710	29,100	21,324
1920–29	33,216	47,191 (1929)	19,086
1930–39	25,864	38,723	14,957 (1933)
1940–49	38,827	43,168	33,800
1950–59	28,861	35,384	18,013
1960–69	24,705	29,961	19,718
1970–79	29,731	32,626	25,568
1980–89	18,557	27,655	8,128 (1987)
1990–99	14,630	18,634	11,308
2000–08	16,055	18,444	12,298

Source: Walter Gomez, *La minería en el desarrollo económico de Bolivia, 1900–1970* (La Paz, 1978); James W. Wilkie and Peter Reich, eds., *Statistical Abstract of Latin America* (Los Angeles, 1980), Vol. X, p. 255 for 1971–76; U.S. Department of the Interio, *Minerals Yearbook, 1978–79* (Washington, 1980), Vol. I, p. 926 for 1977–79; *for 1980–2008* Ministerio de Mineria y Metalúrgica, *Estadística del Sector Mineria y Metalurgica, 1980–2008* (La Paz: 2009) cuadro 11.1 pp. 39–41.

Table 4. *Petroleum & Natural Gas*
Production in Bolivia

Year	Petroleum*	Gas**
1980		79.0
1981		78.0
1982		81.0
1983		84.3
1984		92.0
1985		89.0
1986		92.0
1987		91.4
1988		98.2
1989		107.4
1990		107.0
1991	8.1	105.2
1992	7.8	107.6
1993	8.1	107.6
1994	9.4	115.8
1995	10.4	116.4
1996	10.7	117.6
1997	11.0	106.5
1998	12.6	109.7
1999	10.7	92.2
2000	10.1	127.0
2001	11.4	186.3
2002	11.3	226.7
2003	12.2	261.3
2004	14.2	362.2
2005	15.4	442.7
2006	14.9	474.4
2007	15.0	505.0
2008	14.2	526.0

Notes: * Petroleum is given in milliones of barrels.
** Gas is given in millions of cubic feet.
Source: For 1991 to 2008, INE http://www.ine.gov.bo/indice/general.aspx?codigo=40105 acessed March 20, 2010; for 1980–1990, US Energy Information Administration http://tonto.eia.doe.gov/cfapps/ipdbproject/iedindex3.cfm?tid=3&pid=26&aid=2&cid=BL,&syid=1980&eyid=2008&unit=BCF.

Table 5. Basic Socio-Economic Indicators of Bolivia

Indicator	Amount	Year
Population (Millions) current estimate INE	10,227,300	2009
Population Density per sq. km	8.6	2005
% Urban	58%	2001
% Average Annual Growth of Population	1.9%	2010
Total Fertility Rate (children born to women 14–45 years of age)	3.3	2010
% population 0–14 years	39%	2001
Crude Birth Rate (per 1,000 resident population)	26.3	2010
Crude Death Rate (per 1,000 resident population)	7.3	2010
Maternal Mortality (per 100,000 live births)	180	2008 uw
Life Expectancy at birth (in years)	66.3	2010
Infant Mortality (per 1,000 live births)	41.6	2010
Children (1–5 years) Morality (per 1,000 live births)	10.3	2010 uw
% children underweight for age	6%	2000
% children malnurished under 3 years of age	24%	2003 u
% children under 1 year vaccinated with 3rd DPT shot	72%	2003 u
% children under 1 year vaccinated with 3rd Polio shot	68%	2003 u
% children under 1 year vaccinated with BCGN	93%	2003 u
% Births Attended by Health Professionals	61%	2007 u
% Population which Receives no Medical Attention	22%	2000
UN Ranking Score on Index of Human Development	0.729	2007 un
Income Share of Richest 10% of population	45.3%	2007 wb
Income Share of Poorest 20% of population	2.7%	2007 wb
Percentage of Population living in Poverty	54.0	2005 c
Percentage of Population living in Extreme Poverty	31.2	2005 c
GDP ($ million)	$ 16,674	2008 wb
Gross National Income per capita ($)	$ 1,720	2008 wb
Value of Exports (Goods & Services) $ million	$ 5,382	2009
Value of Imports $ million	$ 4,466	2009
Trade Balance $ million	$ 916	2009
Total External Debt ($ million)	$ 2,443	2008
Perecentage of the Economically Active Population		
in Agriculture	39.2%	2007
in Mining	1.2%	2007
in Construction	5.4%	2007
in Industry	10.5%	2007
in Comerce & Services	43.7%	2007

(cont.)

Table 5. (cont.)

Indicator	Amount	Year
% of EAP in Informal Sector	51.3%	2000 u
% Housing with Access to Drinking Water	65%	2003
% Housing with Access to Interior Sanitation Facilities	31%	2003
% Housing with Access to Electricity	65%	2003
% illiterates both Sexes (over 15 years of age)	13.2%	2001
Population in Public Initial, Primary & Secondary School (in millions)	2,513	2007 u
% of school age children in primary school (net enrollment)	92%	2007 u
% of school age children in secondary school (net enrollment)	57%	2007 u
Average Years of Schooling Completed (20 years and older)	8.7	2007 u
urban population	10.2	2007 u
rural population	5.6	2007 u
Language Most Spoken (6 years and over)		
Spanish	58.3%	2000
Aymara	15.7%	2000
Quechua	22.9%	2000
Guaraní	0.6%	2000
Other Native	0.4%	2000
Foreign	2.0%	2000
Ethnicity of Population 15 years of Age and Older (Self-Identification)		
Quechua	1,555,641	2001
Aymara	1,277,881	2001
Chiquitano	112,216	2001
Mojeño	78,359	2001
Guaraní	43,303	2001
Other Native	75,237	2001
Total National Population (census)	8,274,325	2001
% Population Catholic	78	2001
% Population Protestant	19	2001

Notes: Unless otherwise indicated, all numbers come from the Bolivian Instituto Nacional de Estadística (INE). All statistics given with a "c"are from
CEPAL, *Anuario estadística de America Latina y el Caribe, 2009.* All statistics given with a "wb"are from the World Bank, *World Development Indicators,* found at http://data.worldbank.org/indicator?display=default. All statistics wtih "u"are from Bolivia, UDAPE (La Unidad de Análisis de Politicas
Sociales y Económicas), and all statistics given with "un" come from UNDP
sources, and all statistics with "uw" are from the Institute of Health Metrics &
Evaluation, University of Washington (Seattle).

BIBLIOGRAPHY

I. GENERAL SURVEYS

Bolivia has been well served by its traditional historians, with several general surveys providing a coherent organization of national development. The most important and influential of these earlier histories are: Alcides Arguedas, *Historia general de Bolivia* (La Paz, 1922); and Enrique Finot, *Nueva historia de Bolivia* (Buenos Aires, 1946). More recent works of syntheses have included the constantly updated José de Mesa, Teresa Gisbert, and Carlos D. Mesa Gisbert, *Historia de Bolivia* (4th ed. rev.; La Paz: Editorial Gisbert y Cia, 2001); Clara López Beltrán, *Biografía de Bolivia, un estudio de su historia* (La Paz, 1993); and Alberto Crespo, José Crespo Fernández, and María Luisa KentSolares, eds., *Los bolivianos en el tiempo: Cuadernos de historia* (2nd ed.; La Paz, 1995). A general survey of Bolivian developments in a comparative framework with Peru was undertaken by Magnus Mörner in *The Andean Past: Land, Societies and Conflicts* (New York, 1985), and most recently Brooke Larson, *Trials of Nation Making, Liberalism, Race and Ethnicity in the Andes, 1810–1910* (Cambridge, 2004). An alternative vision of national history was proposed by Xavier Albó and Josep M. Barnadas, *La cara campesina de nuestra historia* (La Paz, 1984), and is further developed in Forrest Hylton and Sinclair Thomson, *Revolutionary horizons: past and present in Bolivian politics* (London, 2007). Some useful recent bibliographical surveys worth consulting are Josep M. Barnadas, *Manual de bibliografía: introducción a los estudios bolivianos contemporáneos, 1960–1984* (Cuzco, 1987); Brooke Larson, "Bolivia Revisited: New Directions in North American Research in History and Anthropology," *Latin American Research Review* 23:1 (1988), and Herbert S. Klein, "Recent Trends in Bolivian Studies," *Latin American Research Review* 31:1 (1996). A good recent introduction to the Bolivian archives is found in Rossana Barragán, *Guía de archivos para la historia de los pueblos indígenas en Bolivia* (La Paz, 1994). Finally, mention should be made of several important national historical journals: These have included *Historia Boliviana*, edited by Josep Barnadas from 1981 to 1986; *Historia y cultura* (La Paz, 1973–), the *Anuario* of the Archivo y Biblioteca Nacionales de Bolivia (Sucre, 1995–); *Data: Revista de Instituto de Estudios Andinos y Amazónicas* (La Paz, 1991–); and *Historias* (La Paz, 1997–). In terms of more specialized works, Luis Peñaloza, *Nueva historia económica de Bolivia* (7 vols.; La Paz, 1981–7), gives a reasonable albeit limited introduction to the field. More schematic, but with important retrospective statistical data, is Eduardo Arze Cuadros, *La economía de Bolivia . . . 1492–1979* (La Paz, 1979). A general survey of organized labor in Bolivian history is provided in Guillermo Lora, *History of the Bolivian Labour Movement, 1848–1971* (Cambridge, 1977). Intellectual thought is dealt with by Guillermo Francovich, *La filosofía en Bolivia* (Sucre, 1945); historians are well covered in Valentín Abecia Baldivieso, *Historiografía boliviana* (2nd ed.; La Paz, 1973). A recent history of Bolivian constitutional legislatures can be found in Rossana Barragán, *Las asembleas constituyentes en la historia de Bolivia* (La Paz, 2006). Political thought is studied in Mario Rolón Anaya, *Política y Partidos en Bolivia* (3rd ed. rev.; La Paz, 1999), which also contains the most complete presentation of party programs and platforms. These in turn can usefully be supplemented with Guillermo Lora, *Documentos políticos de Bolivia* (ed. rev., 2 vols.; La Paz, 1987); and most recently by the party programs as reproduced in Corte Nacional Electoral (CNE) *La representación política en Bolivia. Partidos politicos* (La Paz, 2005). Recently, the first studies of voting behavior have appeared for the modern period; see Salvador Romero Ballivián *Geografía electoral de Bolivia* (2nd ed.; La Paz, 1998), *Geografía electoral de Bolivia así votan los bolivianos* (La Paz, 1993); and most recently his study *El Tablero Reordenado. Análisis de la Elección Presidencial de 2005* (La Paz, 2006) The national electoral court has also sponsored a number of very useful historical studies on elections, voting and voting registration. See for example the detailed analysis by Carlos Hugo Cordero Carraffa, *Historia electoral de Bolivia 1952–2007* (La Paz, 2007); and of electoral representation throughout republican history in Eduardo Leaño Román, *Sistemas electorales en Bolivia. La conversión de votos en cargos del Ejecutivo y Legislativo* (La Paz, 2005); as well as the very useful compliation of voting statistics in "25 Años de evolución electoral en Bolivia," *CNE, Unidad de Análisis e Investigación, Boletín Estadística* III: 7 (Nov. 2007); and the voter registration censuses (Padrón Nacional Electoral or PNE) and their evolution from 1985 to 2005 in *CNE, Unidad de Análisis e Investigación, Boletín Estadística* V (Nov. 2005). One of the more interesting studies on the recent major administrative reform in local governance is Merilee S. Grindle, *Audacious Reforms: Institution Invention and Democracy in Latin America* (Baltimore, 2000); also see Horst Grebe López, et al., *Las reformas estructurales en Bolivia* (La Paz, 1998); and for a detailed analysis of the extraordinary decentralization reforms embodied in the 2009 constitution see Carlos Romero and Carlos Böhrt Irahola, *Autonomías Se hace camino al andar* (La Paz, 2009). All Bolivia's constitutions up to the 1950s are to be found in the compilation and analysis of Ciro Felix Trigo, *Las constituciones en Bolivia* (Madrid, 1958) while traditional constitutional thought is examined in Hormando Vaca Díez, *Pensamiento constitucional boliviano, 1826–1995* (La Paz, 1998). Bolivia's historical legislation on Indians and rural society is in two useful collections: José Flores Moncayo, *Legislación boliviana del indio, recopilación 1825–1953* (La Paz, 1953) and Abraham Maldonado, *Derecho agrario, historia-doctrina-legislación* (La Paz, 1956).

Among the numerous histories of Bolivia's complex international relations, the best is that by Valentín Abecia Baldivieso, *Las relaciones internacionales en la historia de Bolivia* (2nd ed., 2 vols; La Paz, 1986). Also see the recent survey by Eduardo Arze Quiroga, *Las relaciones internacionales de Bolivia, 1825–1990* (La Paz, 1991). Bolivia's close relationship with England is surveyed in Roberto Querejazu Calvo, *Bolivia y los ingleses, 1825–1948* (La Paz, 1971); the analysis by León Enrique Bieber, *Las relaciones económicas de Bolivia con Alemania, 1880–1920* (Berlin, 1984), is a model study on the economic relations between Bolivia and a foreign nation. He has recently expanded this study in his book *Pugna por influencia y hegemonía. La rivalidad germano-estadounidense en Bolivia, 1936–1946* (Frankfurt am Main, 2004). The controversial relations of Bolivia with Chile are seen from the Chilean viewpoint by Francisco Antonio Encina, *Las relaciones entre Chile y Bolivia, 1841–1963* (Santiago, 1963) and for the relations with the United States, see the discussion below.

From different perspectives are the still quite useful studies of national literature by Enrique Finot, *Historia de la literatura boliviana* (4th ed. rev.; La Paz, 1975); and Fernando Diez de Medina, *Literatura boliviana* (Madrid, 1954). Javier Sanjinés C. has surveyed recent literature in two works, *Tendencias actuales en la literatura boliviana* (Valencia, Spain, 1985) and *Literatura contemporánea y grotesco social en Bolivia* (La Paz, 1992). The best survey of the novel is still the works of Augusto Guzman in both his *La novela en Bolivia* (La Paz, 1955) and the work he did for the Pan American Union, *Diccionario de la literatura latinoamericana. Bolivia* (Washington, DC, 1955). There is a general survey of *Literatura virreinal en Bolivia* by Teresa Gisbert (La Paz, 1963), and Perla Zayas de Lima, has examined the *La novela indigenista boliviana de 1910–1960* (Buenos Aires, 1985). There is as yet no single all-encompassing survey of the plastic arts, although as will be made clear in the following sections, the work of José de Mesa and Teresa Gisbert is fundamental for any appraisal of this area in the pre-conquest, colonial, and national periods. A good introduction to Bolivia's architecture is their survey *Bolivia: Monumentos históricos y arqueologicos*

(Mexico, 1970). Recent painting is treated in Pedro Querejazu, ed., *Pintura boliviana del siglo xx* (Milan, 1989); theater in Mario Soria, *Teatro boliviano en el siglo xx* (La Paz, 1980); and film in Alfonso Gumucio, *Historia del cine en Bolivia* (La Paz, 1984); and José Sánchez-H, *The Art and Politics of Bolivian cinema* (Lanham, MD, 1999).

While there are numerous histories of individual religious orders, along with several documentary collections and larger international surveys, the only general history of the Bolivian Church is the cursory survey done by Felipe López Menendez, *Compendio de la historia eclesiastica de Bolivia* (La Paz, 1965). Another institution covered in some detail is the army, done by Julio Diaz A., *Historia del ejército de Bolivia, 1825–1932* (La Paz, 1940); James Dunkerley, *Orígenes del poder militar en Bolivia: Historia del ejército 1879–1935* (La Paz, 1987); and Gary Prado Salmon, *Poder y fuerzas armadas, 1949–1982* (La Paz, 1984). Medicine has been studied in Juan Manual Balcazar, *Historia de medicina en Bolivia* (La Paz, 1956). But the important profession of law has not been adequately treated. An original analysis of the evolution of the engineering profession is found in Manuel E. Contreras, *Tecnología moderna en los Andes minería e ingenería en Bolivia en el siglo XX* (La Paz, 1994).

Given the important role of mining and the extraordinary terrain of the country, Bolivia has been the subject of extensive research by national and foreign scholars in the geological and geographical fields. Much of the very extensive literature is summarized in Jorge Muñoz Reyes, *Geografía de Bolivia* (3rd ed.; La Paz, 1991) and in Federico E. Ahlfeld, *Geología de Bolivia* (3rd ed.; La Paz, 1972). The latest and most comprehensive survey is Ismael Montes de Oca, *Geografía y recursos naturales de Bolivia* (3rd ed.; La Paz, 1997). An interesting attempt recently made to remap the soils and climate of Bolivia using more modern criteria was carried out by the Ministerio de Asuntos Campesinos y Agropecuarios, *Mapa ecologico de Bolivia* (La Paz, 1975); an English study provides a more traditional and quite important analysis of the soils of Bolivia, in Thomas T. Cochrane, *Potencial agricola del uso de la tierra de Bolivia* (La Paz, 1973). Ecological zones are examined in C. E. Brockman, ed., *Perfil ambiental de Bolivia* (La Paz, 1986). Limited but nevertheless useful is the analysis of the distribution of commercial and subsistence plants in Gover Barja Berrios and Armando Cardozo Gonsalvez, *Geografía agrícola de Bolivia* (La Paz, 1971). Still important because of their extensive statistical collections are the government's early twentieth-century surveys: Oficina Nacional de Inmigración Estadística y Propaganda Geografica, *Sinopsis estadística y geográfica de la republica de Bolivia* (2 vols.; La Paz, 1903); *Geografía de la república de Bolivia* (La Paz, 1905); and *Diccionario geográfico de la República de Bolivia* (4 vols.; La Paz, 1890–1904). An interesting political geography of Bolivia dealing with its famous frontier problems is by J. Valerie Fifer, *Bolivia: Land, Location and Politics since 1825* (Cambridge, 1972). The urban geographic setting is explored in Wolfgang Schoop, *Ciudades bolivianas* (La Paz, 1981). Currently, Bolivia also has extensive collections of aerial and satellite photomapping as well as modern demographic and geographic maps available from the Instituto Militar de Geografía and the Instituto Nacional de Estadística. The satellite maps are discussed and indexed in Lorrain E. Giddings, *Bolivia from Space* (Houston, 1977). The only serious, albeit still limited, attempt at providing historical maps is found in Ramiro Condarco Morales, *Atlas histórico de Bolivia* (La Paz, 1985). The large literature on exploration is described in Manuel Frontaura Argandona, *Descubridores y exploradores de Bolivia* (La Paz, 1971). For animals of the region, two basic studies are Raymond A. Paynter, *Ornithological gazetteer of Bolivia* (2nd ed.; Cambridge, MA, 1992) and Sydney Anderson, *Mammals of Bolivia Taxonomy and Distribution* (New York: Bulletin 231, American Museum of Natural History, 1997), and for a detailed analysis of the forests, see Timothy J Killeen, Emilia García E., and Stephan Beck, *Guía de arboles de Bolivia* (La Paz and St. Louis, 1993).

On the evolution of the Bolivian population, see Asthenio Averanga Mollinedo, *Aspectos generales de la población boliviana* (3rd ed.; La Paz, 1998) and Augusto S. Siliz Sánchez, *La poblacion de Bolivia* (La Paz, 2001); and the numerous publications of the National Statistical Institute (Instituto Nacional de Estadística, or INE), especially the *Anuario Estadístico* and the annual economic and social data produced by UDAPE (Unidad de Análise de Políticas Sociales y Económicas, Ministerio de del Planificación de Desarrollo) along with the recent publications on Bolivia by UN agencies, especially those from CEPAL *Anuario estadistico de America Latina y el Caribe* and *Panorama social de América Latina* (both annual multivolume publications which are available online). CELADE (a subdiuvision of CEPAL) is the main source for comparatival demographic statistics, see especially its *Latin American and Caribbean Demographic Observatory (Bulletin)* and its various online databases. Some recent demographic studies include Renata Forste, "The Effects of Breastfeeding and Birth Spacing on Infant and Child Mortality in Bolivia," *Population Studies*, 48:3 (Nov. 1994), pp. 497–511. Finally, the adaptation to high-altitude living has been the subject of recent scholarly interest; see Paul T. Baker and M. A. Little, eds., *Man in the Andes: A Multidisciplinary Study of High-Altitude Quechua* (Stroudsburg, PA, 1976) and various studies in the *American Journal of Physical Anthropology*.

II. PRECOLONIAL AND COLONIAL WORLD

The most exciting recent developments in Bolivian historiography have concerned pre-Columbian themes and colonial social and economic history. Much of this work has been developed by both historians and anthropologists who have interacted with each other to produce major

new interpretations. For early man and his evolution in the region, see
S. J. Fiedel, *Prehistory of the Americas* (2nd ed.; Cambridge, 1992), and,
for the evolution of advanced societies, the work of Luis G.
Lumbreras, *The Peoples and Cultures of Ancient Peru* (Washington, DC, 1974), and
Karen Olsen Bruhns, *Ancient South America* (Cambridge, 1994). A recent
overview of the quickly changing field of Andean archaeology is found
in Terence N. D'Altroy, "Recent Research on the Central Andes," *Journal of Archeological Research*, 5:1 (1997), pp. 3–73. Earlier studies concerned with local preconquest developments include Dick Edgar Ibarra
Grasso, *Prehistoria de Bolivia* (2nd ed.; La Paz, 1973); Arthur Posnansky,
Tiahuanacu (2 vols.; New York, 1945), and the controversial studies of
Carlos Ponce Sanjines, *Descripción sumaria del templete semisubterraneo
de Tiwanaku* (La Paz, 1964) and *Tiwanaku: espacio, tiempo y cultura*
(La Paz, 1972). Full-scale excavations done by fully trained national and
foreign archaeologist have only been permitted recently after decades of closure. This new research has concentrated on Tiwanaku and the agricultural
basis for advanced civilizations in the altiplano and has been summarized
in Alan L. Kolata, *The Tiwanaku: Portrait of an Andean Civilization* (Cambridge, 1993), and the two volumes he edited, *Tiwanaku and Its Hinterland
Archaeology and Paleoecology of an Andean Civilization* (2 vols.; Washington, DC, 1996–2000). There has been a great deal of work on Tiwanaku
settlements north of the Lake, as well as studies by younger Bolivian archeologists on this subject. See Juan Albarracín-Jordán, *Tiwanaku, arqueología regional y dinmica segmentaria* (La Paz, 1996); and Juan Albarracín-Jordán and James Edward Mathews, *Asentamientos prehispánicos
del Valle de Tiwanaku* (La Paz, 1990). The preconquest Aymara kingdoms
were initially studied from surface collections, the results of which were
presented by John Hyslop in "El 'area Lupaca bajo el dominio incaico.
Un reconocimiento arqueologico," *Histórica* (Lima) 3:1 (1979), and "An
Archeological Investigation of the Lupaca Kingdom and Its Origins" (Ph.D.
diss., Columbia University, 1976). An ethnohistory survey was done by
Catherine J. Julien, *Hatunqolla: A View of Inca Rule from the Lake Titicaca Region* (Berkeley, 1983) and new archeological investigations of this
region now include Marc Bermann, *Lukurmata Household Archaeology in
Prehispanic Bolivia* (Princeton, 1994), Charles Stanish, *Ancient Titicaca:
the evolution of complex society in southern Peru and northern Bolivia*
(Berkeley, 2003), Charles Stanish and Brian S. Bauer, eds., *Archaelogical Research in the Islands of the Sun and Moon, Lake Titicaca, Bolivia*
(Los Angeles, 2004), and Charles Stanish, Amanda B. Cohen, and Mark
S. Aldenderfer, eds. *Advances in Titicaca Basin archaeology* (Los Angeles,
2005). The preconquest Aymara groups who controlled the Uyuni salt flats
have been studied by Patrice Lecoq, *"Uyuni prehispanique" archeólogie
de la cordillera intersalar (Sud-Ouest Bolivien)* (Oxford, 1999); and there
is some new work on the valleys by Alvaro Higueras-Hare, "Prehispanic

settlement and land use in Cochabamba, Bolivia" (Ph.D. diss., University of Pittsburgh, 1996).

For interpreting the nature of Andean civilization at its most complete development prior to the Spanish conquest, the work of John Murra has been fundamental. Among his many studies, the most important for the Bolivian perspective include *Formaciones políticos y económicos en el mundo andino* (Lima, 1975), "An Aymara Kingdom in 1576," *Ethnohistory* 15:2 (1968), and his editing of Garcí Diez de San Miguel, *Visita hecha a la provincia de Chuquito* (1576) (Lima, 1964) and most recently of a *Visita de los valles de Sonqo en los yunka de coca de La Paz [1568–1570]* (Madrid, 1991). Work with the recent visitas on the Aymara kingdoms of the Lake Titicaca region has been the source for the studies of Franklin Pease, *Del Tawantinsuyu a la historia del Peru* (Lima, 1978). For a visita in the Cochabmba valley, see José M. Gordillo and Mercedes del Rio, *La visita de Tiquipaya (1573) análisis etno-demográfico de un padrón toledano* (Cochabamba, 1993). On the Inca period of Bolivian history, the works of John Murra, Alfred Metraux, J. H. Rowe, Sally Falk Moore, R. T. Zuidema, Maria Rostworowski de Diez Canseco, Waldemar Espinoza Soriano, Franklin Pease, Nathan Wachtel, and Craig Morris relating to Peruvian developments also have been helpful in understanding the Bolivian experience. For the special role of the Cochabamba region as a crucial granary in the Inca empire, see Nathan Wachtel, "The Mitimas of the Cochabamba Valley: The Colonization Policy of Hyana Capac," in George A. Collier, et al., *The Inca and Aztec States, 1400–1800* (New York, 1982); the question of other ethnic groups under the Inca and Aymara rule has been examined by Thierry Saignes, *En Busca del Poblamiento Etnico de los Andes Bolivianos (siglos XV y XVI)* (La Paz, 1986). On the role of metals in Andean Ameindian societies before and after the conquest see Mary Money. *Oro y plata en los Andes: significado en los diccionarios de Aymara y Quechua, siglos XVI–XVII* (La Paz, 2004).

The theme of the Spanish conquest has drawn a host of fine generalists to write about it, beginning in the English language with the nineteenth-century classic of William H. Prescott, *The History of the Conquest of Peru*. The best modern survey is by John Heming, *The Conquest of the Incas* (New York, 1970). Nathan Wachtel's *The Vision of the Vanquished* (New York, 1977) provides an extremely imaginative reconstruction of the Indian perspective of this event.

In the last three decades, important studies have been undertaken on all aspects of the immediate preconquest and postcontact period in Bolivia. Much of this new work was summarized in John Murra, et al., *Anthropological History of Andean Polities* (Cambridge, 1986). This volume includes studies on the Uru by Nathan Wachtel and on the complex ethnic relations in the Larecaja Valley by Thierry Saignes, along with the study by Thérèse Bouysse-Cassagne on Aymara belief systems. These insights she developed more fully in her study *La identidad aymara: Aproximación histórica (siglo XV, siglo XVI)* (La Paz, 1987). Thérèse Bouysse-Cassagne also reconstructed sixteenth-century Amerindian languages in Bolivia, which appeared as a chapter in Noble David Cook, ed., *Tasa de la visita general de Francisco de Toledo* (Lima, 1975). The most thorough reconstruction of the major highland Indian languages at the time of the Spanish Conquest has been carried out by Alfredo Torero, "Lenguas y pueblos altiplanicos en torno al siglo XVI," *Revista Andina* 5:2 (1987).

The eastern Amerindian frontier has been the subject of quite original works by Thierry Saignes, "Une Frontière chiriguano fossile: la cordillière au XVIe siècle," (2 vols.; 3rd Cycle doctorate, Université de Paris, 1974); *Los andes orientales: historia de un olvido* (La Paz, 1985); and his *Ava y Karai: Ensayos sobre la frontera chiriguano (siglos XVI–XX)* (La Paz, 1990). Also see the classic study of William Denevan, *The Aboriginal Cultural Geography of the Llanos de Mojos of Bolivia* (Berkeley, 1966). More recently has come the work of Ana Maria Lema and Mario Alvarado, *Pueblos indígenas de la amazonía boliviana* (La Paz, 1998), and *Espacio, etnias, frontera atenuaciones políticas en el sur del Tawantinsuyu siglos XV–XVIII* (Sucre, 1995). These groups are dealt with in a comparative perspective in F. M. Renard Casevits, Thierry Saignes, and A. C. Taylor, *Al este de los Andes: relaciones entre las sociedades amazónicas y andines entre los siglos xv y xvii* (2 vols.; Quito, 1988); and in Pilar García Jordán, *Fronteras, colonización y mano de obra indígena, Amazonia andina (siglos XIX–XX) la construcción socio-ecónomico amazónico en Ecuador, Perú y Bolivia (1792–1948)* (Lima, 1998). The non-Aymara and non-quechua groups that existed before and after the Spanish conquest on the altiplano are also being studied. This is the theme of Carmen Beatriz Loza, "Los Quirua de los valles paceño: una tentativa de identificación en la época prehispánica," *Revista Andina*, no. 2 (Dec. 1984). The extensive literature on the Uru was examined by Harriet E. Manelis Klein, "Los urus: el extraño pueblo del altiplano," *Estudios Andinos* 3:1 (1973); and by Nathan Wachtel in a combined archival and ethnographic analysis in his monumental *Le retour des ancetres lesIndiens Urus de Bolivie, XXe-XVI siècle, essai d'historire régressive* (Paris, 1990). He also has explored related themes of this group in *Gods and Vampires Return to Chipaya* (Chicago, 1994).

The early integration of the resident Amerindian peasant populations into the Spanish colonial system has been the subject of much new work in the pages of the short-lived Bolivian review *Avances* (2 vols.; La Paz, 1978), which contained important articles by Tristan Platt, Roberto Choque, and Silvia Rivera. Recently, the essays on the economic and social roles of the Indian noble caciques were reprinted together with a new work by Roberto Choque Canqui, *Sociedad y economia colonial en el sur andino* (La Paz, 1993). This also was the theme in articles by John Murra, "Aymara Lords

and Their European Agents at Potosí," *Nova Americana*, I (1978); Brooke
Larson, "Caciques, Class Structure and the Colonial State in Bolivia," *Nova
Americana*, II (1979); Thierry Saignes in *Cacques, Tribute and Migration
in the Southern Andes* (University of London, Institute of Latin American Studies, Occasional Papers, no. 15, 1985); Silvia Arze and Ximena
Medinaceli, *Imágenes y presagios, el escudo de los Ayaviri, Mallkus de
Charcas* (La Paz, 1991) and, most recently, Laura Escobari de Querejazu,
*Caciques, yanaconas y extravagantes: La sociedad colonial en Charcas, sig-
los XVI–XVIII* (La Paz, 2001). Thierry Saignes also examined early Indian
rebellions and anti-Spanish movements in "'Algun día todo se andará': Los
movimientos étnicos en Charcas (siglo xvii)," *Estudios Andinos* 2 (1985).
Finally, the three major mission frontiers in the eastern lowland Bolivian
region (Moxos, Chuquitos, and the Gran Chaco) have been the object
of major new studies. The first two regions were studied by José Chávez
Suárez, *Historia de Moxos* (2nd ed.; La Paz, 1986), and Alcides Parejas
Moreno in several volumes: *Historia del oriente boliviano: Siglos xvi y xvii*
(Santa Cruz, 1979), *Historia de Moxos y Chuquitos a fines del siglo xviii*
(La Paz, 1976), and his joint volume with Virgilio Suárez Salas, *Chuquitos,
Historia de una utopía* (Santa Cruz, 1992); David Block, *Mission Culture
on the Upper Amazon: Native Tradition, Jesuit Enterprise and Secular
Policy in Moxos, 1660–1880* (Lincoln, NB, 1994); and Pedro Querejazu
and Placido Molina Barbery, *Las Misiones jesuiticas de Chiquitos* (La Paz,
1995). The southern Chaco Indian frontier is examined in James Schofield
Saeger, *The Chaco Mission Frontier: The Guaycuruan Experience* (Tuscon,
AZ, 2000) and by Eric Langer, *Expecting pears from an elm tree: Fran-
ciscan missions on the Chiriguano frontier in the heart of South America,
1830–1949* (Durham, 2009).

Colonial Amerindian demographic history for Bolivia has been totally
revised by the original study of Nicolás Sánchez-Albornoz, *Indios y tribútos
en el Alto Perú* (Lima, 1978), especially as it relates to the question of population growth and internal stratification. Others have used the Amerindian
tribute lists to study population distribution and land tenure: Daniel Santa-
maría, "La propiedad de la tierra y la condición social del indio en el Alto
Peru, 1780–1810," *Desarrollo Económico*, 66 (1977) and his *Haciendas y
campesinos en el Alto Peru colonial* (Buenos Aires, 1988); Brooke Larson,
"Hacendados y campesinos en Cochabamba en el siglo xviii," *Avances* 2
(1978); and Herbert S. Klein, *Haciendas and Ayllus: Rural Society in the
Bolivian Andes in the 18th and 19th Centuries* (Stanford, 1993). Rural
labor also has been the theme of the quite useful collection of notes and
documents by Silvio Zavala, *El servicio personal de los indios en el Perú*
(3 vols.; Mexico, 1978–80); detailed analysis of rural estates is found in
both René Danilo Arze Aguirre, "Las haciendas jesuítas de La Paz (siglo
xviii)," *Historia y cultura* (La Paz) 1 (1973) and in Nadine Sebill, *Ayllus y
haciendas* (La Paz, 1989).

Spanish colonial society has been well studied through recent monographs as well as major collections of documents. Josep M. Barnadas, in *Charcas, origines históricos de una sociedad colonial, 1535–1565* (La Paz, 1973), has examined the first decades of Audiencia rule. A reasonable survey of the published sources for the sixteenth century as a whole is provided in Eduardo Arze Quiroga, *Historia de Bolivia ... siglo xvi* (La Paz, 1969). Alberto Crespo has produced an important series of studies on urban political history: *Historia de la ciudad de La Paz, siglo xvi* (Lima, 1961); *El corregimiento de la Paz, 1548–1600* (La Paz, 1972); and *La guerra entre vicuñas y vascongados, Potosí, 1622–1625* (Lima, 1956). Together with several of his students, he published a major compilation on urban social and economic history in Alberto Crespo et al., *La vida cotidiana en La Paz durante la guerra de independencia, 1800–1825* (La Paz, 1975). An important recent addition to colonial urban history is the chronicle of urban life in seventeenth-century Chuquisaca by Lic. Pedro Ramirez del Aguila, *Noticias políticas de indias [1639]* (Sucre, 1978). The role of urban Indian women also has been studied by Luis Miguel Glave, "Mujer indígena, trabajo doméstico y cambio social en el virreinato peruano del siglo xvii: la ciudad de La Paz y el sur andino en 1684," *Bulletin de l'Institut Français Etudes Andines* 16:3–4 (1988); and Ann Zulawski, "Social Differentiation, Gender and Ethnicity: Urban Indian Women in Colonial Bolivia, 1640–1725," *Latin American Research Review* 25:2 (1990).

Spanish colonial mining and Potosí itself were the subject of numerous chronicles in the colonial period, most of which have been printed only recently, several of them ably edited by Lewis Hanke. The most important are: Luis Capoche, *Relación general de la villa imperial de Potosí* (Madrid, 1959); Bartolomé e Arzans de Orsua y Vela, *Historia de la villa imperial de Potosí* (3 vols.; Providence, RI, 1965; eds. Lewis Hanke and Gunnar Mendoza); and Pedro Vicente Cañete y Dominguez, *Guía histórica geografíca, fisica ... de Potosí* (Potosí, 1952). In the Arzans reprint appear important articles by Gunnar Mendoza, Lewis Hanke, José de Mesa, and Teresa Gisbert on the history of the city. Hanke also surveyed the history of the city in *The Imperial City of Potosí* (The Hague, 1956). Gunnar Mendoza, Bolivia's former national archivist, also has written several monographs on Potosí and its leading figures including *El Doctor don Pedro Vicente Cañete* (Sucre, 1954) and a document collection on *Guerra civil entre vicuñas y vascongados y otras naciones en Potosí, 1622–1645* (Potosí, 1954). A recent study of a seventeenth-century metallurgist and the colony's only distinguished scientist is by Josep Barnadas, *Alvaro Alonso Barba (1569–1662)* (La Paz, 1985). Modern research on the colonial mining industry is dominated by the studies of Peter Bakewell. He has published two major monographs as well as numerous important technical essays. Among these works are Peter Bakewell, *Miners of the Red Mountain: Indian Labour in Potosí, 1545–1650* (Albuquerque, 1984); *Silver and Entrepreneurship in Seventeenth Century Potosí* (Albuquerque, 1988); "Registered Silver Production in Potosí district, 1550–1735," *Jahrbuch für geschichte von Staat, Wirtschaft und Gesellschaft lateinamerikas* 12 (1975); "Technological Change in Potosí: The Silver Boom of the 1570s," *Ibid.*, 14 (1977); "Los determinantes de la producción minera en Charcas y en Nueva España durante el siglo XVII," *HISLA* 8 (1986). This can be supplemented with the older essays of Marie Helmer, *Cantuta recueil d'articles parus entre 1949 et 1987* (Madrid, 1993). David H. Brading and Harry E. Cross, "Colonial Silver Mining; Mexico and Peru," *Hispanic American Historical Review* 52:2 (1972), provided an earlier comparative perspective. The latest study of the minting of monies is Arnaldo J. Cunietti-Ferrando, *Historia de la Real Casa de Moneda de Potosí durante la dominación hispánica 1573–1825* (Buenos Aires, 1995), and on the coins themselves in the colonial and republican period, see Arie Kwacz, *Monedas, medallas y billetes de Bolivia* (La Paz, 1999). The mita labor system has been analyzed in Alberto Crespo, "La mita de Potosí," *Revista Histórica* (Lima) 22 (1955–56); Thierry Saignes, "Notes on the Regional Contribution to the Mita in Potosí in the Early Seventeenth Century," *Bulletin of Latin American Research* 4:1 (1985); and Jeffrey Cole, *The Potosí Mita, 1573–1700: Compulsory Indian Labor in the Andes* (Stanford, 1985); and free wage labor in the mines of Oruro has been the theme of Ann Zulawski, *They Eat from Their Labor: Work and Social Change in Colonial Bolivia* (Pittsburgh, 1995). There also are two important studies on the late colonial mining industry: Rose Marie Buechler, *The Mining Society of Potosí* (Ann Arbor, 1981); and Enrique Tandeter, *Coercion and Market Silver Mining in Colonial Potosí, 1692–1826* (Albuquerque, 1993) Also see Buechler's article "Technical Aid to Upper Peru: The Nordenflict Expedition," *Journal of Latin American Studies*, 5 (1973).

The eighteenth-century debate on the mita is examined in Rose Marie Buechler, "El Intendente Sainz v la 'mita nueva' de Potosí," *Historia y Cultura* (La Paz) 3 (1978), as well as in Tandeter's work. These debates are also reflected in the proposed eighteenth-century mining code of Pedro Cañete, *Codigo Carolina* (ed. E. Martire; 3 vols.; Buenos Aires, 1973–4). The regional economic impact of Alto Peruvian mining has been studied in a magisterial theoretical work by Carlos Sempat Assadourian, *El sistema de la economia colonial. Mercado interno, regiones y espacio económico* (Lima, 1982). Specific trades influenced by Potosí are examined in Carlos Sempat Assadourian, *El trafico de esclavos en Cordoba de Angola a Potosí siglos xvi–xvii* (Cordoba, Argentina, 1966); and Nicolás Sánchez Albornoz, "La saca de mulas de Salta al Peru, 1778–1808," *Anuario del Instituto de Investigaciones Historicas* 8 (Rosario, 1965). The classic study on regional markets and conflicting elites involving Alto Peru was written by Guillermo Cespedes del Castillo, *Lima y Buenos Aires, repercusiones económicas y políticas de la creación del virreinato del Plata* (Sevilla, 1946); while interregional and international trade patterns are studied in Laura Escobari de Querejazu, *Producción y comercio en el espacio sur andino, siglo XVII, Cusco–Potosí 1650–1700* (La Paz, 1985); and Enrique Tandeter et al., "El mercado de Potosí a fines del siglo xviii," in the anthology on markets edited by Olivia Harris et al., cited below.

Recent studies on royal income and the fiscal structure of colonial Bolivia include those by Tibor Wittman, *Estudios históricos sobre Bolivia* (La Paz, 1975); Herbert S. Klein, *The American Finances of the Spanish Empire, 1680–1809* (Albuquerque, 1998); Clara López, *Estructura económica de una sociedad colonial: Charcas en el siglo xvi* (La Paz, 1988); and John J. TePaske, "The Fiscal Structure of Upper Peru and the Financing of Empire," in Karen Spalding, ed., *Essays in the Political, Economic and Social History of Colonial Latin America* (Newark, DE, 1982). The treasury records themselves for the entire colonial period have been reproduced in "Upper Peru," volume 2 of John J. TePaske and Herbert S. Klein, *Royal Treasuries of the Spanish Empire in America* (3 vols.; Durham, NC, 1982).

Work has finally begun on the nonmining economy. Among the studies of this sector are: Mary Money, *Los obrajes, el traje y el comercio de ropa en la Audiencia de Charcas* (La Paz, 1983); and that of a La Paz merchant fortune done by Herbert S. Klein, "Accumulation and Inheritance among the Landed Elite of Bolivia: The Case of Don Tadeo Diez de Medina," *Jahrbuch fúr geschichte von staat, wirtschaft und gesellschaft Lateinamerikas* (Koln) 22 (1985). But there exist few, if any, studies on the construction industry so vital for the building of the urban centers and their monumental churches, on either unskilled or skilled labor, on local trade and credit, or on most aspects of economic urban life. Price history has finally become a serious concern, with the first study being Enrique Tandeter and Nathan Wachtel, *Precios y producción agrarian: Potosí y Charcas en el siglo xviii* (Buenos Aires, 1984).

Of major import in late colonial society was the massive peasant uprising of the early 1780s known as the Rebellion of Túpac Amaru. The most complete narrative of the political and military events that formed these revolts is still the classic work of Boleslao Lewin, *La rebelíon de Túpac Amaru* (Buenos Aires, 1957). More recent interpretations of the causes of this important movement have included Oscar Cornblit, *Power and violence in the colonial city Oruro from the mining renaissance to the rebellion of Túpac Amaru (1740–1782)* (Cambridge, 1995) and Nicholas A. Robins, *Priest-Indian conflict in upper Peru: the generation of rebellion, 1750–1780* (Syracuse, 2007) and those found in Alberto Flores Galindo, ed., *Túpac Amaru II – 1780, Antologia* (Lima, 1976), and Scarlett O'Phelan, *La gran rebelión en los Andes de Túpac Catari* (Cuzco, 1995) An alternative explanation based on a detailed study of the institution of forced sales of imported goods is Júrgen Golte, *Repartos y rebeliones. Túpac Amaru y las contradicciones de la economía colonial* (Lima, 1980). The special nature of the combined mestizo-Indian subrevolt in Oruro is explored by Fernando Cajías, "Los objetivos de la revolucíon indígena de 1781:El caso de Oruro," *Revista Andina* 1:2 (Dec., 1983), and the siege of La Paz and its leader Tupac Catari, was examined by María Eugenia del Valle de Siles beginning with an edition of the 1781 report of Francisco Tadeo Diez de Medina, *Diario del alzamiento de indios conjurados contra la ciudad de... La Paz, 1781* (La Paz, 1981); and most recently her *Historia de la rebelión de Tupac Catari, 1781–1782* (La Paz, 1990). More recent interpretations of these great Indian rebellions are Sinclair Thomson, *We alone will rule: native Andean politics in the age of insurgency* (Madison, 2002), and Sergio Serulnikov, *Subverting Colonial Authority. Challenges to Spanish Rule in Eighteenth-Century Southern Andes* (Durham, 2003).

The extraordinary artistic creativity of the colonial Bolivian society has been the domain of the distinguished pair of art historians, José de Mesa and Teresa Gisbert. Together and separately they have produced a major corpus on painters, sculptors, architects, and artists of all kinds and of all origins who worked in Upper Peru. Among the more important of their joint works are *Holguín y la pintura altoperuana del virreinato* (La Paz, 1956), *Escultura virreinal en Bolivia* (La Paz, 1972), *El pintor Mateo Perez de Alesio* (La Paz, 1972), *Bitti: Un pintor manerista en sudamérica* (La Paz, 1974), and *Arquitectura andina, 1530–1830* (La Paz, 1997). Teresa Gisbert alone has recently written a monumental work on colonial Indian art: *Iconogafía y mitas indígenas en el Arte* (2nd ed.; La Paz, 1994), and most recently the vision of both Indians and non-Indians in *El paraíso de los pájaros parlantes la imagen del otro en la cultura andina* (La Paz, 1999). She also has studied the art of the native textiles in Teresa Gisbert, Silvia Arze, and Marta Cajias, *Arte textil y mundo andino* (La Paz, 1987). Finally, for the general reader, there are two recent works that provide excellent quality reproductions of these materials: Teresa Gisbert, *Bolivian Masterpieces: Colonial Painting* (La Paz and Houston, 1994), and Pedro Querejazu, *Potosí Colonial Treasures and the Bolivian City of Silver* (New York, 1997).

The study of Bolivian colonial history is also aided by more than a century of excellent documentary collections, among the most important of which are Pedro de Angelis, ed., *Colección de obras y documentos relativos a la historia antigua y moderna de las provincias del Rio de la Plata* (6 vols.; Buenos Aires, 1836–37); Marcos Jimenez de la Espada, ed., *Relaciones geográficas de indias: Peru* (4 vols.; Madrid, 1881–97); Victor M. Mauritua, ed., *Juicio de limites entre el Perú y Bolivia* (12 vols.; Barcelona, 1906–7); Roberto Levellier, ed., *La Audiencia de Charcas. Correspondencia de Presidentes y Oidores* (3 vols.; Madrid, 1918–22). Finally, most of the essays of the distinguished historian Humberto Vazquez Machicado gathered together in, *Obras completas* (7 vols.; La Paz, 1988) deal with the colonial period.

III. THE EARLY NINETEENTH CENTURY

The period of the wars of independence and the early years of the republic also has been the subject of major publications in the last few years, which has considerably revised previous interpretations. The recent study by René Danilo Arze Aguirre, *Participación popular en la independencia de Bolivia* (La Paz, 1979), provides the crucial popular background to the elite study by Charles Arnade, *The Emergence of the Republic of Bolivia* (Gainesville, FL, 1957). A detailed examination of the events of the period are contained in Estanislao Just, *Comienzo de la independencia en el Alto Perú los sucesos de Chuquisaca, 1809* (Sucre, 1994); and the most recent surveys include Jorge Silves Salinas, *La Independencia de Bolivia* (Madrid, 1992), and the study by José Luis Roca, *Ni con Lima ni con Buenos Aires: la formación de un estado nacional en Charcas* (La Paz & Lima, 2007). The conflict in one region is examined by Eduardo Arze Quiroga, *Bolivia, el proceso de lucha inicial por la independencia la insurrección de Cochabamba, 1808–1815* (La Paz, 1998). A work on propaganda of the period is Vitaliano Torrico Panozo, *El pasquín en la independencia del Alto Perú* (Mexico, 1997), and a diary of a participant was edited and translated by Nataniel Aguirre, Sergio Gabriel Waisman, and Alba María Paz-Soldán, *Juan de la Rosa memoirs of the last soldier of the independence movement* (New York, 1998). The important role of Sucre has been well illustrated by William Lee Lofstrom, *El Mariscal Sucre en Bolivia* (La Paz, 1983), and complemented by an interesting study of Thomas Millington, *Debt Politics After Independence. The Funding Conflict in Bolivia* (Gainesville, , 1992). The complex role of Santa Cruz has been examined by Philip T. Parkerson, *Andrés de Santa Cruz y la Confederación Peru-Boliviana 1835–1839* (La Paz, 1984), complementing the popular biography of Alfonso Crespo, *Santa Cruz, el condor indio* (Mexico, 1944).

Several volumes of documents of this period have been published by Carlos Ponce S. and R. A. Garcia, eds., *Documentos para la historia de la Revolución de 1809* (4 vols.; La Paz, 1953–4); and Vicente Lecuna, ed., *Documentos referentes a la creación de Bolivia* (2 vols.; Caracas, 1975). Crucial information on this vital period is also provided in such contemporary travel accounts as Alcide D'Orbigny, *Voyage dans l'amerique meridionale* (9 vols.; Paris, 1844); and Edmond Temple, *Travels in Various Parts of Peru* (2 vols.; Philadelphia, 1833). An analysis of the important D' Orbigny travels is the study of Juan Albarracín Millán, *Las exploraciones de Alcides dÓrbigny en Bolivia* (La Paz, 2002). The most important source of early statistical information on Bolivia is the classic study by José Maria Dalence, *Bosquejo estadístico de Bolivia* (Chuquisaca, 1851), supplemented by John Barclay Pentland, *Report on Bolivia, 1827* (Royal Historical Society, 4th Camden Series, vol. 13; London, 1974) – a more complete edition in Spanish was published as *Informe sobre Bolivia* (Potosí, 1975). Finally, much interesting documentation on nineteenth-century rural and urban life in Bolivia has been gathered together by various Peruvian scholars under the direction of Pablo Macera, *Fuentes de historia social americana [Bolivia]* (7 vols. to date; Lima, 1978).

For understanding the complex interaction of political and international history in this first century of independence, the older study by Jorge Basadre, *Peru, Chile y Bolivia independiente* (Barcelona, 1948), remains the classic work. This may be supplemented by the influential works of Alcides Arguedas, *Los caudillos letrados . . . (1828–48)* (Barcelona, 1923); *Le plebe en acción (1848–57)* (Barcelona, 1924); *La dictadura y la anarquía (1857–64)* (Barcelona, 1926); *Los caudillos barbaros . . . (1864–72)* (Barcelona, 1929). All these historical works of Arguedas have been reprinted several times including the Aguilar edition of his *Obras Completas* (2 vols., Mexico, 1957), Vol. II. The most recent survey of this period is by Victor Peralta Ruiz and Marta Irurozqui Victoriano, *Por la concordia, la fusion y el unitarismo: Estado y caudillismo en Bolivia, 1825–1880* (Madrid, 2000). To this can be added studies of individual regimes and leaders, both by nineteenth-century writers such as Ramón Sotomayor Valdes, *Apuntes para la historia de Bolivia bajo la administración del general D. Augustin Morales* (La Paz, 1898), and José Maria Santivanez, *Vida del General José Ballivian* (New York, 1891); or the more recent Manuel Carrasco, *José Ballivian, 1805–52* (Buenos Aires, 1960). Ballivian's famous battle has received a detailed treatment in Fernando Kieffer Guzmán, *Ingavi batalla triunfal por la soberanía boliviana* (La Paz, 1991). But for all their importance, such leading figures as Melgarejo and Belzu still lack serious biographies and few studies exist on the actual functioning of government in the nation. An important and vivid analysis of a major political event of this period does exist in the model study of Gabriel René Moreno, *Matanzas de Yañez* (2nd ed.; La Paz, 1976).

Far more original research has occurred in the economic and social history of the early nineteenth century than in the political area. The major study of government finance by Casto Rojas, *Historia financiera de Bolivia* (La Paz, 1916), was recently supplemented by the study of Millngton. The crucial role of Indian tribute in early republican finance is examined in Jorge Alejandro Ovando Sanz, *El tributo indígena en las finanzas bolivianas del siglo xix* (La Paz, 1986), which should be supplemented with the works cited of Sánchez-Albornoz, Greishaber, Klein, and Tristan Platt, *Estado tributario y librecambio en Potosí* (siglo XIX) (La Paz, 1986), and the study by Eric Langer, "El liberalismo y la abolición de la comunidad indígena en el siglo xix," *Historia y Cultura* 14 (1988). Also see the fine statistical study by Erwin P. Grieshaber, "Survival of Indian Communities in Nineteenth-Century Bolivia: A Regional Comparison," *Journal of Latin American Studies*, 12:2 (Nov. 1980); and his "Resistencia indígena a la venta de tierras comunales en el departamento de La Paz, 1881–1920," *Data* (La Paz) 1

(1991). The crucial role of Bolivian coinage in the early republican regional economy of the other South American republics is explored in an original study by Antonio Mitre, *El monedero de los Andes: Región económica y moneda boliviana en el siglo xix* (La Paz, 1986); and by Gustavo A. Prado Robles, "Efectos económicos de la adulteración monetario," in Rossana Barragón, et al., *El siglo XIX: Bolivia y América Latina* (La Paz, 1997), pp. 299–328. This latter volume also contains several original studies on commerce and trade in the early nineteenth century. Early attempts to revive the mining industry are analyzed in Enrique Tandeter, "Potosí y los ingleses a fines de 1826," *Historia y Cultura* 3 (1978); and William Lofstrom, *Damaso de Uriburu, a Mining Entrepreneur in Early 19th-Century Bolivia* (SUNY Buffalo, Special Studies, no. 35, 1973). A rather complete economic and social history of the early Bolivian development of the littoral is Fernando Cajias, *La provincia de Atacama, 1825–1842* (La Paz, 1975); while the Indian tribute lists have been explored for an original analysis of the native population of the city of La Paz in Rossana Barragán, *Espacio urbana y dinmica etnica, La Paz en el siglo xix* (1990).

IV. THE LATE NINETEENTH CENTURY

The second half of the nineteenth century has been subject to less attention than the earlier period until very recently. Most of the political literature of this period is cited in Herbert S. Klein, *Parties and Political Change in Bolivia, 1880–1952* (Cambridge, 1969, reprinted 2009); in Marta Irurozqui, *La armonía de las desigualdades elites y conflictos de poder en Bolivia, 1880–1920* (Madrid, 1994); and in the works of Basadre and Arguedas. Mariano Baptista, the leading political theorist of the period, has had all his works published in *Obras Completas* (7 vols.; La Paz, 1932–4), and an interesting survey of the political upheavals of the period is catalogued in Nicanor Aranzaes, *Las revoluciones de Bolivia* (La Paz, 1918). A somewhat unsystematic but interesting survey of the society, economy, and political ideas in the last quarter of the nineteenth century is given by Daniele Demelas, *¿Nationalisme sans nation? La Bolivie aux xix–xx siècles* (Paris, 1980). But few serious studies of political life and even fewer biographies or administrative studies exist for this period. There is, however, a superb political novel that captures the era to an extraordinary degree and is one of the best of its genre in Latin America. This is Armando Chirveches, *La candidatura de Rojas* (La Paz, 1909).

The War of the Pacific has produced a series of studies giving the Bolivian interpretation of this important event which include the works of Roberto Querejazu Calvo, *Guano, salitre, sangre: historia de la Guerra del Pacífico* (La Paz, 1979) and his *La Guerra del Pacífico: sintesis historica de sus antecedentes, desarrollo y consecuencias* (La Paz, 1983); and Edgar Oblitas Fernández, *Historia secreta de la Guerra del Pacífico: de 1879 a 1904* (La

Paz, 2001). For the economic origins of the war and its consequences see Heraclio Bonilla, *Un siglo a la deriva: ensayos sobre el Perú, Bolivia y la Guerra* (Lima, 1980) and the two volumes of Oscar Bermúdez Miral, *Historia del salitre desde sus orígenes hasta la Guerra del Pacífico* (Santiago de Chile, 1963), and *Historia del salitre: desde la Guerra del Pacífico hasta la Revolución de 1891* (Santiago de Chile, 1984). An original attempt to measure the impact of the War of the Pacific on the post-war economies of all the participants is Richard Sicotte, Catalina Vizcarra and Kirsten Wandschneider, "The fiscal impact of the War of the Pacific" *Cliometrica* 3 (2009), pp. 97–121. For the impact of the war on internal Bolivian politics see Klein, *Parties and Political Change*.

An excellent analysis of the silver mining industry in the nineteenth century is provided in Antonio Mitre, *Los patriarcas de la plata. Estructura socio-económica de la mineria boliviana en el siglo xix* (Lima, 1981). Several reasonable biographies exist on the leading miners of the period: Ernesto Rück, *Biografía de Don Avelino Aramayo* (Potosí, 1891); A. Costa du Rels, *Felix Avelino Aramayo y su época, 1846–1929* (Buenos Aires, 1942); Jaime Mendoza, *Gregorio Pacheco* (Santiago de Chile, 1924). But the concern is usually with the noneconomic aspects of their lives. Moreover, most of the other sectors of the economy, such as the internal market, regional trade, and public finance are neglected. There is finally beginning to be some interest in the revolution in transportation that occurred in this period: see Harold Blakemore, *From the Pacific to La Paz, the Antofagasta (Chili) and Bolivia Railway Company, 1888–1988* (London, 1990), and a survey of the primary literature is given in Edgar A. Valdes, *Catálogo de folleteria de ferrocarriles del repositario nacional* (La Paz, 1980). But little has yet been undertaken on the modernization of the urban centers.

In contrast to this relative neglect in economic studies, there has been a major renaissance in the social history of this period. This began with an innovative study challenging all the traditional assumptions about the political isolation of the Indian carried out by Ramiro Condarco Morales, *Zarate "El Temible" Wilke: Historia de la rebelíon indígena de 1899* (2nd ed. rev.; La Paz, 1982); and further elaborated on by Marie-Danielle Demelas, "Jacqueries indiennes, politique créole, la guerre civile de 1899," *Caravelle* 44 (1985). This was followed by a critique of the ideas that rural Bolivia was dominated by haciendas in the nineteenth century and was defined by its isolation from the market economy. These assumptions were challenged in two important works: Silvia Rivera, "La expansion del latifundio en el altiplano boliviano: elementos para la caracterizacion de una oligarquía regional," *Avances* 2 (1978); and Erwin P. Greishaber, "Survival of Indian Communities in Nineteenth-Century Bolivia: A Regional Comparison," *Journal of Latin American Studies* 12:2 (1980). A major literature has now developed detailing the complex evolution of rural society in the major regions of the country. Among these works are Brooke Larson,

Colonialism and Agrarian Transformation in Bolivia, Cochabamba, 1550–1900 (Princeton, 1988); Erick D. Langer, *Economic Change and Rural Resistance in Southern Bolivia, 1880–1930* (Stanford, 1989); and Tristan Platt, *Estado boliviano y ayllu andino: Tierra y tributo en el Norte de Potosí* (La Paz, 1982). An alternative model of nineteenth-century growth stressing the role of the forasteros inside the ayllus is given in Klein, *Hacienda y Ayllus* cited above. An overview of this entire struggle over land and indigenous rights is found in Laura Gotkowitz, *Revolution for Our Rights. Indigenous Struggle for Land and Justice in Bolivia, 1880–1952* (Durham, NC, 2007). Finally, a challenge to the post-1880 model of complete destruction of peasant communities is presented in a short and provocative essay by Gustavo Rodríguez, *¿Expansión del latifundio o supervivencia de las comunidades indígenas? Cambios en la estructura agraria boliviana del siglo XIX* (IESE, Universidad Mayor de San Simon, Cochabamba, 1983). There also are several recent studies of regional elites that include Alexis Pérez Torrico, *El estado oligárquico y los empresarios de Atamaca (1871–1878)* (La Paz, 1944); Gustavo Rodríquez O., *Poder central y proyecto regional, Cochabamba y Santa Cruz en los siglos XIX y XX* (La Paz, 1993) and his *La construcción de una región. Cochabamba y su historia siglos XIX XX* (Cochabamba, 1995); and, for the more recent period, the study by Gonzalo Rojas Ortuste, Luis Tapia Mealla, and Oscar Bazoberry Chali, *Elites a la vuelta del siglo. Cultura politica en el Beni* (La Paz, 2000).

V. THE EARLY TWENTIETH CENTURY

With the twentieth century, the pace of research in all areas increased greatly. The first decades of the twentieth century were ones of intellectual ferment. From the initial stirrings of a critique of racist society in the novels and "sociology" of Alcides Arguedas to the more systematic development of an indigenista viewpoint in Franz Tamayo, *La creacíon de una pedagogía nacional* (La Paz, 1910), writers began to challenge the assumptions of their society. A good survey of this activity is found in Guillermo Francovich, *El pensamiento boliviano en el siglo xx* (2nd ed.; La Paz, 1966), and in the literature studies by Díez de Medina and Finot previously cited. For a recent major survey of the entire period, in terms of economic, political, and social history, see the major compendium edited by Fernando Campero Prudencia, *Bolivia en el siglo XX* (La Paz, 1999).

There has been a general neglect of the Liberal era, with the exception of the study of Juan Albarracín Millán, *El poder minero en la administración liberal* (La Paz, 1972). Also see his continuing studies in *Bolivia: el descentrañamiento del estaño. Los republicanos en la historia de Bolivia* (La Paz, 1993), and El *poder financiero de la gran minería boliviana* (La Paz, 1995). The most recent study on the revolt of 1899 that brought the liberals to power is Luis Antezana Ergueta, *La guerra entre La Paz y Chuquisaca (1899)* (La Paz, 1999), which should be supplemented with the older work of Condarco Morales on the Indian leadership in revolt cited above. Political biography has proved more popular, and Bolivian writers have been attracted to the political leaders of the 1920s and 1930s, producing the very best such biographies yet written. There exist two outstanding biographies for this period, one by Benigno Carrasco, *Hernando Siles* (La Paz, 1961), and the other by David Alvestegui, *Salamanca, su gravitación sobre el destino de Bolivia* (3 vols.; La Paz, 1957–62). An overall assessment of this period is provided in Klein, *Parties and Political Change*, and in two outstanding surveys: the first volume of the two-volume history of modern Bolivian political history by Augusto Céspedes, *El dictador suicida, 40 años de historia de Bolivia* (Santiago de Chile, 1956); and in the first three volumes of the five-volume series by Porfirio Díaz Machicado, *Historia de Bolivia. Saavedra, 1920–25* (La Paz, 1954), *Historia de Bolivia, Guzman, Siles, Blanco Galindo, 1925–31* (La Paz, 1954), and *Historia de Bolivia. Salamanca, La guerra del Chaco, Tejada Sorzano* (La Paz, 1955). The major Indian rebellion of the period has been examined by Roberto Choque and Esteban Ticona, *La sublevación y masacre de 1921* (La Paz, 1996), which forms part of a larger multivolume study of the crucial highland Aymara community entitled *Jesús de Machaqa: La marka rebelde.*

The economic history of this period has also been more fully developed than in previous eras. The tin mining industry received an overall economic analysis of some sophistication in the study by Walter Gomez, *La minería en el desarrollo económico de Bolivia, 1900–1970* (La Paz, 1978), and impressive historical reconstructions in Antonio Mitre, *Bajo un cielo de estaño fulgor y ocaso del metal en Bolivia* (La Paz, 1993) and his *El enigma de los hornos la economía política de estadística de la fundiciónde estaño, el proceso boliviano a la luz de otras experiencias* (La Paz, 1993). Complementing these macro-analyses are detailed studies of the early industry by Pedro Aniceto Blanco, *Monografía de la industria minera en Bolivia* (La Paz, 1910); Herbert S. Klein, "The Creation of the Patiño Tin Empire," *Inter-American Economic Affairs* 19:2 (1965), which was updated and published in Spanish in *Historia Boliviana* 3:2 (1983); and Donaciano Ibañez C., *Historia mineral de Bolivia* (Antofagasta, 1943). There are several biographies of the leading miners, among which are Charles F. Geddes, *Patiño: The Tin King* (London, 1972); Alfonso Crespo, *Los Aramayo de Chichas: Tres generaciones de mineros bolivianos* (Barcelona, 1981); and Helmut Waszkis, *Dr. Moritz (Don Mauricio) Hochschild, 1881–1965* (Frankfurt, 2001). The economics of labor in the early tin industry is studied by Manuel E. Contreras, "Mano de obra en la minería estañífera de principios de siglo, 1900–1925," *Historia y Cultura* (La Paz) 8 (1985), who also has surveyed "La minería estañífera boliviana en la Primera Guerra Mundial," in Raul

España-Smith et al., *Mineria y economia en Bolivia* (La Paz, 1984). The early growth of the industry is also studied by John Hillman, "The Emergence of the Tin Industry in Bolivia," *Journal of Latin American Studies* 16 (1984); and its international presence in his essays "Bolivia and the international tin cartel, 1931–1941," *Ibid.* 20:1 (May 1988); "Bolivia and British Tin Policy, 1939–1945," *Ibid.* 22:2 (May, 1990), and in K. E. Knoor, *Tin Under Control* (Stanford, 1945). The political role of the miners is assessed in the previously cited work of Albarracín and William Lofstrom, *Attitudes of an Industrial Pressure Group in Latin America, the "Asociación de Industriales Mineros de Bolivia" 1925–1935* (Ithaca, NY 1968). The nonmining economy of the period is also beginning to be studied; see María Luisa Soux, *La coca liberal: Producción y circulación a principios del siglo XX* (La Paz, 1993) and Antonio Mitre, *Los hilos de la memoria ascensión y crisis de las casas comerciales alemanas en Bolivia 1900–1942* (La Paz, 1996). Finally, Manuel Contreras treats the railroads in his essay "Bolivia, 1900–1939: Mining, Railways and Education," in vol. I of Enrique Cárdenas et al., *An Economic History of Twentieth Century Latin America* (2 vols.; London, 2000).

Good general assessments of the national economy at this time are found in W. L. Schurz, *Bolivia, A Commercial and Industrial Handbook* (Washington, DC, 1921), and Paul Walle, *Bolivia, Its People and Resources* (New York, 1914). Specific aspects of the economy or national economic policy are reviewed in Charles A. McQueen, *Bolivian Public Finance* (Washington, DC, 1925), and most recently in Carmenza Gallo, *Taxes and State Power: Political Instability in Bolivia, 1900–1950* (Philadelphia, 1991). On the history of foreign loans, see the excellent study by Margaret A. Marsh, *Bankers in Bolivia: A Study in American Foreign Investment* (New York, 1928). Among the many surveys on banking history, that by Julio Benavides, *Historia bancaria de Bolivia* (La Paz, 1955), is of some utility. The short-lived Acre rubber boom is examined in Valerie Fifer, "The Empire Builders: A History of the Bolivian Rubber Boom and the Rise of the House of Suarez," *Journal of Latin American Studies* 2:1 (1970).

While the social changes affecting the society with the growth of the tin industry, the modernization of the cities, and the completion of the hacienda expansion have not been seriously analyzed by scholars, there does exist a wealth of data with which to study this problem. Thus, in 1900 came the first and one of the best national censuses: Oficina Nacional de Inmigración, Estadística y Propaganda Geográfica, *Censo nacional de la población de la república de Bolivia, 1° septiembre de 1900* (2 vols.; La Paz, 1902–4). This government office also published numerous geographical studies that have been cited above; and from approximately the late 1880s onward, with increasing tempo under the very efficient Liberals, almost all the government ministries were publishing annual statistics on the national society and economy.

VI. THE 1930S TO THE PRESENT

The Chaco War has produced an enormous literature, from novels to memoirs of individual battles and war experiences. Much of this literature is summarized in Roberto Querejazu Calvo, *Masamaclay: Historia, política, diplomática y militar de la guerra del Chaco* (3rd ed.; La Paz, 1975). For the English reader, a good history of the war itself and of the diplomatic disputes behind it is found in David H. Zook, Jr., *The Conduct of the Chaco War* (New York, 1960). The politics of the war and the radical military regimes that followed are treated in detail in the previously cited works of Díaz Machicado, and Klein, as well as in the second volume of Augusto Cespedes's modern history, *El presidente colgado* (La Paz, 1971), the last two volumes of the history of Porfirio Diaz Machicado, *Historia de Bolivia, Toro, Busch Quintanilla, 1936–1940* (La Paz, 1957) and *Historia de Bolivia Peñaranda, 1940–1943* (La Paz, 1958). On the crucial role of the German military advisers, see Leon E. Bieber, "La politica militar alemana en Bolivia, 1900–1935," *Latin American Research Review*, 29:1 (1994), pp. 85–106, and Eleanor Hancock, *Ernst Röhm. Hitler's SA Chief of Staff* (London, 2008). A detailed study of the military socialist regimes is found in Ferran Gallego Margaleff, *Los orígenes del reformismo militar en América Latina la gestión de David Toro en Bolivia* (Barcelona, 1991) and *Los orígenes del reformismo militar en América Latina la gestián Germán Busch en Bolivia* (Barcelona, 1992). On the financing of the war, see Manuel E. Contreras, "Debt, Taxes, and War: The Political Economy of Bolivia, c. 1920–1935," *Journal of Latin American Studies*, 22:2 (May 1990). The best study of the internal impact of the war, which also contains an innovative oral history of Chaco veterans, is René Danilo Arze *Aguirre, Guerra y conflictos sociales. El caso rural boliviano durante la campaña del Chaco* (La Paz, 1987).

The Chaco War, the rise of the so-called Chaco generation, and the profound political changes in society since the 1930s have been examined by a number of national and foreign scholars. From very different perspectives have appeared: Sergio Almaraz, *El poder y la caida. El estaño en la historia de Bolivia* (2nd ed.; La Paz, 1969); two major studies of René Zavaleta Mercado, *El poder dual en América Latina. Estudio de los casos de Bolivia y Chile* (Mexico, 1974) and *La nacional-popular en Bolivia* (Mexico, 1986). Foreign scholars examining these developments have included Robert J. Alexander, *The Bolivian National Revolution* (New Brunswick, NJ, 1958); James Malloy, *Bolivia, the Uncompleted Revolution* (Pittsburgh, 1970); and Christopher Mitchell, *The Legacy of Populism in Bolivia, from the MNR to Military Rule* (New York, 1977). The most recent political surveys are those by James Dunkerley, *Rebellion in the Veins: Political Struggle in Bolivia, 1952–1982* (London, 1984); James Malloy and Eduardo Gamarra, *Revolution and Reaction: Bolivia, 1964–1985* (New Brunswick,

NJ, 1988); Jean-Pierre Lavaud, *L'instabilité politique de l'Amérique latine le cas bolivien* (Paris, 1991); Catherine M. Conaghan and James M. Malloy, *Unsettling Statecraft: Democracy and Neoliberalism in the Central Andes* (Pittsburgh, 1994); and the volume of essays by Crabtree and Whitehead cited below.

Also of importance in understanding twentieth-century political beliefs are several unique works that have helped define new modes of thought. Of these, the three most important are the previously cited indigenista declaration of Franz Tamayo in 1910, Tristan Marof's *La tragedia del altiplano* (Buenos Aires, 1934), and Carlos Montenegro, *Nacionalismo y coloniaje* (3rd ed.; La Paz, 1953).

Detailed studies of parties and persons are also available for the modern period. The most complete party history are those on the MNR: see Luis Peñaloza, *Historia del Movimiento Nacionalista Revolucionario, 1941–1952* (La Paz, 1963) and Luis Antezana E., *Historia secreta del Moviemiento Nacionalista Revolucionario* (7 vols.; La Paz, 1984–8). Useful for an analysis of the origins of the Trotskyite party is Guillermo Lora, *José Aguirre Gainsborg, fundador del POR* (La Paz, 1960), and most recently the role of POR and the mining unions has been studied by S. Sándor John, *Bolivia's Radical Tradition. Permanent Revolution in the Andes* (Tucson, 2009). No full-scale studies exist on the other Marxist parties, and while numerous campaign biographies exist of all the leading figures in the post-1952 period, few serious works of scholarship have yet to be published. There has, however, been some recent interesting work on populist candidates and groups; see, for example, Fernando Mayorga, ed. *¿Ejemonías? Democracia representativa y liderazgos locales: Percy Fernandez, Mandred Reyes Villa*, Mónica Medina (La Paz, 1997). Useful for particular periods or incidents are the study by Philippe Labrevuex, *Bolivia bajo el Che* (Buenos Aires, 1968), and the collection of Che Guevara's writings of this period in Juan Maestre Alfonso, ed., *Bolivia: victoria o muerte* (Madrid, 1975). The execution of Che is told in a popular format in Henry Butterfield Ryan, *The Fall of Che Guevara: A Story of Soldiers, Spies, and Diplomats* (New York, 1998). The Minister of the Interior under Torres has written a full account of this remarkable period in Jorge Gallardo Lozada, *De Torres a Banzar, diez meses de emergencia en Bolivia* (Buenos Aires, 1972). The background and ideology of the army leadership in this period are analyzed in Jean-Pierre Lavaud, "L'art du coup d'etat: Les militaires dans la société bolivienne (1952–1982)," *Revue française de Sociologie* 30:1 (1989), and he provides a more sustained analysis of the popular protests that helped bring down the military regimes in *La dictature empêhée de la faim des femmes de mineurs, Bolivie 1977–1978* (Paris: CNRS, 1999).

In contrast to the dearth of good works on leaders and parties, the newly politicized movements of workers and peasants have received considerable attention. Aside from the previously cited history of the organized labor movement by Guillermo Lora, there is an original history recently completed by Zulema Lehm and Silvia Rivera, *Los artesanos libertarios y la ética del trabajo* (La Paz, 1988), on the anarchists in the first half of the twentieth century. The central labor federation has recently been treated in Jorge Lazarte Rojas, *Movimento obrero y procesos politicos en Bolivia: historia de la C.O.B., 1952–1987* (La Paz, 1989), and there also exists a survey by John H. Magill, *Labor Unions and Political Socialization: A Case Study of Bolivian Workers* (New York, 1974). The evolution of a professional mining proletariat and its process of unionization and radicalization are considered in Gustavo Rodríguez, *El socavón y el sindicato ensayos históricos sobre los trabajadores mineros, siglos XIX–XX* (La Paz, 1991); René Zavaleta M. "Forma clase y forma multitud en el proletariado minero en Bolivia," in Renée Zavaleta M., ed., *Bolivia, hoy* (Mexico, 1983); Lawrence Whitehead, "Sobre el radicalismo de los trabajadores mineros en Bolivia," *Revista Mexicana de Sociología* 42:4 (1980) and his "Miners as Voters: The Electoral Process in Bolivia's Mining Camps," *Journal of Latin American Studies* 13 (1981). The mine workers also have been the subject of an extraordinary biography by the wife of a miner, Domitila Barrios de Chungara, *Let Me Speak!* (New York, 1978), and an unusual anthropological study by June Nash, *We Eat the Mines and the Mines Eat Us* (New York, 1979) and her rendering of the autobiography of a miner in Juan Rojas and June Nash, *I Spent My Life in the Mines: The Story of Juan Rojas, Bolivian Tin Miner* (New York, 1992). Other autobiographies done by anthropologists include that of Sofía Velasques; see Hans Buechler and Judith-Maria Buechler, *The World of Sofía Velasquez: The Autobiography of a Bolivian Market Vendor* (New York, 1996); Manuela Ari, *Manuela Ari: An Aymara Woman's Testimony of Her Life*, edited by Lucy T. Briggs and Sabine Dedenbach-Salazar Sáenz (Bonn, 1995), and Pedro Condoni and Françoise Estival, *Nous, les oubliés de l'Altiplano témoignage de Pedro Condoni [i.e., Conri], paysan des Andes boliviennes* (Paris, 1996). For the life of an Austrian Jewish family that arrived in Bolivia in the late 1930s, see Leo Spitzer, *Hotel Bolivia: The Culture of Memory in a Refuge from Nazism* (New York, 1998).

Studies on the peasants have been even more numerous than those on the workers. An original survey is provided by Silvia Rivera, *Oprimidos pero no vencidos: Luchas del campesinado aymara y qhechwa de Bolivia, 1900–1980* (4th ed, La Paz, 2003). The two key centers of peasant syndicalization in the Cochabamba Valley and on the altiplano have been studied by Jorge Dandler, *El sindicalismo campesino en Bolivia: Los cambios estructurales en Ucureño* (Mexico, 1969), and Xavier Albó, *Achacachi: Medio siglo de lucha campesina* (La Paz, 1979) – two very fine historical as well as contemporary studies by anthropologists. On contemporary political and ideological developments among the peasant unions, see the numerous essays by Xavier Albó that have been published in several anthologies, as well as his "De MNRistas a Kataristas: Campesinado, estado y partidos, 1953–1983," *Historia Boliviana* 5:1–2 (1985); Javier Hurtado, *El Katarismo* (La Paz, 1986); and Diego Pacheco, *El indianismo y los indios contemporaneos en Bolivia* (La Paz, 1992). The Quechua mobilization is studied in José Antonio Rocha, *Con el ojo de adelante y con el ojo de atrás ideología e tnica, el poder y lo político entre los quechua de los valles y serranías de Cochabamba (1935–1952)* (La Paz, 1999); and Felix Patzi Paco, *Insurgencia y sumisión, movimientos indígeno-campesinos, 1983–1998* (La Paz, 1999). The whole premodern discussion of Indiganista ideology is surveyed in Josefa Salmón *El espejo indígena, el discurso indigenista en Bolivia, 1900–1956* (La Paz, 1997). Also many of the works cited in the section on social conditions below deal with peasant syndicalization and political activities.

Bolivia's strained and complex relations with the United States, the most influential power affecting its development in the twentieth century, is partially surveyed in Bryce Wood, *The Making of the Good Neighbor Policy* (New York, 1961), and Cole Blaiser, *The Hovering Giant: U.S. Responses to Revolutionary Change in Latin America* (Pittsburgh, 1976), and most recently by Kenneth Duane Lehman, *Bolivia and the United States: A Limited Partnership* (Athens, GA, 1999). Specific aspects of that policy have included James W. Wilkie, *The Bolivian Revolution and United States Aid Since 1952* (Los Angeles, 1969) and Eduardo Gamarra, *Entre la droga y la democracia: La cooperacion entre Estados Unidos – Bolivia y la lucha contra el narcotra.co* (La Paz, 1994).

The Bolivian economy since the 1920s also has been the subject of modern studies of exceptional quality. The best general history of the economy from the 1920s to the late 1950s was done by the United Nations Economic Commission from Latin America, CEPAL, *El desarrollo económico de Bolivia* (Mexico, 1957). To this can be added the work by Cornelius H. Zondag, *The Bolivian Economy, 1952–1965* (New York, 1966). Although there is no general synthesis of the modern period, there exist numerous specialized studies on given economic developments. A detailed study by one of the participants in the stabilization program implemented in the late 1950s is that of George Jackson Eder, *Inflation and Development in Latin America: A Case History of Inflation and Stabilization in Bolivia* (Ann Arbor, 1968). The debt crisis as it affects Bolivia has been studied by Oscar Ugarteche, *El estado deudor. Economía política de la deuda: Perú y Bolivia, 1968–1984* (Lima, 1986) and Robert Devlin and Michael Mortimore, *Los bancos transnacionales, el estado y el endeudamiento externo de Boliva* (Santiago de Chile, 1983). The recent "orthodox" shock of the 1980s is studied in Juan Antonio Morales and Jeffrey D. Sachs, "Bolivia's Economic Crisis," in Jeffrey D. Sachs, ed., *Developing Country Debt and the World Economy* (Chicago, 1989); Jeffrey Sachs, "The Bolivian Hyperinflation and Stabilization," American Economic Association, *Papers and*

Proceedings 77:2 (May 1987), and Oscar R. Antezana Malpartida, *Analisis de la Nueva Política Económica* (La Paz, 1988). Estimating the size and shape of the important informal economy is carried out by Samuel Doria Medina, *La economia informal en Bolivia* (La Paz, 1986). A good survey of recent developments is found in Mark Weisbrot, Rebecca Ray, and Jake Johnston, *Bolivia: The Economy during the Morales Administration* (Washington, 2009), and the numerous studies of the Instituto de Investigaciones Socio-Económicas, Universidad Católica Boliviana. See for example the original study from this center by Lykker Anderson, *Baja mobilidad social en Bolivia: Causes y consequencias por el desarrollo* (La Paz, 2002). There also have been numerous surveys of contemporary health, and general conditions of poverty beginning in the 1970s with N. Thomas Chirikos et al., *Human Resources in Bolivia* (Columbus, OH, 1971); USAID Mission to Bolivia, *Bolivia Health Sector Assessment* (La Paz, 1975); and in the 1980s with two UNICEF-sponsored volumes by Rolando Morales Anaya, *Desarrollo y pobreza en Bolivia: Analysis de la situacion del niño y la mujer* (La Paz, 1984) and *La crisis económica en Bolivia y su impacto en las condiciones de vida de los niños* (La Paz, 1985), while the most recent data is found in various national health and household surveys which the Bolivian government has been carrying out since the 1980s. These health surveys (called ENDSA) are carried out every five years and the latest was done in 2008. See Ministerio de Salud y Deportes and INE, *Encuesta nacional de demografía y salud 2008, Informe Preliminar* (La Paz, 2009). The household surveys were initially called MECOVI and now simply "Encuesta de Hogares," and the latest is also for 2008 and the data can be found at http://www.ine.gov.bo/anda/ddibrowser/?id=46#overview. Numerous authors and government agencies have dealt with the question of poverty: among the many works see Rolando Morales Anaya, *Bolivia – política económica, geografía y pobreza* (La Paz, 2000), Naciones Unidas, *¿Donde estamos el 2000? Remontando la pobreza: Ocho cimas a la vez.* (La Paz, 2000). Data on poverty will be found in INE. *Bolivia: Mapa de Pobreza 2001* (La Paz, 2001) and on social conditions at the local level in UDAPSO, *Indices de desarrollo humano y otros indicadores sociales en 311 municipios de Bolivia* (La Paz, 1997), as well as PNUD, *Informe Nacional sobre Desarrollo Humano 2007* (La Paz, 2008).

For mining, the already cited work of Walter Gomez is the standard source of the pre-1970 period, which can be supplemented for the more recent era by Mahmood Ali Ayub and Hideo Hashimoto, *The Economics of Tin Mining in Bolivia* (Washington, 1985). The rise of new medium-sized private mining companies in the modern period is treated in Manuel E. Contreras and Mario Napoléon Pacheco, *Medio siglo de minería mediana en Bolivia, 1939–1989* (La Paz, 1989). Debates over COMIBOL and worker cogovernment of the mines in the 1950s were provided by Amado Canelos O., *Mito y realidad de COMIBOL* (La Paz, 1966), and Sinforosa

Canelas R., *La burocracia estrángula a la COMIBOL* (La Paz, 1960). A detailed survey of the mining tax structure before the current reforms was provided in Malcolm Gillis, ed., *Taxation and Mining. Nonfuel Minerals in Bolivia and Other Countries* (Cambridge, MA, 1978). The older work of Sergio Almaraz, *El petroleo en Bolivia* (La Paz, 1958), should be complemented by the excellent survey of the oil and gas industry by Carlos Miranda Pacheco "Del descubrimento petrolífero a la explosíon del gas," in Campero Prudencio, ed., *Bolivia en el siglo XX*. For current statistical information on the minerals and hydrocarbon industries, see Ministerio de Minería y Metalúrgia, *Estadisticas del sector minero-metalúrgia 1980–2008* (La Paz, 2009).

Detailed studies of the state fiscal structure were carried out in a multi-authored project led by Richard Musgrave, ed., *Fiscal Reform for Bolivia* (Cambridge, MA: Harvard Law School, 1981). Interesting surveys of the several key issues in early post-1952 economic policy appear in Melvin Burke, *Estudios criticos sobre la economía boliviana* (La Paz, 1973), and Carter Goodrich, *The Economic Transformation of Bolivia* (Ithaca, NY, 1955). The agricultural sector received a full-scale modern treatment of some sophistication in E. Boyd Wennergren and Morris D. Whitaker, *The Status of Bolivian Agriculture* (New York, 1975). This work primarily deals with agricultural production after 1952. Analysis of prereform structures and production on the haciendas was done by Edmundo Flores, "Taraco: monografía de un latifundio del altiplano boliviano," *El Trimestre Económico* 22:2 (1955); and Paul Robert Turovsky, "Bolivian and Haciendas Before and After the Revolution" (Ph.D. diss, University of California at Los Angeles, 1980); and most recently Jane Benton, *Agrarian Reform in Theory and Practice: A Study of the Lake Titicaca Region of Bolivia* (Aldershot, 1999). On the profound changes in the economic and social situation produced by the Agrarian Reform of 1953, there now exist numerous studies covering most of the major regions in Bolivia. A good introduction to the problem is found in William J. McEwen, *Changing Rural Society: A Study of Communities in Bolivia* (New York, 1975). More detailed assessments on individual regions can be found in William E. Carter, *Aymara Communities and the Bolivian Agrarian Reform* (Gainesville, FL, 1964); Roger A. Simmons, *Palca and Pucara: A Study of... Two Bolivian Haciendas* (Berkeley, 1974); Daniel Heyduk, *Huayrapampa: Bolivian Highland Peasants and the New Social Order* (Ithaca, NY, 1971); Kevin Healy, *Caciques y patrones: Una experiencia de desarrollo rural en el sud de Bolivia* (Cochabamba, 1983); Barbara Leons, "Land Reform in the Bolivian Yungas," *America Indígena* (Mexico) 27:4 (1967); Melvin Burke, "Land Reform and Its Effect upon Production and Productivity in the Lake Titicaca Region," *Economic Development and Cultural Change* 18 (1970); Dwight B. Heath et al., *Land Reform and Social Revolution in Bolivia* (New York, 1969); Dwight B. Heath, "New Patterns for Old: Changing

Patron-Client Relations in the Bolivian Yungas," *Ethnology* 12 (1973); the Bolivian section in Andrew Pearse, *Latin American Peasant* (London, 1975); Daniel Heyduk, "The Hacienda System and Agrarian Reform in Highland Bolivia: A Re-evaluation," *Ethnology* 13:1 (1974); and a series of recent articles by Ricardo Godoy, "Ecological Degradation and Agricultural Intensification in the Andean Highlands," *Human Ecology* 12:4 (1984); Benjamin S. Orlove and Ricardo Godoy, "Sectorial Fallowing Systems in the Central Andes," *Journal of Ethnobiology* 6:1 (1986), and his joint essay with Jonathan Morduch; and David Bravo, "Technological adoption in rural Cochabamba, Bolivia," *Journal of Anthropological Research*, 54:3 (Fall, 1998). Bolivia is compared to other regions in Ricardo A. Godoy *Indians, markets, and rainforests: theory, methods, analysis* (New York, 2001).

The migration of rural Quechua and Aymara peasants to the eastern lowlands has been a major development within rural Bolivian society in the last three decades, although it is barely keeping up with population growth in the altiplano and highland valleys. As yet there has been no single study encompassing all the features of this complex movement; however, there have been some important dissertations written on this phenomenon. The more interesting of these studies are those by Ray Henkel, "The Chapare of Bolivia: A Study of Tropical Agriculture in Transition" (Ph.D. diss., University of Wisconsin, 1971); Hernan Zeballos, "From the Uplands to the Lowlands: An Economic Analysis of Bolivian Urban-Rural Migration" (Ph.D. diss., University of Wisconsin, 1975); and Connie Weil and Jim Weil, *Verde es la esperanza: colonización, comunidad y coca en la Amazonia* (Cochabamba, 1993). The most recent work on migrations to the Santa Cruz region are by Leslie Gill, *Peasants, Entrepreneurs, and Social Change: Frontier Development in Lowland Bolivia* (Boulder, CO, 1987); Allyn Maclean Stearman, *Camba and Kolla: Migration and Development in Santa Cruz, Bolivia* (Gainesville, FL, 1985); and Michael Redclift, "Sustainability and the Market: Survival Strategies on the Bolivian Frontier," *Journal of Development Studies* 23 (1986). Highland and valley groups also have been the subject of numerous community studies by social scientists and community development people. Unquestionably, the most scholarly of such studies are those carried out in the last three decades by two Jesuit-run research organizations, CIPCA of La Paz and ACLO of Sucre. Urban migration has been the basis of a major CIPCA sponsored statistical survey carried out for La Paz by Xavier Albó, Tomas Greaves, and Godofredo Sandoval, *Chukiyawu, la cara Aymara de La Paz* (4 vols.; La Paz, 1981-7). The city of El Alto and its cholo population were studied by Godofredo Sandoval and M. Fernanda Sostres, *La ciudad prometida: Pobladores y organizaciones sociales en El Alto* (La Paz, 1989); and surveyed in Mauricio Antezana Villegas, *El Alto desde El Alto – II* (La Paz, 1993); while Lesley Gill, has studied various aspects of the city in two recent works,

Precarious Dependencies: Gender, Class, and Domestic Service in Bolivia (New York, 1994), and *Teetering on the Rim: Global Restructuring, Daily Life, and the Armed Retreat of the Bolivian State* (New York, 2000). A recent enthography of the city is given in Sian Lazar, *El Alto, rebel city: self and citizenship in Andean Bolivia* (Durhman, 2008).

Although internal immigration within Bolivia has been constant since 1952, international migration on a very large scale has been relatively recent. The best single study to date on internal migration is that of INE, *Estudio de la migración interna en Bolivia* (La Paz, 2004). The oldest of the international migrations has been the seasonal and permanent migrations to Argentina. See Roberto Benencia and Gabriela Karasik. *Inmigración limítrofe: los bolivianos en Buenos Aires* (Buenos Aires, 1995). The largest recent massive migration has been to Spain, which only began to occur after 2000. This migration is well surveyed by Mercedes Fernández García, "Bolivianos en España," *Revista de Indias*, LXIX: 245 (2009). Unfortunately the smaller contingente of Bolivia migrants to the United States has not been systematically studied.

Bolivia in the last half-century also has been the subject of detailed anthropological investigations on all aspects of Amerindian culture. On the contemporary Aymara populations, for example, the earlier studies of Weston La Barre, *The Aymara Indians of the Lake Titicaca Plateau, Bolivia* (Washington, DC, 1948); Harry Tschopik, "The Aymara," in the *Handbook of South American Indians* (5 vols.; Washington, DC, 1946), vol. II; and Hans and Judy Buechler, *The Bolivian Aymara* (New York, 1971), have been supplemented by a host of new studies on all aspects of contemporary Aymara peasant life. The best single introduction to the new materials is found in Xavier Albó, ed., *Raices de America: el mundo Aymara* (Madrid, 1988). Specific aspects of Aymara culture include older studies on religious belief by William Carter, "Secular Reenforcement in Aymara death ritual," *American Anthropologist* 70:2 (1968); Jacques Monast, *L'Universe religieux des aymaras de Bolivie* (Cuernavaca, 1966), the studies in the anthologies cited earlier edited by Murra. Aymara ritual has been examined recently by Thomas Alan Abercrombie, *Pathways of Memory and Power: Ethnography and History among an Andean People* (Madison, WI, 1998), and Tristan Platt, *Los Guerreros de Cristo cofradías, misa solar, y guerra regenerativa en una doctrina Macha (siglos XVIII–XX)* (La Paz, 1996). Kinship was studied by Xavier Albó, *Esposas, suegros y padrinos entre los aymaras* (2nd ed.; La Paz, 1976); and there exists an older community study by William Carter and Mauricio Mamani, *Irpa Chico, individuo y comunidad el la cultura Aymara* (La Paz, 1982). The high altitude physiology of the Aymara is examined most recently in Tom D. Brutsaert, Jere D. Haas, and Hilde Spielvogel, "Absence of Work Efficiency Differences During Cycle Ergometry Exercise in Bolivian Aymara," *High Altitude Medicine & Biology* 5:1 (2004). The mixture of medical belief systems in the small towns on the altiplano is analyzed in an interesting study by Libbet Crandon-Malamud, *From the Fat of Our Souls: Social Change, Political Process, and Medical Pluralism in Bolivia* (Berkeley, 1991), while the Aymara in an rural town setting was examined by J. R. Barstow, "An Aymara Class Structure: Town and Community in Carabuco" (Ph.D. diss., University of Chicago, 1979). An Aymara group in the multilingual Northern Potosí region is studied in Olivia Harris, *To Make the Earth Bear Fruit: Essays on Fertility, Work, and Gender in Highland Bolivia* (London, 2000) and in Ricardo Godoy, *Mining and Agriculture in Highland Bolivia* (Tuscon, AZ, 1990). A summary of work in Aymara linguistics is found in Lucy Briggs, "A Critical Survey of the Literature on the Aymara Language," *Latin American Research Review* 14:3 (1979); Juan de Dios Yapita and Lucy Briggs, "Aymara Linguistics in the Past 22 Years," *Latin American Indian Literatures Journal* 4:2 (Fall 1988); Harriet E. Manelis Klein and Louisa Stark, eds., *South American Indian Languages: Retrospect and Prospect* (Austin, 1985); and most recently Lyle Campbell, *American Indian Languages: The Historical Linguistics of Native America* (New York, 1997). Studies on Aymara linguistics can be found in the collection edited by Martha J. Hardman, *The Aymara Language in Its Social and Cultural Context* (Gainesville, FL, 1981). Also see Xavier Albó and Layme P.Félix, eds., *Literatura aymara antología* (La Paz, 1992).

The Quechua population of Bolivia is also now being studied intensively, although still less than their Peruvian counterpart. A sociolinguistic study was carried out by Xavier Albó, *Los mil rostros del quechua: Sociolingüística de Cochabamba* (Lima, 1974). The above-cited work of Dandler and Simmons deals with Quechua-speaking communities in the Cochabamba Valley, along with the studies by John F. Goins, *Huayculi: Los indios quechua del Valle de Cochabamba* (Mexico, 1967); and Maria L. Lagos, *Autonomy and Power: The Dynamics of Class and Culture in Rural Bolivia* (Philadelpha, 1994). Tristan Platt has analyzed Quechua symbolism in *Espejos de maiz* (La Paz, 1976) and in an essay in the Murra volume as well as surveyed the historical evolution of these groups in Northern Potosí in the works cited above. Another Potosí Quechua group was recently analyzed by Roger Neil Rasnake, *Domination and Cultural Resistance: Authority and Power among an Andean People* (Durham, NC, 1988).

The unusual medical practices of the Callahuaya Indians located in the altiplano region – a subject of numerous earlier studies – have recently been analyzed in three works by Joseph W. Bastien, *Mountain on the Condor, Metaphor and Ritual in an Andean Ayllu* (St. Paul, MN, 1978); and *Healers of the Andes: Kallawaya Herbalists and Their Medical Plants* (Salt Lake City, 1987); *Drum and Stethoscope: Integrating Ethnomedicine and Biomedicine in Bolivia* (Salt Lake City, 1992); and Louis Girault, *Kallawaya, curanderos itinerantes de los andes* (La Paz, 1987). Also see

Gerardo Fernárez Juárez, et al. *Medicos y yatiris salud e interculturalidad en el altiplano aymara* (La Paz, 1999). The lowland Indians of the eastern frontier have attracted ethnographers for a long time. The classic studies of this region were done at the beginning of the century by Erland Nordenskiold, *The Ethnography of South America Seen from Mojos in Bolivia* (2nd ed.; New York, 1979). There also exists the classic work by A. Holmberg, *Nomads of the Long Bow. The Siriono of Eastern Bolivia* (Washington, DC, 1950). Also on this unusual lowland group is the work by Harold Schefer and Floyd Lounsbury, *A Study in Structural Semantics: The Siriono Kinship System* (Englewood Cliffs, NJ, 1971). Jürgen Riester has studied many of these lowland peoples in *En busca de la Loma Santa* (La Paz, 1976), and *Los Guarasug'we: Crónica de sus útimos días* (La Paz, 1977). A survey of the demography and languages of these numerous groups is found in Pedro Plaza Martinez and Juan Carvajal Carvajal, *Etnias y lenguas de Bolivia* (La Paz, 1985) and in various reports of the World Bank and the United Nations.

Bolivian folklore also has received considerable attention from authors such as M. Rigoberto Paredes, *Mitos, supersticiones y supervivencias populares de Bolivia* (La Paz, 1920); Jesus Lara, *Leyendas quechuas* (La Paz, 1960); Enrique Oblitas Poblete, *Magica, hechiceria y medicina popular boliviana* (La Paz, 1971); and Gustavo Adolfo Otero, *La piedra magica, vida y costumbres de los indios callahuayas de Bolivia* (Mexico, 1951), to mention only a few of the more prolific writers. For the English reader, there is the study by Weston La Barre, "Aymara Folktales," *International Journal of American Linguistics* 16 (1950).

A fundamental theme in modern Bolivia is the question of who is an Indian. The best place to begin studying this crucial theme is the work by Ramiro Molina B. and Xavier Albó, *Gama étnica y lingüística de la población boliviana* (La Paz, 2006), which is based on an exhaustive analysis of the census of 2001. This builds from the earlier study of INE, *Análisis sociodemográfico. Poblaciones nativas* (La Paz 1997) which used the censuses of the 1990s. Albo has also become interested in the origins of elected officials and has produced some fascinating studies. See for example his analysis of the origin of the deputies to the constitutional convention of 2008, Xavier Albó, "Datos de una encuesta. El perfil de los constituyentes," *Tinkazos*, 11 (Mar. 2008); and Xavier Albó and Victor Quispe, *Quienes son indígenas en los gobiernos municipales* (La Paz, 2004).

General historical surveys of the social situation of the Bolivian population are still lacking, but some major areas or specific problems have received considerable attention. Aside from the surveys on poverty and health cited above, contemporary social mobility in rural society was studied by Jonathan Kelley and Herbert S. Klein, *Revolution and the Re-birth of Inequality: A Theory Applied to the Bolivian National Revolution* (Berkeley, 1981). The social structure and labor market of urban populations have been the subject of recent concern in the above-cited works of Albó on La Paz and Sandoval on El Alto; also see Roberto Casanovas Sainz and Antonio Rojas Rosales, *Santa Cruz de la Sierra: Crecimiento urbano y situación ocupacional* (La Paz, 1988); Silvia Escobar de Pabón and Carmen Ledo Garcia, *Urbanización, migraciones y empleo en la ciudad de Cochabamba* (La Paz, 1988); Miguel Urquiola S., *Participando en el crecimiento: Expansió on económica, distribución del ingreso y pobreza en al área urbana de Bolivia:1989–1992 y proyecciones* (La Paz, 1994); and Rolando Anaya Morales, *Desarrollo humano en las montañas: Informe del desarrollo humano de la ciudad de La Paz* (La Paz, 1995).

There is an extensive literature on the use of coca among the peasant populations; see William Carter et al., *Coca en Bolivia* (La Paz, 1980); and an entire issue devoted to coca in *América Indígena* (Mexico) 38:4 (1978). The problem of cocaine has spawned a large literature, most of it highly polemical. Among the more thoughtful studies are the essays in Deborah Pacine and Christine Franquemont, eds., *Coca and Cocaine: Effects on People and Policy in Latin America* (Boston, 1986); Gonzalo Flores and José Blanes, *Donde va el Chapare* (Cochabamba, 1984); Harry Sanabria, *The Coca Boom and Rural Social Change in Bolivia* (Ann Arbor, 1993); and Harry Sanabria, and Madeline Barbara Leons, eds. *Coca, Cocaine, and the Bolivian Reality* (Albany, NY, 1997). An ethnography of the traditional Yungas coca growing regions is found in Alison Spedding, *Wachu wachu cultivo de coca e identidad en los Yunkas de La Paz* (La Paz, 1994), and a good history of the traditional coca industry is found in María Luisa Soux, *La coca liberal producción y circulación a principios del siglo XX* (La Paz,1993). The most reliable data on coca production in Bolivia comes from the annual reports of the United Nations Office of Drugs and Crime [UNDOC], *World Drug Report, 2009* (Vienna and New York, 2009).

Important anthologies of essays also should be mentioned. Several cover political, economic, and social developments in Bolivia since 1952. These include James M. Malloy and Richard S. Thorn, eds., *Beyond the Revolution: Bolivia Since 1952* (Pittsburgh, 1971); J. Lademan, ed., *Modern Day Bolivia: Legacy of the Revolution and Prospects for the Future* (Tempe: Center for Latin American Studies, Arizona State University, 1982); Fernando Calderon and Jorge Dandler, eds., *Bolivia: La fuerza histórica del campesinado* (Cochabamba, 1984); and, most recently the two collections edited by , John Crabtree and Laurence Whitehead, *Towards Democratic Viability: The Bolivian Experience* (New York, 2001); and *Unresolved tensions : Bolivia past and present* (Pittsburgh, 2008). In honor of the fiftieth anniversary of the 1952 revolution, there was published a collection by Merilee Grindle and Pilar Domingo, eds. *Proclaiming Revolution: Bolivia in Comparative Perspective* (Cambridge, MA & London, 2003) and a volume on the first administration of the Morales government: Adrian Pearce, ed., *Evo Morales and the Movimiento al Socialismo in Bolivia: The First*

Term, 2005–2009 (London, 2010). Special issues on Bolivia have appeared in *Problemes d'Amerique Latine* (Paris), 62 (1981), *Caravelle* (Toulouse) 44 (1985); *Cahiers des Ameriques Latines* (Paris), Nouvelle Série, 6 (1987); *Journal of Latin American Studies* (London), vol. 32 (2000); and *Journal of Latin American Anthropology* (Washington, DC) 5:2 (2000). Others containing primarily historical and or ethnographic studies include: J. P. Deler and Y. Saint-Geours, eds., *Estados y naciones en los Andes* (2 vols.; Lima, 1986); and Brooke Larson et al., *Ethnicity, Markets, and Migration in the Andes at the Crossroads of History and Anthropology* (Durham, NC, 1995).

The literature for the past two decades on autonomies, decentralization, citizenship and the indigenous communities has been extraordinary and it is not easily summarized. See for example María Teresa Zegada, *En nombre de las autonomías: crisis estatal y procesos discursivos en Bolívia* (La Paz, 2007); Mario Galindo, *Visiones Aymaras sobre las autonomías* (La Paz, 2007); H.F.C. Manillsa, *Problemas de la autonomía en el oriente boliviano: la ideología de la Nación Camba en el espejo de las fuentes documentales.* (Santa Cruz de La Sierra, 2007); and Jean Paul Guevara Ávila, "Balanza de ocho años de descentralización. Cambios estatales a partir de la descentralización y la Participación Popular en Bolivia," in Manuel De la Fuente, Calude Auroi, and Marc Hufty, eds. *¿A dónde va Bolivia?* (La Paz, 2005). Useful for the special legal aspects of the question of indigenous community autonomy is Xavier Albó, and Carlos Romero, *Autonomías indígenas en la realidad boliviana y su nueva constitución* (2nd ed., La Paz, 2009). There have also been continuos publications of various Bolivian research centers, especiallu FED-ILDIS and the UN Development agency in Bolivia. The debate on the relation of the state and the regions has produced some interesting non polemical works. See for example Rossana Barragán R., "Hegemonías y "Ejemonías": las relaciones entre el Estado Central y las Regiones (Bolivia, 1825–1952)," *Iconos. Revista de Ciencias Sociales*, 34 (2009); Rossana Barragán R. and José L. Roca, *Regiones y poder constituyente en Bolivia* (La Paz, 2006).

From the survey above, it is evident that both national and foreign scholars have been fascinated by the Bolivian experience and have attempted to understand the complex forces that have created this society. Since my primary aim has been to provide the reader with an introduction to basic issues without listing all studies produced in any given subject, I have omitted many works. The books and articles cited, however, will provide the interested reader with further sources for an in-depth investigation. Finally, it is hoped that my comments will have provided interested scholars with some guidelines on what has been done as well as the exciting possibilities that remain in Bolivian studies.

INDEX

346   *Index*

COMIBOL 241; reform 245
COMIBOL (*Corporación Minera de Bolivia*) 213, 214, 217, 221, 224, 238, 241, 245
Commercial crops 285; agricultural crops exports 249
Communal land rights 292
Communism 173
Communist Party 166, 225, 227–8
Community abandonment 48
Compadre 257
Composición de tierra 62
Comunidad indígena 36
Comunidades 22, 121
Comunidades indígenas 257
Concho y Torres 134
Concordancia 193, 197, 204
CONDEPA (Consciousness of the Fatherland) 259, 260
CONDEPA (Consciousness of the Fatherland) party 255, 257
Confederación Peruboliviano 114–15; end of 117
Congress of 1880 143
Conquistadors 27
"Conservative Oligarchy" 153
Conservative Party 146, 151, 154, 155, 157, 160, 162, 169
Constitution: of 2009 291; social constitution 293
Constitutional Convention of 1938 192
Contribución directa 107
Convents, closing of 108
Copacabana Virgin. *See* Virgin of Copacabana

Copacabana, massacre at 130
Copper, artifacts 11
Cordillera Occidental 4
Cordillera Real: climate, 4–5; mineral deposits in 8
Córdova, General 127, 130
Corrales 179
Corregidor 41
Corregidores de indios 44, 82. *See also* Subintendants
Corregimientos 41
Cortés, Hernando 35
Coups d'etat. *See Golpe de estado*
Creole society: establishment of 27; structure of 28–9
Criollo 57
CSUTCB (*Confederación Sindicalúnica de Trabajadores Campesinos de Bolivia*) 242, 246, 252, 257, 260, 261
Cuencas 7
Cultural life 149
Cuzco, siege of 30
Cuzco-Quechua culture 17

Dalence, José María 112, 119, 120, 150
Darío, Rubén 150
Daza regime, overthrow of 145
Daza, General Hilarión 139, 153; rebellion against 142
Debray, Regis 225
Debt servicing 166
Decentralization: program 258; results 259
Decentralized state 264
Decree 21060 (1985) 245
Deficits, government 122–3

44806131R00210

Made in the USA
Lexington, KY
09 September 2015